Reagan and Pinochet
The Struggle over U.S. Policy toward Chile

This book is the first comprehensive study of the Reagan administration's policy toward the military dictatorship of General Augusto
Pinochet in Chile. On the basis of new primary and archival materials
and original interviews with former U.S. and Chilean officials, it traces
the evolution of Reagan policy from an initial "close embrace" of the
junta to a reevaluation of whether Pinochet was a risk to long-term U.S.
interests in Chile and, finally, to an acceptance in Washington of the
need to push for a return to democracy. It provides fresh insights into
the bureaucratic conflicts that were a key part of the Reagan administration's decision-making process and reveals not only the successes but
also the limits of U.S. influence on Pinochet's regime – centered on the
challenge of creating a viable civilian alternative that was acceptable to
both the junta and Washington. Finally, it contributes to the ongoing
debate about the U.S. approach toward democracy promotion in the
Third World over the past half-century.

Morris Morley is an associate professor of politics and international
relations at Macquarie University in Sydney, Australia, and a Senior
Research Fellow at the Council on Hemispheric Affairs, Washington,
DC. His books include *Imperial State and Revolution: The United
States and Cuba, 1952–1986*; *Washington, Somoza and the Sandin-
istas*; and, with Chris McGillion, *Unfinished Business: America and
Cuba after the Cold War, 1989–2001* and *Cuba, the United States and
the Post–Cold War World*.

Chris McGillion teaches in the journalism program at Charles Sturt
University in Bathurst, Australia, and is a Senior Research Fellow at
the Council on Hemispheric Affairs, Washington, DC. He is a former
editorial page editor for the *Sydney Morning Herald*.

Reagan and Pinochet

The Struggle over U.S. Policy toward Chile

MORRIS MORLEY

Macquarie University, Australia

CHRIS McGILLION

Charles Sturt University, Australia

CAMBRIDGE
UNIVERSITY PRESS

CAMBRIDGE
UNIVERSITY PRESS

32 Avenue of the Americas, New York, NY 10013-2473, USA

Cambridge University Press is part of the University of Cambridge.

It furthers the University's mission by disseminating knowledge in the pursuit of education, learning, and research at the highest international levels of excellence.

www.cambridge.org
Information on this title: www.cambridge.org/9781107458093

© Morris Morley and Chris McGillion 2015

First published 2015

Printed in Great Britain by Clays Ltd, St Ives plc

A catalog record for this publication is available from the British Library.

ISBN 978-1-107-08763-7 Hardback
ISBN 978-1-107-45809-3 Paperback

When the [Chilean] Ambassador walked into the Oval Office [in late 1983] to deliver [a] letter [from Pinochet], and sees all of the key cabinet ministers there for an early morning staff meeting waiting to receive him, he almost passes out. Reagan jumps up, greets him and says he has a question that has always puzzled him. The Ambassador starts quaking, thinking he's going to declare war or something but Reagan asks "How do you pronounce your President's name?"

– Senior Department of State Latin American Affairs official,
1983–1988

Contents

Acknowledgments

We would like to thank Deborah Gershenowitz at Cambridge University Press in New York for her encouragement and advice in guiding our manuscript through to its completed form; the two anonymous readers who provided detailed and thoughtful comments on the original draft; the archivists at the Reagan Presidential Library who facilitated a crucial part of our research; and those former U.S. government officials and Chilean political leaders privy to the events described in this study, whom we interviewed. This study was partly funded by a grant from the Australian Research Council.

Abbreviations and Acronyms

AC	Asamblea de la Civilidad (Civic Assembly)
AD	Alianza Democrática (Democratic Alliance)
AFL-CIO	American Confederation of Labor and the Congress of International Organizations
AID	Agency for International Development
AIFLD	American Institute of Free Labor Development
AmEmb	American Embassy
AP	Associated Press
ARA	Bureau of Inter-American Affairs
BDOHP	British Diplomatic Oral History Program
BG	*Boston Globe*
BHN	basic human needs
CCC	Commodity Credit Corporation
CIA	Central Intelligence Agency
CIA/FOIAe, III	U.S. Department of State Collections, Chile Declassification Project, Electronic, CIA Creation Documents
CNT	Comando Nacional Trabajadores (National Workers Command)
CQWR	*Congressional Quarterly Weekly Report*
CSM	*Christian Science Monitor*
CT	*Chicago Times*
CTC	Confederación de Trabajadores del Cobre (Copper Workers Confederation)
CUT	Central Unica de Trabajadores (Central Workers Confederation)

DCM	Deputy Chief of Mission
DDRS	Declassified Documents Reference System
DIA	Defense Intelligence Agency
DINA	Dirección de Inteligencia Nacional (Directorate of National Intelligence)
DJ	Dow Jones
DMN	*Dallas Morning News*
DOS	Department of State
DOS/FOIAe, III	U.S. Department of State Collections, Chile Declassification Project, Electronic, State Chile, Tranche III
DOSB	Department of State Bulletin
DOT	Department of the Treasury
EB	Bureau of Economic and Business Affairs
ECLAC	Economic Commission for Latin America and the Caribbean
FAA	Foreign Assistance Act
FAOHC	Foreign Affairs Oral History Collection
FBIS: DR: LA	Foreign Broadcast Information Service: Daily Report: Latin America
FCO	Foreign and Commonwealth Office
FDA	Food and Drug Administration
FMS	foreign military sales
FPMR	Frente Patriótico Manuel Rodriguez (Manuel Rodriguez Patriotic Front)
FT	*Financial Times*
GDP	gross domestic product
GSP	Generalized System of Preferences
HA	Bureau of Human Rights and Humanitarian Affairs
IADB	Inter-American Development Bank
IMF	International Monetary Fund
IMFA	International Monetary Fund Archives
INR	Bureau of Intelligence and Research
IO	Bureau of International Organizations
JC	*Journal of Commerce*
JDT	James D. Theberge Papers
LARR: SC	*Latin American Regional Reports: Southern Cone*
LAT	*Los Angeles Times*
LAWR	*Latin America Weekly Report*
MDB	Multilateral development bank
MDP	Movimiento Democrática Popular (Popular Democratic Movement)

MH	*Miami Herald*
MIR	Movimiento de Izquierda Revolucionaria (Movement of the Revolutionary Left)
NA	U.S. National Archives
NARA/FOIAe, III.	U.S. Department of State Collections, Chile Declassification Project, Electronic, NARA Chile III
NCN	National Command of the No
NCR	*National Catholic Reporter*
NED	National Endowment for Democracy
NGO	nongovernmental organization
NIE	National Intelligence Estimate
NSA	National Security Archive
NSC	National Security Council
NSDD	National Security Decision Directive
NSSD	National Security Study Directive
NYT	*New York Times*
OAS	Organization of American States
OPIC	Overseas Private Investment Corporation
PCC	Policy Coordination Committee
PCCH	Communist Party (Partido Communista)
PDC	Christian Democratic Party (Partido Demócrata Cristiano)
RNS	Reuters News Service
RRL	Ronald Reagan Library
SAL	structural adjustment loan
SCA	Southern Cone Affairs
SFRC	Senate Foreign Relations Committee
SMH	*Sydney Morning Herald*
TGM	*Toronto Globe and Mail*
TPRG	Trade Policy Review Group
UK	United Kingdom
UN	United Nations
UNGA	United Nations General Assembly
UNHRC	United Nations Human Rights Commission
UPI	United Press International
WBGA	World Bank Group Archives
WP	*Washington Post*
WSJ	*Wall Street Journal*
WT	*Washington Times*

Introduction

During the first three decades of the twentieth century, the United States transformed itself from a dominant regional into a competitive global power, all the while projecting its power abroad driven less by a desire "to make the world safe for democracy" than to put down nationalist threats to an expanding U.S. capital and commerce. Throughout the Cold War era, the gap between idealistic rhetoric and policy practice showed no signs of closing: the verbal commitment to promoting democracy by American presidents "with few exceptions ... was distinctly secondary to the U.S. quest for private economic opportunity and public support for military-dominated regimes that would maintain order."[1]

Between 1898 and 1933, the principal objective of U.S. policy in the Western Hemisphere – based on repeated military interventions and economic pressures – was to create a gaggle of client regimes in Central America and the Caribbean, which culminated in Franklin Roosevelt's announcement of a Good Neighbor Policy. From then on, through the end of the 1950s, Washington's policy toward Latin America gave priority to establishing a "closed economy in an open world." Politically, this translated into supporting "dependable *and weak*" anticommunist regimes, irrespective of their origins or how they ruled.[2] In pursuit of

---

[1] Walter Lafeber, "The Tension between Democracy and Capitalism during the American Century," in *The Ambiguous Legacy*, ed. Michael J. Hogan (New York: Cambridge University Press, 1999), 172. Also see Peter L. Hahn and May Ann Heiss, eds., *Empire and Revolution: The United States and the Third World since 1945* (Columbus: Ohio State University Press, 2001).

[2] David Green, *The Containment of Latin America* (Chicago: Quadrangle Books, 1971), 296 (emphasis original).

this overarching objective, successive administrations approved of, and accommodated, both "stability" achieved within a democratic context and "stability" imposed by brutal, autocratic governments. During the 1960s and early 1970s, maximum flexibility became the justification for diplomatic recognition of armed forces' illegal seizures of power.[3] Starting with the Kennedy administration's approval of the January 1961 military coup in El Salvador, U.S. support for democracy in Latin America, in other words, remained selective and contingent rather than universal and principled.

By the end of the 1960s, the failure of the multibillion dollar Alliance for Progress aid program to satisfy popular expectations of social and economic change triggered a new cycle of nationalist unrest. Featuring a distinct anti–foreign capital, anti-U.S. tinge, political and military forces advocating greater national control over economic resources, and intent on transforming or redefining relations with Washington, assumed power in Bolivia, Peru, and Chile. Additionally, formidable nationalist movements began to emerge in Argentina and Uruguay. Allende's Chile represented the focal point of the new nationalist challenge. Its tentative efforts to move out of the capitalist orbit and its support of ideological pluralism weakened the ties between North and South and directly challenged Washington's ability to secure the continent economically for American interests.

Not surprisingly, as the Vietnam War was drawing to a close, the United States began to refocus its attention on what became a sustained effort to reconsolidate its power and influence 'south of the border.' The Nixon administration moved aggressively to confront perceived 'hostile' governments, utilizing both outsider and insider strategies: economic sanctions complemented political pressures and/or covert operations to either deradicalize or destabilize these regimes. Where regime change was the objective, Washington sought to enlist the support of key state institutions and groups in civil society willing to collaborate in achieving this outcome. At the same time, Henry Kissinger wrote in his memoirs, global conflict with the Soviet Union and its allies "impelled us to maintain a constructive relationship with authoritarian [and anticommunist] regimes of South America."[4] There was no interest in actively promoting a

---

[3] See James Cochrane, "U.S. Policy toward Recognition of Governments and Promotion of Democracy in Latin America since 1963," *Journal of Latin American Studies* 4, no. 2 (1972): 275–291.

[4] Henry Kissinger, *Years of Renewal* (New York: Simon and Schuster, 1999), 754.

strategic shift away from a hemisphere dominated by military regimes to one where democracies flourished. On the contrary, Nixon had enunciated the approach he would adopt early in his tenure: "We must deal realistically with governments in the Inter-American System as they are."[5]

Resurgent Nationalism: Allende's Challenge and Washington's Response

If the 1959 Cuban Revolution had drawn attention to the potential for revolutionary upheaval in Latin America, the September 1970 election of a Socialist-Communist party coalition to political power in Chile – Salvador Allende's Unidad Popular (Popular Unity, UP) – was proof that a Marxist-oriented program of national development could capture the popular imagination and be enacted in a much more conventional fashion. To the United States, a revolution via the ballot box implied the kind of broad-based support that was harder to counter than a guerrilla insurgency, and its democratic origins restricted what means were available to challenge its legitimacy. As well, Chile was a relatively well developed country by Latin American standards and had never descended into the kind of corrupt American satrapy that characterized Cuba prior to the overthrow of the Batista dictatorship. For both reasons, the success of a revolution in Chile had wider implications than Cuba's challenge and raised the prospect of a powerful demonstration effect throughout the region – if not beyond. That was certainly Nixon's perception, clearly articulated during a meeting with Mexico's President, Luis Echeverria, in June 1972. It would be "very detrimental to all of us," Nixon confided to his guest, to have "the Chilean experiment spread through the rest of the continent" and, likening communism to a "poison," he added that in the event of its spread, "it inevitably will infect the United States."[6]

The most senior foreign policy adviser to Richard Nixon and Gerald Ford had an even more inflated view of the contagion effect of outcomes such as Allende's victory in Chile. "It is hard to imagine," Henry Kissinger told a group of U.S. Ambassadors stationed in European capitals, in December 1975, "that if one or the other of these [Communist parties] takes control of a Western government, it will permit the democratic

---

[5] Quoted in Cochrane, "U.S. Policy toward Recognition of Governments," 282.
[6] Transcript of conversation between President Nixon, Mexican President Luis Echeverría Alvarez, and Alexander Haig Jr., June 15, 1972, Conservation no. 735-1, Cassette Numbers 2246–2248, Oval Office, White House, The Nixon Tapes, NSA.

process to operate and thereby face the possibility that it may itself be removed from office."[7] That Nixon and Kissinger were willing to undermine elected governments and work with autocratic regimes as part of their overarching strategic vision reflected not only their contingent attitude toward democracy but also a preoccupation with "the limits of US power" – the driving force behind superpower détente – which demanded a search for alternatives to direct military intervention that would maintain a region (Latin America) firmly within Washington's sphere of influence.[8]

Returning from leave just days after the Chilean election, a senior State Department official encountered a White House that "had gone ape about this – ape. They were frantic, just besides themselves."[9] Nixon denounced Allende's victory at a meeting with Central Intelligence Agency (CIA) Director Richard Helms and Kissinger and instructed the head of the covert agency "to prevent Allende from coming to power or to unseat him by whatever means possible."[10] A similarly apoplectic National Security Council (NSC) Adviser conjured up the specter of dramatic regional consequences for the United States if the vote was allowed to stand.[11]

With the failure of a two-track political-military attempt to prevent Allende's inauguration,[12] the Nixon White House redoubled its efforts to make certain that a government it viewed as profoundly antagonistic to U.S. interests in Chile, in Latin America, and globally did not complete its six-year term of office. When Nixon and his senior foreign policy officials gathered to discuss the "crisis," Undersecretary of State John Irwin addressed the question of tactics. Regime change "could only be achieved in collaboration with internal forces opposed to the new government given the limits on our capability to do it [alone]."[13] Over the

---

[7] Reprinted in Kissinger, *Years of Renewal*, 628.

[8] Jeremi Suri, *Henry Kissinger and the American Century* (Cambridge: Harvard University Press, 2007), 145.

[9] John Hugh Crimmins interview, FAOHC.

[10] Quoted in U.S. Congress, Senate, Select Committee to Study Governmental Operations, *Alleged Assassination Plots Involving Foreign Leaders*, 94th Cong., 2d Sess., Report 94-465, November 20, 1975, 227, 228.

[11] See Henry Kissinger, *The White House Years* (London: Weidenfeld and Nicolson, 1979), 665–670; Kissinger, *Years of Renewal*, 376; Robert Dallek, *Nixon and Kissinger: Partners in Power* (New York: HarperCollins, 2007), 323.

[12] See U.S. Congress, Senate, *Alleged Assassination Plots Involving Foreign Leaders*, 229–254.

[13] Memo of Conversation, NSC Meeting–Chile (NSSM 97), November 6, 1970, NSC Institutional "H" Files, Minutes of Meetings (1969–1974), Folder: NSC Minutes Originals 1970 [1 of 3], Box H-109, NPMS.

next three years, the White House elaborated a multitrack strategy to destabilize and topple the elected UP government from power: an outsider strategy targeting an economy highly dependent on access to short- and long-term sources of foreign funding, especially from U.S. public and private sources, the major U.S.-influenced global lending agencies, and American-origin spare parts needed to maintain its industrial-agriculture infrastructure in optimal working order; and an insider political/covert strategy designed to create a level of political and economic chaos that would induce the armed forces to intervene and terminate the democratic socialist experiment.[14]

The September 1973 coup shattered Chile's democratic tradition and set the stage for an ambitious rightist revolution based on repression and terror. The President and his NSC Adviser were euphoric over Allende's demise, congratulating themselves on their covert role in "help[ing] [to] create the conditions as great as possible" for the coup to succeed.[15] Once the United States had extended official recognition, the junta, headed by army General Augusto Pinochet, accelerated efforts to systematically eliminate all real and perceived opponents. To the extent that the Nixon White House exhibited any concern about the scope and intensity of this state-authored repression, it centered on the generals' failure to comprehend the problem this posed for administration efforts to get a more sympathetic hearing from Congress when it came to military and economic aid requests for Chile.

Gerald Ford had barely moved into the Oval Office when the subject of Chile arose in a top secret State Department briefing paper, which concluded it was "clearly" in America's interests to maintain a positive relationship, especially taking into account the lack of any "acceptable alternative" to rule by the generals.[16] But with momentum on Capitol Hill moving in favor of those legislators opposed to economic and military aid to Chile, there was growing sentiment among State Department officials in favor of a more pro-active approach to dealing with Third World

---

[14] On the U.S. economic blockade, see James Petras and Morris Morley, *The United States and Chile: Imperialism and the Overthrow of the Allende Government* (New York: Monthly Review Press, 1975). For an overall analysis of U.S. policy toward the Allende government, see ibid. and Peter Kornbluh, *The Pinochet File*, updated ed. (New York: New Press, 2013), 79–115.

[15] Telcon, Nixon to Kissinger, September 16, 1973, Digital NSA.

[16] Briefing Paper, Department of State, "Latin America and Human Rights," August 17, 1974, attached to Memo, NSC, Davis to Kennedy et al., August 19, 1974, NSA, NSC Latin American Affairs Staff: Files, 1974–1977; Folder: President Ford-Briefings, August–September 1974, Box 11, Gerald R. Ford Library, Ann Arbor, MI.

recipients who were major human rights abusers amid a concern that, otherwise, "Congress would take the matter out of the Department's hands."[17] Appointed Secretary of State in September 1973, Kissinger blustered that allowing legislators to dictate U.S. policy toward Chile could trigger falling dominos across Asia and a profound weakening of America's global position.[18]

By early 1975, the Ford White House was forced to acknowledge that a reluctance to censure or find serious fault with the junta's method of rule was not producing the sought-after results, above all, congressional approval for adequate funding of a Chilean economy in serious trouble and an end to the country's pariah status within the international community. With the political left decimated, physically and organizationally, the Christian Democrats disoriented, and the regime's hold on power uncontested, Kissinger decided that the most immediate and pressing task was to improve the credibility of the administration's policy. This led to a mild tactical shift from uncritical support of the military regime to selective statements of disapproval about specific abuses perpetrated by the Chilean security forces. But Kissinger still rejected the notion "that human rights interests *per se* outweighed other US interests and objectives in Chile," even as he conceded that Chile's record constituted a major obstacle to achieving these "interests and objectives."[19]

In June 1976, Kissinger arrived in Santiago to address an Organization of American States (OAS) conference. At a much anticipated prior meeting with Pinochet, the Secretary went out of his way to allay any fears the dictator might have harbored that Chile would be subjected to a major dressing down over the junta's human rights performance. In so many words, he told his host that none of the critical remarks in his speech should be taken seriously – that they were nothing more than a sop to American domestic opponents of the regime and did not reflect his views or those of the Ford administration: "The speech is not aimed at Chile . . . *but we have a practical problem we have to take into account*."[20]

Three months later, the "practical problem" reached new heights: the targeted assassination of one of the most influential Chilean critics of the

---

[17] Quoted in Patrick Breslin, "Human Rights: Rhetoric or Action?," WP, February 27, 1977, C4.
[18] Transcript, DOS, The Secretary's Principals and Regionals Staff Meeting, December 23, 1974, Digital NSA.
[19] Telegram, Kissinger to Popper, June 20, 1975, ibid.
[20] Memo of Conversation, Kissinger, Pinochet, Carvajal, Rogers et al., Santiago, June 8, 1976, DOS/FOIAe, III (our emphasis).

Pinochet regime, former Allende government Foreign Minister Orlando Letelier, and his American colleague Ronni Moffitt, in a car bombing in downtown Washington, D.C., only blocks from the White House. Carried out by agents and accomplices of the Dirección de Inteligencia Nacional (Directorate for National Intelligence, DINA), Chile's security organization, it was part of Pinochet's Operation Condor, a program to wage war against prominent Chilean exiles – civilian and military – seeking to mobilize international opposition to the authoritarian regime.[21] As the Ford administration prepared to leave office, U.S. Ambassador to Chile David Popper characterized bilateral relations as "difficult, formal, and largely static."[22]

Carter, Latin America, and Chile

Well before Jimmy Carter took office in January 1977, the combined effects of the U.S. defeat in Vietnam, the Nixon-Kissinger role in toppling Chile's democratic government, and revelations about U.S. covert operations abroad under the guise of national security had exhausted the electorate's tolerance for an interventionist foreign policy – particularly one justified in terms of countering Soviet activities wherever they might be said to occur in the Third World. Congressional reaction to the arrogant abuse of foreign policy powers had already produced legislative restrictions on executive branch prerogatives in this area, and the public outcry at the exposure of those same excesses meant that any new administration would have to exercise great caution in what latitude remained to pursue U.S. interests abroad or risk once again stoking domestic political opposition. To the incoming President, the lesson was clear: the days of the unrestrained projection of American power abroad were over.

The Carter White House thus confronted the challenge of how to relegitimate American foreign policy domestically and internationally. Beginning with his inaugural address, Carter repeatedly emphasized a connection between a nation's (military) strength and a foreign policy that was always "strongest and most effective when [it emphasized] morality

---

[21] See Kornbluh, *The Pinochet File*, 331–363; John Dinges, *The Condor Years* (New York: New Press, 2004).
[22] Telegram, Popper to Kissinger, January 28, 1977, DOS/FOIAe, I; Telegram, Popper to Kissinger, January 18, 1977, Chile Human Rights Documents, File: DOS, Human Rights in Chile, Vol. 20, Folder 1, Box 12, NA.

and a commitment to freedom and democracy."[23] His critique of Nixon-Ford was not that they had been less than vigorous in promoting U.S. interests but that at times they had misconstrued what these interests were, deceived the American people about how they were pursuing them, and acted in ways that undermined confidence at home and abroad in the U.S. commitment to the values it claimed to champion. The new President bemoaned the "inordinate fear of communism" that had seen the United States "willing to adopt the flawed and erroneous principles and tactics of our adversaries, sometimes abandoning our own values for theirs."[24] Carter, in other words, was determined to break with the realpolitik of the Nixon-Ford-Kissinger era and to substitute for secret diplomacy, covert politics, and automatic support for authoritarian anticommunist regimes an ideology of morality based on the pursuit of human rights. Yet, this commitment to human rights was never as "absolute" or principled as the President insisted it would be in his inaugural address. It was conceptually flawed in seeking to separate the behavior of the regime from the nature of the regime. Instead of challenging the origins or legitimacy of repressive allied regimes, it focused primarily on their methods of governance.[25] As well, the administration made "ample use" of the "extraordinary circumstances" clauses written into human rights legislation ("loopholes") to minimize or circumvent aid cutbacks.[26]

One of the transition option papers prepared by the State and Defense departments for the President-elect defined the "fundamental question" to be addressed in devising policy toward Latin America as "how best to protect and advance U.S. interests and values in a situation of growing estrangement and waning U.S. hegemony."[27] What priority democracy and human rights would be accorded in implementing this approach was far from clear. Deputy Secretary of State Warren Christopher insisted

[23] Jimmy Carter, *Keeping Faith* (London: Collins, 1982), 142. Also see Jimmy Carter, Inaugural Address, January 20, 1977, American Presidency Project.

[24] Jimmy Carter, Commencement Day Speech at Notre Dame University, May 22, 1977, ibid.

[25] For a comprehensive analysis of Carter's regional human rights policy, see Lars Schoultz, *Human Rights and United States Policy toward Latin America* (Princeton: Princeton University Press, 1981).

[26] David Carleton and Michael Stohl, "The Foreign Policy of Human Rights: Rhetoric and Reality from Jimmy Carter to Ronald Reagan," *Human Rights Quarterly* 7, no. 2 (1985): 216.

[27] State and Defense Transition Options Papers, Volume 2, "The U.S. and Latin America," November 1976, Plains File, Subject File, Folder: Transition: State and Defense Options Papers [3], 11/76, Box 41, Jimmy Carter Library, Atlanta, GA.

that human rights "will be woven, we are determined, into the fabric of American foreign policy."[28] In a major speech at the University of Georgia in April 1977, Secretary of State Cyrus Vance provided a detailed exposition of the administration's human rights policy, reiterating the emphasis on specific techniques of governing, not on questions of regime origins or legitimacy. Brutal or autocratic rulers would never be opposed on the grounds of their essential nature. Vance underlined the importance of pursuing human rights in a "realistic" and calculated fashion based on each particular case, the possibilities for taking "effective action," and its impact on national security interests.[29] This, he later wrote, could best be achieved through "quiet diplomacy."[30] To a senior colleague, it appeared to differ little, if at all, from the Kissinger position: "to wit, you're much better off if you are quiet on the subject and put pressure on behind the scenes."[31] In retrospect, however, a number of department officials concluded that the administration never resolved how this would happen because the policy was "never really set down, thought out and planned"[32] and that even the President himself "never really" understood what it meant.[33]

If the core Carter White House message was that the United States would no longer turn a blind eye to human rights abuses in its relations with other governments, the idea developed few strong roots in the foreign policy bureaucracy. Treasury adhered to the policy but did so only grudgingly whenever it determined Washington's position on multilateral development bank (MDB) loans,[34] Commerce resisted any attempts to link human rights and trade in ways that might threaten U.S. access to export markets, and the Pentagon traditionally opposed any foreign policy 'innovation' that threatened weapons transfers to Third World armed forces and, by extension, reduced its influence with their officer corps. At the middle and lower rungs of the State Department, there was a good deal of disagreement about the interpretation and application of

---

[28] U.S. Congress, Senate, Committee on Foreign Relations, Subcommittee on Foreign Assistance, *Human Rights*, 95th Cong., 1st Sess., March 4, 7, 1977, 62.

[29] Vance Speech on Law Day before the University of Georgia's Law School, April 30, 1977, DOSB, May 23, 1977, 505–508.

[30] Cyrus Vance, *Hard Choices* (New York: Simon and Schuster, 1983), 46.

[31] Interview with James M. Wilson Jr.

[32] U.S. Ambassador to the UN Andrew Young, quoted in David S. Broder, "Pushing Human Rights: To What Consequence?," WP, June 15, 1977, 17.

[33] Interview with Stephen Cohen.

[34] For convenience, the terms *multilateral development bank* (MDB) and *international financial institution* (IFI) are used interchangeably.

the policy between the career foreign service officers in the geographic bureaus and the mainly political appointees located in the newly elevated Bureau of Human Rights and Humanitarian Affairs (HA), a number of whom were recruited from Congress, where they had worked on legislation restricting economic and military aid to countries with lamentable records in this area.[35]

Throughout his run for the White House, Carter appeared to single out Chile for special attention in his critique of U.S. foreign policy during the Nixon-Ford era. In the second campaign debate, he repeated his charge that U.S. policy toward Chile – its role in the "destruction" of a democratic government and "strong support" of a military dictatorship – had failed to reflect American values.[36] While these comments were essentially directed at past U.S. policy, they raised expectations of a significant shift in America's relations with the Pinochet regime. Such optimism was reinforced by the absence of any overriding threats to U.S. interests, which meant that Chile posed a fairly 'no loss' target of Carter's commitment to human rights.

At the outset of his presidency, U.S.-Chilean relations ranked far from the top of Carter's list of hemisphere concerns. Nonetheless, he did put an end to his predecessors' cozy relationship with Pinochet, but the alternative he offered did not encapsulate a commitment to redemocratization in Chile. NSC official David Aaron recalled, "We weren't going to try to overthrow Pinochet. As far as the Carter White House was concerned the focus was on human rights abuses. There were no plans of how you get to democracy."[37]

After January 1977, economic aid programs to Chile were terminated, military relations were scaled back, and U.S. officials began opposing Chilean loan requests to the MDBs. Simultaneously, Carter officials embarked on a combined public and private diplomatic offensive to embarrass the Pinochet regime over its style of governance and, for the first time since the coup, opened up lines of communication with prominent opposition leaders, at the very least acknowledging that they had legitimate grievances and ambitions. But these meetings were not intended

---

[35] On the conflict between HA and the geographic bureaus, see Caleb Rossiter, *Human Rights: The Carter Record, the Reagan Reaction* (Washington, DC: Center for International Policy, 1984).

[36] Transcript, "The Second [Presidential] Debate, San Francisco, October 6, 1976," in *The Great Debates*, ed. Sidney Kraus (Bloomington: Indiana University Press, 1979), 480.

[37] Telephone interview with David L. Aaron.

to encourage the opposition to ratchet up its challenge to the regime or to force the junta to open genuine negotiations with their opponents, and were certainly not an attempt to undermine Pinochet in any substantive fashion.

Time and again, before scheduling these meetings, Carter officials stated that Washington was not searching for an alternative to Pinochet and reassured junta officials that there was no major policy shift under way. Irrespective of the human rights issue, the administration had "no intention whatsoever" of attempting to destabilize the military regime.[38] Not even irrefutable evidence that the regime had authorized and carried out an act of international terrorism in the heart of the American capital was sufficient to shake Carter's reluctance to break ties with the military regime. While American diplomats continued to tell Chilean officials that "our overall mood is one of disappointment" at the lack of sufficient progress on the human rights front,[39] maintaining a "cool" relationship and keeping cooperation to a minimum remained the preferred policy option.

Nevertheless, by early 1978, the revelations of Chilean government involvement in the Letelier-Moffitt killings had begun to cast an increasingly wide shadow across bilateral ties. Robert Steven, State's Chile Desk Officer between 1977 and 1979, "could not emphasize enough how much Letelier now dominated everything. If I went to a meeting of any sort in the Department and tried to argue for any consideration on another Chile issue, I was shot down."[40] Ambassador George Landau "was never called back to Washington for consultations over any other issue. Letelier was it."[41]

On May 13, 1979, bilateral ties took a dramatic turn for the worse. The Chief Justice of the Chilean Supreme Court rejected Washington's request for the extradition of the DINA officers implicated in the Letelier-Moffitt murders. The State Department termed the judgment "deplorable" and denounced the three released officers as "terrorists."[42] The NSC's Robert Pastor called the decision "much worse than any one

---

[38] Memo of Conversation, DOS, Cauas, Luers, Barnebey, May 24, 1977, DOS/FOIAe, I.
[39] Telegram, Vance (Christopher) to AmEmb Santiago, December 7, 1977, Chile Human Rights Documents, File: DOS, Human Rights in Chile, Vol. 24, Folder 2, Box 14, NA.
[40] Interview with Robert Steven.
[41] Interview with George W. Landau.
[42] Quoted in "U.S. Assails Chile Court's Refusal to Extradite Three in Letelier Case," *NYT*, October 3, 1979, 4.

of us had anticipated."[43] Secretary of State Vance recalled Landau to participate in a "thorough review of all facets of our relations" with the Latin regime.[44] Senators Edward Kennedy (D-MA) and Frank Church (D-ID) pressed for consequential economic and military sanctions if the regime was unwilling to rescind the decision.[45] The eventual White House response, however, fell considerably short of such proposed or threatened measures, including the imposition of any, let alone rigorous, controls on U.S. private bank lending to the dictatorship which had played a key role in keeping the Chilean economy afloat. More significant, and directly linked to the Letelier case, was Carter's decision in 1980 to exclude Chile from participation in the annual UNITAS naval exercises with other Latin American allies – the first time in twenty-one years that a regional ally had not been invited to participate in UNITAS on political grounds. This was the final straw for Pinochet and his junta colleagues, recalled then U.S. Ambassador to Chile George Landau: "They were just hoping and praying that Reagan would win the November presidential election."[46]

Inside Chile, the practical impact of Carter's human rights policy was evident in terms of the number of lives saved, the periodic easing of repression (release of prisoners, return of exiles), the dissolution or reconfiguration of the more appalling instruments of repression (closing down detention/torture centers, abolishing DINA, lifting of states of emergency), the identification of DINA as responsible for the Letelier-Moffitt murders, and the extradition of its security operatives who actually carried out the terrorist act. But whether Carter's initiatives facilitated the growth of the political opposition by encouraging the dictatorship to engage in pseudo-democratic "reforms" is less clear. Pinochet's July 1977 decision to move toward a new "protected democracy" (the Chacarillas Plan), for instance, was less a response to U.S. entreaties or pressures than part of a broader effort to translate the regime's brute force into some kind of legitimacy to govern – its one constant Achilles' heel. On balance, nonetheless, these gains were less impressive than those Pinochet could boast. The dictator managed to survive the departure of his strongest

---

[43] Memo, NSC, Pastor to Brzezinski, May 25, 1979, Vertical File, Chile-Human Rights, Folder: Chile-Human Rights (3), June 30, 1979, JCL.

[44] Quoted in "U.S. Recalling Envoy Over Chile's Refusal to Extradite 3," *NYT*, May 16, 1979, 8.

[45] Telegram, Vance to AmEmb, Santiago, "Text of Letter," May 16, 1979, DOS/FOIAe, III.

[46] Interview with George W. Landau.

and most powerful overseas supporters (Nixon, Kissinger, and Ford) and weathered the worst of Carter's shift to a 'cool but correct' relationship without making any major domestic concessions.

Reagan and the Anticommunist Resurgence

Reagan's decision to jettison the human rights–driven Carter policy toward the Pinochet regime stemmed largely from a worldview he brought to the White House, what one scholar summarized as a "life-long conviction" that the Soviet Union sought "world domination and therefore must be resisted on all fronts."[47] Speaking to reporters only days after his inauguration, the new President declared that every Soviet leader since 1917 had expressed the view "that their goal must be the promotion of world revolution and a one-world Socialist or Communist state." Moscow's favored concept of morality was limited to whatever would "further their cause, meaning they reserve unto themselves the right to commit any crime, to lie, to cheat, in order to attain" its ultimate end.[48] Two years later, before an audience of Christian evangelical leaders, Reagan went so far as to characterize the Soviet Union as nothing less than an "evil empire" that constituted a profound threat to worldwide American and Western interests.[49]

These kinds of statements were music to the ears of a virulently anticommunist armed forces leadership in Chile who saw themselves as locked in a mortal conflict to preserve not only the country's national integrity but also Western civilization from the influence of the 'Marxist virus.' Indeed, as far back as the late 1960s, many Chilean officers expressed irritation at what they considered Washington's failure to treat them as equal partners in this wider conflict – epitomized by the refusal to provide sophisticated weapons transfers – and were equally alarmed by Nixon's détente policies and Carter's decision to prioritize human rights as signs of a flagging commitment to the moral effort the global struggle against Communism necessarily required.[50]

---

[47] Michael Turner, "Foreign Policy and the Reagan Administration," in *Reagan's First Four Years*, ed. John D. Lees and Michael Turner (Manchester: Manchester University Press, 1988), 126.

[48] The President's Press Conference, January 29, 1981, American Presidency Project.

[49] President Reagan's Speech before the National Association of Evangelicals, Orlando Florida, March 8, 1983, http://www.hbci.com.

[50] Frederick M. Nunn, *The Time of the Generals* (Lincoln: University of Nebraska Press, 1992), 25–27.

To a greater or lesser extent, each of Reagan's senior policy advisers shared the President's robust anticommunist outlook. They also interpreted America's relative decline as a global power as a consequence of superpower détente, arguing that the decision to pursue a new relationship with Moscow (and Beijing) during the 1970s based on 'engagement' had weakened the U.S. militarily and constrained it from more forcefully projecting its power abroad in defense of the country's national interest. In this view, the costs of détente were both moral and strategic: moral, because détente had accorded a permanent recognition to the Soviet Union and its oppressive system of rule; strategic, because détente had led to a series of setbacks for the United States in Central America, the Middle East, and southern Africa that were attributed to the Carter White House refusal to decisively and effectively confront Soviet 'aggression.' Reagan policy makers focused much of their criticism on Jimmy Carter himself over his alleged "failure of leadership" and his penchant for substituting a "theology" of human rights policy "for a healthy sense of self-preservation."[51]

One of the most influential contributions to this interpretation of events was a November 1979 article, "Dictatorship and Democracy," authored by a neoconservative Georgetown University professor Jeane Kirkpatrick and published in *Commentary Magazine*. After savaging Carter's human rights policy for destabilizing friendly Third World allies, Kirkpatrick distinguished between two types of regimes: "authoritarian" pro-American and anticommunist governments (such as Pinochet's Chile) pursuing domestic and foreign policies acceptable to Washington and which were capable of "moving toward democracy"; and "totalitarian" communist governments (such as Cuba or Nicaragua's Sandinista government) that were relentlessly hostile to U.S. interests and were never likely to become democratic.[52] According to Kirkpatrick, America's best interests were served by a policy approach combining fulsome support of the "authoritarians" with active political, covert, and military aid to anticommunist "freedom fighters" attempting to topple the "totalitarians" – not by Carter's "utopian" policy.[53] This reasoning profoundly

---

[51] James L. Buckley, Undersecretary of State for Security Assistance, quoted in Rossiter, *Human Rights*, 22.

[52] Jeane Kirkpatrick, "Dictatorships and Double Standards," Commentary, November 1979, 34–45. This article built on ideas outlined a year earlier by Ernest Lefever in his article "The Trivialization of Human Rights." See Stefan Halper and Jonathan Clarke, *America Alone* (New York: Cambridge University Press, 2005), 57.

[53] Quoted in Carleton and Stohl, "Foreign Policy of Human Rights," 209.

influenced Reagan's articulation of a foreign policy "doctrine" that attempted "to provide a coherent conceptual framework for explaining American policy [by] welding together lofty moral goals of support for freedom, democracy, and human rights with more concrete political-military aims of rolling back Soviet-supported 'Marxist' regimes."[54] It also included an equally determined commitment to ensure the survival of pro-American regimes confronting serious internal challenges to their hold on political power. Reagan was so taken with Kirkpatrick's analysis that she was enlisted as a foreign policy adviser during the 1980 presidential campaign, recruited to the NSC after the election, and eventually appointed U.S. Ambassador to the United Nations and a member of Cabinet.

In May 1980, a group of Reagan supporters, members of the so-called Committee of Santa Fe, launched a focused assault on Carter policy toward Latin America in a document titled "A New Inter-American Policy for the Eighties." Further elaborating on Kirkpatrick's critique, the document warned that the United States was engaged in "World War III" with the Soviet Union and that Central America was the "soft underbelly" in this conflict that had to be protected at all costs. Carter's regional policy was dismissed as nothing more than "camouflaged escapism to Soviet imperialism" that disproportionately "target[ed]" U.S. allies for human rights abuses and so "must be reversed."[55] This policy proposal was no less than a clarion call to revive the Roosevelt Corollary to the Monroe Doctrine and give Washington the right to intervene anywhere in the Western Hemisphere at its choosing. Reagan was sufficiently impressed by the document's analysis that three of its five coauthors later joined his foreign policy team.

In the period between Reagan's election and inauguration, sentiment among his advisers and supporters for downgrading the role of human rights in foreign policy decision making had been palpable. Senior Latin

---

54 Raymond Garthoff, *The Great Transition* (Washington, DC: Brookings Institution Press, 1994), 693. For excellent critical discussions of the Reagan Doctrine and its application to the Third World, see ibid., 678–715; Odd Arne Westad, *The Global Cold War* (New York: Cambridge University Press, 2005), 331–363; David F. Schmitz, *The United States and Right-Wing Dictatorships* (New York: Cambridge University Press, 2006), 194–240. Reagan's approach to democracy promotion in Latin America is analyzed in Thomas Carothers, "The Reagan Years: The 1980s," in *Exporting Democracy: The United States and Latin America (Themes and Issues)*, ed. Abraham F. Lowenthal, 90–122 (Baltimore: Johns Hopkins University Press, 1991).

55 The Committee of Santa Fe, "A New Inter-American Policy for the Eighties," May 1980, 9, 37.

American adviser Roger Fontaine – who subsequently joined the NSC staff – declared that the new administration would employ "quiet diplomacy" in dealing with human rights abuses so as not to "irritate" regional allies.[56] A report jointly prepared by a member of the transition team and a legislative aid to the conservative Senator Jesse Helms (R-NC) recommended a need to "reduce influence of human rights advisers and 'social reformers'" in State's Bureau of Inter-American Affairs (ARA).[57] At his initial press conference, newly appointed Secretary of State Alexander Haig announced that the war against "international terrorism" would take precedence over human rights concerns because the latter's "extraordinary role" under Carter had produced "distortions" that had undermined U.S. policy objectives.[58]

The Southern Cone military dictatorships were seen as key allies in the wider hemispheric struggle against communism and radical nationalism. With indecent haste, Reagan embraced the dictatorships in Argentina, Brazil, Chile, and Uruguay, lauding their free market, neoliberal economic model and accommodating their autocratic and highly repressive style of governance as necessary to combat what State Department and CIA officials referred to as the "Moscow-Havana" axis.[59]

Despite the President's clearly, if simplistically, articulated foreign policy objectives, he had limited experience in the area, arguably less interest, and an "almost negligent management style" when it came to dealing with his bureaucracy.[60] Over time, these personal attributes played a not

---

[56] Quoted in Penny Lernoux, "Latin Reaction to Election Shows Split," NCR, November, 21, 1980, 4.

[57] Quoted in Juan de Onis, "Reagan's State Dept. Latin Team Asks Curb on 'Social Reformers,'" NYT, December 4, 1980, 1, 17.

[58] Quoted in Don Oberdorfer, "Haig Calls Terrorism Top Priority," WP, January 29, 1981, A1, A4. In a withering editorial, the WP observed that "scarcely had the administration announced its crusade against 'state-sponsored terrorism' than it embraced the one state, Chile, which has incontrovertibly sponsored terrorism on American soil." Editorial, "Our Pal Pinochet," WP, February 23, 1981, A14.

[59] See Michael Schaller, *Reckoning with Reagan: America and Its President in the 1980s* (New York: Oxford University Press, 1992), 142. The first-term Reagan image of the Soviet Union as an aggressive, interventionist power seeking to challenge the United States in its traditional sphere of influence seemed sharply at odds with Moscow's actual behavior, which was cautious, pragmatic, and reactive, willing to provide limited economic and military aid to its political allies but determined to avoid any commitment that threatened the possibility of a confrontation with the United States in its own backyard. See Nicola Miller, *Soviet Relations with Latin America, 1959–1987* (Cambridge: Cambridge University Press, 1989), esp. 148–216.

[60] Asaf Siniver, *Nixon, Kissinger, and U.S. Foreign Policy Making* (Cambridge: Cambridge University Press, 2008), 228. On Reagan's detached management style, also see Lou

unimportant role in allowing less ideological and more pragmatic conservatives to gain control over Chilean policy making. Reagan tended to be aloof and passive in discussions over the details of particular policies, initiated few of them himself, and was generally averse to issuing orders to his subordinates. If his senior advisers reached a consensus, he would usually endorse it; if not, he would typically defer making any decision. When a policy decision had been reached, he rarely took the time to check on its implementation.[61] Alexander Haig complained about the President's sheer lack of responsiveness: an early suggestion that the two meet weekly for briefings simply went unanswered, and the Secretary was never sure whether his daily reports were even read. Reagan closeted himself behind White House staffers so that it was not "government by Cabinet, but government by staff," and no one could ever be sure who was responsible for policy directives.[62] In those circumstances, presenting a case for a change of policy direction or emphasis was rarely a simple matter – often it would become a hotly contested affair between departments, agencies, and individuals each trying to advance arguments they hoped Reagan or those close to him would find compelling – because it was all too often impossible to ascertain precisely what the President was thinking or where his sympathies might lie.[63]

Decision making was further muddied by Reagan's initial reliance on a foreign policy "directorate" of key advisers that had no formal nomenclature and generally met on an ad hoc basis. The group comprised Haig, Kirkpatrick, Caspar Weinberger (Defense Secretary), William Casey (CIA Director), Richard Allen (NSC Adviser), George Bush (Vice President), Edmund Meese (White House Counselor), James Baker (White House Chief of Staff), and Michael Deaver (Deputy White House Chief of Staff). Of these, Casey, who was given an early mandate (and sizeable budget)

Cannon, *President Reagan: The Role of a Lifetime* (New York: Simon and Schuster, 1991), 172–185, 339.

[61] Michael Schaller, "Reagan and the Cold War," in Deconstructing Reagan, ed. Kyle Longley et al. (Armonk, NY: M. E. Sharpe, 2007), 8.

[62] Alexander M. Haig Jr., *Caveat: Realism, Reagan and Foreign Policy* (London: Weidenfeld and Nicolson, 1984), 91–92, 82, 85.

[63] One striking early example of this laxity was the fate of National Security Decision Directive 1(NSDD) – a blueprint for restructuring and streamlining the bureaucratic framework to provide the President with advice on foreign policy and security matters. It was not until January 1982 that Reagan finally signed a revised version of the original document. But it had little effect, as the foreign policy bureaucracy continued to function in the absence of "orderly decisionmaking" procedures or with clear "lines of responsibility." Richard A. Best Jr., *The National Security Council: An Organizational Assessment* (Washington, DC: Congressional Research Service, 2009), 18.

to rebuild the CIA into a formidable instrument of U.S. foreign policy, and Weinberger, who presided over a major armed forces renovation and rebuilding program, were arguably the most influential voices. Although Haig may have possessed the more impressive foreign policy credentials among the group, he also had the least personal connection to Reagan – a factor that played an unusually important role when it came to the President's high-level appointments. Haig's abrasive and combative personality, and his ambition to exercise a Kissinger-type control over policy making, alienated him from a number of the President's closest senior advisers inside and outside the White House.[64]

The advice Reagan received (and numerous decisions made) would often come down to the force of personalities – and individual access to the President. It was not until George Shultz was appointed Secretary in June 1982 that the State Department began to have an effective advocate within the "directorate."

The Congressional Challenge

For all its ideological chest thumping, the Reagan White House was never given free rein to conduct foreign policy as it saw fit. In the November 1980 elections, Republicans gained a majority in the Senate and picked up thirty-three seats in the House of Representatives. On the surface, the voters returned a Congress basically sympathetic to the incoming President's worldview, thus apparently providing him a strong mandate to conduct policy on his own terms. But what subsequently occurred defied these expectations. While a small coterie of legislators considered Pinochet an anticommunist hero, Reagan's relations with Capitol Hill were never trouble-free. "Congress," observed I. M. Destler, "remained open, fragmented, decentralized, and therefore hard for anybody to manage." The Senate Foreign Relations Committee (SFRC) had added six new "moderate-to-liberal" members, while the chairmanships of regional subcommittees (including Western Hemisphere Affairs) of the House

---

[64] See David Rothkopf, *Running the World* (New York: Public Affairs, 2006), 218. For a useful overview of the Reagan foreign policy bureaucracy, see Barry Rubin, *Secrets of State* (New York: Oxford University Press, 1987), 208–222. Reagan's White House advisers were never enamored of Haig, whose strident anticommunist posturing "scared the shit" out of Reagan and prompted those close to the President to undermine the Secretary from the beginning of his tenure. Assistant Chief of Staff Michael Deaver, quoted in Schaller, *Reckoning with Reagan*, 123.

Foreign Affairs Committee (HFAC) passed to "activist liberals" who would become vocal opponents of the administration's more belligerent policies.[65]

An early indicator that Reagan was dealing with a far from compliant Congress was the fate of his first nominee to fill the position of Assistant Secretary of State for HA. In May 1981, the President submitted the name of Ernest Lefever, a right-wing ideologue who had waged a systematic campaign against Carter's "public preaching and punitive policies directed against friendly and allied regimes," including Chile. Lefever advocated a greater emphasis on "quiet diplomacy" and argued that the very office he had been nominated to head should be "abolish[ed]."[66] During confirmation hearings before the SFRC, Lefever was rigorously questioned by senators all too aware of the irony of appointing someone to this position who, as Alan Cranston (D-CA) put it, "ha[d] made a career out of promoting a diminished, muted role for American human rights advocacy," opposed any human rights constraints on U.S. foreign aid, encouraged closer ties with the most repressive regional governments, and "generally displayed a blindness towards human rights violations by rightwing dictatorships."[67] Lefever was unrepentant, and the Committee voted 13–4 to reject his nomination. This was a humiliating outcome for the administration because not only was the Committee chaired by a Republican but the White House had mounted an aggressive lobbying campaign in defense of the nomination.[68] The result indicated at least to some Reagan officials that, when it came to dealing with Congress, "saying we don't care about human rights is a loser."[69]

---

[65] I. M. Destler, "Reagan, Congress, and Foreign Policy in 1981," in *President and Congress: Assessing Reagan's First Year*, ed. Norman J. Ornstein (Washington, DC: American Enterprise Institute, 1982), 68.

[66] Ernest W. Lefever, *Human Rights and Foreign Policy* (Washington, DC: Ethics and Public Policy Center, 1980).

[67] U.S. Congress, Senate, Committee on Foreign Relations, *Nomination of Ernest W. Lefever*, 97th Cong., 1st Sess., May 18, 19, June 4, 5, 1981, 3, 4, 68, 129–130. A memorandum originating in Cranston's office prior to the hearings provided a blunt summary of Lefever's human rights views: "[He] opposes any human rights legislation; opposes public US support for human rights; opposes Human Rights Bureau; views human rights in Communist countries as Red-baiting opportunities." Quoted in Sarah Snyder, "The Defeat of Ernest Lefever's Nomination: Keeping Human Rights on the United States Foreign Policy Agenda," in *Challenging U.S. Foreign Policy*, ed. Bevin Sewell and Scott Lucas (Basingstoke: Palgrave Macmillan, 2011), 140.

[68] Destler, "Reagan, Congress, and Foreign Policy in 1981," 69.

[69] Quoted in Kathryn Sikkink, *Mixed Signals: U.S. Human Rights Policy and Latin America* (Ithaca: Cornell University Press, 2004), 155.

While the executive branch succeeded in winning greater flexibility in deciding the terms of economic aid and arms sales to repressive anticommunist Third World regimes, legislators never gave Reagan carte blanche to fund these rulers as he saw fit. Congress was always more critical of these regimes per se and was more inclined to view them, and not merely their human rights records, as the problem, which partly explained the persistent disagreements between the two branches over the amount of pressure that should be applied on the Chilean and other Latin military dictatorships. Reagan officials would soon discover that a number of influential legislators considered how the administration approached the Chile 'problem' – a litmus test that could affect the support it could expect for other, more important regional (and global) initiatives.

Individual Rights versus Institutional Reform

Within the foreign policy bureaucracy were pockets of resistance to abandoning human rights considerations entirely. The top post in the State's HA Bureau remained vacant until late November 1981, when Elliott Abrams, a staff aide to New York Democratic Senator Daniel Patrick Moynihan, was confirmed by the Senate as the new Assistant Secretary. This failure to make an appointment for almost a year ensured that the Bureau carried virtually no weight during the early foreign policy debates. Secretary Haig was not in the least perturbed, dismissing human rights as "a rather foolish subject."[70]

Those State Department officials less hostile to the idea that human rights should not be summarily dismissed from future foreign policy decision making, in contrast to the Carter approach, saw it primarily as a weapon to use against the Soviet Union and its allies. A memo drafted by Abrams within days of his nomination to the HA post, and authorized by Deputy Secretary of State William Clark and Undersecretary Richard Kennedy, advocated the restoration of human rights to a core role in U.S. foreign policy practice because it equated with the fundamental moral and ideological objective of the anti-Soviet struggle, which was to spread "political liberty" around the world.[71] The memo was also intended to signal Congress that the administration was intent on pursuing a coherent

---

[70] "Transcript of Interview with Elliott Abrams," November 16, 1990, in Kenneth W. Thompson, ed., *Foreign Policy in the Reagan Presidency*. Lanham: University Press of America, 1990, 106; interview with Elliott Abrams.

[71] Quoted in John Ehrman, *The Rise of Neoconservatism* (New Haven: Yale University Press, 1995), 157. The memo and its recommendations were approved, reportedly by

human rights approach to minimize opposition to other "important foreign policy initiatives."[72] Abrams promised to limit public criticism of friendly abusers and defined opposition to the global spread of communism as "an essential part of human rights policy." Where he diverged from the Kirkpatrick-Haig view was in a belief that "you cannot make a clear distinction between East and West on the basis of freedom if the U.S. is supporting dictatorships around the world."[73]

Unlike some Reagan officials who dismissed Carter's human rights policy as little more than politics of useless gesturing, Abrams offered a slightly more generous assessment, seeing it as a combination of "a kind of foolish idealism and also what Jeane [Kirkpatrick] called 'Blame America first.' My criticism was not of [Carter policymakers'] intention but of the outcome. They didn't achieve much." In contrast, the Reagan White House intended to support pro-U.S. regimes in the Third World without necessarily overlooking completely their human rights violations. In his introduction to the 1981 *Country Reports on Human Rights Practices* that served as the framework for White House policy, Abrams laid out the general approach, essentially along the lines of the Clark-Kennedy memo. The Soviet Union was the primary target, "quiet diplomacy" would be the vehicle for encouraging Third World allies to improve their performance without allowing such criticism to affect U.S. interests or undermine U.S. influence and, reflecting continuity with Carter policy, the focus would be largely confined to promoting political freedoms, "effectively excluding economic and social rights from consideration as basic human rights."[74]

Pinochet and the Chilean Armed Forces

Even though the bureaucratic debate over Chile policy revealed Reagan officials to be largely uninformed about the fundamental nature of the country's armed forces – its institutional memory, global outlook, self-perception, values, and ideals – the shifts and changes in U.S. policy cannot be fully comprehended without attention to the history and

Reagan himself. Ibid. Also see "Human Rights Revisited," *New Republic*, November 25, 1981, 5–6.

[72] Quotes in Jesús Velasco, *Neoconservatives in U.S. Foreign Policy under Ronald Reagan and George W. Bush* (Baltimore: Johns Hopkins University Press, 2010), 101; Cynthia Brown, ed., *With Friends Like These* (New York: Pantheon Books, 1985), 5.

[73] Interview with Elliott Abrams.

[74] Rossiter, *Human Rights*, 24. Other quotes in Christopher Madison, "Abrams, State's Human Rights Chief, Tries to Tailor a Policy to Suit Reagan," *National Journal*, May 1, 1982, 763.

culture of this coercive institution, which had long viewed itself as the very repository of national values, interests, and goals.[75] During the twentieth century, all three services played key roles in laying the economic and political foundations of the modern Chilean state, including the adoption of the 1925 Constitution. Beginning in the 1920s, the twin ideas of the state playing a key role in industrial and economic development, and the importance of social justice to avoid instability and the political radicalization of the lower classes, began to permeate the thinking of the army's officer corps.[76] So also did a nationalist outlook reflected in a strand of thinking opposed to foreign economic domination and in favor of domestic control over strategic resource sectors. None of this, however, inclined the armed forces to jettison an innate anticommunism combined with a more generalized distrust of mass movements and the potential dangers of popular democracy.

The other distinctive feature of the Chilean armed forces was a deeply instilled institutional discipline: each service placed a premium on armed forces unity, and officers were imbued with a belief in "order, hierarchy, and authority."[77] This was a critical factor influencing the armed forces' behavior following the 1973 coup: it partly explained the discipline, unity, and shared sense of purpose that characterized the dictatorship and the extraordinary impenetrability of the junta itself. In consequence, as Robert Barros has persuasively argued, based on an examination of transcripts of the junta's meetings, external actors (both inside and outside Chile) had limited knowledge of the internal dynamics of decision making within the highest levels of the Pinochet regime, and this often produced demands, requests, expectations, and responses that were based on a fundamental misreading of the junta's intentions and behavior.[78]

---

[75] For comprehensive analyses of the Chilean armed forces history and culture, see Frederick M. Nunn, *The Military in Chilean History* (Albuquerque: University of New Mexico Press, 1976); John Bawden, "Outlook of the Officers: Military Thought in Chile, 1960–1990" (PhD thesis, University of California, Riverside, June 2009). The latter study is largely based on a detailed analysis of Chilean military thinking as expressed in intraservice journals and periodicals.

[76] After more than seven years of the Pinochet regime, despite a program of large-scale denationalization, the remaining state enterprises still generated a greater share of GNP than the state sector did in 1965. See Juan Gabriel Valdés, *Pinochet's Economists* (New York: Cambridge University Press, 1995), 269–270.

[77] Liisa North, "The Military in Chilean Politics," in *Armies and Politics in Latin America*, 2nd ed., ed. Abraham F. Lowenthal and J. Samuel Fitch (New York: Holmes and Meier, 1976), 181.

[78] Robert Barros, *Constitutionalism and Dictatorship: Pinochet, the Junta, and the 1980 Constitution* (Cambridge: Cambridge University Press, 2002).

A formative experience of the generation of military officers who came to power in the 1970s was their key role in crushing nationwide strikes in the mines during 1947, which they interpreted as part of an effort by the Communist Party to topple the government.[79] During the 1950s and 1960s, the teaching of geopolitics in Chile's war academies by, among others, two junta members – Augusto Pinochet and the navy's José Merino – served to reinforce nationalist, statist, and anticommunist sentiments. Geopolitical thinking was based on "the idea of the state as a living organism engaged in a constant struggle for survival" against the forces of economic decline and political and moral decay.[80] Marxist notions of internationalism and class conflict were seen as threats that weakened the nation by destroying its social cohesion.[81] Chilean military studies of insurrectionist movements from Algeria to Vietnam reinforced the idea that civil society was a battlefield on which, left unchecked, Marxists "inveigled themselves into power by making tactical alliances with various political factions, by using xenophobia, nationalism, or legitimate demands for social justice to mobilize people around a popular revolution they could eventually hijack and steer towards communism."[82]

This thinking partly explained the military's interest in economic development – poverty empowered revolutionaries – and constituted a further reason for it to suspect both democracy's "excesses" and politicians who were tempted to exploit that system for their own ends. But an ingrained belief that matters of security (however exaggerated) took precedence over other considerations (human rights, international opinion) made the Chilean armed forces extremely resistant to outside appeals to "moderate" their behavior or return to barracks before they themselves could be satisfied that their mission had been accomplished. Although Pinochet was often regarded by U.S. officials as obstinate, thickheaded, or concerned only with his own power, the General's ability to maintain his position for so long after the coup resulted in large measure from his capacity to represent, articulate, and defend these essential cultural and historical characteristics of the most powerful coercive institution of the Chilean state. From the perspective of U.S. officials, however, the result was often frustration that Pinochet simply 'wasn't getting the message.'

---

[79] See Bawden, "Outlook of the Officers," 75; Carlos Huneeus, *The Pinochet Regime* (Boulder: Lynne Rienner, 2007), 111.

[80] Bawden, "Outlook of the Officers," 42, 103–106, 110.

[81] See John Child, "Geopolitical Thinking in Latin America," *Latin American Research Review* 14, no. 2 (1979): 89–111.

[82] See Bawden, "Outlook of the Officers," 152.

On September 11, 1980, seven years to the day after the overthrow of Salvador Allende, Chileans went to the polls to approve a new Constitution drafted on the instructions of Pinochet. Although held in controversial circumstances (under a state of emergency and with all political parties outlawed), the document was approved by a majority of voters. It ratified the military's social and economic reforms, entrenched Pinochet's rule as President of the Republic for a further eight years, and severely circumscribed Chilean politics well into the future. But the Constitution also contained temporary dispositions that laid out a clearly defined timetable for a return to elected government, including a plebiscite in 1988 to decide whether a regime candidate (eventually Pinochet) would continue in office for a further eight-year term or, failing that, competitive elections the following year for the presidency and a new Congress. In 1981, few U.S. officials paid as much as lip service to this transition plan that eventually would be accepted by the Reagan administration as a road map for pursuing the restoration of civilian rule in Chile and, particularly in its second term, would pressure Pinochet to achieve the necessary milestones along the way – an end to harassment of political opponents, lifting states of exception, legalizing political parties, allowing his opponents access to the mass media, and, finally, honoring the outcome of the process.

This study documents and explains why the policy shift from a "close embrace" to a more complex approach that put Chilean democracy on Washington's agenda, though dramatic in appearance, was consistent with, indeed ultimately dictated by, the same fundamental interests that shaped U.S. regional policy since the beginning of the twentieth century. It represented a shift in tactics, not a change in historic overarching policy objectives. As long as Pinochet presided over an environment conducive to U.S. trade and investment interests, and supportive of its regional political and security priorities, the Reagan administration was initially prepared to actively support – or at least not actively oppose – the Chilean dictator. But influenced by a new cycle of transitions from dictatorship to democracy across the region, concerned that Pinochet's ambitions might undermine support for the junta's economic reforms, and encouraged by the emergence of a civilian alternative potentially acceptable to both Washington and Pinochet, the White House and State Department shifted track and began to encourage redemocratization in Chile. The process by which the administration came to accept that this moment had arrived and would require a new policy approach, nevertheless, was far from effortless. Apart from the difficulties encountered in getting Pinochet to accept a transition program, it challenged long-held inclinations, witnessed differences in the interpretation of basic facts, engendered personality conflicts, and triggered a vigorous interagency debate before consensus was achieved.

I

In from the Cold

The Reagan administration came into office so determined to reverse the tone and nature of U.S. foreign policy as it had developed under President Jimmy Carter that one senior official in the ARA imagined his new superiors "felt that they were conducting a hostile takeover." The atmosphere, he said, "was very much that nobody here could be trusted."[1] Transition team members, recalled Carter's Deputy Assistant for National Security Affairs David Aaron, "were not interested in being briefed on anything."[2] Robert Pastor, the NSC's Latin American staffer, encountered the icy nature of the transition environment in a meeting with incoming NSC Adviser Richard Allen: "Even though these people who were coming in represented much of what I disagreed with, I felt that as an American official I should be prepared to help them and brief them. Not only did Dick Allen express disinterest at best but he said to me 'You'd better be out of that office at noon on January 20 or police are going to come and take you out of that office.'"[3] On the other hand, Reagan's Secretary of State, Alexander Haig, had quite a different view of the transition dynamics. "I found no great enthusiasm in the Department of State for the Reagan Administration," he would later write. "The fear

---

[1] Interview with George F. Jones.
[2] Telephone interview with David L. Aaron.
[3] Interview with Robert Pastor. "The new crowd who came in on the transition team," recalled a State Department HA official at the time, "oh, it was a very nasty transition. The assumption was that anyone who had worked with the Carter administration was obviously a kind of lefty, and the idea that you could be loyal to the president regardless of who the president was was something alien to some of the more extreme people there." Theresa A. Tull interview, FAOHC.

was abroad that a legion of right-wing activists was going to march in and start conducting American diplomacy according to the rules of a political rally."[4] The predominant view of Carter's Latin American policy among the newcomers, according to a senior career Foreign Service Officer at the time, was that it had angered political allies, especially military regimes, and that "we should stop meddling and telling them what they ought to do with respect to their own internal situations and human rights. They were good anti-communists and wanted to be our friends. We should make the most of it."[5]

Motivated by these kinds of sentiments, the new administration was determined to pull the State Department into line. ARA and its career staff members were a principal target of what one Reagan official described as a transition team "witch hunt." Within twenty-four hours of the formal transfer of power, "everybody was pretty much gone from the [ARA] front office."[6] The majority were replaced by political appointees ideologically opposed to Carter policies south of the border or else career officers lacking expertise or experience in regional affairs.[7]

In Chile, the ruling junta was euphoric over the election result. "The military were dancing in the streets," Ambassador George Landau remembered, "because Reagan had finally won, they had finally gotten rid of Carter and everything had changed."[8] Interviewed by *El Mercurio* in early December, Foreign Minister René Rojas predicted an "open and closer dialogue" with Washington once Reagan was ensconced in the White House.[9] Charles Grover, then Deputy Chief of Mission (DCM) in the U.S. Embassy in Santiago, predicted more of a wait-and-see approach, unconvinced that General Pinochet allowed himself the same sense of elation. Secretary Haig may have given the impression that Ronald Reagan

---

[4] Haig, *Caveat*, 63, 64.
[5] Robert Service interview, FAOHC.
[6] Robert B. Morley interview, FAOHC.
[7] See Kai Bird, "Ronald Reagan's Foreign Service," *APF Reporter* 7, no. 3 (1984). U.S. embassies around the world soon got the message that the Reagan White House and State Department were not receptive to viewpoints that diverged from the ambassadors' assessments. The result was a dramatic decline in the number of "dissent cables" to Washington: from twenty-eight during 1977 to fifteen in 1981 to a mere five in 1983. Said one State Department official, this "reflect[ed] a feeling among [Foreign Service] officers that policy making ha[d] been polarized and therefore alternative ideas [were] less welcome [and] that espousing ideas on their own merits [was] apt to put your career at risk." Quoted in ibid.
[8] Interview with George W. Landau.
[9] Quoted in "Minister Rojas Discusses OAS, U.S. Relations," FBIS: DR: LA, December 3, 1980, p. E2.

was going to adopt a "more favourable attitude to ad hoc regimes" in Latin America, but Grover's impression was that Pinochet had not "fooled himself for one moment on that."[10]

With a Republican President in the White House, the frosty relationship between Washington and Santiago began to thaw almost immediately. Reagan officials quickly signaled that improved ties with the Chilean dictatorship were high on the administration's regional agenda. Lauding the generals' anticommunism and free market economic model, the arm's-length policy Carter had adopted largely over the issue of human rights was to be replaced by a 'close embrace.' Deputy Assistant Secretary of State for Inter-American Affairs John Bushnell – appointed to the position by Carter in 1977 and retained by Reagan – told the HFAC that "in Chile we believe our interests, including human rights, are best served by a less confrontational approach than has characterized policy in recent years."[11] To put ties on a more constructive basis, the administration intended to move quickly to remove many of the obstacles to normalized relations imposed during the previous four years.[12]

At the same time, this desire to engage the junta was accompanied by an uneasy feeling among some members of the foreign policy bureaucracy that getting Pinochet to implement even limited changes to his repressive governance would be difficult. "If I were to prioritize our goals in the Southern Cone area during Reagan's first year," said a middle-level State Department official in ARA, "I think that we thought there was more hope for change in Argentina than any other country. We thought that both Chile and Paraguay were hard cases and not likely to see change in the foreseeable future."[13] In Santiago, U.S. Embassy officials subscribed to a more dire prognosis: that Pinochet might further polarize Chilean society and thereby force the political center "to choose between the right or the left."[14]

Reaching Out to Pinochet

Understanding Chile's internal dynamics appeared to rank low among Haig's priorities. The day after Reagan's inauguration, Ambassador

---

[10] Interview with Charles W. Grover.
[11] U.S. Congress, House, Committee on Foreign Affairs, Subcommittees on International Economic Policy and Trade and on Inter-American Affairs, *U.S. Economic Sanctions Against Chile*, 97th Cong., 1st Sess., March 10, 1981, p. 41.
[12] Briefing Paper, "Chile," drafted ARA/SC, June 22, 1981, DOS/FOIAe, III.
[13] Interview with Robert B. Morley.
[14] Charles W. Grover interview, FAOHC.

George Landau received a call from the new Secretary's Office to return to Washington immediately for a meeting. As one of those rumored to be on Reagan's hit list, Landau assumed his diplomatic career was about to end. Much to his surprise, Haig offered him the ambassadorial posting to El Salvador instead (which Landau declined). What particularly struck Landau was the absence of any reference to Chile during the entire conversation. Secretary Haig "never asked me a single question about Chile," the Ambassador reminisced. "It was not on their minds."[15]

Haig nevertheless spelled out the administration's intention to improve ties with the military regime publicly and emphatically in early February 1981. "We will strengthen our relations with the Chilean government," he told the Santiago-based magazine *Cosas*. "I want that to be very clear."[16] The revival of an active diplomatic relationship symbolized the policy shift in Washington. "We found we were suddenly receiving a lot of visitors," DCM Grover remembered, "principally military people but also CODELs [congressional delegations]." Some aspects involved in building the new relationship, however, received low priority: it was not until April 1982, for instance, that staff levels at the Embassy were brought back to where they had been prior to the reductions made by Carter as part of a package of sanctions imposed on Chile in November 1979, after its supreme court rejected a U.S. request for the extradition of three Chileans wanted in connection with the assassination of former Chilean Foreign Minister Orlando Letelier and his assistant Ronni Moffitt in Washington in 1976.[17]

Economic relations between the United States and Chile underwent a significant change as Washington moved to roll back a number of sanctions imposed by the Carter White House. Testifying before two House subcommittees in March, Bushnell vigorously defended this aspect of the policy shift, highlighting, among other factors, the incongruity between Carter's selective sanctions against the Pinochet regime and the latter's settlement of claims by expropriated U.S. firms "on an equitable basis," as well as the regime's support of U.S. positions "on many hemispheric and global issues." Chile continued to be the subject of a "blatant double standard" that overlooked recent improvements, Bushnell insisted, and

[15] Interview with George W. Landau.
[16] Quoted in William R. Long, "Reagan Held Inviting Chile Back to Fold of US Friends," JC, March 4, 1981, p. 11A. Six days later, Pinochet announced there would be no political opening during his eight-year transition government.
[17] Interview with Charles W. Grover. For a detailed analysis of the murders and their aftermath, see John Dinges and Saul Landau, *Assassination on Embassy Row* (New York: Pantheon Books, 1980).

maintaining the 1979 prohibition on Export-Import Bank (Eximbank) financing of American overseas investors in particular could only serve to damage the prospects for potential U.S. investors. This sanction had already played a role in undermining a number of U.S. project bids, and the need to move swiftly was dictated by "the fact that there are several large projects coming up for final tender in Chile over the next few months."[18] Significantly, revocation of the prohibition was not accompanied by any assurances from Santiago of greater cooperation regarding the Letelier case. Effectively, the White House had removed this as a major obstacle to improved ties because, as one U.S. official bluntly explained, there was "no likelihood of any further cooperation from Chile on this case, so why extend the agony?"[19]

At the Treasury Department, Secretary Donald Regan moved with equal speed to get the Carter policy of opposing or abstaining on MDB loans to Chile and other Third World countries on human rights grounds overturned. In a memo to Haig he requested a thorough examination of the policy in relation to these "problem countries."[20] Under the Harkin amendment to the 1977 International Financial Institutions Act, Treasury-appointed U.S. executive directors were required to oppose loans to any country whose government engaged in a consistent pattern of gross violations of internationally recognized human rights, unless the program to be funded met basic human needs. There was a consensus among senior State Department officials on the need to reassess the role that human rights considerations should play in determining votes in the MDB's, but this did not extend to the involved bureaus where deep divisions existed. The result was that loan applications would, for the moment, be treated on a case-by-case basis pending the outcome of interagency discussions. On Chile, HA initially favored abstention votes because of the persistence of widespread abuses and the formidable congressional and public opposition to Pinochet's rule. State's Policy Planning Bureau (S/P) concurred with HA, but for tactical reasons only – specifically a belief that supporting Chilean loan requests could either "complicate" administration efforts to ease the restrictions on military aid to the regime or have a "negative" impact on getting Congress to lift

---

[18] U.S. Congress, House, "U.S. Economic Sanctions against Chile," pp. 37, 51; quoted in Edward Walsh, "Administration Defends Lifting of Aid Sanctions," *WP*, March 11, 1981, p. A16.

[19] Quoted in James Nelson Goodsell, "Reagan Team Breaks Ice on Chile, Saying 'What's the Use of Sanctions,'" *CSM*, February 28, 1981, 9.

[20] Memo, Regan to Haig, February 23, 1981, Executive Secretariat, NSC, "Human Right Feb 1981–March 1982," Box 6, RRL.

similar restrictions in the case of El Salvador. ARA and the Bureau of Economic and Business Affairs (EB), conversely, advocated "yes" votes, contending that there had been "significant human rights progress" and that to support the loans would have no impact on legislation related to El Salvador.[21]

Preparing for a June meeting with Chilean Foreign Minister René Rojas, Secretary Haig received a "talking points" memo from his Assistant Secretary for Inter-American Affairs, Thomas O. Enders, that began: "The Reagan administration wants to *normalize relations with Chile as quickly as possible; we're your friends; there will be no public posturing* by any official."[22] A Department briefing paper for Vice President George H. Bush's meeting with Rojas stressed the Chilean government's equally strong determination "to expand all types of official and private relations." The major obstacle on the U.S. side was the 1974 Kennedy amendment to the Foreign Assistance Act (FAA) prohibiting security assistance and sales to Chile, and the lack of any prospect of influencing Congress to overturn or modify it in the medium term. The one point of "continuing tension" from the Chilean side was the junta's perception that U.S. policy was "tilt[ing]" toward Argentina in the border dispute centered on the Beagle Channel.[23] Nonetheless, such was the warm reception given Rojas by senior U.S. government officials that *El Mercurio* editorialized about "a new attitude of the U.S. Government toward Chile and Latin America in general."[24]

Following a major review of the human rights landscape across much of the Third World during the first half of 1981, the State Department announced that the U.S. government would no longer oppose loans to military regimes in Korea, Argentina, Chile, Paraguay, and Uruguay for non–basic human needs (BHN) because "the administration view is that there is not a consistent pattern of gross violation to be found in these countries."[25] In the specific case of Chile, Haig justified reversing

---

[21] Memo, Palmer, Hormats, Enders, Wolfowitz to Haig, June 26, 1981, DOS/FOIAe, III.
[22] Memo, ARA Enders to Haig, June 5, 1981, ibid. (our emphasis).
[23] Briefing paper, DOS, "VP's Meeting with Rojas," June 8, 1981, Executive Secretariat, NSC, Country File, "Chile Vol. 1, 1/2081–7/31/84 (5)," Box 91868, RRL.
[24] "Paper on Foreign Minister's Visit to Washington," FBIS: DR: LA, June 15, 1981, E1.
[25] Undersecretary of State for Political Affairs Walter Stoessel Jr., in U.S. Congress, House, Committee on Foreign Affairs, Subcommittee on Human Rights and International Organizations, *Implementation of Congressionally Mandated Human Rights Provisions,* Vol. 1, 97th Cong., 1st Sess., July 14, 30, September 17, 1981, 13. The Reagan White House viewed relations with Argentina as entering "a bright new day." Robert E. Service interview, FAOHC. This was no doubt enhanced by the generals' decision to actively

the Carter policy by quoting a Department assessment that there had been "significant improvements" in the country's human rights situation, including "dramatic, dramatic reductions" in violence against its civilian population.[26] On that basis, Haig cabled the Santiago Embassy in early July that Washington intended to vote in favor of a $126 million Inter-American Development Bank (IADB) loan for highway maintenance. He admitted that the loan "does not meet basic human rights criteria" but invoked the post-1976 "improvement" rationale to justify the decision.[27] The legal requirement to consult with Congress prior to making decisions of this kind was in effect deemed no longer operative.

The issue of human rights and U.S. policy in the MDBs was the subject of a lengthy House subcommittee hearing later that month, where administration officials attempted to spell out in more detail the case for asserting that the four Southern Cone governments were not at the time perpetrating gross human rights abuses. One exchange in particular illustrated the different interpretations that could be given to that term. Subcommittee chair Jerry Patterson (D-CA) expressed particular skepticism about the alleged improved conditions in Chile. He found it difficult to comprehend why a positive determination had been made given that the information provided to his office, which he assumed State was privy to as well, revealed that the situation was actually deteriorating. Senior Deputy Assistant Secretary Ernest Johnston conceded that there had been recent increases in arrests but insisted that, in quantitative terms, there had been "a big improvement." Patterson tartly responded, "[But] is 'improvement,' improvement by torturing fewer people than before, really the standard we want to use for assessing human rights? Or is it stopping the practice?" As the hearing proceeded, the chair exhibited

cooperate with U.S. policy in Central America, including a willingness to help to train and arm the Nicaraguan contras. See Roy Gutman, *Banana Diplomacy: The Making of American Policy in Nicaragua, 1981–1987* (New York: Simon and Schuster, 1988), 49–54. By contrast, the Chileans offered little more than verbal support for Reagan's subregional policy. See, for example, Lieutenant Colonel Oliver North's less than successful effort to get active Chilean support of the anti-Sandinista war during 1985. Peter Kornbluh, "The Chilean Missile Caper," *The Nation*, May 14, 1988, 667–669.

26   Quoted in Judith Miller, "U.S., in Change Is Backing Loans to 4 Latin Lands," *NYT*, July 9, 1981, 1; John. M. Goshko, "Administration Reiterates Aim of Scuttling Carter Rights Policies," *WP*, July 10, 1981, A12.

27   Telegram, Haig to AmEmb Santiago et al., July 6, 1981, DOS/FOIAe, III. Over the next seven days, U.S. representatives in the MDBs cast favorable votes for another five non-BHN loans to these countries. W. Frick Curry and Joanne Royce, *Enforcing Human Rights: Congress and the Multilateral Banks* (Washington, DC: Center for International Policy, 1985), 12.

increasing frustration over Johnson's refusal to specify the thresholds for determining whether a consistent pattern of abuses existed. Pushed on the issue of prolonged detention without charges, Johnson thought the administration would consider "longer" than twenty days falling into that category. His interrogator was singularly unimpressed: "You can do a lot in 20 days. I would hate to be 20 days incommunicado without any opportunity to get counsel or to be charged or to know why you're there and get beat up three times a day." Patterson was just as unconvinced by Johnson's insistence that the decline in absolute numbers of human rights abuses was an appropriate yardstick for talking about "improvements": "if they are still today torturing, if they are still today detaining, without trial or reference to basic civil liberties [and] if they have been doing it for 3 years and they are still doing it today, it does seem to me that there is a consistent pattern."[28]

Clashes between the Reagan White House and Congress over Latin American policy seemed inevitable from the outset. Victor Johnson linked his appointment as Staff Director of the House Western Hemisphere sub-committee to a strong perception on the Hill "that the Reagan administration was going to make Latin America almost a wedge issue, an area where they were going to emphasize their differences with the Democrats, with the Carter administration, and overthrow many of the presumptions that used to guide policy and put in place their own." He described Republican efforts to "stack the Foreign Affairs Committee with right wing members" contrary to a long tradition of appointing bipartisan inter-nationalists from both parties. As foreign policy issues assumed a more partisan quality, the membership started changing "partly to reflect that and partly as a cause of it. That's basically the way they tried to influence the committee. The Republicans took up the administration's talking points on whatever it was on the table." Yet, despite the enthusiasm displayed by senior Reagan policy makers for normalizing relations with Chile, and a determined effort to convince Congress, the executive branch was hard put to mobilize an influential constituency on whom it could depend to rally around the cause. On the contrary, the refusal or failure to consult the Hill on the Eximbank and MDB decisions, Pinochet's reluc-tance to contemplate any major human rights initiatives, and Congress's

[28] U.S. Congress, House, Committee on Banking, Finance and Urban Affairs, Subcommittee on International Development Institutions and Finance, *Human Rights and U.S. Policy in the Multilateral Development Banks*, 97th Cong., 1st Sess., July 21, 23, 1981, 79–80, 81, 82, 84, 85, 90.

insistence that until there was evidence of declining abuses by the regime, U.S. aid spigots would remain largely shut down promised to generate ongoing tensions between the two branches of government. "Especially in the House," Johnson explained, "people didn't buy into assumptions that an alliance with the Pinochets of the region advanced the national interest."[29]

That, nonetheless, was precisely how senior Reagan officials viewed the situation. The visit by Reagan's United Nations (UN) ambassador, Jeane Kirkpatrick, to Chile and a number of other countries in August 1981 was intended to serve a dual purpose, said a member of her delegation: "to demonstrate that the U.S. would no longer object to a government's internal affairs, and to take a swing around some of the principal countries and let them know there's a new group in Washington, and we're all your friends, and we'll get along and so on." Kirkpatrick's meeting with Pinochet, unaccompanied by Ambassador Landau, and her refusal to meet with the opposition leadership – "for fear of offending our friends in the Chilean government," as one of her entourage recalled – conveyed a powerful symbolic message. After conferring with the junta leader, Kirkpatrick reported back to Landau, "'You know, you can do business with them. We can work with Pinochet.'" The visit "showed the Chileans, it showed the opposition, it showed the government," Landau observed, "that things had changed. Pinochet figured, after he talked to Jeane, that everything was hunky-dory."[30] Kirkpatrick then told a Santiago press conference that Washington desired to "normalize completely its relations with Chile in order to work together in a pleasant way," dismissing the Letelier case as "no impediment whatsoever" to improved bilateral ties. Except for some minor loose ends, the case had been effectively "solved" in Kirkpatrick's eyes – a view not shared by many in Congress or among all of her State Department colleagues.[31] Some of the UN Ambassador's closest ideological bedfellows were equally unhappy with her dismissive attitude toward the antigovernment forces. "Let's put it this way," said United Nations Human Rights Commission (UNHRC) representative Richard Schifter. "I was taking a position somewhat different to hers."[32] Less than forty-eight hours after Kirkpatrick left Chile, several prominent members of the political opposition, including the

---

[29] Interview with Victor C. Johnson.
[30] Interview with George W. Landau.
[31] Quoted in John Dinges, "Kirkpatrick Trip Upsets Opposition in Chile," *WP*, August 13, 1981, A25.
[32] Interview with Richard Schifter.

President of the Chilean Human Rights Commission, Jaime Castillo, whom she had declined to meet, were sent into exile for approximately fifteen months. Nor did Kirkpatrick's message or Pinochet's actions in the aftermath of her visit help administration efforts to ease congressional restrictions on military aid to Chile. Undersecretary of State for Political Affairs Walter Stoessel Jr. told the new Chilean Ambassador to the United States, Enrique Valenzuela, that if Pinochet continued to take such harsh measures, it would make the job of lobbying Congress to repeal the Kennedy amendment more arduous than it already was.[33]

Given Congress's determination to maintain the linkage between military aid and human rights progress in Chile, White House efforts to improve bilateral relations were going to prove difficult. The one early exception involved a decision that did not require congressional assent. In 1980, in response to Santiago's lack of cooperation in the Letelier investigation, the Carter administration decided not to invite the Chilean Navy to participate in the annual Operation UNITAS joint exercises in the South Pacific. Following Reagan's election, that decision was reversed. Peter Whitney, the State Department's Chile Desk Officer between 1979 and 1981, recounted that, despite repeated efforts by the Department of Defense, the Carter White House could not be persuaded "to make the call on what to do about UNITAS exercises" for quite some time. By contrast, when Whitney and his superior John Bushnell met with Reagan's Deputy Secretary of State William Clark, they were told simply to lay out the pros and cons and Clark would get Reagan to make a quick decision. "We wrote a short memo," said Whitney, "and Ronald Reagan approved it."[34]

Throughout 1981, administration officials repeatedly and publicly stated that the human rights situation in Chile had significantly improved and that abuses perpetrated under the military dictatorship were "by no means unique, either in Latin America, among nations on other continents, or in totalitarian states."[35] In his annual report on Chile, the UN Special Rapporteur failed to confirm Washington's upbeat assessments. On the contrary, the report excoriated the regime over the continuation of the torture, murder, and disappearances of unionists, academics, church people, and political dissidents carried out by the security agencies and

[33] See Memo of Conversation between Stoessel and Valenzuela, September 10, 1981, DOS/FOIAe, III.
[34] Interview with Peter Whitney.
[35] USUN delegate Michael Novak, quoted in "U.S. Opposes U.N. Plan on Rights Issue in Chile," *NYT*, February 27, 1981, 8.

their paramilitary allies, and concluded that there had been no improvement in the overall situation during the previous twelve months. Justifying its votes against draft texts on Chile, and an amended resolution adopted by the UN General Assembly (UNGA) in early December expressing "grave concern at the persistence and even deterioration of the human rights situation in Chile," the U.S. delegation accused the Special Rapporteur of giving limited attention to the release of most political prisoners, and to other gains, "concentrating instead on those areas where there has been limited progress or where there has been an increase in government powers not subject to judicial review." It offered a similar justification for opposing an extension of the Rapporteur's mandate. As far as the U.S. government was concerned, the situation had "improved considerably," and Chile was being unfairly singled out for special attention.[36]

When the administration nominated career diplomat James Theberge, former head of the Nicaraguan Embassy during the Somoza era in the mid-1970s, as U.S. Ambassador to Chile, Senator Paul Tsongas (D-MA) spoke for many of his colleagues in describing the selection as "a clear symbol of the administration's changing perception of the Chilean regime." At his December 1981 Senate confirmation hearing, Theberge repeated the administration mantra that "there has been a significant improvement in the human rights situation in Chile" since 1976 and suggested that presidential certification of progress might be enough to satisfy Congress and persuade it to resume aid to the military regime. Senator Edward Kennedy (D-MA) angrily dismissed the idea, characterizing the White House attitude as one of "'see no evil, hear no evil' when evil is there to be seen by all."[37] Nonetheless, after an extended debate in both chambers, Congress endorsed a compromise provision that would

---

[36] Quotes in *Yearbook of the United Nations 1981*, vol. 35 (New York: United Nations, Department of Public Information, 1985), 951–953; Telegram, Shultz (Stoessel) to USUN Mission, December 3, 1981, DOS/FOIAe, III.

[37] U.S. Congress, Senate, Committee on Foreign Relations, *Theberge Nomination to Be Ambassador*, Unpublished Transcript, December 7, 1981; *Congressional Record – Senate*, 97th Cong., 1st Sess., Vol. 127, Part 24, December 16, 1981, 32133. Tsongas quoted in *Congressional Record – Senate*, 97th Cong., 2d Sess., Vol. 128, Part 3, March 2, 1982, 2803. Archconservative Jessie Helms (R-NC) opposed the nomination, accusing Theberge of allegedly playing a significant role in the withdrawal of U.S. support for the Somoza regime in Nicaragua during his stint as Ambassador. The Committee's most liberal member, Edward Kennedy, attacked Theberge's failure to acknowledge the serious nature of reports on the deteriorating human rights situation in Chile and his insistence that there had been "substantial improvement" since 1977. *Congressional Record – Senate*, 97th Cong., 2d Sess., Vol. 128, Part 3, March 4, 1982, 2798, 2799. Ultimately, the full Senate voted 83–12, with five abstentions, to confirm Theberge as the new U.S. Ambassador to Chile.

remove the restrictions on security assistance, arms sales, and military aid if the President could certify that Chile had made "significant progress" in complying with internationally recognized standards of human rights and the junta cooperated in the arrest and prosecution of Chilean operatives indicted by a U.S. federal grand jury in the Letelier case.[38]

Certifying Chile on human rights grounds posed no particular problem for the White House: its attitude was well illustrated by the decision to send the now former Ambassador George Landau as its representative to the funeral of ex-Chilean President Eduardo Frei. "For a former ambassador to attend the funeral of an important head of state," explained a then State Department official, "was about the lowest possible person you can send. If you really want to send a message you send the Vice President or the Secretary of State."[39] Landau himself interpreted the decision as essentially a pragmatic one: "Frei died the week after I left Chile [on January 16, 1982] and the question arose 'Who are we going to send?' [ARA's] Bob Service suggested that I go. It was very simple." Landau found it somewhat telling that Reagan "didn't know who Frei was."[40] Justice Department officials were not so casual in their approach to Chile, privately warning the State Department that they would thwart any attempt to whitewash the Letelier-Moffitt murders by testifying against presidential certification until the regime proved more cooperative.[41]

The Economic Crisis: 1982

Of more immediate concern to Pinochet was the impact of the 1982 global recession on the Chilean economy, made worse by the increased costs of petroleum imports flowing from the Organization of Petroleum Exporting Countries' (OPEC) fourfold rise in the price of oil. The severe impact bought to an abrupt end the late-1970s economic boom based largely on the free market formula of a deregulated financial system, large-scale foreign investment, and excessive foreign borrowings. The contraction in world trade saw the market price of copper alone fall in real terms to its lowest level since the 1930s. As the country plunged into a

---

[38] See William Chapman, "Reagan Wins Qualified Aid Victories," *WP*, December 16, 1981, A7; "Debate on International Security and Development Act of 1981," in *Congressional Record—Senate*, 97th Cong., 1st. Sess., Vol. 127, Part 19, October 22, 1981, 25002–25050.

[39] Interview with George F. Jones.

[40] Interview with George W. Landau.

[41] See Kornbluh, *The Pinochet File*, 419.

devastating economic crisis, the Pinochet-appointed team of University of Chicago–educated economic advisers led by Finance Minister Sergio de Castro initially opted for a do-nothing response – believing the crisis would be short-lived and that their market reforms were sufficiently anchored to withstand any profound setbacks. When Interior Minister Sergio Fernández presented Pinochet with a "solution" (heavily influenced by de Castro) based on "deepening reforms, with an emphasis on privatizations," the military leader rejected the plan, relieved both officials of their cabinet posts in April 1982, and replaced them with more pragmatic advisers sympathetic toward the neoliberal, free market policies but prepared to adopt a more flexible approach than that espoused by the 'Chicago Boys.'[42]

As it turned out, it was a case of too little, too late. By year's end, Chile's gross domestic product had suffered an "unprecedented" decline in excess of 14 percent as a result of falling production levels in virtually every major economic sector. The official employment rate rose from approximately 8 percent in mid-1981 to nearly 22 percent by December 1982, while another 8 percent of the workforce were enrolled in the government's minimum (make-work) employment program. Inflation trended upward for the first time in eight years, while the value of exports, which had fallen by close to 16 percent in 1981, declined a further 4 percent in 1982.

During 1982, more than 800 private firms went bankrupt (compared with an average annual number of 277 between 1975 and 1981), and over 50 percent of private bank loans fell into default. The Central Bank suffered a catastrophic fall in its international reserves of more than 30 percent, from $3.8 billion to $2.6 billion. Meanwhile, total foreign debt, much of it accumulated through luxury imports ("conspicuous consumption") and speculation, blew out from approximately $6 billion in 1978 to more than $17 billion in 1982, seriously compromising Chile's international credit rating. The nation's $1.2 billion balance of payments surplus in 1980 deteriorated over the next two years and could only be financed by new foreign borrowings at skyrocketing interest rates.[43] By

[42] Huneeus, *The Pinochet Regime*, 362.
[43] ECLAC, *Economic Survey of Latin America and the Caribbean, 1982*, vol. 1 (Santiago: United Nations, 1984), 271, 291, 296; Greg Grandin, *Empire's Workshop: Latin America, the United States and the Rise of the New Imperialism* (New York: Metropolitan Books, 2006), 171; World Bank, Office Memo, Francisco Aguirre-Casaca, Acting Director, LAC 1 to Sidney Chernick, "Chile – Note on Eligibility for Special Assistance," October 21, 1983, Loan Committee: Chile-General, Box: File Folder 1058371,

year's end, Chile had one of the highest per capita debt ratios in the world.[44]

With Latin America accounting for more than 55 percent (approximately $300 billion) of Third World debt and Chile's banking system on the verge of total collapse, Central Bank Chairman Carlos Cáceres traveled to Toronto for an International Monetary Fund (IMF) meeting, which, he said, "was like a wake": Mexico had just declared that it was unable to meet its debt interest repayments, and other Latin debtors "raised their hands and said 'We're not going to pay our debt.'" The global banking system was facing a crisis, and some of the largest U.S. banks were in danger of collapsing. Only Chile, said Cáceres, "sat down with the banks and said 'We want to restructure.'" Pressure from foreign private creditors on the Chilean Central Bank to assume the debts owed by the nation's private banks met with initial resistance, even though the banks cited the precedent of a 1978 decision to guarantee the external debt of one bankrupt institution, which was repeated for several others in 1981. Exhibiting a surprising degree of flexibility, the Pinochet regime eventually agreed on massive state intervention in the economy to guarantee the debt of the financial sector (at a cost of $7 billion), then balked at a subsequent demand by foreign creditor banks to assume the total debt owed by private local companies. Having made clear that this was a nonnegotiable decision, said Cáceres, debt-restructuring negotiations were successfully concluded. The peso was devalued and an accord was negotiated with the IMF for funds to revive domestic industry, which, in return, committed Chile to a series of "economic adjustments" that guaranteed the Fund would play a key role in the military regime's economic policy making over the next two years.[45] The government's willingness to cooperate with Chile's foreign creditors and bail out the financial sector was not simply an exercise in financial expediency but was also dictated by political concerns. In the words of the Central Bank Chairman, "Chile was under great and important pressure because of the Pinochet regime

WBGA; Office Memo, S. T. Beza to Managing Director, Deputy Managing Director, "Chile – Briefing for Mission," October 21, 1983, Central Files, C/Chile/810, Mission Van Houten and Staff, October–December 1983, IMFA; Briefing Paper, "Chile: Domestic Situation/Foreign Policy," May 3, 1983, DOS/FOIAe, III; Valdés, *Pinochet's Economists*, 26–28, 262; DOS, INR, "Chile: From Theory to Practice – More Flexibility in Economic Policies," January 11, 1983, DOS/FOIAe, III.

[44] Kenneth N. Gilpin, "The Maze of Latin America's Debt," *NYT*, March 13, 1983, F4.

[45] Valdéz, *Pinochet's Economists*, 263; Barbara Stallings, "Politics and Economic Crisis: A Comparative Study of Chile, Peru, and Colombia," in *Economic Crisis and Policy Choice*, ed. Joan M. Nelson, 113–167 (Princeton: Princeton University Press, 1990).

and we didn't want to open another door of vulnerability. So, for us it was not only economically important but also politically important to try to negotiate a restructuring of the debt."[46]

American investors in Chile were not exempt from the effects of the economic downturn. Exxon projected a $90 million loss in 1982, Dow Chemical decided to close its $32 million petrochemicals plant, Firestone shut its tire factories and declared bankruptcy with $22.5 million in outstanding debts, and General Motors closed down two of its four auto plants.[47] The following year, only $182.3 million of $328.3 million in direct foreign investment authorized by the Chilean government actually entered the country.[48]

As this financial crisis was unfolding, the U.S. Embassy had cabled the State Department that the regime "fac[ed] a growing credibility gap" over its economic policies, its continued human rights abuses, and its refusal to budge on even a limited opening up of the political system. "What is most striking about this double-barrelled barrage" of opposition to the regime's economic performance, the document explained, was that it ranged across the "national spectrum" from business, industrial, and financial sectors to organized labor, agriculture, and small entrepreneurs.[49] The wider stakes involved with respect to a possible region-wide debt default made Washington only too keen to lend its support to Chile's efforts to reach an agreement with its creditors. Put simply, according to Cáceres, "it was quite important for the U.S. government to show that at least one country in Latin America was ready to negotiate the process."[50]

Dialogue of the Deaf

Plans to resume military aid to Chile, most vigorously supported by the ideological hardliners in the administration and in the Congress, were running up against new reports of human rights abuses. In March 1982, the UNHRC once again expressed "serious concern at the persistence and, in certain respects, deterioration of the human rights" in Chile, based on the Special Rapporteur's latest report highlighting a rise in the number

---

[46] Interview with Carlos Cáceres.
[47] See Jackson Diehl, "Exxon, Others Find Projects Awry in Chile," *WP*, October 3, 1982, A1, A13.
[48] U.S. Embassy, Santiago, "Chile: Economic Trends Report," April 1984, Chilean Economic Documents 1984, Box 47, JDT Collection.
[49] Telegram, Theberge to Haig, March 1, 1982, DOS/FOIAe, III.
[50] Interview with Carlos Cáceres.

of detainees tortured and ill-treated, and how this was done with "the tolerance of the administrative and judicial authorities."[51]

On Capitol Hill, anti-Pinochet legislators signaled that they would launch a frontal attack on the administration's entire regional policy (threatening military support for right-wing regimes in El Salvador, Guatemala, and Honduras) in the event that the White House ignored such reports and certified Chile for the purposes of resuming military aid. The response by State evidenced its concern. The day after James Theberge was sworn in as the new U.S. Ambassador to Chile, Assistant Secretary Thomas Enders made a flying forty-eight-hour visit to Santiago "to see if there was any possibility of getting the regime to be a little light on the human rights abuses."[52] During a meeting with Pinochet, Enders spelled out the bottom line for certification: it could be justified on the basis of "substantial progress" in human rights and with reference to the U.S. "national interest," but he emphasized (directly contradicting Kirkpatrick's statement a year earlier in Santiago) that no movement was possible unless Washington was convinced that Pinochet's government had taken "appropriate steps ... by all legal means available" to prosecute those implicated in the Letelier case. The junta leader refused to specify any possible new initiatives on either front.[53]

Enders' visit confirmed State Department suspicions that, despite the ostensible thaw in relations, the chances of making much of an impression on Pinochet were slight. Still, the Assistant Secretary described his meeting with the Chilean leader as "very cordial." DCM Grover had his own explanation for this affability: "Pinochet didn't fool himself" that anything would come of the meeting, and so he turned it into "purely a courtesy call."[54]

Chile's lack of cooperation with U.S. investigators in the Letelier case and the ongoing arrests, murders, reports of torture, and other "negative incidents" forced even Secretary Haig to concede that the country had "not helped its case."[55] Newly installed Assistant Secretary for HA Elliott Abrams went further, stating that the administration should withhold support for certification on the grounds that "everyone ... on the Hill will be saying that there is no stability now but rather a real regression on

---

[51] United Nations, *Yearbook of the United Nations, 1982*, vol. 36 (New York: United Nations, Department of Public Information, 1986), 1119–1120.

[52] "Enders and Chilean Chief Meet," *NYT*, March 11, 1982, 18.

[53] Telegram, Theberge to Shultz, March 11, 1982, DOS/FOIAe, III.

[54] Interview with Charles W. Grover. Enders quoted in "Enders and Chilean Chief Meet."

[55] Telegram, Haig to AmEmb, Santiago, March 27, 1982, DOS/FOIAe, III.

human rights [which means] the political costs to us will be very high."
Moreover, a failure to withhold support would likely raise questions
about "the credibility of our Latin American policy" in light of U.S.
opposition to human rights certification in El Salvador.[56] Abrams insisted
that these kinds of arguments were often constructed simply to win the
bureaucratic policy debate: "I remember in 1981 a meeting on military aid
to Guatemala, and I remember the argument that we shouldn't be giving
aid to these people because they are bad was not a winning argument.
The argument that this [aid] is never going to happen because Congress
will pass a law forbidding it, so why is this smart? – that was a winning
argument."[57] Justice Department officials remained scathing about the
responsibility of Chilean officials for the lack of progress in the Letelier
case and were prepared to say so publicly. "[The Chileans] haven't done
spit since the day this thing happened," the Assistant U.S. Attorney in
charge of the case, Lawrence Barcella, told the *Washington Post*. "In
fact, they have been dilatory and obstructionist."[58]

On his return from Santiago, Enders nonetheless curiously described
bilateral ties as "excellent,"[59] even if presidential certification seemed
far away, and the obstacles (congressional hostility, Chilean inaction,
interagency divisions) to any policy shift were as formidable, as ever.
In a memo to Undersecretary for Political Affairs Lawrence Eagleburger
within days of Enders' return, Abrams wrote that the Department of
Justice "seems strongly opposed" to certification on the grounds of the
Letelier case. Frustrating as that was, Abrams despaired even more about
getting Congress to change its mind: "I don't know whether there is
anything the Chileans can do for us to satisfy the (foolish) demands
of Congress."[60] How much the Chileans wanted to assist was another
matter. Even U.S. Ambassador-at-Large Vernon Walters (a Pinochet confidante) was unable to convince the General that "nothing has poisoned
American-Chilean relations like the Letelier case [which] remains one

---

[56] Memo, Abrams to Stoessel, February 12, 1982, ibid.
[57] Interview with Elliott Abrams.
[58] Quoted in John M. Goshko, "Administration Reviews Plan to Renew Chile Aid," *WP*, March 5, 1982, A13.
[59] Quoted in Jackson Diehl, "Enders Visit to Chile Leaves Aid in Doubt," *WP*, March 12, 1982, A20. Enders repeated an earlier (January) assessment by a visiting congressional delegation headed by Senate Majority Leader Howard Baker (R-TN): "Without exception, each [Chilean] official with whom the delegation met expressed satisfaction at the improvement of the relationship." U.S. Congress, Senate, *Developing an American Consensus, Report by Howard H. Baker Jr.*, 97th Cong., 2d Sess., March 1982, 16.
[60] Memo, Abrams to Eagleburger, March 13, 1982, DOS/FOIAe, III.

of the primary obstacles to the loosening of the restrictions on sales of arms to Chile." Pinochet, Walters noted unsurprisingly, "did not like this."[61] Unwilling to pay more than lip service to Washington's entreaties, Pinochet confronted the White House with a major dilemma. With Congress insisting that movement on the Letelier case was needed for certification and the administration reluctant to use its debt leverage to force the issue, State's options had effectively been reduced to lobbying Santiago in the hope it might be persuaded to improve its human rights performance.[62] Abrams delivered the message personally during a meeting with Chilean Embassy officials in early May: in the absence of movement on human rights and the Letelier case, he told them, the prospects for certification "in the short run" were negligible.[63]

NSC official Roger Fontaine attributed State's "very cautious" approach to Chilean certification to congressional hostility and fear that it might compound the difficulties in certifying other countries, notably El Salvador, and to "the need to couple Chilean certification with a similar move for Argentina." In his response to a memo from the Secretary of State, Fontaine's superior William Clark (appointed NSC Adviser in January 1982) agreed that "the Argentine factor must be carefully weighed in any decision to proceed." Nonetheless, it was the President's desire that State prepare a strategy leading to certification of both Chile and Argentina within a reasonable time period. That strategy should take into account how best to achieve human rights improvements in Chile and to "minimize the fallout with Congress and the Argentines."[64] Whatever optimism may have existed about a positive outcome was quickly doused by Santiago's determination to resist outside pressure. Reporting on his visit to Chile in late July, Fontaine described a government that would not make any human rights "concessions" "if they were directly linked to certification." The Embassy concurred that any attempt to publicly make this connection "will fail."[65] Ambassador Theberge urged Washington simply to "cut the Gordian knot" and certify Chile on the grounds of U.S. national interest, significant improvements in human rights, and

[61] Memo of Conversation between Pinochet and Walters, May 13, 1982, ibid.
[62] Memo, DS, Exec Sec L. Paul Bremer III, to William P. Clark, WII, "Certification...," July 2, 1982, NSA, Office of Assistant to the President, Country File, Chile Vol. 1 1/20/81–7/31–84 [4], Box 91868, RRL.
[63] Haig to AmEmb Santiago, May 11, 1982, DOS/FOIAe, III.
[64] Memo, NSC, Roger Fontaine to Clark, July 8, 1982, Oliver L. North Collection, Chile, Box 62, RRL; Memo, White House, Clark to Shultz, July 8, 1982, ibid.
[65] Memo, NSC, Fontaine to Clark, August 6, 1982, ibid.

the regime's "partial" cooperation with the Letelier investigation.[66] His advice was rejected as politically impossible to take seriously.

Reviewing bilateral issues with Chilean Ambassador Enrique Valenzuela in mid-September, Thomas Enders indicated that getting Congress to ease its opposition to certification in the absence of some positive action on the junta's part would remain "a difficult problem."[67] Getting this message through to Chilean officials, though, was proving to be no simple task. As with Pinochet, observed one U.S. official, they failed to "understand our predicament and our position" vis-à-vis Congress, which he attributed to "a certain amount of incomprehension [about the U.S. political system that] exists in Santiago."[68]

Chile's cooperation with Britain during the 1982 Falklands (Malvinas) War likely had a major impact on the junta's sense of confidence and independence at this time. Under the terms of a secret pact negotiated with air force General Fernando Matthei when war seemed inevitable, Chile agreed to provide the British with intelligence on Argentine troop movements, early warning of air attacks and weather reports, permit reconnaissance planes to fly over Chilean territory, and offered to allow the use of its ports. At the request of Whitehall, the Chilean Navy dispatched two submarines to apply pressure to Argentina's southern sea flank. Additionally, the junta secretly repatriated an Special Air Service unit that had made a forced landing near Punta Arenas – raising speculation that the British may have been allowed to use Chilean territory for refueling purposes. There is even some evidence to suggest that Chilean intelligence officers participated in the interrogation of captured Argentine soldiers. Whether for their own reasons or as part of the cooperation extended to the British, the Chilean Army deployed forces along the border with Argentina during the conflict, requiring Buenos Aires to divert its most highly trained troops from the Falklands theater to counter a possible attack. In return for its assistance, Whitehall made advanced weaponry available to Santiago cost-free or at much reduced prices. This included Hawker Hunter fighter jets, three Canberra PR-9 reconnaissance aircraft, long-range radar, anti-aircraft missiles, and over-the-horizon intelligence-gathering equipment – helping to fill a gap in Chile's weapons procurement program created by U.S. and French

---

[66] Diplomatic Note, Theberge to Dam, November 3, 1982, DOS/FOIAe, III.
[67] Telegram, Shultz to AmEmb, Santiago, September 16, 1982, ibid.
[68] Memo, Smith to Enders, December 7 1982, author declassified FOIA.

bans on arms transfers.[69] Having earned Thatcher's gratitude, the junta now had a powerful and indebted friend in London. Perhaps most importantly, the military outcome of the war and the subsequent collapse of the Argentine dictatorship eliminated any serious threat to Chile from its most powerful neighbor for the foreseeable future. These developments could only have reinforced the Chilean junta's disposition to ignore pressure from Washington for concessions over human rights and progress on democracy.[70]

Signs of Change in Washington

There were two developments within the U.S. foreign policy establishment that laid the foundation for an eventual rethink of Washington's approach toward Pinochet during 1982. The first was the replacement of Alexander Haig as Secretary of State with George Shultz in March; the second was Reagan's June speech to the British Parliament outlining his global democracy crusade. In Shultz, Reagan chose someone with

[69] See Paolo Tripodi, "General Matthei's Revelation and Chile's Role during the Falklands War: A New Perspective on the Conflict in the South Atlantic," *Journal of Strategic Studies* 26, no. 4 (2003): 116, 118–119; Sir Lawrence Freedman, *The Official History of the Falklands Campaign: Vol. 2. War and Diplomacy*, rev ed. (London: Routledge, 2007), 394–403; Charles Moore, *Margaret Thatcher: The Authorized Biography*, vol. 1 (London: Allen Lane, 2013), 692–699. Chile's decision to support the British was also influenced by its ongoing dispute with Argentina over the Beagle Channel Islands, awarded to Chile by arbitration – an outcome Buenos Aires refused to accept – and by the fear that a quick and successful Argentine victory in the Falklands would embolden the Dirty War generals to launch a military attack on Chile soon after. See Sir Lawrence Freedman, *The Official History of the Falklands Campaign: Vol. 1. The Origins of the Falklands War*, rev ed. (London: Routledge, 2007), 80–81; Freedman, *Official History, Vol. 2*, 396. Thatcher made no reference to the cooperation Britain received from Chile in her memoirs. See Margaret Thatcher, *The Downing Street Years* (London: Harper-Collins, 1993), 173–235. It was not until a speech to the 1999 Conservative Party conference that she publicly acknowledged Chile's "enormously valuable assistance" during the crisis. Speech, Conservative Party Conference, October 9, 1999, Margaret Thatcher Foundation, http://www.margaretthatcher.org.

[70] At the senior policy-making level, there was no consensus on what stance the United States should adopt. Reagan himself "was very confused," a senior British diplomat recalled. "He had Jeane Kirkpatrick on one side telling him relations in the hemisphere were all that mattered, forget Britain and its old imperialism, they've go no business to be out here; it's a bunch of rocks on the South Atlantic. Who needs that? On the other side, there were the pro-Europeans like [Undersecretary of State Lawrence] Eagleburger who was saying we've got to support the Brits and so on." Sir Derek M. D. Thomas Interview, BDOHP. In his memoir, Secretary of State Haig described as "unreconcilable" his differences with Kirkpatrick over the conflict. Haig, *Caveat*, 269.

superior people skills than those of the former Secretary as well as a more pugnacious attitude in challenging the ideologues' dismissive opinion of diplomacy. To Elliott Abrams, Shultz's arrival was a pivotal moment in the development of a human rights policy. Here, finally, was someone with the ability to exert influence at the highest levels of the administration who was prepared to give a fair hearing to the view that "there should be a greater distancing from, and opposition to, President Augusto Pinochet."[71] But as someone who had been instrumental in devising the program to train the 'Chicago Boys' in the University of Chicago Economics Department, Shultz's attitude toward the Pinochet regime was bound to be tempered by his connections to these individuals, and his general inclination was not to upset reforms they had introduced that had made Chile a "pioneer in opening the markets."[72]

Shultz was trusted by Reagan and shared the basic thrust of his foreign policy outlook. This extended to the speech the President delivered to the British Parliament, in which he outlined what he called "a plan and a hope for the long term – the march of freedom and democracy which will leave Marxism-Leninism on the ash-heap of history." Declaring that it was "time that we committed ourselves as a nation – in both the public and private sectors – to assisting democratic development" throughout the world, he proposed to do this by fostering "the infrastructure of democracy, the system of a free press, unions, political parties, universities, which allows a people to choose their own way to develop their own culture, to reconcile their own differences through peaceful means." The linkage between human rights, the anticommunist crusade, supporting "freedom fighters," and democracy promotion was Reagan's central message: "If the rest of this century is to witness the gradual growth of freedom and democratic ideals," he told the assembled legislators, "we must take actions to assist the campaign for democracy. The objective I propose is quite simple to state: to foster the infrastructure of democracy [in civil society]."[73] Although it was unclear how this objective would be translated into policy practice, it did accelerate a process leading to the creation of a National Endowment for Democracy (NED), which was incorporated as a private grant-funding institution in November 1983, with almost its entire annual budget provided from congressional

---

[71] "Transcript of Interview with Elliott Abrams," 107.
[72] Interview with Carlos Cáceres.
[73] Address to Members of the British Parliament, June 18, 1982, in *Public Papers of the Presidents of the United States, Ronald Reagan, 1982, January to July 2, 1982* (Washington, DC: U.S. Government Printing Office, 1983), 745, 746.

appropriations. As an instrument for waging the Cold War, the NED's "democracy-building" mission was to provide assistance to private and political organizations seeking to promote regime changes supportive of U.S. interests.

Richard Schifter maintained that the intellectual genesis of this "pro-democracy" position was embedded in the 'Kirkpatrick Doctrine.' "Democracy promotion," he recalled, "really reflected the point of view of a good many of us who were associated with neo-conservatism [who] believed in the strong advocacy of democracy against, above all, the major threat of the Soviet Union and the Communists. When Jeane wrote her article she wrote down what we all felt."[74] While the predominant view among Reagan's advisers was that the Westminster speech had its origins in the neoconservative critique of Carter, some officials also interpreted it as a clarion call to go beyond the rigidity of the Kirkpatrick Doctrine in raising options and formulating a new conceptual foreign policy framework.[75] The impact on the U.S. Congress was double-edged. "The Democrats just loved it," said Victor Johnson, "but then it became much harder for us because then we had to fight the policy based on nuance. 'Is this thing with democracy in the name being run in a way that actually promotes democracy?' It was much harder to win that debate with the public because it was nuanced."[76]

As regards Chile, Reagan's speech incorporated a specific message: that "U.S. 'understanding' of Pinochet had its limits [primarily because] quiet diplomacy was not producing any visible results."[77] By year's end, it was clear that Chilean officials were already picking up on that message. In early December, the Chilean Foreign Ministry's Director General, Fernando Zegers, visited the U.S. Ambassador's residence in Santiago to convey the regime's profound unease "at signs of shift in U.S. foreign policy," based on statements by Reagan, Shultz, and other senior officials about the importance of political democracy. Theberge emphatically denied that this was part of an attempt to increase the pressure on Chile to quicken the transition away from military rule. On the contrary, he explained, "every effort was being made to strengthen our bilateral relations." Theberge ascribed the "extreme touchiness" of the regime leadership to a

---

74 Interview with Richard Schifter.
75 Harry G. Barnes Jr., "U.S. Human Rights Policies and Chile," in *Implementing U.S. Human Rights Policy*, ed. Debra Liang-Fenton (Washington, DC: U.S. Institute of Peace Press, 2004), 310.
76 Interview with Victor C. Johnson.
77 Barnes, "U.S. Human Rights Policies and Chile," 310.

combination of domestic political and economic problems and an "increasing irritability with the USG [U.S. government] over the absence of progress on certification."[78]

Publicly, the administration was not shifting its policy at the UN despite the fact that after nearly a decade of military rule, state-authored repression remained widespread, according to human rights organizations, the Catholic Church, and Western diplomats in Santiago.[79] Reporting on developments in the second half of 1982, the UN's Special Rapporteur painted a bleak picture of a country where hundreds of arrests were still taking place "without a judicial or administrative warrant" and procedural guarantees "continued to be seriously restricted within the legislative framework of the double state of emergency."[80] His end-of-year report was overwhelmingly adopted by the UNHRC and the General Assembly, which "reiterated its grave concern at the persistence of human rights violations in Chile."[81] Unmoved by this impressive array of hard evidence, Washington refused to budge from its position that the overall situation had improved and again accused the UN of "singling Chile out for special treatment."[82] That same week, Chile's Catholic bishops issued a letter that referred to "a severe social crisis whose signs are growing misery, violence, lack of confidence and fear."[83] At the end of Reagan's second year in the White House, even a U.S. Embassy official remarked that the ongoing failure to make sufficient progress in eliminating human rights abuses still "casts a long shadow" over U.S.-Chilean relations[84] – although not enough of one to invite public censure. Weeks later, the new

---

[78] Telegram, Theberge to Shultz, December 3, 1982, DOS/FOIAe, III. Frustrated by Pinochet's refusal to make any contribution to White House efforts to gain congressional certification, State Department officials began describing him as someone totally "impervious to outside influence" and even compared him unfavorably with those obdurate allies who lost power in Nicaragua and Iran. AmEmb Santiago to DOS, "Proposed Certification Scenario," March 9, 1983, ibid. One of Pinochet's advisers offered a particularly cutting explanation of his behavior: "Basically he doesn't believe in democracy" – a point further evidenced in a mid-1983 speech, when Pinochet "criticized politicians as being irresponsible and said that democracy was the 'culture dish' of Communism." Quoted in Edward Schumacher, "Unrest in Chile Brings Pinochet First Tough Test," *NYT*, June 27, 1983, 7.

[79] See Edward Schumacher, "Chile Rights Abuses Persist, Monitors in Country Report," *NYT*, December 6, 1982, 1, 13.

[80] *Yearbook of the United Nations, 1983*, vol. 37 (New York: United Nations, Department of Public Information, 1987), 882, 883.

[81] *Yearbook of the United Nations, 1982*, vol. 36, 1120.

[82] Telegram, USUN Mission to Shultz, December 13, 1982, DOS/FOIAe, III.

[83] "Bishops Issue Letter on Country's Situation," FBIS: DR: LA, December 22, 1982, E1.

[84] Quoted in Peter Kornbluh, "U.S. Befriends Chile," *NCR*, December 31, 1982, 4.

Chilean Foreign Minister Miguel Schweitzer used strong words to inform Ambassador Theberge that human rights were "not of primary importance in the government's foreign policy."[85]

The High Price of Finance

Predictably, in lieu of Pinochet's refusal to take Washington's human rights concerns seriously, attempts by senior junta officials to lobby Congress and the President to lift the arms ban and to provide a $390 million bridging loan to deal with the nation's economic problems were unsuccessful. Undersecretary of State for Economic Affairs Allan Wallis told Chilean Ambassador Valenzuela that Treasury "would be as forthcoming as possible" regarding the loan request, but the human rights situation "hampered" White House efforts to make anything happen.[86] With Foreign Minister Schweitzer scheduled to visit Washington in late March 1983 to discuss certification, the Santiago Embassy suggested that Secretary Shultz remind him of the U.S. role in Chile's successful external debt renegotiations and the administration's recent decision to approve $144.5 million in Commodity Credit Corporation (CCC) credits for the Latin nation.[87]

The regime's broader relations with the major global lending organizations were another matter. The World Bank was a minor presence in the Chilean economy during the first three years of Reagan's presidency. Apart from disbursing some loans already in the pipeline, the institution did not engage in "aggressive lending" to Chile, partly because, in the words of one involved Bank official, "they didn't want us," and also because of the refusal of the Chileans to abide by the World Bank charter, which required that governments guarantee the borrowings by state

[85] Telegram, Theberge to Shultz, February 24, 1983, DOS/FOIAe, III. Argentina's certification prospects were much more advanced based on a "greatly improved" human rights record, "no serous threat" of a renewed Falklands conflict, and a commitment to hold elections and return government to civilians in January 1984. As well, the armed forces institution remained "a bastion of anti-Communism in an unstable domestic environment." Memo, Shultz to Reagan, March 9, 1983, ibid.
[86] Telegram, Shultz to AmEmb Santiago, March 9, 1983, ibid.
[87] Telegram, Theberge to Shultz, March 23, 1983, ibid. In 1983, the administration also signed a general agreement with the Pinochet regime allowing the Overseas Private Investment Corporation to insure future American investors in Chile despite the lack of human rights certification, which, not surprisingly, triggered congressional criticism and may explain why no actual contracts were signed as of late 1987. See David P. Forsythe, *Human Rights and U.S. Foreign Policy* (Gainesville: University Press of Florida, 1988), 59.

enterprises.[88] It was not until late 1983 that Chile indicated its preparedness to provide this guarantee, thus "effectively [eliminating] a major constraint to Bank involvement in many areas of lending in Chile."[89] While
sectors of Chile's capitalist class were critical of the government's more
draconian efforts to weather the economic crisis, Bank officials complemented the regime on its response insofar as the changes implemented did
not fundamentally affect the neoliberal economic model. "To its credit,"
wrote Acting Regional Director Francisco Aguirre-Casaca, "Chile retains
an open, market-oriented economy with a minimum of economic distortions." This adherence to "generally sound policies" justified continuing
Bank support.[90] But the reality for much of the period prior to 1982,
explained Carlos Cáceres (appointed Chile's Finance Minister in early
1983), was that the government "didn't worry about the World Bank or
the Inter-American Development Bank because with all the credit coming
in from private foreign banks we didn't need it." Among the government's senior economic officials, "support from the IMF was much more
important."[91]

In January 1983, after protracted negotiations, the Chilean government and the IMF reached agreement on a two-year standby program
to provide $564 million in Fund credits and a Compensatory Financing
Facility of about $325 million. In return, Chile agreed to a set of austerity
measures for 1983–84 that were more onerous than those the private
banks would have imposed.[92] Any optimism that the regime could fulfill
its commitments was short-lived. In mid-March, a visiting Fund mission reported that capital outflows, corporate bankruptcies, and banks
lacking funds to meet their responsibilities had resulted "in a sharp devi-
ation from the stand-by program." Unimpressed by the government's
presentation of an austerity "shadow program," largely confined to some

---

[88] Interview with Paul M. Meo.
[89] World Bank, "Chile: 1983 Annual Meetings Briefing Paper," September 20, 1983,
    Clausen's – Chile, Vol. 2, Box 209488B, WBGA.
[90] World Bank, Office Memo, Francisco Aguirre-Casaca, Acting Director, LAC 1 to Sidney
    Chernick, Chile – Note on Eligibility for Special Assistance, March 31, 1983, File Unit:
    Loan Committee, Chile-General, Box 1058371, WBGA.
[91] Interview with Carlos Cáceres. "We had very good relations with the Executive Director
    of the IMF, Jacques de Larosière," said Cáceres, and this held Chile in good stead when
    differences over economic strategies occurred. Ibid.
[92] U.S. Embassy, Santiago, Chile: Economic Trends Report, April 1984; Office Memo,
    M. J. van Houten to Acting Managing Director, "Chile-Short Visit," February 23, 1983,
    Central Files: C/Chile/810, Mission – Van Houten and Staff, March 1983, IMFA.

new revenue-raising measures, the mission told Chilean authorities that
continuing IMF support was dependent on the "implementation of a
strong emergency plan designed to return to the path of the stand-by program in the near future."[93] With no option other than compliance, the
regime increased taxes, deregulated the price of goods, and implemented
more spending cutbacks, together with another devaluation of the peso.[94]

In view of the regime's initial failure to meet economic targets required
under the Fund standby loan, a successful outcome to ongoing negotiations between Chile and its private bank creditors became all the more
difficult. After weeks of discussion, Chilean government officials and a
twelve-bank advisory committee agreed on a financial plan to put before
the country's 550 commercial bank creditors. If all the creditors agreed
to the plan, said the IMF Executive Director Jacques de Larosière, the
Fund would grant "a waiver from compliance with the original program's quantitative performance criteria," so long as it received written
assurances from banks by mid-June.[95] Only weeks later, another mission
concluded that the financial crisis "appears to have been brought under
control and a measure of stability has returned to the domestic financial
system."[96] Soon after, the IMF agreed to a Chilean request for a waiver
that allowed it to receive all 1983 standby disbursements, reschedule its
debt agreement with the foreign banking community, and "temporarily
disregard" some of the January standby conditions.[97] Cáceres maintained
that Washington's strong and consistent support of Chile during debt
negotiations certainly blunted U.S. criticism about the pace of political
reform. In any event, Pinochet was impervious to such pressure: "he was
not going to be thrown out from the government, he was commander of
all the armed forces in Chile, so the U.S. government could say anything
it wanted to but he was quite sure that trying to press him to leave the

[93] Office Memo, Jan van Houten to Managing Director, Deputy Managing Director,
"Chile – Consultation under Stand-by," March 21, 1983; Central Files: C/Chile/810,
Mission – Van Houten and Staff, March 1983, IMFA; Office Memo, Francisco Aguirre-
Casaca, Acting Director, LAC 1 to Sidney Chernick, "Note on Eligibility for Special
Assistance."
[94] See Edward Schumacher, "Chile Raises Tariffs and Devalues Peso," *NYT*, March 24,
1983, D13; James Petras and Fernando Leiva, *Democracy and Poverty in Chile* (Boulder:
Westview Press, 1994), 29.
[95] Quoted in "Chile, Banks Agree on Financing Plan," *WSJ*, May 2, 1983 (Factiva).
[96] Office Memo, Jan van Houten to Managing Director and Deputy Managing Director,
"Chile-Review Mission," July 12, 1983, Central Files, C/Chile/801, Mission Van Houten
and Staff, March, July 1983, IMFA.
[97] "IMF Grants Request Submitted by Government," FBIS: DR: LA, July 29, 1983, E3.

government before the time that was approved in the Constitution of
1980 – that was not possible."[98]

Still, as long as Washington remained committed to supporting Chile
as a model Latin debtor, U.S. officials had few options other than to
keep pressing the regime on human rights rather than promote a return
to civilian rule. The reason remained pragmatic rather than altruistic:
no other issue, Thomas Enders wrote to Lawrence Eagleburger, posed a
greater obstacle to "our desire to establish completely normal relations"
and help bail out the slumping Chilean economy.[99] More worrying for
State Department officials was the rising tide of political discontent that
had accompanied the country's economic collapse. This had emboldened
opposition groups to increase the number and size of anti-regime demonstrations at a time when there was still no "credible alternative" to the
regime that would allow its opponents "to attract sufficient active support to threaten GOC [Government of Chile] stability." In these circumstances, the Embassy reported, it was "thus not surprising that Pinochet
has opted for no drastic change in direction and a 'muddle through'
approach to his problems."[100]

A May 1983 State Department briefing paper described Chile's military
regime as "firmly entrenched" with no serious challenge to its authority from within the armed forces or civil society on the horizon. And
despite problems in U.S.-Chilean relations, Pinochet remained a valuable ally and, in most respects, a consistent supporter of U.S. economic
and foreign policy objectives: "Chile's strongly anti-Soviet/Cuban foreign policy and its market oriented economic policies facilitate bilateral
hemispheric and global cooperation." The paper singled out Pinochet's
endorsement of both Reagan's Central America policy and Washington's
determination to resist efforts to oust Israel from membership in international organizations.[101] Those positive factors had to be weighed against
a looming challenge from the streets that would pose the most serious
threat to Pinochet since the 1973 military coup.

The Economic Crisis Turns Political

What was missing from State's May briefing paper was attention to
the deepening impoverishment of the majority of the Chilean populace,

[98] Interview with Carlos Cáceres.
[99] Briefing Memo, Enders to Eagleburger, May 23, 1983, DOS/FOIAe, III.
[100] Telegram, Theberge to Shultz, March 21, 1983, ibid.
[101] Briefing Paper, April 25, May 3, 1983, ibid.

further exacerbated by the IMF austerity strictures. The burden of the "adjustment" strategy fell most heavily on the lower socioeconomic classes. In 1983, real wages fell by almost 11 percent, and the median family income in Greater Santiago by a staggering 28 percent, while per capita income was lower than at any time since 1970.[102] And as the cost of living spiraled upward, wage levels declined, jobs disappeared, and bankruptcies continued to hit the small property-owning petty bourgeoisie, opposition to Pinochet's policies broadened – and calls for fundamental change grew louder.

Confidence in State's assessment about Pinochet's unshakeable hold on political power was tested almost immediately when the first of a series of monthly nationwide "days of protest" over worsening economic conditions and the slow pace of political reforms took place under the leadership of the Confederación de Trabajadores del Cobre (Copper Workers Confederation, CTC). Beginning with its 1981 call for strike action at the El Teniente mine, the CTC had assumed a leading role in mobilizing an increasingly broad-based opposition to the regime's free market economic policies. Over the next four years, the CTC and other unions, loosely organized into the Comando Nacional Trabajadores (National Workers Command, CNT), would play a key role in coordinating public protests against the junta. Invariably, these protests took the form of venting deep-seated economic grievances and demanding comprehensive political changes that the junta was not about to countenance or the White House encourage. Another, more dramatic expression of the divisions reopening in Chilean society was the growth in urban guerrilla warfare. Back in 1980, the Partido Comunista (Communist Party, PCCH), buoyed by the possibility of translating antiregime protests by the urban poor into "insurrection," began to advocate a strategy of "mass popular rebellion."[103] By 1982, more than one-third of all urban youths in Chile were jobless, and hundreds had joined the armed wing of the Movimiento de Izquierda Revolucionaria (Movement of the Revolutionary Left, MIR) while others affiliated with the Communist Party–supported Frente Patriótico Manuel Rodríguez (Manuel Rodriguez Patriotic Front,

---

[102] Stallings, "Politics and Economic Crisis," 131; ECLAC, *Economic Survey of Latin America and the Caribbean, 1983* (Santiago: United Nations, 1985), 271; Patricio Meller, *The Unidad Popular and the Pinochet Dictatorship* (New York: St. Martin's Press, 2000), 90–91.

[103] Edward Schumacher, "Copper Miners in Chile Defy Regime," *NYT*, June 17, 1983, 3; Mark Ensalaco, *Chile Under Pinochet* (Philadelphia: University of Pennsylvania Press, 2000), 149.

FPMR) established in late 1983. Between then and 1986, actions by these groups – distributing stolen food to the poor, bombings, assassinations, kidnappings – reinforced the perception of a society sliding into civil war.

It was the outbreak of significant demonstrations against the regime beginning in May 1983 that prefigured the transformation of an unwieldy and disparate multiclass, antigovernment movement into a more organized force far more difficult for the regime to control. At first, an intelligence assessment prepared by the CIA was skeptical about the possible emergence of "a massive, unified, antigovernment labor offensive," because the unions had "borne the brunt of [a decade of] military repression" and were still constrained by government restrictions, and their members were among the most vulnerable in the current economic circumstances.[104] Secretary of State Shultz saw things differently, cabling regional embassies that he discerned the possibility of "a viable and broadly based civilian alternative to military rule."[105] The participation of large numbers of middle-class and some upper-class Chileans in the early protests may have strengthened this perception.

Responding to the first of these large-scale civil disobedience actions, the regime cracked down brutally.[106] Those particularly targeted included copper workers (the army, for example, took over the state-owned El Salvador and Chuquicamata mines), union leaders and cadres, and the radical left-wing parties and their urban shantytown supporters (*pobladores*). Publicly, U.S. officials maintained a line of least resistance in commenting on the regime's behavior. During his confirmation hearing, Assistant Secretary of State for Inter-American Affairs–designate Langhorne Motley told the SFRC that Washington was reluctant to aggressively pressure the junta to bring the election timetable forward because Chile "is a friendly country and our relations with it are good."[107] Privately, the prospect of a polarized civil society in which the moderate political opposition would lose control of the protest movement to the left social movements and political parties was never far from U.S. policy makers'

---

[104] CIA, "Chile: Prospects for Pinochet," Intelligence Assessment, May 17, 1983, DOS/FOIAe, III.

[105] Telegram, Shultz to All American Republic Diplomatic Posts, May 26, 1983, ibid.

[106] For a discussion of the strikes and the regime response, see Manuel Antonio Garretón, "Popular Mobilization and the Military Regime in Chile," in *Power and Popular Protest*, ed. Susan Eckstein (Berkeley: University of California Press, 2001), 266–270.

[107] Quoted in "Washington Stays on the Fence over the Rising Protest," *LAWR*, July 15, 1983, 5.

minds. Another wave of civil disobedience in mid-June involving hundreds of thousands of participants did nothing to ease those fears. In a nationally televised speech, Pinochet announced that he had no intention of relinquishing power ahead of schedule and only agreed to some limited concessions, such as easing the process for exiles to return and ending book censorship.[108] In the State Department, though, alarm bells were ringing as senior officials began to express concern about a "serious polarization" and doubts that the regime "can hold the country in line until the scheduled elections in 1989."[109]

The view from the Department was that responsibility for preventing a further deterioration of the situation inside Chile resided with the junta. In a confidential briefing memo for a meeting with Chilean Ambassador Valenzuela at the end of June, Undersecretary of State Eagleburger was urged to stress the point that unless the Chilean military showed "moderation and political vision to avert a dangerous polarization," the traditional democratic parties "may be radicalized and weakened." In that circumstance, the only beneficiaries would be "the Communists or other extremists."[110] Eagleburger agreed and pressed the Chilean diplomat to lobby his government to "consider political dialogue or other steps" as the best means of circumventing such an outcome.[111]

What concentrated the minds of Reagan officials were two concerns: that the junta's refusal to respond to some opposition demands might intensify and radicalize the social-class conflict; and a desire to avoid any negative comparison with its hard-line response (including economic sanctions) to the suppression of the Solidarity trade union movement by Poland's communist military regime. By moving in what one U.S. official called "subtle, incremental steps," the idea was to indicate White House

---

[108] Edward Schumacher, "Foes of Pinochet in Mass Protests in Chilean Cities," *NYT*, June 15, 1983, 1, 11; Jackson Diehl, "Pinochet Seems to Waiver in Face of Protests," *WP*, June 19, 1983, A15; Edward Schumacher, "Chilean Makes Concessions to Protesters," *NYT*, June 18, 1983, 3. Former Chilean Mines and Labor Minister José Piñera ascribed Pinochet's reluctance to give up power to a "lack of confidence that the U.S. would support him" if political changes "unleash[ed] social forces he might not be able to control." This he traced to Pinochet's interpretation of the Carter White House role in the demise of the Shah of Iran: it had "encouraged internal changes on human rights grounds, and when this unleashed anti Shah forces, the USG [U.S. government] not only was not there to lend support but pulled the rug out from under him [and] and abandoned him to his own luck." Draft, "Chilean Transition, September 22, 1982," Chron 1982, Box 13, JDT Collection.

[109] Briefing Memo, Michel to Eagleburger, June 21, 1983, DOS/FOIAc, III.

[110] Ibid.

[111] Telegram, Shultz (Dam) to AmEmb Santiago, June 30, 1983, author declassified FOIA.

displeasure with Pinochet's strategy and, it was hoped, encourage the armed forces' moderates to lobby for a more rapid transition timetable. At the same time, administration officials cautioned that there were limits to what could be achieved. Irrespective of the internal challenge, said one, the regime's hold on power remained firm, meaning that there would be "no big Carter-type push [because] it would be counterproductive to make a lot of noise."[112]

In the aftermath of a second nationwide antiregime social mobilization in July 1983, calling for political and economic change, the cable traffic from Santiago reinforced Washington's deepening unease over Pinochet's rule. "[The] growing political pressures for change and Pinochet's immobility," Theberge informed Shultz, "are sharpening the divisions and tensions with[in] the society." The leadership of the opposition movement was in danger of passing from the moderate political and labor leaders to the radicals because of a growing "polarization and radicalization of Chile politics" that are taking place. In this new "political-psychological climate," the moderates "are being pushed to adopt more radical postures in order to defend their positions against proponents of the most extreme solutions." Theberge urged a review of U.S. tactics to avert these worst fears from becoming reality. The Embassy even initiated a limited series of meetings with moderate union leaders and conservative politicians on the need to forge a center-right coalition of political parties that might constitute an opposition movement acceptable to the junta – and attractive to Washington. Nonetheless, the Ambassador cautioned that the White House focus should remain on "cooperative ties" with the military government and insisted that quiet diplomacy remained the best means of achieving U.S. goals: "Our influence can be made far more effective by quiet, private and friendly action than by public posturing."[113]

Although some Embassy officials had begun to develop regular contacts with opposition labor and political figures over the previous year, the Ambassador himself had remained aloof from such contacts. In fact, his close ties with Pinochet and senior government officials contrasted sharply with his reluctance to engage such groups as the Catholic Church or the Chilean Commission on Human Rights, which maintained working ties with other Embassy officials and, together with the Church's human rights organization, the Vicariate of Solidarity, provided what the Country Team acknowledged were the most accurate statistics on

---

[112] Quotes in John M. Goshko, "U.S. Escalating Criticism of Chile Regime," *WP*, July 15, 1983, A19.
[113] Telegram, Theberge to Shultz, July 18, 1983, DOS/FOIAe, III.

human rights abuses.[114] While Theberge socialized with cabinet ministers on weekends,[115] he "didn't see his role as being popular with the opposition. That wasn't what he was sent there to do," recalled a senior American diplomat. "He was sent there to have good relations with the government and slowly, carefully, gradually push them in the direction of a democratic opening. He was pursuing the first Reagan administration policy of 'You achieve what you want with these dictatorships by not gratuitously offending them.'"[116] The Socialist Party's Heraldo Múñoz remembered the Ambassador as someone who "didn't want any dealings with the opposition" so as to avoid upsetting the Chilean head of state and the bilateral relationship.[117]

As the demonstrations showed no signs of abating, however, this issue suddenly catapulted to the forefront of the Chile policy debate in Washington. Under instructions from Motley, Theberge now began to meet with centrist trade union leaders, opposition party leaders, and American Federation of Labor (AFL) and American Institute of Free Labor Development (AIFLD) officials active in Chile as part of an effort to promote an alliance between the Christian Democrats, the moderate Social Democrats, and right-wing political groups to minimize the possibility that they might pursue their own deals with the left.[118] At the end of June, Theberge met with Partido Demócrata Cristiano (Christian Democratic Party, PDC) President Gabriel Valdés and other party officials and was impressed by their "moderate and pragmatic" views and, just as importantly, their understanding as to why the United States refused to "align itself against the Pinochet government." During the talks, Valdés described the protests and strikes "as both necessary and dangerous": the former because the government would have to negotiate with the moderates "in order to find a peaceful way out of the crisis;" the latter because the conflict could trigger a "direct confrontation between the

[114] See Edward Schumacher, "Silent Diplomacy of U.S. Irks Latin Rights Activists," *TGM*, April 18, 1983, 13.

[115] Charles W. Gillespie interview, FAOHC.

[116] Interview with George F. Jones.

[117] Telephone interview with Heraldo Múñoz.

[118] See James Brooke, "Mild Criticism by Reagan Shakes Pinochet's Support," *MH*, August 15, 1983, 10A; Edward Schumacher, "Truckers in Chile Begin a Walkout," *NYT*, June 24, 1983, 3; "Theberge Hints at US Definition," *LAWR*, July 23, 1983, 7; Testimony by Deputy Assistant Secretary of State James Michel and Assistant Secretary Elliott Abrams in U.S. Congress, House, Committee on Foreign Affairs, Subcommittees on Human Rights and International Organizations, and the Western Hemisphere Affairs, *Human Rights in Argentina, Chile, Paraguay, and Uruguay*, 98th Cong., 1st Sess., October 21, 1983, 181–182.

people and the army in which the moderate leaders in the government
and in the opposition would be displaced by extremists."[119]

Pinochet's attempts to crush the protest movement included the proposed reimposition of a state of siege. This was rejected by other members
of the junta, who questioned whether a repressive response was the best
instrument for terminating the protests and worried that it could have
a negative impact on current debt talks, make a negotiated transition
to civilian rule more difficult, and ratchet up external demands for an
accelerated return to democracy.[120] Restrained by his junta colleagues,
Pinochet was nonetheless determined to crack down as harshly as possible on the opposition movement. "It's all over gentlemen," he declared
in a message to opposition leaders, while announcing that no further
demonstrations would be permitted.[121] Trade unions, political parties,
and employer associations were neutralized or dismantled, dozens of
union leaders were sacked, and hundreds of workers were jailed. Pinochet
utilized sophisticated tactics to detach labor unions and employer organizations from the protest movement. When copper union leaders, under
pressure from the rank and file, lobbied to have their sacked workers
reinstated, the government responded that a decision would be made the
day after the next (mid-July) national protest. As a result, the copper
workers did not participate in the organization of that or subsequent
demonstrations. Likewise, following its failed national strike, the regime
successfully induced the National Truckers Association to eschew further
open confrontation by agreeing to refinance $120 million of truck own-
ers' debts. PDC leaders arrested for their role in organizing protests were
released, and to mollify the Catholic hierarchy, the Church was allowed
to appoint a new rector of the Catholic University of Valparaiso for the
first time since the 1973 military coup.[122]

---

[119] Telegram, Theberge to Shultz, July 1, 1983, DOS/FOIAe, III.
[120] Barros, *Constitutionalism and Dictatorship*, 280. Under a "state of siege," a government
places restrictions on the movement of people in or out of cities and gives the coercive
institutions, usually the police, the authority to arrest individuals without charges or
warrants. This differs from the declaration of a "state of emergency," whereby governments suspend normal constitutional (executive, legislative, and judicial) procedures
that can, in turn, be used to justify the suspension of individual rights and freedoms to
regain control of a particular situation it deems a threat to its authority.
[121] Quoted in Jackson Diehl, "Chileans Protest Despite Curfew, Troops in Streets," *WP*,
July 13, 1983, A15.
[122] See Jackson Diehl, "Protests Seen Revitalizing Opposition Forces in Chile," *WP*, July
14, 1983, A24; DOS, INR, Current Analysis Series, I-A Highlights, July 18, 1983,
LAAD, NSC, Chile [2 of 2], Box 90512, RRL.

In a mid-year cable to Shultz, Theberge assessed recent developments in Chile and their implications and possible consequences for U.S. policy making. Over the previous six months, he wrote, the regime's "moral authority and credibility" had deteriorated. The days of national protest and antigovernment mass mobilizations had "exceeded expectations" and, more troubling, had "escaped the control of their labor and political organizers." Pinochet's response to the unrest – targeted repression and minor concessions – was unlikely to halt the eroding legitimacy of his regime over the medium term because of a continuation of the economic crisis and the escalating political challenge. That said, the opposition was divided over how best to achieve a political transition. Whereas the moderates wanted key amendments to the 1980 Constitution and its transition plan, a growing sector was advocating a strategy "of popular mobilization and peaceful protest with the hope of compelling Pinochet to resign, or spurring the Army to remove him from power." The possibility that the moderates could lose control of the leadership of this mass movement to the left was all the more likely if the political challenge to military rule became more polarized and radicalized. Already, the moderate antiregime leaders were being pressured "to adopt more radical postures in order to defend their positions." While Theberge considered it "imperative" that Washington "clarify [its] policy goals, priorities and tactics" to deal with this more "complicated" environment, his own proposed solution was to maintain the status quo by sticking with "quiet, private and friendly action" to influence the regime.[123] If Pinochet was a problem, in other words, the United States should continue to work with him to find a solution.

Even Assistant Secretary Motley, himself a proponent of retaining the "quiet diplomacy" approach in dealing with the junta, was having second thoughts about the situation in Chile. In a memo to Undersecretary Eagleburger, he detailed his concerns: the regime's legitimacy was unraveling; the economic crisis had even antagonized traditional elite sectors; and more conservative elements had publicly aligned themselves with the opposition movement, which now incorporated groups and parties across the political spectrum. The domestic U.S. fallout of the junta's deepening political isolation and refusal to moderate its human rights abuses had contributed to the growth of a formidable anti-Pinochet lobby in Washington supported by a significant part of the American electorate, "mak[ing] closer ties politically costly in terms of the credibility of U.S.

---

[123] Telegram, Theberge to Shultz, July 18, 1983, DOS/FOIAe, III.

objectives in Central America, Poland and elsewhere." Diplomatic efforts, public and private, had made little headway in convincing the regime to change its ways, and the army's loyalty to Pinochet based on institutional discipline and personal ties remained a fundamental constraint on the U.S. ability to influence or pressure him. Nonetheless, America's economic and security interests in Chile remained undeniably important, as did the "considerable symbolic importance" the Reagan administration attached to a government that had toppled a Marxist regime and implemented a free market model of development.[124]

Despite a reluctance to excessively criticize the junta because of a belief that this could undermine Washington's already limited influence, a failure to press for some changes would expose the White House to attack for supporting the harsh punishment meted out to the opposition. This explained the vigorous response to the temporary arrest and incarceration of PDC President Gabriel Valdéz and two other party leaders in July, after they testified in court on behalf of youths in possession of leaflets supporting the protests: the State Department called their treatment "regrettable" and communicated its unhappiness directly to senior Chilean officials.[125] During a mid-August meeting, Motley again reminded Ambassador Valenzuela that "bad news coming out of Chile" increases pressure on the administration and constricts its options in dealing with Congress.[126]

The effort to cultivate ties with the Chilean armed forces "to get them to use their influence to moderate the practices of the regime" was *the* most exasperating and difficult of problems, remembered one Reagan official.[127] The Embassy found the military "the hardest possible target simply because it would not discuss politics with foreigners."[128] So did Pentagon officials visiting Chile, who refused to play a "second game" by espousing a position contrary to that of the State Department in the absence of any real and immediate threat to U.S. interests in Chile.[129] Thus Chileans were hearing the same story about the need for political

---

[124] Memo, Motley to Eagleburger, July 28, 1983, ibid.
[125] Quoted in "State Department Changes Tune after 12 July Protests," *LAWR*, July 30, 1983, 5.
[126] Memo, Motley to Eagleburger, August 19, 1983, DOS/FOIAe, III.
[127] Confidential telephone interview 2 (our emphasis).
[128] George F. Jones interview, FAOHC.
[129] Interview with Langhorne Motley. In other words, while the country's situation "needed to be rectified . . . nobody [including the Defense Department] was going to shed any blood over it." Ibid.

reform from both U.S. civilian and defense officials. Neither, however, was making any impact.

On the fourth day of a national protest organized by sectors of the labor movement in mid-August, demonstrations against the regime reached record numbers, forcing Pinochet to deploy eighteen thousand troops onto the streets of the capital to impose order, followed by a ruthless crackdown on the political left and its major social base in the shantytowns.[130] In an effort to deescalate the political crisis, reassert control without having to depend exclusively on force, and make some changes in economic policy, Pinochet appointed Sergio Jarpa, a moderate nationalist and former President of the right-wing National Party, as Interior Minister and named a new civilian cabinet, replacing some of the rigid neoliberals with less ideologically inclined officials. Jarpa was then instructed to open a dialogue (*aperatura*) with "responsible" (i.e., non-Marxist) opposition leaders. For the moment, this was enough of a political opening to satisfy the Reagan administration that its minimal prodding of the regime was working. There were encouraging and conciliatory signs as well from within opposition ranks: prior to the August protests, six political parties, ranging from the moderate left to the moderate right, formed the Alianza Democrática (Democratic Alliance, AD) and now agreed to enter into negotiations with Jarpa as a bloc. Perhaps most surprising was the inclusion of Socialist Party moderates (the Altamirano wing) in the AD. Whether to join provoked a "heated debate" within party ranks, said Heraldo Múñoz, and it was not until Pinochet named Jarpa to negotiate with the opposition that "we thought that this was perhaps the beginning of the end." What proved to be the most persuasive argument in favor of joining the dialogue was the repeated violent state responses to the mass mobilizations over the previous four months.[131]

---

[130] For an excellent discussion of protests in the *poblaciónes*, see Cathy Lisa Schneider, *Shantytown Protest in Pinochet's Chile* (Philadelphia: Temple University Press, 1995), 153–189.

[131] Heraldo Múñoz, *The Dictator's Shadow* (New York: Basic Books, 2008), 179; telephone interview with Heraldo Múñoz. Carlos Altamirano was Secretary General of the Socialist Party during the Allende era and a leading advocate of armed struggle in the 1972–1973 internal UP debates over whether to confront the antigovernment forces or consolidate the gains already made and negotiate, at least with the Christian Democrats. In exile, Altamirano renounced his earlier belief that Allende had been toppled from power owing to a failure to engage armed struggle, embraced a social democratic outlook, and now advocated developing an alliance with the Christian Democrats. See Múñoz, *The Dictator's Shadow*, 124–125; Lois Hecht Oppenheim, *Politics in Chile*, 2nd ed. (Boulder: Westview Press, 1999), 74, 8.

In facilitating a dialogue with the moderate political parties, the regime's objectives were multiple: to get the opposition "off the streets" and regain the political initiative; to appeal to those members of the middle class who had joined the protesters because of the severity of the economic crisis; and to exploit the increasingly tenuous relationship between the center-right and the left social movements and parties over the effectiveness of mass mobilization politics – to seek a deal with the former on the government's terms. In allowing the *aperatura* to go ahead, Pinochet did so with limited enthusiasm, most likely because of the growing influence of a group of hard-line nationalists inside and outside of the cabinet.[132]

A CIA National Intelligence Estimate (NIE) labeled the AD "weak in terms of purpose, leadership and organization," even though its dialogue with Jarpa represented the "best means of ensuring a peaceful transition to democracy . . . acceptable to a broad spectrum of Chilean moderates."[133] While disavowing the agenda and tactics of the radical left, the AD insisted on Pinochet's resignation, the restoration of civil liberties, a more rapid transition to democracy, revocation of the 1980 Constitution, and a softening of the regime's economic policies. The first of the dialogues produced some grounds for optimism as the AD was encouraged to lay out its proposals, but it quickly became clear that Jarpa had no real authority to negotiate on any issue of substance. His responses, Washington judged, were "positive but deliberately vague, reflecting Pinochet's basic unwillingness to consider any transition formula other than the slowly paced process outlined in the 1980 Constitution."[134]

On September 9, the AD suspended negotiations, following a national day of protest centered in the *poblaciónes*. The junta's response to the protest had been predictably ham-fisted, raising moderate opposition concerns that Pinochet was simply playing into the hands of the radical left by bringing the country closer to a social explosion that they couldn't control.[135] Citing the government's foot dragging on a specific agenda and timetable for an ongoing dialogue, as well as the level of state repression, the AD leadership began to view Jarpa as part of Pinochet's strategy to

[132] Marcelo Pollack, *The New Right in Chile 1973–1989* (Basingstoke: Macmillan, 1999), 87.
[133] NIE, CIA, "Chile: Days of Protest," September 27, 1983, CIA, FOIAe, III. Also see Memo, Motley to Eagleburger, September 19, 1983, DOS/FOIAe, III; interviews with AD leaders, in Mark A. Uhlig, "Pinochet's Tyranny," *New York Review of Books*, June 27, 1985, 35–40.
[134] Telegram, Shultz (Dam) to USDEL, November 24, 1983, DOS/FOIAe, III.
[135] Jackson Diehl, "Limited Liberalization Pays Limited Dividends for Gen. Pinochet," *WP*, September 11, 1983, A21. Also see NIE, CIA, "Chile: Days of Protest."

deepen existing tensions within the opposition, in the hope that he could negotiate a separate peace with the center-right on his terms.

Two days after the AD suspended talks, and on the tenth anniversary of the 1973 coup, a confident and unapologetic Pinochet attacked the opposition leaders as "agents of violence" and made not the slightest concession to growing demands that he relinquish political power.[136] In Washington, doubts were being expressed about Ambassador Theberge's ability to get "a clear message" through to the Chilean government on the importance of acting decisively if the radicals were to be denied "a psychological and tactical opening." Realistically, Motley concluded in a memo to Eagleburger, the United States had only one option: to "exert gentle but firm pressure" on the regime to initiate a dialogue with "non-extremist members" of the opposition and "clearly define and move toward" a democratic transition.[137] "Let's face it, we haven't got many cards to play in Chile," another senior official had put it bleakly some weeks earlier. "Our influence with Pinochet is minimal and our credibility with the opposition is thin."[138]

Questions about Theberge's competence, or reluctance to follow orders, reflected growing differences between the Ambassador and the Department over how to deal with Pinochet. As he prepared to return to Washington for consultations, Theberge renewed his criticism of HA's Elliott Abrams, accusing the Assistant Secretary of wielding undue influence on certain Department offices "to reinterpret or back away" from the administration's commitment to eliminating the ban on military assistance to Chile. Theberge exhorted the Department "to grasp the nettle" and certify Chile and Argentina simultaneously.[139] This set the stage for an inevitable clash with Abrams during the Ambassador's round of meetings at State. Abrams's response to Theberge's "strong preference" for delaying Argentina's certification "as long as possible in order to build a case for Chilean certification" was short and emphatic, in the knowledge that Shultz was on his side: HA would "strongly oppose" any move to certify Chile for the moment.[140]

---

[136] Quoted in Stephen Kinzer, "Pinochet Is Firm in Anniversary Speech," *NYT*, September 12, 1983, 3.

[137] Briefing Memo, Motley to Eagleburger, September 14, 1983, DOS/FOIAe, III.

[138] Quoted in Philip Taubman, "U.S. Wears a Hato amid Chile Unrest," *NYT*, August 25, 1983, 11.

[139] Letter, Theberge to Motley, September 14, 1983, Oliver L. North, "Chile," Box 62, RRL.

[140] Memo, Motley to Dam, "Chile – Your Meeting with Ambassador Theberge," October 4, 1983, "Chron Chile 1982–1985," Box 16, JDT Collection.

Toward the end of September, Motley again wrote to Eagleburger proposing a number of short- and medium-term courses of action the administration should pursue in addressing political developments in Chile. Despite the refusal of Pinochet to contemplate stepping down, Motley predicted that the General was likely to be removed from office before his term expired in 1989. The key question, then, was whether the circumstances of Pinochet's departure would most benefit the "moderate civilian leadership" or the radical left. The initial dialogue between Jarpa and the moderates "achieved some success in dampening down confrontation; in all other respects it [had] proved disappointing." First, Pinochet exploited the contradictory goals of the negotiating parties "to perpetuate his mandate." Second, one premise of the dialogue – that a functioning electoral system could coexist with a Pinochet presidency until 1989 – was an "untenable" scenario. Third, the antiregime moderates were a diverse coalition, not a unified political movement, "whose only common denominator [was] the removal of Pinochet from power."

Despite his belief that Washington was left with no alternative but to exert a modicum of pressure on the regime to engage with the nonradical opposition, Motley still remained far from hopeful about a successful outcome given the obstacles that had to be surmounted. The U.S. government's restricted ability to wield much influence with either side, he complained, was particularly exasperating. Not even the efforts of high-level, sympathetic administration officials such as Reagan's Ambassador-at-Large Vernon Walters or UN Ambassador Jeane Kirkpatrick had been able to push Pinochet toward "preferred U.S. behaviour." The certification impasse and "our perceived uneasiness with Pinochet and his policies" had merely reinforced a deeply held skepticism within Chilean ruling circles about "our intentions." The lack of certification, together with the restrictions on military aid and training, had also created a situation where American officials did "not have ready political entrée to key military figures" to influence regime decision making.

Nothing could more sharply reflect Washington's quandary than Motley's admission that, deep into the third year of the Reagan presidency, the "primary asset" for influencing Santiago was "symbolism [and] symbolic actions." This being the case, he warned against "overplay[ing] our hand [by] attempt[ing] to intervene too actively," recommending instead that U.S. policy over the next four to six months concentrate on bolstering the moderates in the government and civil society "as a hedge against radicalization," discouraging joint actions between the moderate opposition and the left and seeking "where possible to enhance our leverage by continuing cooperative relations with the GOC on issues of mutual interest." Eagleburger agreed that as long as the dialogue between the regime and the opposition continued, the administration should maintain a "relatively balanced posture" in close consultation with NATO and Latin American countries, and expand official and unofficial communications with Chile's government and "acceptable" opposition leaders.

Having already instructed Ambassador Theberge to "seek more frequent visible meetings with the opposition" to push a transition agreement along, Motley suggested using "unofficial emissaries as channel[s] of communication to both sides" to ensure the success of the dialogue. The most difficult task remained extracting concessions from the regime that might satisfy congressional certification requirements. Motley perceived a situation not totally bereft of possibilities for applying pressure on Pinochet: while visits by senior U.S. officials may "have failed to move him," the Chilean leader was "weaker and more vulnerable now," a reality that might be exploited to Washington's advantage. To do so, he advocated a "two-pronged diplomacy" of maintaining cooperative bilateral relations while seeking to exert influence with "key personalities" inside the government supportive of a democratic political transition.[141] Whether this proposal had any greater chance of success seemed unlikely, especially given the earlier failures of senior Reagan officials to make much headway in convincing Pinochet to take U.S. concerns seriously.

Two subsequent meetings between Jarpa and the AD further underscored the former's limited mandate, making it difficult for State Department officials to avoid concluding that the *aperatura* was "primarily a subterfuge for Pinochet to retain power as long as possible." The regime did make some token concessions, including a decision not to renew the state of emergency, thereby restoring the right to assemble. These and other small political openings were well and good, wrote Deputy Secretary of State Kenneth Dam, but "the closer discussions came to the true kernel of the problem – Pinochet's continuance in office – the more apparent it became that the dialogue had evolved into little more than a government stall."[142]

That was not Jarpa's interpretation of events. He would subsequently accuse PDC officials in particular of using contacts in the United States to "spread the idea that only they could solve the problems faced by Chile."

---

[141] Memo, Motley to Eagleburger, "Chile Policy Memorandum," September 23, 1983, DOS/FOIAc, III.

[142] Telegram, Shultz (Dam) to USDEL, November 24, 1983, ibid.

The government was also convinced that the PDC had joined forces with the Marxists and were sending emissaries to governments in Europe advising them not to invest in Chile because of the instability they had helped create. "Under these conditions," said Jarpa, "there were no possibilities for the Christian Democrats to cooperate in solving problems." In the same breath, he admitted that the government "was not willing to compromise or transfer power to a specific party."[143] The moderate opposition now felt itself between a rock and a hard place. With no significant gains to show from the dialogue, the only pressure it could bring to bear on the regime was renewed social mobilization that risked almost certain violence. If the struggle moved in this direction at a time when the unemployment rate among urban shantytown dwellers had risen to around 60 percent, the prospects of the center-right maintaining control of the opposition movement and avoiding lower-class radicalization would diminish with each passing day.[144] Yet the moderates remained "extremely suspicious" that Pinochet would renege on concessions once protests were ended, leaving them adrift and "open to leftist charges of sellout."[145]

Any prospects that negotiations would resume soon were dashed in late October, when frustrated and angry AD negotiators finally broke off the dialogue with Jarpa altogether, convinced that Pinochet was not prepared to contemplate a rapid transition to civilian rule and that Jarpa simply lacked the authority to negotiate. The Embassy cabled State that moderate opposition leaders were no less apprehensive than Washington that failure to win concessions could "radicalize the political process and drive the poor and much of the middle class into the arms of the far left."[146] As if to demonstrate the point, the leftist Movimiento Democrática Popular (Democratic Popular Movement, MDP), the other coalition that emerged in this renewed political struggle, supported by the CNT, took the initiative in organizing another series of antiregime mobilizations on October 11–13 despite a government ban on actions of this kind. Nearly

---

[143] Quoted in Patricia Arancibia Clavel et al., *Jarpa: Confesiónes Politicas* (Santiago: Editorial Sudamericana Chilena S.S., 2002), 362.

[144] See Jackson Diehl, "Moderate Opposition Warns of Growing Anger among Chile's Poor," *WP*, September, 19, 1983, A15.

[145] CIA, Directorate of Intelligence, "Prospects for Chile," September 2, 1983, Executive Secretariat, NSC, Country File, Chile Vol. 1, 1/20/81–7/31/81 [3], Box 91868, RRL.

[146] Telegram, AmbEmb, Santiago (Matthews) to Shultz, November 7, 1983, DOS/FOIAe, III.

a hundred thousand Chilean protesters filled the streets of Santiago in response.[147]

As Reagan's third year in office drew to a close, the administration's initial determination to restore amicable relations with the Pinochet dictatorship confronted several obstacles. Foremost among them was opposition among significant and influential sectors of the U.S. Congress to the idea of normalizing ties with a regime universally condemned as a major human rights abuser. Although the legislators had agreed to remove the restrictions on security assistance and arms sales to Chile in 1981, dependent on White House certification that "significant progress" was occurring on the human rights front and that the junta was cooperating on the Letelier-Moffitt investigation, this constituted little more than a pyrrhic victory for the administration so long as Pinochet turned a deaf ear to U.S. appeals for progress in both areas. No amount of lobbying by Washington and its diplomats in Santiago, or limited material and symbolic assistance, was able to extract more than counterfeit concessions such as Jarpa's dialogue with the AD. Pinochet's intransigence – his dismissive attitude toward criticism and advice – against the backdrop of renewed social mobilization by the opposition forces led increasingly frustrated American officials to begin to contemplate the need for a different approach that diverged from one committed to essentially unqualified support of an anticommunist ally.

[147] Cynthia Brown, "Protest in Chile – The Road Ahead," *The Nation*, December 3, 1983, 563; Jackson Diehl, "Chilean Opposition Splits; Left Dominates Protests," *WP*, October 12, 1983 (Factiva).

2

Turning the Tide

Following the collapse of negotiations involving Interior Minister Sergio Jarpa and the AD, State Department Counselor Edward Derwinski arrived in Santiago in early November 1983 carrying a singular message for the Chilean government: with the recent transition from military rule to democracy in Argentina the previous month, Chile risked being the "odd man out" in the region vis-à-vis relations with Washington.[1] Derwinski's instructions from Motley were to "exert gentle but firm pressure" on the regime to negotiate an agreement with the moderate opposition on a transition timetable.[2] In meetings with the opposition, Derwinski encountered an AD leadership that was "uniformly pessimistic" about the future of any dialogue, convinced that Jarpa's "good intentions" would inevitably fall victim to Pinochet's refusal to accept any erosion of his "dictatorial powers" and that this, in turn, would almost certainly "radicalize the political process" in ways that could only benefit "the far left." The severity of the socioeconomic crisis reinforced the appeal of the more radical sectors of the opposition movement. Until further notice, Derwinski was told, the AD saw no alternative to returning to civilian disobedience and mass mobilization politics to put maximum pressure on the regime to make concessions, otherwise nothing would change.[3] Nevertheless, at a press conference before his departure, Derwinski saw no contradiction in reaffirming the existing U.S. policy approach: "silent

---

[1] Quoted in "Reagan Urges Chile to Restore Democracy," *NYT*, November 2, 1983, 7.
[2] Briefing Memo, Motley to Derwinski, October 27, 1983, DOS/FOIAe, III.
[3] Telegram, AmbEmb Santiago (Matthews) to Shultz, November 7, 1983, ibid.

diplomacy is something we prefer."[4] A State Department policy review did not suggest otherwise. The "uncertainty" surrounding the domestic political landscape, it concluded, dictated that in the short term, U.S. interests "would be best served by maintaining a cooperative bilateral relationship with Chile" (meaning the junta) and working behind the scenes to get the regime and the nonradical opposition to agree on a transition timetable.[5]

To the Reagan administration, Chile was now becoming just as much a regional as a bilateral problem, particularly in view of successful democratic transitions in Peru (1980) and Argentina (1983) and similar processes well advanced in Brazil and Uruguay. In mid-November, Ambassador-at-Large Vernon Walters was asked by the White House to deliver a letter to Pinochet urging some compromise in his approach. When Walters read the initial draft of the letter from ARA, he "felt it was much too strongly worded," said one of its authors. As the messenger, and someone with close ties to the dictator, "we had to take his criticisms seriously and so we had to redraft the letter and some of the harsher language was taken out of it."[6]

Prior to leaving for Santiago, Walters received a thorough briefing from the State Department about the purpose of his meeting with Pinochet: "the primary objective of your mission is to urge Pinochet to commit himself to a peaceful democratic government [which] is necessary to the maintenance of stability in Chile and the Southern Cone." Walters was further instructed to assuage any possible concerns the dictator might have about U.S. motives. The administration did not question the "legitimacy" of the 1980 Constitution, it did not want Pinochet "to resign now," and Walters should reassure the General that the lack of certification of Chile's human rights situation for the purpose of releasing military aid was simply a result of the regime's failure to meet the requirements of U.S. law and

---

[4] Transcript of Press Conference, Santiago, November 3, 1983, in *American Foreign Policy: Current Documents* (Washington, DC: Department of State, 1985), 1444.

[5] Memo, Hill to McFarlane, November 25, 1983, Executive Secretariat, NSC, Country File, Chile Vol. 1, 1/20/81–7/31/84 [1], Box 91868, RRL.

[6] Confidential telephone interview 2. Pinochet insisted that his response be delivered personally to Reagan by the Chilean Ambassador. Some weeks passed before a meeting could be scheduled. "When the Ambassador walked into the Oval Office to deliver the letter, and sees all of key cabinet ministers there for an early morning staff meeting waiting to receive him, he almost passes out. Reagan jumps up, greets him and says he has a question that has always puzzled him. The Ambassador starts quaking, thinking he's going to declare war or something but Reagan asks 'How do you pronounce your President's name?'" Ibid.

"in no way alters our desire to maintain and, where possible, improve our cooperative relationship." What Washington sought was "an early definition of a timetable" for implementing the measures discussed by Jarpa and the moderate political leaders such as the legalization of political parties (officially banned since 1977) and details governing the conduct of the plebiscite that would decide whether Pinochet remained in power beyond 1989.[7] This was the first of a number of fundamental miscalculations by Reagan officials that, as then Embassy DCM George Jones put it, "if we say the right things to Pinochet, Pinochet will respond."[8]

On November 18, just days prior to Walter's visit, the AD participated in the largest antigovernment demonstration since the coup, organized again by the leftist MDP and the labor unions. Hundreds of thousands of Chileans "across generational, socio-economic and political lines" took to the streets, where they encountered the standard brutal junta response. While Theberge highlighted the substantial middle-class participation, he nevertheless refused to attach any broader significance to the rally. "[It] does not form part of a sustained pattern of increasing mass mobilization against the Pinochet government," he cabled Washington. "Thus its impact is likely to be limited and short-lived."[9] Pinochet paid the demonstrators little heed, and the same was true of his attitude to the message Walters delivered. In fact, Pinochet told his visitor that Washington's eventual decision to certify Argentina's human rights record for the purposes of resuming aid was one more example of a lack of reciprocity in U.S. policy. Speaking "more in sorrow than in anger," he complained to Walters that while Chile had consistently supported U.S. foreign policy, "you have not reciprocated. Your policy towards Chile is really not much different from that of the Carter administration."[10]

Back in Washington, congressional demands for progress in the Letelier case continued to make no impression on Pinochet. Justice Department officials accused him and the other members of the junta of "actively imped[ing]" the investigation, while State's Director of Southern Cone Affairs described their behavior as "stonewalling [and] not about to concede anything on this because they didn't need us for anything."[11] Testifying before Congress, Assistant Secretary of State for HA Elliott

---

[7] Telegram, Shultz to AmEmb, Jakarta and Santiago, November 15, 1983, DOS/FOIAe, III. Also see Briefing Memo, Eagleburger to Walters, November 16, 1984, ibid.

[8] Interview with George F. Jones.

[9] Telegram, Theberge to Shultz, November 22, 1983, DOS/FOIAe, III.

[10] Telegram, Theberge to Shultz, December 12, 1983, ibid.

[11] Memo, Hill to Clark, October 7, 1983, ibid.; Robert B. Morley interview, FAOHC.

Abrams stated that "we continue to receive credible reports of violence and torture by the police and security forces."[12] If Pinochet had "been put on notice that in the absence of further movement toward democracy in Chile, relations with the U.S. are not likely to improve," as Assistant Secretary Langhorne Motley insisted was the case, the General appeared unmoved.[13] The outlook was not promising.

Pressure without Leverage

As the Pinochet dictatorship entered its eleventh year, inter- and intra-agency disagreements on Chile policy were widening. The major combatants in the bureaucratic debate – State and the NSC – continued to offer sharply differing interpretations of Pinochet's behavior, his importance to U.S. interests, and how the administration should deal with him. To NSC officials, Pinochet was a pivotal bulwark against communism and Soviet influence in Latin America and warranted continued support; in State the growing view was that his determination to remain in power until at least 1989 was a recipe for potential disaster and had to be challenged by a more active U.S. effort to promote a democratic political transition. A senior Inter-American Affairs official elaborated, "There were people within the NSC staff who felt that Chile represented a stalwart ally in the Cold War and that we should do whatever we could to maintain a friendly and cooperative relationship. Then there were others, mostly within the [State] Department, in the Human Rights Bureau and elsewhere, who felt that we had to do whatever we could to pressure or induce Chile to clean up its human rights record and to undo some of the harsher elements of the regime. Langhorne Motley was kind of in the middle."[14] In Santiago, the Country Team overwhelmingly supported the anticommunist interpretation, remembered an Embassy official, with "only a couple" of officers advocating the democracy strategy.[15]

---

[12] U.S. Congress, House, *Human Rights in Argentina, Chile, Paraguay, and Uruguay*, 145. The UN Special Rapporteur's report on Chile (covering the period September to December 1983) described a country where state-authored torture remained an "habitual practice," where judicial protection "remained inadequate," and where arbitrary detentions and arrests had jumped more than fourfold between 1982 and 1983. The report concluded that "prospects for the protection of human rights and freedoms continued to be bleak." United Nations, *Yearbook of the United Nations 1984*, vol. 38 (New York: United Nations Department of Public Information, 1988), 862, 863.

[13] Briefing Memo, Motley to Shultz, December 20, 1983, DOS/FOIAe, III.

[14] Confidential telephone interview 2.

[15] Confidential telephone interview 1.

Proponents of a tougher line seemed to have scored one victory in December when the United States opposed a $268 million loan (which nonetheless was approved) to Chile's state-owned Codelco copper enterprise in the IADB. Treasury Secretary Donald Regan instructed the U.S. Executive Director to vote no, even though staff officials, including Undersecretary Beryl Sprinkel, had argued in support of the loan.[16] While Treasury had voted in favor of past BHN loans, it more than the other executive branch departments had to be sensitive to Congress, which determined the annual replenishment of funds for the MDBs.[17] On Capitol Hill, the degree of hostility toward the Pinochet dictatorship – influenced by continuous pressure exerted by Chilean exile groups and their allies in the human rights, religious, and independent research organizations (Council on Hemispheric Affairs, Washington Office on Latin America, etc.) monitoring events in Latin America, as well as the yearly condemnation of the Pinochet government at the UN – virtually guaranteed a negative response to non-BHN Chile loan submissions. A further incentive may have been that Chilean copper imports to the United States doubled in 1982 and 1983, adding further pressure on American copper producers struggling in a depressed market. As mines closed and workers were laid off, these domestic producers began appealing for restrictions on Chilean imports.[18]

The elimination of obstacles to improved bilateral ties continued to founder on the twin rocks of Pinochet's reluctance to simultaneously pursue his "war on terror" and redemocratization – and the Reagan administration's lack of sufficient instruments to pressure Pinochet to move in that direction. By 1984, a senior regional official in State recalled, "it was quite clear that [Pinochet] resented our repeated efforts to try to get him to moderate his behavior. He certainly wanted to show that he was not vulnerable to American pressure and he certainly let us know that he felt that we didn't understand what was going on in his country."[19] In mid-May, he reinforced this stance, promulgating a new

---

[16] Memo, Motley, McCormack, and Eaglebuger, December 2, 1983, DOS/FOIAe, III.

[17] During the 1980s, the U.S. Congress was not reluctant to apply pressure during these negotiations with the IMF and World Bank by "threaten[ing] to reduce or withhold the funds" to force acceptance of demands in return for the release of its contributions. Ngaire Woods, *The Globalizers* (Ithaca: Cornell University Press, 2006), 32.

[18] For the view of American copper producers, see Daniel F. Cuff, "Talking Business with George Munroe of Phelps Dodge; the Bid to Cut Copper Imports," *NYT*, June 19, 1984, D2.

[19] Confidential telephone interview 2.

"antiterrorism law" that significantly expanded the definition of terrorism and increased the penalties for engaging in such behavior. Having determined that in the wake of the Falklands defeat and the collapse of the military dictatorship, the Argentine "threat" was receding, not even "the carrot of an enhanced military relationship" bolstered efforts by U.S. emissaries to convince the junta to quicken the pace of political reform, said State's Director of Southern Cone Affairs Robert Morley. "We had no meaningful leverage to get them to speed up the process of return to democracy."[20] As a consequence, the policy approach still concentrated on low-key diplomacy, largely confined to ongoing discussions with the Chilean Ambassador in Washington. In Santiago, access to regime officials was much more limited. Whenever Embassy officials attempted to convey U.S. concerns, they "ran into a buzz-saw" of resistance, not helped by Ambassador Theberge's reluctance to do anything that might upset the junta. "Instructing him to go in and push for something was always a problem."[21]

In mid-February 1984, a House Armed Services Committee delegation visited a number of hemisphere nations, including Chile, to review security-related matters. Given the congressional prohibition on bilateral military cooperation with Chile, the junta had turned to alternative supply sources, purchasing equipment primarily from Israel and the United Kingdom. The delegation noted that this shift to other suppliers was not without its downside: the mismatch in weapon systems "increased logistical problems and increased vulnerability to disruption of deliveries of equipment and spare parts." In addition, a good deal of the junta's older military hardware was of American origin and dependent on access to U.S. spare parts to maintain it in optimal working order.[22] American suppliers' prospects for recapturing this market were low in the absence of presidential certification. The administration had been able to circumvent legislative sanctions on one occasion only, convincing Congress to reclassify ejection seat parts to the junta for American-built military aircraft as "safety related," making them no longer subject to the Kennedy

---

[20] Robert B. Morley interview, FAOHC.
[21] Confidential telephone interview 2. Theberge was a Cold War ideologue obsessed with keeping the Soviet Union out of the Western Hemisphere. See, for example, James Theberge, *Russia in the Caribbean* (Washington, DC: Center for Strategic and International Studies, 1973); *The Soviet Presence in Latin America* (New York: Crane Russak, 1974).
[22] U.S. Congress, House, Committee on Armed Services, *Report of the Delegation to Eastern Caribbean and South American Countries*, 98th Cong., 2d Sess., No. 16, Committee Print, February 1984, 33.

amendment to the FAA. This "victory" was due largely to the efforts of State's Langhorne Motley, who personally lobbied the Massachusetts Senator that the parts had to be replaced every two years, irrespective of the amount of use, and could only be purchased from the American firm of Martin-Baker. Kennedy eventually "relented" and the materiel was "quietly" exported to Santiago. "When it came down to practical issues," Motley said, "Kennedy could be very practical." Although the dollar value of the parts was minimal, the symbolism was important. As well as establishing a precedent, the sale itself sent a positive signal to the Chilean military.[23]

The executive branch was just as determined to overcome the legislative obstacles to providing economic aid to the junta through the instrumentalities of quasi-government corporations that were less subject to congressional scrutiny or oversight. The CCC, the Overseas Private Investment Corporation (OPIC), and the Eximbank all "continued to subsidize and encourage private-sector dealings with Chile." Between fiscal years 1981 and 1984, for instance, the Eximbank authorized just under $144 million in loan guarantees and insurance to U.S. investors wanting to do business in Chile.[24]

Nonetheless, efforts to bolster U.S. aid programs faced continuing obstacles. When the new Chilean Ambassador to the United States, Hernán Errázuriz, called on Elliott Abrams in January 1984, he discovered that the requirements for certification had, in effect, become more demanding. The Argentine experience, where democratization preceded certification, Abrams told his visitor, meant that "practically speaking it might not be possible to certify Chile until after an election is held there as well."[25] If the Chileans were unhappy with this statement, Ambassador Theberge was positively furious, accusing Abrams of responsibility for a "creeping escalation of the certification requirements . . . to fit the interests of different bureaucratic sectors in Washington." Having already expressed his opposition to the "unrealistic" demand that the regime "take new steps" in the Letelier case, this apparent decision to link certification to "progress towards democracy," a requirement that was not mandated by statute, was the last straw for the Ambassador.[26]

[23] Interview with Langhorne Motley; W. Frick Curry, *Subsidizing Pinochet* (Washington, DC: Center for International Policy, 1985), 3, 4.
[24] Ibid., 5.
[25] Telegram, Shultz to AmEmb Santiago, January 6, 1984, DOS/FOIAe, III.
[26] Letter, Theberge to Abrams, January 10, 1984, Executive Secretariat, NSC, Country File, Chile Vol. 1, 1/20/81–7/31/81, Box 91868, RRL.

Technically, Theberge's interpretation of the law governing Chilean certification was correct, but Abrams's political sense was closer to the mark. As NSC officials pointed out, in a December 7, 1983, letter to NSC Adviser Robert McFarlane (appointed in October), the President linked human rights improvements and movement toward redemocratization in terms of Chilean certification.[27] Indeed, democracy promotion had by now supplanted the Kirkpatrick Doctrine in shaping administration thinking about Chile. Speaking before a Boston World Affairs Council meeting in February 1984, Secretary of State George Shultz referred to Chile as one of the countries "sticking out like a sore thumb" in the hemisphere's new democratic landscape.[28] Another Department official described Pinochet as "a lightning rod everywhere, the most hated man in the world, the symbol of authoritarian repression" in a region moving away from dictatorial rule.[29] None of these sentiments had the least impact on Theberge's outlook. He remained convinced that Abrams was engaged in a deliberate effort to make certification "harder not easier" as part of a broader policy of treating Chile as "a pariah state." A colleague in the Latin American Bureau sought to convince Theberge that Motley was "not about to allow [a hardening of certification requirements] to happen" and had already begun to rein Abrams in for "encroaching bureaucratically on ARA turf, trying to make and change policy towards Chile."[30] Tensions between the Bureau and Abrams were not confined to Chile, although in that case "we thought he was pressing too hard."[31]

In ARA's Office of Southern Cone Affairs (SCA), Robert Morley grappled with the question of whether State should attempt to substitute, amend, or delete the Chilean certification requirements in the 1985 FAA. While acknowledging that the prospects of success were "poor," he advocated a course of action that would eliminate certification and in its place agree to a congressional line item veto over all Chilean Munitions Control export license applications, foreign military sales (FMS), and security assistance programs. Whether or not the legislators supported this option, SCA strongly opposed the existing certification demands because they exposed Chile alone "to such singular, and unwarranted, scrutiny."[32] On

[27] Memo, Thompson to McFarlane, January 27, 1984, Executive Secretariat, NSC, Country File, Chile Vol. 1, 1/20/81–7/31/84 [1], Box 91868, RRL.
[28] Telegram, Shultz to AmEmb Santiago, February 22, 1984, DOS/FOIAe, III.
[29] Confidential telephone interview 1.
[30] "Morley Talk," January 18, 1984, January–April 1984, (IB), Box 19, JDT Collection.
[31] Confidential telephone interview 2.
[32] Memo, Morley to Kilday, February 21, 1984, DOS/FOIAe, III.

March 14, 1984, the HFAC – as Abrams had foreshadowed – responded
by approving an additional certification requirement that "an elected government is in power in Chile." When asked by NSC Adviser McFarlane
"where we should go from here," staff aides Raymond Bughardt and
Constantine Menges could only answer that recent developments were
"going in reverse." They reported that State had decided to withhold any
challenge to the new certification requirement until it reached the joint
conference committee because they already had their "hands full with El
Salvador," which was about to stage a presidential election. Their advice
to McFarlane was that the best strategy would be to devise a coordinated approach for fighting approval of the new amendment when the
1985 FAA reached the floor of the full House of Representatives. The
NSC Adviser concurred with "the substance" of the memo.[33]

Weeks earlier, one of Washington's most important European allies
had exposed the tensions within the foreign policy bureaucracy over Chile
policy. On that occasion, West German Chancellor Helmut Kohl cabled
Reagan that Pinochet's refusal to budge from the 1989 election timetable
was "playing into the hands of left-wing and communist forces." The
NSC's Jacqueline Tillman wrote the initial draft response, advising the
President to inform Kohl that "the most effective manner of achieving
progress in Chile is quietly and discreetly."[34] State Department revisions
of the draft letter produced a mixed response from Elliott Abrams, who
considered them "an improvement" but flawed in two respects. First, the
letter still conveyed "too strong a sense of support for Pinochet," and second, it failed to seriously address Kohl's disquiet over the potential consequences of a long, drawn-out transition process. After all, said Abrams, a
key U.S. objective is "to avoid polarization which pro-Soviet/Cuba groups
will exploit." Moreover, any reluctance to encourage European support
for accelerating the democratization process in Chile did not bode well
for the administration's Central America policy, where "we can use all the
help we can get from the WG's [West Germans] and other key allies."[35]

Assessing the political balance in Chile in early 1984, Theberge predicted more "social unrest and political agitation," and deepening frustration and anger among all social classes "over the slow pace of economic progress as well as the limited nature of the political opening."

---

[33] Memo, Burghardt and Menges to McFarlane, March 15, 1984, Executive Secretariat,
    NSC, Country File, Chile Vol. 1, 1/20/81–7/31/84 (1), Box 91868, RRL.
[34] Memo, Tillman to McFarlane, February 24, 1984, DDRS (2001: 2272).
[35] Memo, Abrams to Eagleburger and Motley, February 29, 1984, DOS/FOIAe, III.

Another cycle of protests and growing political polarization seemed inevitable, not least because Pinochet appeared incapable of developing a credible longer-term strategy for dealing with the opposition, preferring instead a mixture of short-term tactics to fracture and control the social movements.[36] Pinochet's "natural inclination," said one member of the Country Team, was "to batten down the hatches and not make any movement toward democratization because that would be interpreted as a sign of weakness."[37] Although he displayed a sporadic willingness to combine brutal repression of the left social movements, unions, and political parties with some limited concessions to the center-right antiregime political class and its organizations, Pinochet was determined to stay in power until at least 1989 – and resist all external or internal pressures so long as he retained the confidence of the Army High Command. To this end, he used the most recent round of military promotions to "retain his closest confidants in key positions."[38] But the mass protests had "diminished" his popular support base, and the concern among State officials was that any further erosion, amid a severe economic downturn, could lead to "renewed unrest" unless the junta responded to U.S. efforts to actively promote, rather than just outline, a transition process.[39] The chances of that happening were slim.

Isolating the Left

Reagan policy makers sympathized with regime efforts to crack down on the radical left movements and parties in the name of "combating terrorism." However, they desired an equal commitment to a redemocratization process that would prove attractive to the majority of Chileans and so eventually make possible the handover of power to a "right of center [civilian] government."[40] Rather than pursuing the latter course of action, Pinochet was treating all sectors of the opposition movement in a manner that risked forcing them into an alliance with the very internal forces that the White House believed would open Chile up to Soviet and Cuban influence. When Theberge warned that "nothing that Pinochet has

---

[36] Telegram, Theberge to Shultz, March 13, 1984, NSC Secretariat, Constantine C. Menges, Chile (3), Box 90376, RRL.
[37] Wade Matthews interview, FAOHC.
[38] Briefing Paper, DOS, INR, "Eight Months of Protest in Chile," January 26, 1984, DOS/FOIAe, III.
[39] Memo, Michel to Shultz, January 11, 1984, ibid.
[40] Memo, Abrams to Eagleburger and Motley, February 29, 1984, ibid.

said or done [over the past three months] has restored confidence in his political leadership or reveals an effective strategy for dealing with the increasingly intense opposition he faces,"[41] he was engaging in a subtle critique of administration attempts to encourage progress on a transition process as much as he was damning Pinochet. Reluctant to impose new sanctions, Washington remained hopeful it could convince the regime to reach an accommodation with the center and center-right opposition groups by judicious prodding alone – a strategy that had yielded few positive results to date, which both sides largely attributed to the U.S. government's inability to shift from its fundamentally "ambivalent" policy toward Chile. For the regime, dissatisfaction resulted from the failure to certify Chile and "public statements in support of a democratic transition"; for the opposition, it stemmed from a belief that the United States was "deliberately not pressuring Pinochet to move forward on the transition."[42]

In late March 1984, the AD called its members back into the streets, organizing another round of national protests in collaboration with the CNT. The day before the civil disobedience was to begin, the government declared a ninety-day national state of emergency and mobilized thousands of police and troops to confront the demonstrators, who, in Pinochet's mind, were once again being "engineered by forces which are directly or indirectly at the service of Soviet imperialism."[43] Undeterred by this formidable projection of coercive power, Santiago was brought to a standstill as urban workers, *pobladores*, and students, supported by unions and the organizations of the professional class and propertied petty bourgeoisie, "engage[d] in strikes, hunger strikes, marches, demonstrations, and confrontations with police" that continued through much of April.[44]

On April 12, Principal Deputy Assistant Secretary of State for Inter-American Affairs James Michel outlined the administration's policy on Chilean democratization in a speech at the University of Arkansas. Quiet diplomacy, he insisted, was the touchstone of Washington's approach, the preferred means for achieving the twin U.S. policy objectives of "the

---

[41] Telegram, Theberge to Shultz, March 13, 1984, ibid.
[42] Briefing Memo, Motley to Eagleburger, March 16, 1984, ibid.
[43] Quoted in "Destiny Gave Me the Job," interview with Pinochet, *Newsweek*, March 19, 1984, 67. Also see "Security Measures Strengthened," *FBIS: DR: LA*, March 27, 1984, E2; Jackson Diehl, "Chile's Pinochet Veers between Crackdowns and Conciliation," *WP*, April 13, 1984, A25, A31.
[44] Schneider, *Shantytown Protest in Pinochet's Chile*, 174.

emergence of a centrist political consensus and a soft transition into democracy." More aggressive measures in dealing with situations like that in Chile would be counterproductive, "totally isolating ourselves from regimes and thus making them fair game for the left." This was not tantamount to the "unconditional acceptance of authoritarian regimes," because, as in the case of Chile, the administration made "a clear distinction between accommodation to the status quo and a relationship based on the presumption of change." This was a public and unambiguous statement that the White House now expected the military regime to change its behavior in such a way as would usher in a new civilian government – a long way removed from the initial close embrace policy. But high on the list of actions impeding executive branch attempts to encourage that outcome, Michel told his audience, were those constraints imposed by Congress, notably certification of human rights improvements as a precondition for increased military aid. All that this "policy of denial" had achieved was Chile's shift to alternative arms suppliers while providing the United States with no "leverage" to accelerate a democratic transition in a country where its influence was already extremely limited.[45]

Congressional hostility toward the dictatorship and the administration's reluctance to jettison a Chile policy based on "quiet diplomacy" also posed a problem for the moderate anti-Pinochet opposition parties. The day before another national protest was set to begin on May 11, Undersecretary of State for Political Affairs Michael Armacost met with these party leaders in Washington. He had little to offer other than a statement of the administration's unqualified support for a return to democracy and further advice on how the "democratic forces" could best contribute to achieving this outcome. First, the party leaders were urged to resolve all internal differences before entering into a new dialogue with the government. Second, they should refuse any cooperation with "anti-democratic elements" of all political persuasions. Third, they were encouraged not simply to concentrate on the "Pinochet problem" at the expense of offering "positive statements of alternatives." Fourth, the parties should be pragmatic by agreeing to begin talks with the government on the basis of the 1980 Constitution without conceding the legitimacy of the document. Finally, they were cautioned to avoid putting nonnegotiable demands on the table.[46] While the AD decided against

[45] James Michel, "U.S. Support for Democracy in Chile," University of Arkansas, Fayetteville, Arkansas, April 12, 1984.
[46] Briefing Memo, Motley to Armacost, May 8, 1984, DOS/FOIAe, III.

participation, they endorsed the May 11 protests in the hope that this "symbolic" initiative would "force the regime to negotiate." In contrast, the MDP parties viewed the protests as the forerunner to a prolonged national strike leading to a revolutionary upheaval. Pinochet answered this latest popular challenge to his authority with another heavy-handed response that cleared the streets but did neither the government's reputation nor its certification prospects any favors.[47]

The moderate opposition's perceived failure to make headway with the junta was an ongoing concern among American officials. A July Embassy cable to Secretary Shultz lambasted their "inability [to] project a credible leadership image, develop a convincing political alternative to the left or successfully mobilize Chilean society." By falling down on all these criteria, they had allowed the radical left, now playing a prominent role in the protests, to assume the leadership mantle because it was "the only visible source of direct pressure" on the regime.[48] In other words, their failure made it much more likely that the "radicals" would eventually consolidate their leadership of a burgeoning mass movement – once again raising the specter of the very systemic social, political, and economic changes that the 1973 coup was meant to forestall.

Until the left was dismembered (or at least seriously "tamed") as a major political force in Chilean politics, the armed forces leadership remained more than just hesitant about a return to the barracks, and the Reagan administration was less inclined to force the issue.[49] Taking the left out of the transition equation would reassure the junta (and the White House) that there was nothing to fear from a return to civilian government; it would also leave the opposition political parties with little incentive to continue flirting with "extremists" in their efforts to leverage the military back to the barracks. For Washington there were added benefits: it would limit the terrain on which any future election was held to political and legal (as distinct from social and economic) issues; ensure that only the center-right would inherit power; lend apparent legitimacy

---

[47] Schneider, *Shantytown Protest in Pinochet's Chile*, 174.

[48] Telegram, AmEmb Santiago to Shultz, July 24, 1984, LAAD, NSC, Chile [2 of 2], Box 90512, RRL.

[49] The leaders of the Communist Party, the Socialist Party, and the MIR had been comprehensively repressed or exiled by 1978. While U.S. intelligence and military contacts clearly understood the impact of this state-authored terrorism, and the extent to which the left had been decimated, there was still a concern among some Reagan officials as late as December 1984 about the potential reemergence of a direct radical challenge to the regime. See Kornbluh, *The Pinochet File*, 415.

to this result by marginalizing the social forces most likely to oppose it; and eventually lead to the complete disintegration of any serious radical challenge to the system put in place by the junta.

For these reasons, U.S. officials refused to legitimize mass protests by acknowledging their importance or by meeting with the representatives of the left social movements and political groupings. Instead, they sought to discredit mobilization tactics as violent, chaotic, and crisis prone and typically condemned or dismissed the participants as playing into the hands of a Soviet-Cuban conspiracy to destabilize Chile. On these grounds, among others, U.S. officials were willing to implicitly tolerate, if not condone, the military state's targeted repression. Washington's overarching objective was to split the radical left from the moderate opposition and isolate it from participation in the transition process.

In other words, the Reagan administration's message to the junta was that some forms of state-authored abuse were less serious than others – that it was sufficiently discriminating about human rights so as to appear sympathetic to Pinochet's systematic repression of the "antisystem" opposition leaders (political, labor, human rights, students, teachers, etc.) under the rubric of countering terrorism. Conversely, public revelations of widespread torture were more difficult to ignore. It was, in the words of Elliott Abrams, "perhaps the most troublesome [problem] and the most significant in terms of Chile's image in the U.S. and elsewhere."[50] Two years later, the regime would still be hearing from Washington that "some aspects" of the human rights situation were complicating U.S. efforts to support Chile.[51] At least implicitly, these kinds of ambiguous messages weakened U.S. attempts to encourage an overall improvement. This, in turn, further undercut White House efforts to make any progress in convincing Congress to permit a resumption of military assistance, thereby limiting U.S. access to, and influence with, members of the armed forces' officer corps.

Of course, Washington's actual (and perceived) support for an antiterrorist policy went along with efforts to get Pinochet to understand that the state-authored repression must serve a larger political purpose. Regime violence – eliminating the left as a major political-electoral force – could be rationalized and accommodated so long as it accelerated progress toward a return to democracy in Chile. The mid-year emergence of the Group of Eight (G-8), a loosely organized collection of rightist parties critical

---

[50] Telegram, Shultz to AmEmb Santiago, June 25, 1984, DOS/FOIAe, III.
[51] Telegram, Shultz (Whitehead) to AmEmb Santiago, June 23, 1986, ibid.

of Pinochet himself and/or the military government, gave added hope to
the moderate opposition in their respective efforts "to promote political
dialogue and consensus." The U.S. Embassy praised the formation of
the G-8 as part of a necessary "intellectual process" in the development
of a "durable political consensus," while warning that the fundamental
question – "whether the political process can advance enough to contain the pressures and frustrations arising from serious socio-economic
problems, or whether many Chileans will lose hope in rational political
solutions and turn toward more radical approaches" – was no closer to an
answer.[52]

Divisions within the Junta

The security forces' crackdown on antiregime militancy across Chile during August coincided with a renewed opposition debate over the most
effective strategy for achieving a stable democratic transition. Held under
the auspices of the Center for Development Studies – a think tank established by Gabriel Valdés in 1981 and directed by the economist and PDC
member Edgardo Boeninger – the positions taken ranged from those who
believed in a united front of all anti-Pinochet forces designed to bring
down the regime to those who supported a "transition with continuity" in which democratic government would arise out of the institutions
created by the regime. The Socialist Party's Ricardo Lagos championed
an agreement between "all political forces, without exception, which
strongly reject the dictatorship and desired democracy." His colleague,
Eduardo Ortiz, argued that social mobilization should be the central
component of a movement that resulted in the "abolition of the authoritarian model." Proponents of a negotiated transition included the PDC's
Gutenberg Martínez and Eugenio Ortega, who argued for a coalition of
"players from the right, the middle and the left side of politics" committed to an "agreed rupture" with the institutional arrangements imposed
by the armed forces. Delegates disagreed on other matters, including how
much reform of the 1980 Constitution would be needed before it was
acceptable. Not surprisingly, the debate concluded with no strong consensus on how to proceed.[53]

---

[52] Telegram, AmEmb Santiago (Matthews) to Shultz, June 8, 1984, ibid.
[53] Quoted in Patricio Aylwin Azócar, *El Reencuentro de los Democratas: Del Golpe al
triunfo Del No* (Santiago: Ediciones B. Chile, 1998), 268–270.

In September, a day of protest organized by the AD led to two days of violent confrontation between police and demonstrators, during which 10 people were killed, 150 were wounded, and 1,000 were arrested – including, once again, the PDC President Gabriel Valdés.[54] These continuing large-scale protests indicated that forcing the genie of civil disobedience back into the bottle using strong-arm tactics was proving a more difficult task than the generals had envisaged. Furthermore, the regime's knee-jerk coercive response merely papered over ongoing tensions within the junta over how to deal with the opposition movement once the "iron fist" had achieved its immediate purpose of restoring a temporary order. By the end of the month, disagreements were being aired publicly: while Pinochet continued to insist he would remain in power until at least 1989 and refused to countenance renewed negotiations with the opposition – a position that only strengthened the hardliners within opposition ranks – his junta colleague air force General Fernando Matthei issued a statement supporting a renewal of the dialogue and drawing up a specific transition timetable.[55] In an interview with *El Mercurio*, Matthei raised the specter of dire consequences for the military if a transition were not completed prior to 1989 and indicated that, under certain circumstances, he would even be prepared to invite the Marxist left (as distinct from the "radicals") to the negotiating table. There were, he said, only three preconditions for a revival of talks: a consensus that the Communists would be excluded from any new civilian government and that private property rights would be guaranteed; an AD agreement to drop its demand that the 1980 Constitution be abandoned; and agreement that if the armed forces returned to barracks, they would do so without loss of their status or traditional prerogatives, and no officer would be prosecuted for human rights abuses.[56]

The response – more widespread demonstrations than previously   was not what Matthei welcomed. On October 29–30, a tenth national protest provided the clearest evidence yet to the junta and Washington of the

[54] Figures in ibid., 273.

[55] On Matthei's statement, see "Air Force Commander Favors Talks with Opposition," *FBIS: DR: LA*, September 26, 1984, E1; on Pinochet's stance, see interview in Edward Schumacher, "Chile's Leader, Belittling Foes, Vows to Stay On," *NYT*, August 8, 1984, 1, 4. Mid-year CIA reports described the junta and the armed services as "more willing than Pinochet to work out a peaceful political solution." CIA, Intelligence Assessment, "Chile: Pinochet under Pressure," July 1, 1984, CIA/FOIAe, III.

[56] Telegram, Theberge to Shultz, September 26, 1984, DOS/FOIAe, III.

growing strength and organization of the opposition social movements. Organized by the left parties, unions, and social movements, largely over economic measures (including a 23 percent devaluation of the peso, the imposition of new import duties, and food price increases of up to 55 percent[57]), this latest protest brought the country to a virtual standstill. Pinochet's countermeasures were swift and savage: on November 6, he imposed a ninety-day state of siege and proceeded to apply maximum force "to put down the demonstrations, [including] massive shanty-town raids to prevent the radicalization of the poor, and violent intimidation of labor leaders, student activists, and human rights defenders and priests working among the shanty-town poor."[58] In the process, hundreds of opposition leaders and thousands of *pobladores* were arrested.[59] Once again, the AD supported but did not participate in the protest, in all likelihood a compromise position resulting from disagreements within the coalition over its decision to reestablish a tactical alliance with the MDP – a move opposed by the AD's more conservative and right-wing elements.[60]

The junta consensus on the need to invoke state-of-siege powers was arrived at without much, if any, discussion; how forcefully those powers should be applied or whether the regime's entire response should be confined to repression was another matter altogether. For instance, the U.S. Embassy reported that both the air force's General Matthei and the navy's Admiral Merino told Pinochet "they would not accept a hardliner to replace Jarpa," who had stepped down as Interior Minister in early November. The outcome was Jarpa's reappointment and increased powers ("partial control") in determining what measures would be taken to restore stability and order.[61]

By now Washington's frustration over the lack of progress on the transition was palpable. Prior to the October days of protest, Assistant

---

[57] Lydia Chavez, "Is State of Siege Enough to Keep the Lid on Chile?," *NYT*, November 11, 1984, 19.

[58] Ensalaco, *Chile under Pinochet*, 137. For an extended discussion, see ibid., 137–155.

[59] Cynthia Brown, "Chile's Road to Crisis," *The Nation*, December 8, 1984, 601; Jackson Diehl, "Pinochet Targets Political Movements," *WP*, November 10, 1984, A14; John M. Goshko, "Chile's 'Siege' Discomfits White House," *WP*, November 18, 1984, A32; Schneider, *Shantytown Protest in Pinochet's Chile*, 180.

[60] See "AD to Develop More Active Opposition Role," *FBIS: DR: LA*, August 14, 1984, E2–E3.

[61] Telegram, AmEmb Santiago (Matthews) to Shultz, November 16, 1984, DOS/FOIAe, III; Anthony Boadle, "Pinochet Reinstates State of Siege in Chile," *NYT*, November 7, 1984, A26.

Secretary Motley had asked the Embassy for a sounding on whether Pinochet and the opposition were capable of "taking advantage" of a dialogue opening of their own accord, which would allow the United States to maintain its "low-key posture." Otherwise, it might be time for a "sharply focused, controlled diplomatic effort [by the U.S. and other foreign governments] to help the Chileans help themselves."[62]

Following the reimposition of a state of siege on November 6, the administration postponed a scheduled visit to Santiago by Army Chief of Staff General John Wickham Jr. At a regional foreign ministers' meeting in Brasilia that same month, George Shultz's diplomatic language could not conceal Washington's profound disappointment over Pinochet's uncompromising approach. Shultz termed the state of siege and the wave of arrests "very disappointing to us" and added that he was "sure that General Pinochet is well aware of that fact." Harry Barnes, soon to be appointed as new U.S. Ambassador to Chile, said that Washington's unusually critical reaction demonstrated the fallacy of Pinochet's longstanding case for unqualified U.S. support: that only he stood between stability and chaos. If this change in tone represented, as Barnes predicted, the beginning of the abandonment of quiet diplomacy, little substantive change in policy was immediately apparent.[63] While the State Department announced that it was "reviewing carefully how recent developments may affect U.S. interests," officials privately cautioned against interpreting the review as portending any major policy shift because, as they readily acknowledged, Washington's ability to influence developments inside Chile was confined to persuasion and appeals for "moderation." In the absence of tougher measures, Pinochet could maintain his inflexible stance and ignore U.S. calls for dialogue in the knowledge that there was little or nothing the Reagan administration could or would do about it.[64]

Chilean Ambassador Hernán Errázuriz gave no indication that the United States could expect any change in Pinochet's behavior during a meeting with White House Ambassador-at-Large Vernon Walters. Pinochet, said Errázuriz, was "shock[ed]" at Washington's "indignation" over the imposition of a state of siege and other emergency measures, which were forced on the government to deal with "the problem of terrorism and violence which exists in Chile." Pinochet was also "disappointed"

[62] Telegram, Shultz, from Motley to Theberge, October 18, 1984, DOS/FOIAe, III.
[63] Barnes, "U.S. Human Rights Policies and Chile," 311.
[64] Quoted in John M. Goshko, "Chile's 'Siege' Discomforts the White House," *WP*, November 18, 1984, A32.

at the administration's failure to "acknowledge in any positive way" his decisions to ease restrictions on opposition parties organizing and expressing their views in the mass media. What the United States would define as "positive steps," Walters responded, were a rapid lifting of the state of siege, revived dialogue with the moderate political parties, and concrete steps in the transition process. Errázuriz countered that Pinochet was intent on carrying out a "controlled decompression," and there was little chance that the state of siege would be terminated for at least three months. Objecting that this was "much too long," Walters was then given a lesson in Chilean military thinking: the institution totally supported the President's "tough stand," and the snap cancellation of General Wickham's visit "had been regarded as a slap in the face of the Armed Forces and had further hardened their stance."[65]

Signs that the State Department was considering a more aggressive diplomacy toward Chile triggered a swift response from its most prominent and combative advocate of a "softly, softly" approach. Any reversion "to a policy of public criticism, pressures and sanctions," Ambassador Theberge fulminated in a telegram to Shultz, was only likely to "contribute to a prolongation of the present intransigent line."[66] The Ambassador had earlier made the same point in a memo to Motley, invoking the authority of Church officials and "prestigious moderate conservatives," who had advised him that there was "little else the U.S. can and should do at present."[67] To clinch his argument, Theberge dredged up the Carter administration's resort to "penalties, sanctions and threats like that [which had been] futile and counter-productive" and declared that any attempt to replicate those actions would only result in the same negative outcome.[68]

In a memo to Deputy Secretary of State Kenneth Dam, however, Motley recommended approval of the less cautious of two policy options that proposed an expanded diplomatic initiative, including cooperation and coordination with European governments, especially of a Christian Democratic and Social Democratic persuasion, who "have access to the

---

[65] Memo of Conversation, Walters and Errázuriz, November 23, 1984, LAAD, NSC, Chile, Box 91181, RRL.

[66] Telegram, Theberge to Shultz, for Armacost and Motley, November 20, 1984, DOS/FOIAe, III.

[67] Telegram, Theberge to Motley, October 24, 1984, ibid. Theberge "had never stuck his fingers in Pinochet's eyes and I don't think would have been effective if he did." Interview with Langhorne Motley.

[68] Telegram, Theberge to Shultz, November 19, 1984, DOS/FOIAe, III.

Chilean opposition that we do not have." Other suggested measures to pressure Pinochet and the junta ranged from exploiting the nation's foreign debt burden to voting against, or abstaining on, Chilean loan requests to the IFIs.[69] Informed that the Department was considering a joint initiative on Chile with the Europeans to revive the dialogue process, an agitated Theberge cabled the Secretary's Office that the Embassy considered this option unattainable. European socialist and social democratic governments, he asserted, did not support Washington's policy of "encouraging concessions by both [sides] that will permit genuine negotiations."[70] Theberge was especially bewildered as to why State's Seventh Floor would consider taking up an offer of help from the French government, which he alleged had supported the "terrorist" MIR and exhibited a deep hostility toward the Pinochet regime.[71]

Undeterred by Theberge's protestations, the Department, in a comprehensive report on bilateral relations toward the end of 1984, concluded that Pinochet and the moderate opposition political parties now bore equal blame for the instability and lack of progress toward a transition. If, as the Embassy Country Team concluded, Pinochet had no intention of presiding over a smooth, stable democratic transition, officials in State were prepared to label the civilian opposition as "no guarantee that [U.S. national interests] will be better served." In these circumstances, unless Washington applied maximum pressure on both sides to renew the dialogue, the only beneficiaries of an ever-widening split would be the Communist Party and other movements of the radical left that could transform Chile into another Nicaragua. As well, what was happening in Chile "could tilt the balance in [newly emerging democracies] in Bolivia and Peru, both of which are confronting fragile political situations vis-à-vis the military and leftists."

The question State's report posed was whether a dictator who "has served tangible [American] interests in the U.N., OAS, on Israel, Puerto Rico, Grenada, etc.," well in the past could "on balance . . . cost us more in the future." Worldwide, the starkest contradiction in U.S. foreign policy centered on perceptions of an aggressive promotion of democracy and human rights in some countries (Nicaragua, Poland) but not in others (Chile). The report characterized U.S. efforts to influence Chilean domestic politics as marginal at best, while stressing that this alone was not

---

[69] Memo, Motley to Dam, November 21, 1984, ibid.
[70] Telegram, Theberge to Shultz, November 21, 1984, ibid.
[71] Telegram, Theberge to Shultz, for Motley, December 6, 1984, ibid.

grounds for concluding "that since there is nothing constructive we can do in Chile, we should do nothing." To contemplate "walking away from Chile out of sheer frustration" was unthinkable. Whether future policy should concentrate on "getting rid of Pinochet" or try to work with him to achieve "an orderly transition" – a clear indication that while both options were now in play, the die had not yet been cast on either of them – it was imperative to avoid "*get[ting] out front publicly in working to change the situation.*" Working with allies and through third parties offered some leverage, but the key to exerting influence rested on Washington's ability to communicate with Pinochet and army generals who, in the absence of a guaranteed amnesty for human rights abuses, would continue to support him "out of sheer self-preservation" – a stance reinforced by the loss of authority and reputation suffered by the Argentine military following that country's transition to democracy. Irrespective, the report continued, the biggest single obstacle to achieving U.S. policy objectives remained Pinochet himself: "Over the past eleven years, every conventional overt policy approach imaginable has been tried [and failed]." When visited by senior U.S. officials, Pinochet had listened to their words "and then told us to mind our own business." Unless he could be pressured to put as much effort into a managed political transition as the armed forces were exerting in waging the war on "terror," prospects for a satisfactory resolution of the conflict seemed poor.

Perhaps surprisingly, the report was highly critical of Pinochet's "inadequate appreciation of the terrorist problem," reflected in his failure over the previous twelve months to crush the armed insurgency, especially the radical leftist FPMR. The task at hand, therefore, required careful handling to maintain Pinochet's "*usefulness as a foil to the communists/terrorists while we bring pressure to bear in support of a controlled democratic transition process.*" Another impediment to U.S. efforts to promote the transition dialogue was Pinochet's uncompromising attitude toward the Communist Party. Equating democracy exclusively with anti-communism and refusing to negotiate with the center-right opposition largely because it was unwilling to accept the 1980 constitutional provision banning the Communist Party outright epitomized the bankruptcy of junta policy. The dictator's failure to adequately "fight terrorism" and establish a clear democratic timetable had effectively "undercut" the moderate opposition forces "to the benefit of the [Chilean Communist Party]."

Finally, the report observed that while Pinochet and his junta colleagues remained in agreement about "combating terrorism," there was a "growing split" over the need to move forward on the transition process. Whether that offered new opportunities for Washington to exploit was unclear. Pinochet's actions had politically isolated the regime among most social classes, including many of its own traditional supporters. Defections by "most of the political right" and a more ambiguous relationship between the middle class and the junta assumed even greater significance when placed alongside the Communist Party's key role in mobilizing the lower classes against the government in the period leading up to the state of siege. It was a scenario that conjured up the specter of a revolutionary change similar to Cuba or Nicaragua, where in each case the middle disappeared and the left assumed the leadership of the anti-dictatorial struggle. The White House did not want to confront another situation where the transition process foundered because centrist forces were too weak and the authoritarian head of state moved too late to prevent an unacceptable alternative from capturing political power.[72]

Scarcely had State's report been tabled when a broad-based center-left coalition of political and labor groups, defying the three-week-old state of siege during which hundreds of mid-level political leaders had been arrested and nearly five hundred Chileans sent into internal exile, organized a further two days of national protest (November 27–28), put down only after another formidable application of the state's coercive power, especially in Santiago.[73] Theberge's assessment of culpability for what had occurred contrasted markedly with that of the Department's own report. As far as he was concerned, the ongoing political impasse was largely due to "intransigent and irreconcilable positions" taken by PDC-dominated AD. Having a year earlier described PDC leaders, including Gabriel Valdés, as "moderate and pragmatic," the Ambassador now claimed that as long as they remained in charge of the Christian Democrats and, by extension, the AD, the latter would oppose amnesty guarantees for the military and support legalization of the Communist Party in a democratic Chile[74] – thereby making a transition impossible.

Again appearing to contradict his own earlier assessments, Theberge took issue with those Reagan officials who warned of a potential radicalization of the opposition movement unless Pinochet adopted a more flexible and less obdurate approach. While fragmented politically, he was adamant that Chile "is neither dangerously polarized nor moving in

---

[72] Report, DOS, "Chile: Political Overview," November 23, 1984, ibid. (emphasis original).
[73] Lydia Chavez, "Chileans Defying Army, Stage Protests," *NYT*, November 28, 1984, 3.
[74] Telegram, Theberge to Shultz, November 29, 1984, DOS/FOIAe, III.

the direction of dangerous polarization."[75] This interpretation received strong support from Chile's Ambassador to the U.S. Hernán Errázuriz, who summarily dismissed "this theory that Pinochet was polarizing the situation and the extremes were the ones who would win the transition." That scenario, he said, was "never a reality."[76]

Theberge was not alone in demonstrating how difficult it would be to achieve a genuine intrabureaucratic consensus on State's Chile policy review. A major disagreement had already erupted between two senior officials, the Director of Policy Planning Peter Rodman and HA's Assistant Secretary Elliott Abrams. In a memo to the Deputy Secretary of State, Rodman characterized Washington's "ability to influence Pinochet [a]s almost nil." The application of strong U.S. sanctions could "send the Chilean economy into a downward spiral" and most likely see the armed forces close ranks behind the President, who "would probably resort to increased repression and try to tough it out." The end result would be "a full-blown crisis on our hands with no solutions in sight." Rodman was skeptical of achieving a satisfactory outcome even if the United States resorted to carrots instead of sticks. He doubted "that we can put together a package of economic rewards attractive enough to affect Pinochet's calculations." Therefore, he continued, the overriding strategic objective should be to ascertain whether the "moderate center" could be strengthened to a point where its leadership was capable of taking power if Pinochet were ousted, and whether they could be pressured "to split decisively from the extreme leftists with whom they are now allied." Rodman dismissed ARA's support of a more activist policy with a few well-chosen and sarcastic words: "[It] may well have the saving grace that it is really ineffectual and therefore harmless." Nonetheless, it would be the height of irresponsibility *"to launch a campaign to accelerate the pace of events when we do not have a clue about what forces could replace Pinochet if we undermined him."* He advocated the adoption of a more "cautious" approach – based on high-level visits, media statements, and symbolic initiatives in response to developments in Chile – combined with a longer-term strategy "to strengthen the democratic moderates and split them from the hard core left."[77]

An incensed Abrams fired back, denouncing the memo as nothing more than a series of "vague and unproven assumptions" that underestimated a

[75] Telegram, Theberge to Shultz, December 19, 1984, ibid.
[76] Interview with Hernán Errázuriz.
[77] Memo, Rodman to Deputy Secretary of State, November 29, 1984, DS/FOIAe, III (our emphasis).

possible junta move against Pinochet and the ability of a center-right coalition to emerge as a unified and formidable political alternative. To argue that simply because Pinochet opposed a democratic transition, "there is just nothing to be done," was defeatist and "a counsel of doom." The "risks of inaction," Abrams warned, could only lead to a more polarized society and serve the interests of the radical left: to accept the likelihood of at least another decade of military rule "may guarantee that Pinochet is followed by the very forces from which he claims to be saving Chile."[78] Rodman's analysis was grounded in the objective facts of the Chilean situation, Abram's analysis in the frustration that those facts were generating in Washington. In Chile, meanwhile, domestic political trends were narrowing the gap between the two views.

Enlisting Outside Pressure

While administration officials were under no illusions that Pinochet was making matters worse by intensifying state-authored violence and, in the process, alienating even traditional conservative supporters, they took no comfort from the fractious behavior of the opposition parties, mired in personality and policy conflicts and united only around the single issue of getting rid of the head of state. "We decided that both are to blame," said an American official, "and one thing we're not going to do is just swat Pinochet on the head. That won't do it." Instead, the United States settled on a new round of high-level diplomacy. In Santiago, Principal Deputy Assistant Secretary of State James Michel delivered an unambiguous message: the warring parties must take "some constructive steps to help themselves before it is too late for us to help them."[79] If a luncheon meeting with AD leaders was any indication, this was not going to happen soon or easily: the AD complained to the visiting American diplomat that "dialogue with Pinochet is impossible"[80] – which suggested little enthusiasm for unilateral concessions on the AD's part.

Undersecretary Michael Armacost supported Abrams and ARA on the "need to take a more activist approach" to keep the "far left" at bay. The key to developing a "viable strategy" and lending more legitimacy to the process, he suggested, was enlisting the Vatican – which shared

[78] Memo, Abrams to Deputy Secretary of State, November 30, 1984, ibid.
[79] Quotes in Bernard Gwertzman, "Mediation in Chile Termed Essential by U.S. Officials," *NYT*, December 2, 1984, 4.
[80] AD member and Socialist Party president Ricardo Lagos, quoted in Jackson Diehl, "Repression by Pinochet Seen Driving His Traditional Supporters Away," *WP*, December 7, 1984, A32.

Washington's concern about reining in the more "radical" elements within Chile – and the Catholic Church as mediators between the protagonists. This underscored the importance of Ambassador-at-Large Vernon Walters's upcoming meeting with the Pope: "If the Church's reaction is lukewarm," Armacost wrote to Kenneth Dam, "then it may be best to let the cauldron simmer a while longer."[81] Walter's briefing paper for his trip to Rome on December 14 described the principal objective as gaining the Pope's agreement to act as "a catalyst for breaking the political impasse in Chile and ensuring [an] orderly political transition that blocks Soviet/Communist influence." By directly encouraging both sides "to abandon intransigent positions and move towards a negotiated settlement," the briefing paper noted, the Pope could lay the groundwork for follow-up efforts by the United States and its European allies.[82] In Santiago, Ambassador Theberge discussed a possible 1985 papal visit to Chile with the Papal Nuncio, noting that it would provide "an opportunity for the Pope to [privately] encourage Pinochet to commit himself to internal liberalization and progress on the transition to democracy."[83] Another Embassy official previously cautioned that such a visit would have to be "manage[d]" with great care to ensure that Pinochet "can least exploit it."[84]

Under the leadership of Cardinal Raúl Silva, the Church had become something of a thorn in the government's side, with its increasing attacks on the latter's human rights abuses and criticism of the impact of economic reforms on the poorest Chileans. A confidential report by the Catholic bishops in the early 1980's, for instance, bluntly criticized Pinochet's "authoritarian and arbitrary mentality, his personalism, and his contempt for those who dissent."[85] Silva's retirement in September 1982 and the appointment of Juan Francisco Fresno as Archbishop of Santiago in June 1983 had buoyed government hopes of a more congenial relationship with the Church hierarchy. A high visibility public meeting

---

81 Note, Armacost to Dam, December 4, 1984, DOS/FOIAe, III. At his November 30 meeting with Hernán Errázuriz, Assistant Secretary Motley was specifically asked whether the United States had been in contact with the Church (which it had). Motley's response was evasive to say the least: "We had nothing to report on this issue" beyond acknowledging that the Church "is a key element in the current equation." Telegram, Shultz to AmEmb Santiago, December 6, 1984, ibid.
82 Telegram, Shultz to AmEmb, Rome, for Walters, December 13, 1984, ibid.
83 Telegram, Shultz, Info AmEmb Rome, From Theberge, December 7, 1984, ibid.
84 Telegram, AmEmb Santiago (Matthews) to Shultz, November 8, 1984, ibid.
85 Quoted in "Paper Reports Bishops' 'Secret Agreements,'" *FBIS: DR: LA*, January 4, 1984, E1.

between Fresno and Pinochet soon after the former's appointment and a perceived easing of the tough position on human rights formerly taken by Silva appeared to bear out these hopes.[86] Having displayed a "personal contempt for and distrust of" the retiring Archbishop,[87] Pinochet actively cultivated Fresno, convincing him to host two of the dialogues between Interior Minister Jarpa and the AD. Getting Fresno's cooperation in limiting Church activism and easing criticism of the regime's human rights abuses proved more difficult to achieve. Like his predecessor, the new Archbishop faced considerable pressure from priests, nuns, and other Church leaders "to speak more forcefully against continuing military repression and in support of rights for the poor and a return to democracy."[88] According to one priest, when the dialogue failed to produce results, Fresno finally began to "wis[e] up."[89]

More generally, relations between the Vatican and Pinochet had abruptly deteriorated in mid-January 1984, after the Nunciature granted asylum to four MIR militants and the regime refused them safe conduct to leave Chile, disregarding a personal plea from Pope John Paul II. Relations with the Chilean Church soured further some weeks later at Punta Arenas, when Pinochet accused priests of participating in demonstrations and was booed and jeered by hundreds of people. Several bishops publicly defended their clergy in contrast to Fresno's more low-key response to regime attacks on the Church, interpreted in some quarters as a reluctance to antagonize the junta because of his desire to play a prominent role in any future mediation initiative.[90]

Although Fresno and the other moderate bishops continued to espouse the need for dialogue and reconciliation, tensions between the regime and

---

[86] In the poor neighborhoods, where the popular church flourished, Fresno was soon being referred to as *Frenos* (Brakes), implying that he wanted to slow the burgeoning anti-Pinochet protest movement. See Tim Frasca, "Top Chilean Prelate 'Wise to Local Politics,'" *NCR*, December 23, 1983, 19.

[87] Telegram, AmEmb Santiago (Matthews) to Shultz, November 16, 1984, DOS/FOIAe, III.

[88] Jackson Diehl, "New Leader Moves Chilean Church toward Center," *WP*, September 23, 1983 (Factiva).

[89] Quoted in Frasca, "Top Chilean Prelate 'Wise to Local Politics,'" 19. Subsequently, Fresno did take action when approximately thirty thousand urban poor occupied two vacant lots owned by the University of Chile, built tent cities, and petitioned for permission to build permanent settlements. The initial police response was a mixture of "tear gas and beatings" to force the settlers to vacate the sites. The Church intervened on the side of the squatters, including visits to the sites by Fresno and his predecessor Raúl Silva and the provision of health and nutritional services. Ibid.

[90] See Tim Frasca, "Chile: State Puts Church on Defensive," *NCR*, June 22, 1984, 22.

the Catholic hierarchy continued to deepen through mid to late 1984. In September, air force leader General Matthei opined that the Church-State relations were "as cold as [they] can be."[91] With the reintroduction of the state of siege, even Fresno's patience appeared to reach its limits. Before a mid-November meeting attended by fifteen hundred priests and nuns in Santiago, he read a pastoral letter highly critical of the government's human rights violations and the failure to move toward a democratic transition, and took the unprecedented (post-1973) step of calling on all Catholics to take part in a day of fasting and prayer.[92] This moment effectively marked the end of Pinochet's efforts to curry favor with Fresno. The Embassy reported, incorrectly as it turned out, that the Archbishop no longer believed the Church could "play a direct [or effective] role in promoting a dialogue."[93]

State Department officials were now publicly accusing the junta of deliberately "putting their relationship with the U.S. at risk" by stalling on the democracy issue and were questioning whether Santiago really was concerned about better ties with Washington. On November 30, Assistant Secretary Motley warned Ambassador Errázuriz that unless the state of siege was lifted, the junta risked Chile again becoming a major target of renewed congressional criticism. The recent crackdowns, Motley said, were not only "counterproductive [but] could be taken straight out of a script written by Castro."[94] Even so, the administration remained steadfast in its reluctance to impose "any kind of [aid] sanctions" or publicly and vociferously denounce the regime's human rights abuses, determined to avoid a replay of Carter policy when strident public attacks and no votes in the MDBs "had little impact" and failed to "turn Pinochet around on things."[95] This reluctance probably explained Errázuriz's relaxed attitude toward U.S. threats to toughen the line on Chile; nor was he worried about the congressional advocates of sanctions as he was convinced they were more than counterbalanced by influential regime supporters on both sides of the political aisle.[96]

---

91   Quoted in "Air Force Chief on Church-Government Relations," *FBIS: DR: LA*, September 17, 1984, E2.
92   "Santiago Archbishop Supports National Fast Day," *FBIS: DR: LA*, November 15, 1984, E2.
93   Telegram, AmEmb Santiago (Matthews) to Shultz, November 17, 1984, DOS/FOIAe, III; Telegram, Theberge to Shultz, November 21, 1984, ibid.
94   Telegram, Shultz to AmEmb Santiago, December 6, 1984, ibid.
95   Quoted in "U.S. Officials Pressuring Chile to Allow Democracy," *Atlanta Journal*, December 3, 1984, 5.
96   Interview with Hernán Errázuriz.

The debate over how the United States should vote on a Chile human rights resolution submitted to the UNGA in December reflected the Reagan administration's impasse between the felt need that the regime had to moderate its behavior and a reluctance to force the issue. The resolution incorporated the latest findings and recommendations of the Special Rapporteur, who again found that the situation in Chile had deteriorated over the previous twelve months. If the U.S. United Nations (USUN) delegation in New York was unified in advocating a no vote, the sentiment in State was divided. ARA sided with UN Ambassador Jeane Kirkpatrick, and was joined by the Bureau of International Organization Affairs (IO), which initially supported an abstention vote but subsequently deferred to the USUN delegation. HA, conversely, forcefully argued that abstention was a far better option because it would assist the effort to win European support for a positive human rights resolution on El Salvador, be consistent with White House support for Special Rapporteurs in Afghanistan and Poland, and avoid a result (a U.S. no vote) that could be "seriously misused by Pinochet to undercut moderates within his government." HA pointed out that most of America's European allies were intent on voting yes, which would leave the United States "virtually alone" if it decided to cast a no vote.

After considerable discussion, Kirkpatrick ultimately convinced then temporary Acting Secretary of State Motley "that we should continue to oppose the singling out of Chile for special treatment and the establishment of a double standard for Latin American countries."[97] Without exhibiting great enthusiasm, the United States joined twelve other nations in voting against the resolution. As Undersecretary Armacost told Errázuriz at a December 7 meeting, the double standard justification was unlikely to convince a majority of America's allies that its vote was not "an expression of support for a repressive government."[98] While

---

[97] Memo, Kilday to Acting Secretary, December 6, 1984, DOS/FOIAe, III. Also see Telegram, USUN Mission (Kirkpatrick) to Shultz, December 8, 1984, LAAD, NSC, Chile [2 of 2], Box 90512, RRL.

[98] Telegram, Shultz to AmEmb Santiago, December 8, 1984, LAAD, NSC, Chile (11/20/1984–12/11/1984), Box 91713, RRL. In the space of a month, Errázuriz was called to the Department on four occasions "to receive expressions of U.S. concern over the deteriorating situation in Chile" centered around his government's perceived failure to keep to its promise of taking "tangible steps" toward a transition to democracy. After the last of these meetings (December 7), an angry Ambassador declared that Santiago "did not care" about U.S. votes in the UN and warned it to "back off" its criticism or risk an endless state of siege and regime hardliners gaining increased influence with Pinochet. Ibid.

critical of restrictions on freedoms, the excesses of state repression, and the state of siege, the USUN delegation once again chose to "reproach the UN for its double standards claiming that the text [was] a mixture of truths, falsehoods and statements that the UN was clearly not competent to make [and] would require Chile to respect criteria not universally applied."[99]

UNHRC Representative Richard Schifter offered a simple explanation for this constant U.S. quest for balanced resolutions on Chile: it was all about "how we could bring Pinochet's regime to an end, but not have it be succeeded by something that involved the Communists." The idea was to see "whether we could come up with a formula that would achieve that result by not being so antagonistic toward the junta, but also not to be so forthcoming as to get Pinochet to be able to say 'We have no problem.'"[100] State Department officials sought to "capitalize" on the U.S. vote and "extract some leverage/credibility with Pinochet...by characterizing it as a tough vote in which we are virtually alone in defending the principle [that one standard should not be applied to Chile while another is applied to other human rights abusers] and 'supporting' Chile."[101] Pinochet was not impressed by arguments of that kind.

A More Activist Policy?

In the weeks following Reagan's November reelection victory, what to do about Chile was high on the State Department's agenda. While ARA emphatically opposed any "'get Pinochet policy' or a 'pressure Pinochet only' policy," there was widespread frustration at the Chilean leader's "intransigence" when it came to supporting a "controlled" transition to democracy as well as the failure of the "acceptable" opposition groups "to agree to a common...platform to force Pinochet into negotiations."[102] Abrams took the initiative in advocating a shift to a more activist democracy-promotion effort, which he justified on the basis that "you can't go around saying you're for freedom but we don't care about South Korea, we don't care about South Africa, and bashing only the Soviets and Cubans." Democracy promotion had to be part and parcel of the broader

---

[99] *Yearbook of the United Nations 1984*, 866.
[100] Interview with Richard Schifter.
[101] Memo, Michel, to Armacost, December 8, 1984, DOS/FOIAe, III.
[102] Memo, Motley to Deputy Secretary, "US Policy toward Chile," December 20, 1984, ibid.; Action Memo, Motley to Shultz, "US Policy toward Chile," attached to Memo, INR, Montgomery to DeWitt, December 19, 1984, ibid.

anti-Soviet Cold War strategy, and "Chile was a particularly attractive case." The main source of bureaucratic resistance to a policy shift was the NSC, where anticommunist concerns were still paramount. Abrams and Secretary of State Shultz, however, were convinced that there was little risk of a communist takeover in Chile because within the moderate opposition there now existed the potential for a viable democratic alternative to Pinochet. "We knew those guys through the Embassy," said Abrams, "all the Christian Democrats came to Washington. Later, of course, the Socialists came too. But initially we're talking about the most moderate centrists. These were our guys."[103]

In late December, following weeks of discussion and analysis, Motley submitted a draft action memo on U.S. policy toward Chile to Shultz, proposing that Washington pursue "an activist but gradual approach to try to influence an orderly and peaceful transition to democracy." The memo indicated that, finally, a strong interagency consensus had developed around five key strategic initiatives: sustained diplomatic pressures on the Pinochet regime and the moderate opposition to reach agreement on a transition scenario that avoids taking sides or provoking "an intransigent response" by either side; greater efforts to induce the moderate opposition to "distance" itself from the left parties and social movements "and arrive at an accommodation with the junta leaders"; simultaneous attempts to wrest a "transition timetable" from the regime while continuing to strongly support its "antiterrorist" activities; encouraging those European allies, principally West Germany and Great Britain, who "essentially share our views on the situation in Chile," to constructively engage with both sides; and the implementation of a flexible public diplomacy strategy in support of a return to democracy.[104] The memo acknowledged the dilemmas and obstacles the United States faced inside and outside Chile when it came to achieving its objectives, foremost among which was overcoming Pinochet's resistance to democratization, which was "creating instability in Chile inimical to U.S. interests." The administration's limited ability to influence internal political developments was also cited, along with the ongoing disagreements between transition supporters in the government and opposition that could only strengthen the Communist Party's belief in the viability of armed

[103] Interview with Elliott Abrams. Abrams recalled regular meetings with Kissinger in Washington during that period when "he would sort of say to me, 'What are you doing to General Pinochet? Why are you trying to destabilize Chile? How is it possibly in the interests of the U.S. to have, you know, those Communists?'" Ibid.

[104] Action Memo, Motley to Shultz, "US Policy toward Chile."

struggle, the legal constraints on bilateral economic and military assistance that restricted Washington's leverage over the process, and the likelihood that Congress would introduce new punitive legislation targeting Chile on returning from its summer recess. The longer it took the transition advocates on both sides to reach an agreement, Motley warned, the more encouraged the Communist Party would be to pursue a policy of "violent opposition" toward Pinochet.[105]

While expressing "few qualms about an activist policy," State's Bureau of Intelligence and Research (INR) identified a major contradiction in the memo's key argument. At one and the same time, wrote INR's John Dewitt, Motley supported the application of stronger diplomatic pressures on Pinochet and acknowledged the importance of avoiding any initiative that would make the dictator even more intransigent than he already was. The reality was, as the Santiago Embassy was particularly keen to emphasize, "*any* pressure makes Pinochet intransigent."[106] If no one took particular exception to this criticism, the same could not be said of NSC comments on the draft memo that urged greater cooperation between Washington and Santiago and downplayed the human rights situation in Chile. This produced an angry riposte from Abrams, who termed the NSC response "unacceptable and violative of several fundamental points" on which the State Department had agreed. "What world is the NSC talking about," Abrams asked, when it said that the United States should share certain relevant information with the junta, "provided there is no pattern of human rights violations by Chile?" The documentary evidence of a clear pattern of abuse was overwhelming, not least the regime's persistent use of torture. If the Council's "foolish" proposal to exempt the dictatorship from public criticism were adopted, "we [would be] virtually begging for congressional initiatives which will tie our hands and destroy our policy."[107]

Any State Department consensus, in other words, belied a persistent yawning gap that existed between State and the NSC over how to proceed. And even within State, the agreement on policy ends began to erode as discussion turned to policy means. In seeking to influence Chile's internal politics, Washington's senior diplomats generally conceded that the U.S. had "very limited leverage with Pinochet." Only the economy suggested

---

[105] Ibid.
[106] Memo, INR, DeWitt to Montgomery (emphasis original).
[107] Memo, Abrams to Deputy Secretary of State, Motley, Rodman, December 27, 1984, DOS/FOIAe, III.

itself as a pressure point that might be exploited.[108] Indeed, Motley's discussion paper noted that Pinochet could be "vulnerable" to economic inducements or pressures.[109] But Shultz was extremely reluctant to contemplate any measures of this kind, if only because "he was very admiring of the government's economic management and he knew the economic managers."[110]

Indeed, the painfully slow revival of the Chilean economy was an added concern to the Reagan White House, which was committed to maintaining the country's global creditworthy status, particularly given the still highly fragile Latin debt situation.[111] Despite an upswing in the economy beginning in the last quarter of 1983, Chile remained caught between low world copper prices and high debt service payments, which made it difficult to meet IMF standby targets and encourage new foreign direct investment sufficient to make a real dint in the country's balance of payments deficit.[112] Another problem was the nation's foreign private bank creditors, who were refusing to sign agreements covering official payments due in 1984 unless the dictatorship continued to subsidize "the servicing of private sector debts." In May, the regime gained some relief. After the IMF staff agreed to ease restrictions on borrowings, the Executive Board approved the resumption of drawings by the junta government.[113] A mid-year IMF mission to Chile provided a reality check. It warned of dark clouds on the horizon and concluded that "unfavorable external factors threaten to cut short the economic uptrend."[114]

---

[108] Action Memo, Motley to Shultz, "US Policy toward Chile."

[109] Ibid.

[110] Interview with Elliott Abrams. Despite active lobbying by Ambassador Errázuriz, the State Department refused to budge from its stance that "you're doing the right thing with the economy and the wrong things with the political side." Interview with Hernán Errázuriz.

[111] The economy began to rebound to a limited extent beginning in late 1983 and during 1984: GDP grew modestly, unemployment declined somewhat, inflation remained steady, and there was a small balance of payments surplus in 1984, in contrast to the previous two years, when international reserves fell by more than $1.5 billion. ECLAC, *Economic Survey of Latin America and the Caribbean 1984* (Santiago: United Nations, 1986), 243.

[112] World Bank, Office Memo, Rainer B. Steckhan, Acting RVP, LAC, to A. W. Clausen, "Chile: Briefing for Meeting with Ambassador Hernán Felipe Errázuriz," July 26, 1984, Clausen's – Chile, Vol. 2, Box 209488B, World Bank Group Archives.

[113] James M. Boughton, *Silent Revolution: The International Monetary Fund, 1979–1989* (Washington, DC: International Monetary Fund, 2001), 407.

[114] Office Memo, Jan van Houten to Managing Director and Deputy MD, "Mission to Chile," July 20, 1984, Central Files: C/Chile/810, Missions, 1984–1985, International Monetary Fund Archives.

Concurrently, the junta was grappling with another economic problem: fending off a major threat to Chile's copper export industry from domestic American producers after the U.S. International Trade Commission (USITC) confirmed that the interests of local producers had been damaged by foreign imports. The USITC left open whether the imposition of quotas or tariffs was the best way to resolve the issue. In Congress, legislators sympathetic to the domestic producers, including the powerful chair of the Senate Budget Committee, Pietro 'Pete' Domenici (R-NM), were demanding international lending institutions (including the IMF and IADB) be required to press copper producers to voluntarily cut their production levels in return for financial support.[115] From Santiago, Theberge cabled his strong opposition to quotas, arguing that "it could have a major catalytic effect" harmful to U.S. interests in Chile and region-wide, deepen Chile's economic woes "with the resultant political polarization," and contradict the administration's commitment to the free market. The armed forces would be "particularly bitter," given that a significant part of their budgets depended on copper export revenues.[116] In Washington, Chile's Ambassador Hernán Errázuriz accused the Department of ignoring Theberge's argument and encouraging proponents of an embargo on Chilean copper. "We had lots of meetings about our economic program with U.S. officials in Treasury, Defense, and the CIA who all supported us," he explained. "But there was pressure from the State Department."[117]

Brushing off possible domestic political fallout in the midst of his presidential reelection campaign, Reagan announced in September that he would not impose quotas on copper imports on the grounds that to do so would raise the price of copper domestically and thereby harm those industries that processed copper as well as foreign countries highly reliant on copper earnings and burdened by onerous debt obligations.[118] Had such restrictions been imposed, the impact on the Chilean copper industry and the country's economy in general would have been severe at

---

[115] Nancy Dunne, "Commodities and Agriculture: Reagan Takes Advice on Ways to Help Copper Industry," *FT*, August 8, 1984 (Factiva).

[116] Telegram, Theberge to Shultz, July 24, 1984, LAAD, NSC, Chile [2 of 2], Box 90512, RRL.

[117] Interview with Hernán Errázuriz.

[118] "Memorandum on the Denial of Import Relief for the Copper Industry," September 6, 1984, American Presidency Project.

a time of falling world prices, a rising foreign debt, a skyrocketing budget deficit, and continuing large-scale unemployment.[119]

Scarcely had the copper threat been lifted when Chilean negotiations with the IMF again foundered. In late October and early November, Fund officials recorded considerable progress "in determining the medium-term adjustment required to re-establish a viable balance of payments," only to see this optimism punctured by acrimonious discussions between Pinochet government officials and a visiting IMF mission in December over the size of the 1985 adjustment. The Chileans proposed a current account deficit of approximately $1.7 billion, whereas the IMF staff considered $1.4 billion an upper limit given the country's high level of indebtedness. Junta officials rejected this figure as incompatible with the 1985 economic growth rate goal of at least 4 percent. The IMF staff challenged Chilean projections on inflation and the current account deficit as well as the economic growth rate, declaring them neither "feasible [n]or acceptable."[120] As a result, the mission was unable to reach a final agreement on an economic program. This was not good news to Washington, where the IMF program was considered vital if Chile was to maintain its "credibility in international financial markets and prevent a mass defection by smaller bank lenders."[121]

A related U.S. concern was the possibility that a worsening political instability might induce Chile's foreign bank creditors to demand a new Paris Club (an informal grouping of creditor nations) agreement "as a precondition to disbursement of new money." Although the regime was extremely reluctant to participate in another gathering of what it characterized as a highly politicized, European-dominated organization, and saw few benefits flowing from an official rescheduling, the State Department was inclined to a more positive, not to say self-interested, interpretation. The financial rewards of a new agreement would at least maintain "an undesirable but sustainable situation and [avoid] economic disaster." Moreover, if this occurred, Washington's "economic leverage to support the political transition would be multiplied without putting

---

[119] "Treasury Minister Raps U.S. Copper Protectionism," *FBIS: DR: LA*, May 18, 1984, E1; "U.S. Copper Import Limit to 'Aggravate' Economic Crisis," *FBIS: DR: LA*, June 21, 1984, E1.

[120] Office Memo, Jan Van Houten to Managing Director, Deputy MD, "Chile – Negotiation of an Extended Arrangement," December 21, 1984, Central Files: C/Chile/810, Missions, 1984–1985, IMFA.

[121] Action Memo, Motley to Shultz, "US Policy toward Chile."

up any U.S. resources [and] could form an integral part of the initiative with the Europeans."[122]

The "basic human needs" caveat in determining the U.S. position on MDB loan applications helped explain Washington's continued support for some Chilean loan requests even as U.S. officials acknowledged the "recent deterioration" in the human rights environment.[123] Also working in Pinochet's favor was a White House generally unconvinced that muscle flexing in the MDBs "was a very effective way to bring pressure on countries for the purpose of improving their human rights performance."[124] During November, the Reagan administration voted in favor of two Chilean requests to the IADB. State and Treasury officials justified the first, a $35.7 million roads loan approved unanimously by the Bank's executive directors, because of its perceived economic benefits and "uncertainty about whether punitive U.S. action at this time would help improve the human rights situation."[125] One day after State Department spokesman John Hughes had commented that a "cycle of terrorism, repression and protest" was impeding the democratic process in Chile, the U.S. executive director cast a second yes vote for a $125 million loan to Chile, primarily to fund health, educational, and sanitation projects for the poor. This decision was preceded by a "heated" bureaucratic debate between those officials (principally in HA) advocating a no or abstention vote to punish the junta for the worsening human rights climate and their colleagues (especially ARA) wary of giving ammunition to the Pinochet regime's hardliners. Ambassador Theberge reportedly played a key role in persuading Washington to the (unlikely) notion that a yes vote would give the United States increased leverage with the junta.[126] According to an Embassy paper, supporting the loan was a consensus view among a Country Team that was "firmly opposed to putting pressure on the Chilean government by vetoing loans" in the international financial institutions.

---

[122] Memo to Files, DOS, "Economic Overview," November 23, 1984, DOS/FOIAe, III.
[123] Quoted in Clyde H. Farnsworth, "U.S. View on Loans for Chile," *NYT*, November 20, 1984, D15.
[124] Elliott Abrams, in U.S. Congress, House, Committee on Banking, Finance and Urban Affairs, Subcommittee on International Development Institutions and Finance, and Senate, Committee on Foreign Affairs, Subcommittee on Africa, *Human Rights Policies at the Multilateral Development Banks*, 98th Cong., 1st Sess., June 22, 1983, 82; Curry and Royce, *Enforcing Human Rights*, 17.
[125] John M. Goshko, "Administration Supports Loan for Chile Despite Rights Record," *WP*, November 22, 1984, A43.
[126] Quoted in "U.S. Backs Loan Despite State of Siege," *CT*, November 30, 1984, 5; John M. Goshko, "Chile Criticized, Aided," *WP*, November 29, 1984, 30.

To do so would be "counterproductive," eroding what minimal influence the White House had with the regime and ensuring that the latter would no longer do "favors," such as voting with the United States in international and regional organizations.[127]

Theberge's apparent failure to carefully weigh the likely impact of yes votes on Congress was particularly concerning to Secretary of State Shultz and other State Department officials. In a memo to the Ambassador, Shultz pointed out that the administration could come under fire from the new Congress when it reconvened in early 1985 over U.S. voting practices in the MDBs. The House Foreign Affairs Committee had already listed a hearing on the subject, and several legislators would take the White House to task over the way it had applied Section 701 of the IFI Act requiring the United States to vote against loans to gross violators of human rights that do not meet BHN criteria.[128] In the case of Chile, legislators were also planning hearings to pursue several courses of action, given added impetus by the reimposition of the state of siege, a tightening of certification requirements for arms sales and security assistance, the introduction of additional Chile-specific amendments or resolutions imposing new economic sanctions, a toughening of the language in Section 701 "to specify which human rights violations trigger compliance with the law," and the submission of nonbinding "sense of the Congress" resolutions that criticized administration policy in international lending bodies from a human rights perspective.[129]

As the first Reagan administration approached its end point, the key question that Chile policy makers had to answer was put succinctly in State's December action memo: "whether we wish and/or are able to substantively affect the situation in Chile to bring about a real transition to democracy or whether we admit to a lack of influence on this issue and only see the public perception of such a policy."[130] As far as intention was concerned, the administration remained divided over what, if any, pressure to bring to bear on the Chilean junta, and even those policy makers most keen on pushing for a greater respect for human rights and a transition to democracy lacked anything remotely resembling a clear

---

[127] Report quoted in Jack Anderson, "On Chile, the U.S. Is Silent," *WP*, December 30, 1984, C7. In December, the United States voted in favor of a $48 million Chilean loan request to the IADB, only to have it rejected by the Executive Board, "With Theberge, The US in Chile Talks Tough, Carries Small Stick," *LARR: SC*, December 21, 1984, 1.

[128] Telegram, Shultz, to AmEmb Santiago, December 7, 1984, DOS/FOIAe, III.

[129] Memo, Bennett to Deputy Secretary, January 12, 1985, ibid.

[130] Action Memo, Motley to Shultz, "US Policy toward Chile."

strategy on how to proceed – except for a deeply held aversion to wielding high-impact economic sanctions as an instrument of foreign policy. As for dangling aid and trade carrots, instead of sticks, as an incentive to the junta to change its outlook, Congress had ruled that out with a series of legislative restrictions.

With Congress preparing to take the offensive on Chile policy, it was perhaps unsurprising that in a speech marking International Human Rights Day, Reagan attempted to mollify his critics by labeling the "lack of progress toward democratic government" in the Latin nation an "affront."[131] More importantly, the reference to Chile could be interpreted as a sign that the President was now willing to give more credence to the views of those State Department officials impatient with Pinochet's obstinate refusal to respond to U.S. appeals to lift the state of siege, open a genuine dialogue with the opposition, and take serious steps toward a democratic transition. Further evidence that Reagan's attitude might be changing occurred sooner than two weeks after his speech, during a meeting with Secretary of State Shultz. In the course of their discussion, Shultz unveiled plans to appoint new Ambassadors to approximately one-third of all regional embassies (including Chile) and to make a series of personnel changes at the Department's Assistant Secretary level. Asked by reporters to comment on complaints that Shultz was intent on stacking the Department with officials who were less ideological and more pragmatic and moderate in their political outlooks, the President categorically dismissed the suggestion and indicated his approval of the Secretary's actions.[132] The implications for Chile policy were potentially far-reaching. Theberge's replacement would remove a vocal critic of those in State pushing for a tougher line on Pinochet, while the Department changes promised to further shift the balance of power in their favor.

---

[131] Proclamation 5287, Bill of Rights Day, Human Rights Day and Week, [December 10] 1984, American Presidency Project.

[132] See John M. Goshko and Lou Cannon, "Conservatives Suspicious of Shultz Purge: Takeover Attempt at State Is Seen," *WP*, December 23, 1984 (Factiva).

3

Dead Ends in Chile Policy

By the beginning of Ronald Reagan's second term, a number of factors were conspiring to make a gradual change in U.S. policy toward Chile inevitable. Prominent among these, in the most general sense, had been Reagan's speech to the British Parliament in June 1982, in which he committed the United States to promoting "freedom and democracy" as a matter of principle throughout the world. The context for, and background to, this speech was the American President's deeply held belief that the Soviet Union was an "evil empire," utterly untrustworthy, and should eventually be consigned to history unless it was willing to fundamentally transform its society, politically and economically. The more immediate trigger was Reagan's support for the Solidarity movement in Poland, which was posing a major challenge to the Soviet-backed government of General Wojciech Jaruzelski.[1]

That speech had important repercussions. First, Reagan's commitment did not sit well with the wholehearted support of a military strongman such as General Augusto Pinochet and left the White House open to the charge of double standards – supporting democracy where it served U.S. interests in the struggle against leftist movements and regimes, especially in Central America, but exempting dictatorships perceived as valued allies for strategic, political, or economic reasons. Indeed, in the closing months of 1984, pressure was again building inside Congress to apply tougher measures against Chile in response to the concern of some legislators that the administration, despite its lofty rhetoric, was simply choosing

[1] See Edmund Morris, *Dutch: A Memoir of Ronald Reagan* (New York: Random House, 1999), 460.

to ignore Pinochet's continued repression. Second, the London speech gave some latitude to those State Department officials eager to pursue policy approaches beyond the strictures of the Kirkpatrick Doctrine and what it implied for Washington's relations with anticommunist Third World autocrats. Jeane Kirkpatrick's departure in early 1985 provided an opportunity to contest her interpretation and influence, especially in the White House. "[W]e started taking a different approach to Chile," recalled a senior U.S. official, and simultaneously "started to draw new lessons from the fall of the Shah in Iran and of Somoza in Nicaragua."[2]

Global and regional trends also undermined old certainties about East-West conflict and provided new opportunities for U.S. policy makers. In March 1985, Mikhail Gorbachev became Secretary General of the Communist Party in the Soviet Union and almost immediately set about outlining a new kind of foreign policy that emphasized cooperation with the United States rather than competition in contested regions of the Third World. Meanwhile, in Asia and Latin America, multiclass political movements were posing serious challenges to entrenched authoritarian regimes. In Turkey, South Korea, and the Philippines, dictatorial governments were in the process of conceding to popular demands for transitions to civilian rule; in Argentina, electoral democracy had already supplanted military rule, and it was well on the way to doing so in Brazil and Uruguay.

Though Chile remained a low-priority issue for the Reagan White House, key U.S. officials regarded it as a "standout" exception to the democracy trend sweeping the hemisphere and/or expressed frustration that Pinochet simply "wasn't getting the message" about the need to improve the human rights situation and implement political reforms. This encouraged a perception that Chile was witnessing an "endless cycle" in which the political situation was never getting better, only worse.[3] The rise of mass mobilization politics in 1983–1984 triggered an additional concern about the resurgence of the left social movements and the need to hasten the transition to democracy as a way to prevent further political polarization with all its attendant risks. Even those Reagan officials

---

[2] Quoted in E. A. Wayne, "US Looks at Chile as the Next Place to Promote Democracy," *CSM*, March 23, 1988, 1. The belief that Pinochet might suffer a similar fate to that which befell Nicaragua's dictator Anastasio Somoza in July 1979 was unrealistic in the extreme. Despite the renewed social mobilization politics, Pinochet still had the support of a unified and formidable armed forces, together with a significant sector of the population, and a monopoly of coercive power. But while the comparison was fundamentally flawed, the fact that it was nevertheless discussed and raised the interesting question as to whether Reagan officials took it seriously or used it for their own purposes.

[3] Interviews with Elliott Abrams and Harry G. Barnes.

less concerned by a Somoza-type outcome worried that a continuation of Pinochet's rule would discredit what Secretary of State George Shultz described as "the best economic policies you can find anywhere" in the Third World.[4] Chile, he observed, was a paradox: "it had an open economy that was doing well and a political system that was not what we would like."[5]

But if a change in policy approach was now on the agenda, it was going to be managed with great caution. Over time, and after considerable bickering among individual agencies and officials, a gradual shift occurred, based on two key operational premises: that power could only be transferred by the military in an orderly fashion, rather than by popular pressure from below that might produce another leftist government intent on shifting Chile out of the U.S. politicoeconomic orbit, and that this outcome depended on the ascendancy of the center-right opposition forces, who posed no threat to fundamental Chilean (or U.S.) military and economic interests. The ultimate goal remained as outlined by Deputy Assistant Secretary of State for Inter-American Affairs James Michel in April 1984: to facilitate "the emergence of a centrist political consensus and a soft transition into democracy."[6] For this to happen, his colleague, Southern Cone Director Robert Morley, told PDC officials early the following year, demanded an organized opposition that could present "a viable alternative to Pinochet" and a regime willing to dialogue with it, while simultaneously eliminating the "terrorists."[7]

Frustration Builds in State

As far as Pinochet was concerned, the widespread popular unrest of 1983 and 1984 had failed to alter the essential political balance in Chile and certainly had done nothing to dent his confidence or temper his distaste for compromise. In November 1984, under the aegis of restoring order, he reimposed a state of siege for a period of ninety days as the prelude to a harsh crackdown targeting both the radical political left and the moderate political forces, including PDC members.[8] Washington

---

[4] Minutes of Meeting, NSC, Cabinet Room, Chile, November 18, 1986, LAAD, NSC, NSC Meeting on Chile 11/18/1986, Box 91172, RRL.

[5] Telephone interview with George P. Shultz.

[6] Michel, "U.S. Support for Democracy in Chile."

[7] Telegram, Shultz to AmEmb Santiago, January 26, 1985, LAAD, NSC, Chile (01/02/1985–02/14/1985), Box 91713, RRL.

[8] See Peter D. Bell, "Democracy and Double Standards: The View from Chile," *World Policy Journal* 11, no. 4 (1985): 719.

responded in a contradictory fashion to this latest wave of repression: on one hand, the State Department characterized the regime's human rights performance as "the greatest disappointment" in Latin America;[9] on the other, the White House was still reluctant to support UNGA resolutions critical of Chile. Within the ranks of the moderate opposition, the cumulative impact of the violent state response to the protests over the past year was starting to force a reconsideration of the continuing effectiveness of the direct confrontation tactic. However, none of the party leaders was yet prepared to accept that the transition plan Pinochet had outlined in the 1980 Constitution was an acceptable route to democracy or that it represented anything more than an attempt by the dictator to prolong his rule indefinitely.

On State's Seventh Floor, George Shultz drew his own lesson from recent events: "By the start of the second Reagan term," he wrote in his memoirs, "I was convinced that the U.S. approach was not working. We understood Pinochet: he was not changing. But he did not understand us: we wanted a more open government, the rule of law and a government headed by elected officials." Shultz readily admitted that this was not yet a consensus view within the administration and that he "was not really on the wavelength of the President and many of his advisers: to them, Pinochet was a friend of the U.S. and a bulwark against communism." Although the Chilean dictator "made everyone uneasy," it was difficult to mobilize support for devising a new approach. The White House was reluctant to criticize Pinochet's governing style because "he was on our side" in the struggle against communism and radical nationalism.[10] The NSC was similarly inclined, and this interpretation did not lack sympathizers in the Pentagon. When it came to human rights and democracy versus security and economic interests, Reagan, the NSC, the Pentagon, and many in the State Department were still not ready to cut Pinochet loose.

Shultz's strongest advocate within State was Elliott Abrams, HA's neoconservative Assistant Secretary who, paradoxically, had a track record

---

[9] Quoted in Pamela Constable and Arturo Valenzuela, *A Nation of Enemies* (New York: W. W. Norton, 1991), 290.

[10] George P. Shultz, *Turmoil and Triumph: My Years as Secretary of State*. New York: Charles Scribner's Sons, 1993, 970. Elliott Abrams arrived at a similar conclusion about Reagan: "the President's instincts [regarding Chile] were not good [because he] continued to think of the Chilean leader as a loyal anticommunist friend who deserved U.S. support." Quoted in Thomas Carothers, *In the Name of Democracy: U.S. Policy toward Latin America during the Reagan Years* (Berkeley: University of California Press, 1991), 156.

of supporting the most violent and autocratic regimes in the Third World, especially in Central America, in the name of anticommunism and democracy promotion. But, on this occasion, he was convinced that the time had come to turn a page on Chile because "the only alternative to Pinochet was democracy."[11] Yet even the most insistent proponents of quiet diplomacy, such as Assistant Secretary for Inter-American Affairs Langhorne Motley, now conceded that, at best, this approach had only resulted in limited progress and "needed to be rectified" in some way.[12]

Pinochet, as one U.S. official told the *Christian Science Monitor*, "simply hasn't a democratic bone in his body."[13] Given his obvious disdain for politicians, it was not surprising that words such as *dialogue* and *negotiation* were absent from his vocabulary. Nor was he particularly vulnerable to outside pressure. Abrams conceded that Washington "lacked the ability to influence events on a day-to-day basis" but, attempting to put the best gloss on the situation, maintained that it might be possible to shape the broader "evolution" of developments in Chile.[14] The question was how. "We were 'kind of stumbling along,'" observed another U.S. diplomat involved with Latin American policy. "We didn't have enough instruments of influence at our disposal to bring about the desired result."[15]

In a January 1985 meeting with Chile's Foreign Minister Jaime del Valle, Interior Minister Sergio Jarpa, and Finance Minister Luis Escobar, Ambassador James Theberge could only tell the three civilian ministers what they already knew about the political impact of the reimposed state of siege: it had produced "a wave of critical moment in the U.S. press, the Congress, and ha[d] made it increasingly difficult for [the administration] to maintain a cooperative relationship with the Chilean Government." Theberge could not understand why it was necessary to prolong martial law when the government already had "all the means necessary" to maintain internal security.[16] The same message was delivered later that month to Chilean Foreign Ministry officials by a visiting delegation of congressional Democrats (Peter Kostmayer, D-PA, James Jeffords, R-VT, and Robert Torricelli, D-NJ), who added that they would support legislation to further reduce U.S. cooperation with Chile on loans and military

---

[11] Interview with Elliott Abrams.
[12] Interview with Langhorne Motley.
[13] Quoted in James Nelson Goodsell, "US Slaps Pinochet's Hand for Extending State of Siege in Chile," *CSM*, February 13, 1985, 10.
[14] Interview with Elliott Abrams.
[15] Confidential telephone interview 2.
[16] Telegram, AmEmb Santiago (Theberge) to Shultz, January 18, 1985, DOS/FOIAe, III.

contacts unless Chile "demonstrated an intention to improve its human rights performance and pursue a political opening leading to democratic rule."[17]

Washington's efforts to influence events inside Chile were not helped by the country's "very negative international image."[18] The human rights situation in the six months since June 1984 had deteriorated according to Treasury Assistant Secretary David Mulford, which, he implied, should therefore trigger U.S. opposition to all Chilean loan requests to the MDBs. Although the State Department was reluctant to dump a flexible policy of assessing Chile submissions "on a case-by-case basis,"[19] in the absence of human rights improvements, this was ultimately a "politically untenable" stance.[20] Acting on State's recommendation, the White House tried to put some mild pressure on Santiago by twice requesting the IADB to postpone the vote on a Chilean $130 million industrial recovery loan submission. When that failed, the United States abstained on the vote, a decision ARA's James Michel termed a "prudent" gesture, particularly in view of growing congressional sentiment for further tightening U.S. sanctions on Chile.[21] "We felt it was time to send a signal," said an administration official.[22] Motley reassured the U.S. investment community in Chile that the vote was primarily a response to pressure from the Hill and did not signify any larger policy shift.[23] The loan was approved, and days later, Pinochet, in a signal that he cared little for U.S. posturing and was in no mood for moderation, extended the state of siege and sacked Jarpa and Escobar – both of whom had opposed the extension and were the most pro-transition cabinet members. In a telegram to Shultz, Ambassador Theberge suggested that Jarpa's ouster further contracted Pinochet's civilian political base by alienating the traditional right and numerous *gremios* (or professional associations) – "who strongly supported [Jarpa's] more nationalistic economic plan." But his solid backing from the armed forces, contrasted with an impotent and

---

[17] Telegram, AmEmb Santiago (Matthews) to Shultz, January 29, 1985, ibid.

[18] Memo, Michel to Deputy Secretary of State, February 1, 1985, Ludlow "Kim" Flower, Chile: Economy, Box 91258, RRL.

[19] Talking Points on Chile for meeting of Inter-Agency Working Group on Human Rights and Foreign Assistance, drafted ARA/SC, January 14, 1985, DOS/FOIAe, III.

[20] Memo, Michel to Deputy Secretary of State, February 1, 1985.

[21] Ibid.

[22] Quoted in Joel Brinkley, "U.S. to Abstain on Loan to Chile to Protest Human Rights Abuses," *NYT*, February 6, 1985, 4.

[23] Lydia Chavez, "U.S. Envoy, Ending Chile Visit, Avoids Any Criticism of Pinochet," *NYT*, February 21, 1985, 4.

disorganized opposition, "apparently convinced Pinochet that he is firmly in control."[24] The danger now was that an overconfident dictator would only make matters worse by seeking to prolong his rule – thus playing into the hands of the radical left.

Inside State, officials in the ARA and HA bureaus began work in earnest on new policy recommendations that included stepped-up public criticism of Pinochet, more U.S. abstentions in MDBs – although without blocking loans or encouraging other nations to do so – and a more activist, and potentially difficult, "tightrope act" by the Embassy to develop more lines of communication with the political opposition as well as Chilean government officials.[25] To implement the "tightrope act," Shultz went ahead with his decision to replace Theberge, who had completely "used up his credit on both sides" of the political divide in Chile, with a new ambassador who could "start fresh" with the regime and its opponents. Executive branch officials, bemoaning the fact that they had "so little leverage left with Pinochet," also began canvassing congressional support for a resumption of limited military aid to Chile to win influence with members of the junta who might be more inclined to listen to outside advice, especially if it came with the offer of substantive rewards. That idea generated limited enthusiasm at best among liberals, as well as a number of conservative House Republicans.[26]

In a February cable to the U.S. Mission in Geneva ahead of the annual UNHRC resolution on Chile, Deputy Secretary of State Kenneth Dam emphasized the growing sense of frustration in dealing with a junta that refused to budge from a conviction that it must first defeat the "terrorists" before it could begin the transition process. What the Chileans failed to understand was that successful transitions were invariably those "where the two issues of security and democracy are addressed simultaneously." The problem was not confined to Pinochet alone. Dealing with a fractured opposition was equally problematic. "If there were a widespread consensus among the political opposition on the transition, the Chilean military would probably have to accommodate this pressure. In the absence of such pressure, the military are able to pursue their own agenda and insist on their own timetable." Dam warned that the Communists

---

[24] Telegram, Theberge to Shultz, "Jarpa's Future and the Future of Chile," February 19, 1985, LAAD, NSC, Chile-1985 (8), Box 91713, RRL.

[25] Quoted in Jack Anderson, "U.S. Planning Tougher Line on Chile," *WP*, January 24, 1985, DCi1.

[26] Quotes in Tim Golden, "U.S. May Ask for Military Aid to Chile," UPI, February 10, 1985.

were working to ensure that neither side moderated its position; their goal was to "polarize the situation," leading the Chilean military to believe that only "tough security measures" could prevent an explosion. This could only lead to increased human rights abuses "and failure to distinguish between the legitimate opposition and the terrorist element." State Department officials tried vainly to impress upon the regime that its refusal to pursue both tracks in tandem would have the effect of letting the Communists "define the rules of the game."[27]

In an attempt to break this dynamic and encourage a return to democracy, State proposed to send its senior Latin American diplomat, Langhorne Motley, to Santiago for discussions with both sides in the conflict. This move drew a cautious White House response and was not wholeheartedly embraced by the NSC. Determined to keep Motley on a short leash, NSC Adviser Robert McFarlane and his deputy, Admiral John Poindexter, reportedly arranged for Latin American staffer Jackie Tillman – hardly supportive of a tough line with Pinochet – to accompany Motley and sit in on his meetings with government officials and political party leaders. Theberge was informed of this last-minute arrangement and was left with the distinct impression that the NSC "didn't trust" Motley and that the State Department and the White House remained in "competition over policy control."[28]

Motley Visits Santiago

Publicly, the Department insisted that no particular event triggered the Motley trip, although the sacking of Jarpa and the persistence of "torture and police brutality" were matters of serious concern. The possibility that Pinochet's autocratic rule might strengthen the radical left and lead to "another Nicaragua" further exercised some American officials.[29] Motley himself ascribed the timing of the visit to Secretary Shultz's "wonderful theory of not getting bogged down on the item of the day or what he called 'gardening': every now and again you sit back and look at other things you haven't been spending a lot of time on. And he took this gardening approach toward Chile, 'you know, we haven't done anything on Chile, let's think about it for a while.'" The outcome of these discussions turned

---

[27] Telegram, Shultz (Dam) to U.S. Mission Geneva, February 16, 1985, DOS/FOIAe, III.
[28] Motley Visit, February 17–22, 1985, "Jan 1985–March 1985 (Vol. 1)," Box 24, JDT Collection.
[29] Quotes in "U.S. Official to Press Chile on Elections," *NYT*, February 16, 1985, 3.

on the idea that Chile was the last military domino that needed to fall in Latin America:

The challenge was that Pinochet was very good on terrorism and on anti-Soviet/Cuban activities and [his] was a staunch anti-Communist government. So Pinochet gets credit for that. On the other hand, it was the lack of a democratic kind of evolution that was happening in Brazil. And once it happened in Argentina with the election of [Raúl] Alfonsín, everybody said, "Well, maybe it's Chile's turn." That's what brought Chile up on Shultz's radar screen.[30]

With Chile now firmly on Shultz's "radar screen," and on the evening of his departure, Motley received a long briefing paper prepared by ARA's Robert Morley that outlined the Department's overall hopes for the visit and how they should be pursued. "Our specific and concrete goal," Morley wrote, "should be to keep Pinochet in power through the next four years but to turn him around from reliance on military command to reliance on political governance." If Pinochet did not respond, "our alternative will have to be damage limitation that leaves the Pinochet question open in a public political sense, but that, in fact, does not make him fair game from the left." It may be necessary, he continued, "to run a complicated policy" that avoids giving Pinochet the idea that the prime objective of the trip is to apply pressure on him to implement reforms that were likely to have precisely the opposite effect. "Drawing on Dick Walter's advice," Morley concluded, "our Chile policy may end up based in large measure on constructive ambiguity."

The briefing paper advised Motley to keep the focus on U.S. support for a return to democracy and the benefits likely to accrue from regime initiatives toward this end: it would have the effect of "enhancing the political credibility of our Chile policy in the U.S." and give the administration greater flexibility in its dealings with Congress to assist Chile. It was suggested that he use the Communist Party's support for armed insurrection as a point of contrast "to turn Pinochet around from reliance on security to equal emphasis on democracy and security" and that he employ the same threat "to drive a wedge between the Communists and the moderate center-left." Another piece of advice was to "pressure the military to pressure Pinochet by calling into question their loyalty to the [1980] Constitution as opposed to their loyalty to Pinochet." Finally, the Assistant Secretary should be aware that the opposition's "mounting

---

[30] Interview with Langhorne Motley.

frustration" had produced some "increasingly bizarre and fanciful thinking" on how to break the impasse:

When David Dlouhy and David Cox visited Chile in mid-October [1984] the
game for the opposition was to conclude a grand Constitutional Pact uniting
all elements, including the Communists. This effort was a failure since it went
to the heart of the problem they have been unable to resolve, i.e. Communist
participation. When Jim Michel and Bob Morley visited in November, the game
for the moderate opposition was to go around Pinochet and appeal to the military
service chiefs for talks with the opposition. This effort was so poorly conceived
and so clumsily handled that it lasted a mere 72 hours. The next phase was for the
government to raise the possibility of an appointed Congress. That lasted about
a week.[31]

Motley's program in Santiago included meetings with Pinochet and a
range of senior military personnel, government officials, opposition parties, trade unions, and representatives of the Church. During an uncomfortable encounter with the Chilean President, he received "a 45 minute
tirade about how Chile had supported the U.S. in the UN."[32] In response,
Motley dutifully "emphasized that successful political transitions were
marked by equal attention to the advances toward democracy and security," without demanding the implementation of explicit democracy
measures or human rights initiatives. This restraint was attributable,
in part, to Motley's reluctance to go beyond the quiet diplomacy
approach – even though its value was being questioned in Washington –
and partly because he did not consider it "'appropriate' for an American 'gringo' [as a visitor] to try to 'muscle' the country's President."[33]
Nonetheless, Motley left the meeting convinced that he had at least "laid
down a marker for [Pinochet] of our interest in seeing that the military
fulfill their commitment to return Chile to democracy" and suggested in
a report to Shultz that now might be the time to open "other constructive
steps" with Washington's European allies "to jointly press Pinochet and
[the] opposition to get on with the political transition."[34] Still, the General's demeanor did not leave his American visitor overly encouraged.
"Pinochet is in no danger of being overthrown in the next two years,"

[31] Memo, Morley to Motley, "Your Trip to Chile, Feb 17–20, February 16, 1985," "Jan
     1985–March 1985 (Vol. 1)," Box 24, JDT Collection.
[32] Interview with Langhorne Motley.
[33] Quoted in Howard Kurtz, "U.S. Official Receives Little Assurance from Chile's
     Pinochet," *WP*, February 23, 1985, A12.
[34] Telegram, Theberge to Shultz on Motley meeting with Pinochet, February 19, 1985,
     DOS/FOIAe, III.

Motley cabled Shultz at the conclusion of his four-day visit. "The opposition is not organized, either in a political or armed sense, and the military is highly trained and disciplined." In the absence of any change in direction and tempo, "Chile and therefore our interests are headed for trouble over the long haul." The problem was not Pinochet's "will and determination" but the military's "ability to sustain the same determination." If Pinochet was in power beyond the 1989 transition deadline, Motley thought his "departure, removal or overthrow" could be "messy." Realistically, though, there was "precious little we can do to influence the immediate situation (no bilateral aid) so we need to think of the long haul... and how we act now to hold our own." Working through the Church to "quietly help influence the situation internally" should be considered.[35] The Embassy had drawn much the same conclusion: the key sticking point, Theberge informed Shultz, remained Pinochet's refusal to "advance toward democracy" while "combat[ing] terrorism."[36]

Motley took up this issue with Admiral José Merino, telling him that "terrorism was insidious [but] that, while the GOC was doing well in the physical fight with terrorism, he was concerned about the psychological aspects of the struggle."[37] He delivered a similar message to the Presidential Secretariat's minister, General Santiago Sinclair, noting that since the approval of the 1980 Constitution, "nothing concrete had been done [regarding the transition plans] and that the government of Chile's understandable desire to maintain flexibility on the transition had undermined its credibility." Moving the transition process along by eliminating restrictions on freedom of expression would have the effect of "lancing a boil," in the process easing "political frustration" at home and improving the regime's international image. Motley concluded by insisting that "the suppression of terrorism and the transition must be carried out together[,] not sequentially."[38]

During conversations with opposition leaders, Motley pressed them to accept the 1980 Constitution and the other basic transition parameters the junta's General Matthei had outlined six months earlier (to *El Mercurio*) as a starting point and warned that "street protests and mass mobilizations played into the hands of the Marxists and should

[35] Memo, Motley to Shultz, February 21, 1985, ibid.
[36] Telegram, Theberge to Shultz, from Motley, February 19, 1985, ibid. Also see Telegram, Shultz (Dam) to U.S. Mission, Geneva, ibid.
[37] Telegram, Theberge to Shultz on Motley meeting with Merino, February 21, 1985, ibid.
[38] Telegram, Theberge to Shultz on Motley meeting with Sinclair, February 21, 1985, ibid.

be stopped immediately."[39] Such advice did not elicit a strong positive response because shifting the struggle from the streets to the negotiating table eliminated the opposition's one avenue of admittedly limited pressure on the regime – social mobilization – and would risk effectively surrendering control of the streets to the radical left.[40] Motley's overall impression of the opposition was not encouraging: "We met with the so-called conservatives, who would say 'We wish things would go faster.' We met with the truckers, especially those who were conservative and capitalistic in a sense. Then you would have the fringe groups saying 'Everything's wrong since the sun came up this morning.'" The Christian Democrats alone impressed him as being "ready for advancements and change." But the larger picture remained fraught with difficulty. Motley conveyed his sense of personal frustration to Archbishop Juan Fresno in a few well-chosen words: "There's a role reversal here: you have my prayers."[41]

At various times during his visit, Motley's actions seemed to undercut the toughness of his message. During a meeting with Foreign Minister Jaime del Valle, he waxed sympathetic about how Chile was a "victim of international circumstances," referring to the vagaries of public opinion in a strangely dismissive way: "A bull frog leaps from lily pad to lily pad to avoid the water. The bull frog no longer jumps on the lily pads of El Salvador, Guatemala and Uruguay because the problems there are on the way to solution. So the Chile lily pad is the one place to jump. International opinion is the bull frog." The Foreign Minister responded by appealing to the United States "not to help the bull frog."[42] Interviewed by *El Mercurio*, Motley offered what appeared to be a more direct endorsement of the regime, conceding that the transition to democracy was "particularly difficult when there are violent, antidemocratic terrorist attacks" and that the military and its supporters were owed "a debt of gratitude

---

[39] Quoted in "Motley's Visit Delights Chile," *LAWR*, March 1, 1985, 10.

[40] See "Motley Visit Viewed As 'Not Very Successful,'" *FBIS: DR: LA*, February 25, 1985, E1.

[41] Interview with Langhorne Motley.

[42] Telegram, Thebege to Shultz on Motley meeting with de Valle, February 21, 1985, DOS/FOIAe, III. Motley used the same analogy during a conversation with reporters on his return to Washington. His visit had not raised "the decibel level," he said, in dismissing any major change in U.S. policy. What had changed in the Western Hemisphere was the disappearance of "any more lily pads for those in the human-rights game to jump on – no more nuns getting killed in El Salvador." This explained why "suddenly Chile ha[d] become the focus of public attention." Quoted in Pamela Constable, "US Is Pushing Chile to Ease Its Policies," *BG*, February 24, 1985, 8.

for what they did in 1973."[43] His parting comment to reporters that the nation's future was "in good hands" allowed Chilean government officials to label the visit "positive" and presume that the U.S. envoy "must have left with favorable impressions."[44]

In Washington, the evident impasse in Chile's political situation was not lost on HA's Elliott Abrams. The day before Motley returned from Santiago, Abrams told the *Miami Herald* that "we have said from the very beginning that quiet diplomacy is not a principle but a tactic. We try it first and if it works, great. If it doesn't, then you shift to other tools." In the context of a deteriorating human rights situation in Chile, those other tools meant that "we need to move beyond quiet diplomacy."[45] These comments angered Motley, still a strong advocate of quiet diplomacy, who complained to Shultz about the "growing problem" of Abrams making freelance public statements at odds with agreed-on policy toward Chile.[46] His patience exhausted, Motley moved to metaphorically take hold of the problem and solve it:

It was a turf issue. Elliott was in charge of human rights: I was on a very tricky mission with the full blessing of Shultz and the White House. And so I play this balancing act I was going into, and I come out of it and I make my statements, and I find out that apropos of whatever Elliott feels he is compelled to make some kind of public statement on the issue in *my* region. And that irritated me. And so I sorted it out when I came back. And he made no more statements on it.[47]

Following close on the heels of Motley's visit, the Pentagon's senior Latin American affairs specialist, Néstor Sánchez, ventured to Santiago to continue the dialogue with regime officials. Explaining the significance of this decision to send a hard-line ideologue like Sánchez, a State Department official said that "different elements of our government have different lines of communication" and that Sánchez would be delivering a message to "a different case of characters [compared to Motley]." This did not represent any fundamental change in policy, the official insisted, but only a "change of tactics."[48] In meetings with Pinochet and other ranking

---

[43] Quoted in "Top U.S. Official Lauds Chile Regime," *CT*, February 25, 1985, 3.

[44] See "Departure Statement Viewed," *FBIS: DR: LA*, February 22, 1985, E1.

[45] Quoted in Alfonso Chardy, "U.S. Abandons 'Quiet Diplomacy' with Chile," *MH*, February 21, 1985, 9A.

[46] Memo, Motley to Shultz, February 21, 1985.

[47] Interview with Langhorne Motley; Langhorne Motley interview, FAOHC (our emphasis).

[48] Quoted in Terri Shaw, "U.S. Stepping Up Effort to Promote Talks in Chile," *WP*, February 27, 1985, A1. Sánchez was Deputy Assistant Secretary of Defense.

members of the armed forces, Sánchez expressed interest in improving military-military cooperation within the current legislative restrictions. The Embassy reported that this did not please the political opposition because they perceived it "as improving U.S.-Chilean ties." But whether the opposition appreciated it or not, the real significance of the visit was that Pinochet and senior Chilean military officers had received the same unqualified message from a senior Defense Department official as that conveyed by Motley.[49] Conversely, Gabriel Valdés, then running for the PDC presidency (and reelected by a large majority in early June) had a very different interpretation of Sánchez's message: the Pentagon envoy viewed the world exclusively through the prism of the Cold War conflict, which translated into "the [U.S.] are out to destroy the Nicaraguans but Pinochet is not a problem."[50] Irrespective of these various assessments, Theberge would later conclude that Pinochet "had not taken seriously" either visit, let alone "U.S. appeals for [a] transition to democracy."[51]

On Capitol Hill, Motley's visit failed to impress Edward Kennedy, who termed the administration's approach "more smoke than fire." Addressing the Senate in early March, he declared that "unless the United States is willing to use its substantial economic leverage by blocking MDB loans to Chile, the Pinochet regime will not budge from its stubborn refusal to carry out democratic reforms."[52] The following week, Senators Kennedy and Tom Harkin (D-IA) and Representatives Ed Feighan (D-OH) and Bruce Morrison (D-CT) introduced legislation calling for economic sanctions against Chile. One key provision in the bills required the United States to vote no on Chilean loan requests to the MDBs; another would make Chile ineligible for the Generalized System of Preferences (GSP), affecting approximately $40 million annually in Chilean imports, and OPIC benefits at a time when Chile was OPIC's largest customer, with guarantees covering $290 million in U.S. investments and loans for 1986.[53]

En route to New York in mid-March to begin debt renegotiation talks, Chile's new Finance Minister, Hernán Büchi, took time out to confer

---

[49] Telegram, Theberge to Shultz, March 19, 1985, DOS/FOIAe, III.

[50] Quoted in "Wavering CD Picks Leader," *LAWR*, May 17, 1985, 10.

[51] "GV's Statement on the USA," May 11, 1985; "Handwritten Notes, March–June 1985," Box 24, JDT Collection.

[52] Quoted in *Congressional Record – Senate*, 99th Cong., 1st Sess., Vol. 131, Part 4, March 5, 1985, 4418.

[53] Statement of Senator E. M. Kennedy introducing economic sanctions against Chile, March 10, 1985, from Office of the Senator, DOS/FOIAe, III.

with State Department officials in Washington, who made it clear that democracy initiatives "would have a bearing on Chile's relationship with the international community and the country's creditworthiness." The nation's ongoing dependence on international finance could be gauged by the fact that even after debt rescheduling arrangements were agreed to, the IMF estimated that Chile would require nearly $2 billion in additional funds to meet its balance of payments shortfall in 1985–1986 because of inaccurate forecasts of copper prices and the high interest rates on its overseas borrowings.[54] When asked by Kenneth Dam if his government contemplated an official Paris Club rescheduling to deal with the problem, Büchi responded in the negative, saying that he was hoping for bilateral rescheduling agreements on the grounds that this was more likely to facilitate new foreign investments and official trade credits.[55] Either way, Chile was seeking to raise funds via a World Bank structural adjustment loan and an unprecedented World Bank guarantee for new commercial bank loans as well as a substantial amount in nonguaranteed private bank loans.

The same month, the U.S. abstained on a separate $11 million public sector loan application by Chile before the World Bank to demonstrate its dissatisfaction with Pinochet's maintenance of the state of siege and refusal to talk to the opposition.[56] This was the second MDB loan abstention in as many months, although the U.S. representative again stopped short of any attempt to actually block the loan going through. Some officials characterized the abstention vote "as a tilt toward the tactical approach advocated by Elliott Abrams."[57] The Assistant Secretary depicted it as a change of tactics that indicated Washington's displeasure with Pinochet, although in a way that was preferable to voting against such loans, which "might send a stronger signal but would tend to restrict further flexibility on our part." Future loan decisions, Abrams told reporters, would depend "on what will work, on what policies the [Chilean] government follows, what the overall political situation is, how the democratic opposition is acting, how much unity there is in the

---

54 Peter Montagnon, "Credits and Euronotes: World Bank May Back 1.95 Billion Dollars Chile Loans," *FT*, May 13, 1985 (Factiva).

55 Telegram, Shultz to AmEmb Santiago, "Acting Secretary Dam Meeting March 12 with Chilean Finance Minister Büchi," March 19, 1985, LAAD, NSC, Chile-1982 (2), Box 91713, RRL.

56 "U.S. Abstains from Vote on Chile Loan Political Concerns Are Underscored," *WP*, March 15, 1985, A25.

57 Telegram, Shultz to AmEmb New Delhi, March 15, DOS/FOIAe, III.

opposition, and how much terrorism there is in Chile."[58] Shultz was
equally hard to pin down when describing administration intentions in
testimony before a House subcommittee: "The Pinochet regime is facing a challenge and from our standpoint what we are seeking to do is
to help those who are in opposition have some coherence and separate
from the Communists, and encourage the Pinochet regime to interact
with them as they were starting to do."[59] Legislators, however, were
more interested in how the State Department intended to pursue this
goal and whether it was using all the resources at its disposal. Later,
over executive branch objections, a House Foreign Affairs subcommittee,
influenced by the "marked deterioration" in the human rights situation,
endorsed a resolution calling for new economic and military sanctions
against Chile. Although nonbinding, the resolution was a clear indication
that White House policy was getting as little traction on the Hill as it was
in Santiago. Deputy Assistant Secretary of State James Michel charged
that Congress was attempting to impose an undesirable straitjacket on
how the United States should respond to a complex situation.[60] In April,
Congress rejected the resolution. Some of the country's most influential
newspapers accused the administration of engaging in a "deceptive public
relations game in its conduct of quiet diplomacy" as applied to Pinochet
(*New York Times*), others that its policy represented a series of "empty
gestures" designed "to impress liberals in Congress" (*Boston Globe*).[61]

Ratcheting up the Pressure

During the early months of 1985, American diplomats in Washington
and Santiago presented rather dismal assessments of the prospects for a
return of democracy in Chile. To ARA's Langhorne Motley, the dictator's power and control, based on a loyal cabinet of military officials and
technocrats, seemed as strong as ever. As a consequence, he was under
no pressure to "seriously" engage with the political opposition, whose

---

[58] Quoted in Don Oberdorfer, "Official Says U.S. Is Changing Tactics, Not Policy, in
      Human Rights Arena," *WP*, March 20, 1985, A14.
[59] U.S. Congress, House, Committee on Appropriations, Subcommittee on Foreign Oper-
      ations and Related Agencies, *Foreign Assistance and Related Programs Appropriations
      for 1986, Part 3*, 99th Cong., 1st Sess., March 21, 1985, 285.
[60] Quoted in John M. Goshko and Don Oberdorfer, "House Panel Endorses Sanctions
      against Chile," *WP*, March 21, 1985, A29. Also see "New Rebukes to Chile," *CQWR*,
      March 23, 1985, 548.
[61] Editorial, "Four More Years in Chile?," *NYT*, February 25, 1985, 16; Editorial, "Stage-
      Show Diplomacy," *BG*, February 22, 1985, 14.

"ineffectual, disoriented political activities have nurtured Pinochet's confidence." Given this impasse, Motley concluded, the United States had little option but to rely on the military regime's economic problems – making interest payments on its foreign debt, falling copper prices, and the repair bill from a major earthquake that had struck the coast near Valparaiso – if any challenge to his rule were to emerge.[62]

The Embassy offered an equally cheerless picture, highlighting the "failure of the opposition's social mobilization goals, the AD's continuing paralysis and loss of momentum, and its incapacity to offer credible guarantees of a moderate viable alternative to military rule, [which] played into the hands [of] Pinochet." The dictator's own "intransigent stance and conviction that the political opening had failed, achieved such ascendancy within 'the government of the armed forces' that other senior military officials and cabinet offices no longer had room to stake out independent positions." Hence Pinochet and his supporters "justifiably feel stronger now than at any period since early 1983." The Embassy did identify potential pressure points, notably the right-wing political parties, high-profile independents, and business groups who had become disenchanted with the regime, and the fact that a "large sector, perhaps the majority, of the population, albeit unorganized and difficult to mobilize, appear to have gone to the sidelines but potentially could throw its weight behind the opposition." Nonetheless, it cautioned, the obstacles to ending military rule remained formidable. First, "the decline in popular support for organized demonstrations [had] dispelled the urgency of negotiations," and the military was now less inclined to deal with a moderate opposition that had participated in what it termed "irresponsible actions and adopted confrontational attitudes." Second, though Chile's economy was vulnerable to internal pressures, there were no obvious access points that could be exploited to press demands for reform. Third, organized labor was "intimidated, fearful for jobs, [and] hard to mobilize." Fourth, the Catholic Church – the one avenue of influence Motley had identified and urged the administration to pursue – was calling for reconciliation and dialogue, had not sought to pressure the regime for "concrete political concessions," and so was easily dismissed as an instrument for change. Overall, the Embassy concluded, "the balance of forces has shifted in favor of Pinochet although not as much as the government appears to think."[63]

---

[62] Cable/Analysis, AmEmb Santiago to DOS, April 24, 1985, author declassified RRL.
[63] Telegram, AmEmb Santiago (Matthews) to Shultz, April 1, 1985, DOS/FOIAe, III.

Pinochet could certainly outgun his armed opponents, and he had managed to outfox the political opposition by directing its energies through the latter part of 1983 into talks with Jarpa and so away from the work of mobilizing grassroots social action against the regime. However, this did not mean that the junta leader could act with impunity, unencumbered by any constraints, for at least three key reasons. Given the "constitutional dictatorship" that the junta had created to help legitimate its rule, he lacked the formal power to reverse the growing independence of key institutions such as the courts. In August 1985, for instance, an investigation by appeals court judge José Cánovas into the brutal murders of three Communist Party members forced the resignation of Carabineros Director César Mendoza, a leading figure in the coup against Allende. His replacement, General Rodolfo Stange, did not advantage Pinochet insofar as the new director became an ally of Merino and Matthei in committing the junta to abide by legal norms. Furthermore, while Pinochet's position within the Chilean Army was unassailable – an estimated twenty-nine of the fifty-two serving army generals were considered as "hard-line unswerving supporters of the President," and their number included almost all generals "occupying troop commands or other key positions in either the army or the government"[64] – his junta colleagues were known to be defenders of the 1980 Constitution and its timetable for the transition, and increasingly nervous about Chile's international isolation and the effect this might have on the country's long-term economic welfare.

Lastly, although the regime could suppress popular resistance, it could not guarantee that, over the longer term, a movement uniting civic, trade union, and party groups would not emerge and effectively challenge its rule. Jarpa's ill-fated dialogue with opposition political leaders had, after all, lifted the public profile of political parties, even though they were still officially outlawed, and one of the most prominent party leaders, the PDC's Gabriel Valdés, remained willing to cooperate with left-wing groups, including the Communist Party, in support of strikes and street protests to put pressure on the regime.[65] Opportunities for U.S. policy makers to push for a return to democracy did exist, in other words, even if, for now, abandoning Pinochet himself was not an option. One high-level State Department official remarked, "We think it's important to

[64] Telegram, Theberge to Shultz, April 29, 1985, ibid.
[65] Handwritten notes, "AD & Gabriel Valdés," March 1985, March–June (II) 1985, Box 24, JDT Collection. Also see "Wavering CD Picks Leader," 10.

maintain a situation where we can talk to him – even if his response is unprintable."[66]

It was at about this time that Motley finally fell foul of his superiors. Having come under mounting criticism from both ends of Pennsylvania Avenue over his handling of Latin American affairs, the White House decided to replace him after the President received "a continuous and growing stream of critical reports" about his conduct and after the Assistant Secretary had given what was considered "flippant and indifferent" congressional testimony in support of Reagan's Nicaraguan contra initiatives prior to a crucial House vote on aid to these anti-Communist insurgents.[67] On April 30, Shultz announced Motley's resignation and offered the position to Abrams, who was looking to move out of HA.[68] That removed one opponent to new thinking on Chile policy and substituted, as head of ARA, a strong advocate of tackling the Chile problem in a more direct and forceful manner to encourage the transition to democracy.

The administration now stepped up both its public and private pressure on the Pinochet regime. On May 7, President Reagan issued a statement naming Chile, along with Nicaragua and Cuba, as an exception to the democratic tide sweeping Latin America. At the policy implementation level, the frustration over Pinochet's refusal to take seriously U.S. admonitions or prodding was palpable. "We feel that Pinochet's actions play into the hands of the extremists by creating a clandestine opposition which the Communists can control," said one State Department official. "In Chile," said another, "we have a choice between a dead horse and a snail. We've chosen the snail. But it isn't getting us anywhere."[69] Three days after Reagan's statement, the administration took the far more dramatic step of hosting an "unprecedented" meeting in Washington attended by senior State Department officials and a group of seven Chilean opposition

---

[66] Quoted in Doyle McManus, "U.S. Chile Policy Mired in Dilemma," *MH*, May 18, 1985, 5.

[67] Motley was also the subject of criticism from close U.S. ally, President Roberto Suazo, and other Honduran government officials over his alleged unpleasant demeanor, from the Nicaraguan contra leadership, who accused him of indifference to their cause, and from the Florida's Cuban-American community, for showing no interest in getting Radio Marti on air. Most senior administration officials were also mistrustful of his performance. See Action Memo: Executive Secretary to Shultz, "Dismissal of Ambassador Motley and His Replacement," "Amb. Chron Files: Aug 1985–Dec 1985," Box 26, JDT Collection.

[68] Note, "Motley Resignation," April 30, 1985, "May–June 1985, Vol. V," Box 25, ibid.

[69] Quoted in ibid.

leaders ranging from the moderate right to the moderate left. This was
the latest, and to date highest-profile, initiative in a State program to
fund regular visits by political party leaders to "participate in high-level
meetings" with senior Reagan officials.[70] It signaled that Washington
now regarded the opposition not simply as the object of repression but
as a possible alternative government. This had the effect of making it
"increasingly clear as to what side we were on," Abrams recalled, which
meant indicating to these individuals that the United States would no
longer mount an "ideological defense of Pinochet."[71]

In planning the meeting, Department officials ignored complaints from
Gabriel Valdés that he did not want to be in the same gathering with representatives of the center-right parties: the overriding objective was to
ensure that all of the acceptable opposition leaders received what would
be a "tough message" about the need to "agree on a common agenda
for engaging the military." Undersecretary for Political Affairs Michael
Armacost, who chaired the meeting, was instructed to tell the Chileans
that, given their present weak position with respect to Pinochet, they had
to be "more imaginative in the search for a transition to democracy." For
the same reason, it was important they not present the military with "nonnegotiable demands." This meant the opposition leaders must "resolve
[their] differences [and] work together," denouncing both left-wing terrorists and right-wing death squads and agreeing to open talks with the
junta based on the provisions of the 1980 Constitution "as a pragmatic
first step."[72]

Following assurances that the administration took its views seriously
and was committed to encouraging a political transition, Armacost told
the group that Washington's most immediate priority was to get the
state of siege (which had again been renewed in early May for another
ninety days) lifted. He referred to the "success" in the Philippines, where
the Department had urged the democratic opposition to unite to work for
what practical changes were possible, adding that "we gave this advice not
because we liked the Constitution they had to work with, but because it
was a place to start." He concluded his remarks by exhorting the group to

---

[70] Telegram, Shultz (Armacost) to AmEmb Santiago, May 10, 1985, State Department
Collections, FOIA released documents.
[71] Interview with Elliott Abrams.
[72] Memo, Motley to Armacost, "Meeting with Chilean Political Party Leaders," May 10,
1985, "Chron File: Chile 1982–1985," Box 16, JDT Collection.

maintain contact and to "work to disassociate themselves from the advocates of violence and non-democratic ideals," as these actions only "play [into] the hands of the [Pinochet] government." Abrams, who accompanied Armacost, told the Chileans that his nomination to replace Motley, along with the appointment of a new ambassador to Santiago, would not herald any weakening of support for Chilean redemocratization but that it would be necessary "to make compromises with the military" to achieve that outcome, as had occurred in the cases of Brazil and Uruguay. Although the opposition's frustration was understandable, Abrams urged the parties to pursue realistic goals by working "pragmatically for what is possible, accepting that it can be less than ideal," and promised that the United States would collaborate with them to achieve "that pragmatic solution."[73]

The two sides came away from the meeting with rather different interpretations of what had occurred. The PDC's Valdés left with the impression that U.S. officials "were concerned" about a transition to democracy in Chile in some abstract sense, "but nothing more."[74] When Armacost urged opposition leaders, once again, to cut all ties with the MDP and the Communists and accept Pinochet's 1980 Constitution as a basis for future negotiations with the regime, the Socialist Party's Manuel Antonio Garretón interpreted the request as, in effect, asking the opposition to "legalize the dictatorship."[75] State Department officials were, nonetheless, pleased with the results of the discussion. To Armacost, it "greatly served U.S. foreign policy interests in Chile."[76] The embrace may have appeared limited, said State's Chile Desk Officer, James Swigert. Yet, it was definitely a turning point: "for the U.S. government to make a decision to treat an opposition grouping as a serious player in an authoritarian situation was a big step."[77]

Four days after meeting the opposition leaders, Armacost tried to leverage some concessions from the regime. In discussions with Admiral Merino, he stressed the importance of Santiago and Washington

---

[73] Telegram, Shultz (Dam) to AmEmb Santiago, May 18, 1985, DOS/FOIAe, III.

[74] Quoted in Mimi Whitfield, "U.S. Takes Role of 'Neutral Power Broker' in Chile," *MH*, May 28, 1985, 5A.

[75] Quoted in Jackson Diehl, "U.S. Pressures in Chile Are Said to Fail," *WP*, May 28, 1985, A10.

[76] Telegram, Shultz (Armacost) to AmEmb Santiago, May 10, 1985, State Department Collections, FOIA released documents.

[77] Interview with James Swigert.

"work[ing] together to create the conditions under which the USG [U.S. government] can be helpful [in military and economic areas]." That would require the regime to take "concrete steps on the political transition and in the human rights area."[78] The Undersecretary had also been advised to put some none-too-subtle pressure on the ruling junta over Chile's negotiations with its twelve commercial creditor banks for an emergency debt financing package to cover the country's balance of payments deficit for 1985–1986. Without U.S. support, an ARA briefing memo indicated that the plan to have the World Bank guarantee commercial bank loans might not be approved and, as much as the administration desired to help, it "need[ed] some tools to work with." Foremost among these was the lifting of the state of siege. Washington, the memo suggested, "would welcome this step and [we] are prepared to be as helpful as we can on your financing requirements once this is accomplished."[79]

In mid-June, Pinochet did lift the state of siege and eased some restrictions on the press. Prior to that decision, the government had released all persons being held in indefinite detention and reduced the number in internal exile from 257 to 39. ARA was in no doubt that the perceived threat to key parts of Chile's 1985–1986 foreign financial package convinced Pinochet to adopt these measures, specifically a concern that otherwise loans currently being negotiated with the IMF and the private commercial Bank Advisory Group (BAC) might be voted down by the United States and other member countries.[80] A tougher stance, in other words, had produced results.

Twenty-four hours later, State's Nicholas Platt informed the Treasury Department that although the human rights situation in Chile remained "very poor and a source of great concern," it was his Department's view that "the deterioration brought on by the state of siege has stopped." On that basis, State had no objections to pending loan requests before the World Bank and its International Finance Corporation totaling $495 million.[81] Treasury, fearing Chile might default on its $20 billion foreign debt, agreed to ease its objections to the idea of the World Bank underwriting commercial bank risks, on the understanding that the

---

78 Telegram, Shultz to AmEmb Santiago on Armacost meeting with Merino, May 21, 1985, DOS/FOIAe, III.

79 Briefing Memo, Motley to Armacost, May 11, 1985, ibid.

80 Memo, Michel to Shultz, June 17, 1985, ibid.

81 Memo, Nicholas Plat, DOS to Edward Stucky, DOT, June 18, 1985, "Chile: Chron Files and Articles 1984–1985," Box 22, JDT Collection. Also see Memo, DOS, To Files, June 18, 1985, DOS/FOIAe, III.

original amount would be reduced to $150 million and tied to specific Bank-financed projects.[82] A senior Treasury official explained that his department did not want "to put Chile to the wall and play Russian roulette with the banks."[83] In July, IMF managing director Jacques de Larosière told a bankers' meeting in Chile that the country had been "up to date with its external financial commitments despite the serious difficulties it has faced" and that having "met deadlines and made progress," it deserved "the necessary resources to ensure it keeps growing."[84] The following month, Chile reached agreement with the IMF on a three-year loan program totaling $850 million, of which $750 million comprised special drawing rights from the IMF's extended facility. This emergency financial package followed news of Chile's success in negotiating new loans from commercial banks totaling more than $1 billion for 1985–1986, together with $300 million in funds for a highway project (of which $150 million was guaranteed by the World Bank).[85]

Without consulting Congress, the White House decision to support World Bank cofinancing for Chile almost immediately after the state of siege had been lifted made mute any determination as to whether the regime was still engaged in a recurring pattern of gross human rights violations as required by law. This triggered a sharp response from the anti-Pinochet forces on Capitol Hill. Their most prominent spokesman, Senator Edward Kennedy, took "strong exception" to Treasury Secretary James Baker's view that merely lifting the state of siege constituted significant progress toward improving the human rights situation, observing that forty-eight hours was "hardly adequate time" for executive directors to assess whether improvements had taken place, let alone that a positive shift in the pattern of state behavior had occurred.[86] Over the next six months, legislators' concerns about human rights in Chile received

---

[82] "World Bank to Ease Chile's Debt Problems," *SFC*, June 21, 1985, 40; Martin Mittelstaedt, "World Bank Okays Loan to Chile," *TGM*, June 21, 1985, B11; James. L Rowe Jr., "Banks to Lend Chile $1 Billion," *WP*, June 29, 1985, D1, D2.

[83] Quoted in S. Karene Witcher, "U.S. Backs Plan by World Bank for Chile Loans," *WSJ*, July 1, 1985, 16.

[84] Quoted in Carlos Portales, "DE 1985 a 1986: Estados Unidos y la Transición a la Democracia en Chile," *CONO SUR* 5, no. 2 (1986): 4.

[85] "International Report: IMF Approval," *TGM*, August 20, 1985 (Factiva); "IMF Formally Approves Loan Program for Chile," Dow Jones, August 16, 1985 (Factiva). Chile signed formal agreements with its commercial bank creditors for $1.1 billion later that same year. See Peter Montagnon, "Chile Signs 1 Billion Loan Accord with Bankers," *FT*, November 2, 1985 (Factiva).

[86] Letter, Senator Edward Kennedy to Secretary of Treasury, James Baker, December 9 1985, DOS/FOIAe, III.

powerful validation. Between June and December, the Chilean Human
Rights Commission documented almost thirty-four hundred victims of
arrests, internal exile, torture, and violent deaths, which Tom Harkin
observed was "hardly a significant change" compared with the state of
siege period.[87]

Divergent Outlooks

If Pinochet's decision to lift the state of siege encouraged U.S. officials, the
reelection of Gabriel Valdés as PDC President in June drew the opposite
reaction. Valdés, said Elliott Abrams, was "certainly viewed as not particularly friendly to us."[88] At the 1983 inauguration of Argentine President
Raúl Alfonsín, Langhorne Motley was told by Valdés "in essence that the
U.S. should take military [action] against Chile."[89] James Theberge had
junked his earlier positive assessments and now labeled Valdés "the single major obstacle to the unification of the democratic, anti-communist
forces, and to a negotiated transition with the armed forces," blaming
the "political paralysis and incoherence" of the democratic opposition on
the "anachronistic and destructive attitudes of the left-wing of the PDC,"
which the Ambassador attributed primarily to its leader.[90] This changed
view of Valdés was mirrored in Washington, where he was now basically
regarded as erratic, obstructionist, and uncooperative. This assessment
was only reinforced by his determined prodding of Congress for harsher
sanctions against Pinochet – which made life more difficult for the administration in its attempt to formulate a nuanced policy approach. Deputy
Secretary of State for South America Robert Gelbard went so far as to
accuse the PDC President of responsibility for Pinochet's machinations,
of living "in a time warp" and representing "a different kind of politics"

---

[87] U.S. Congress, House, Committee on Banking, Finance and Urban Affairs, Subcommittee
on International Development Institutions and Finance, *Human Rights and U.S. Voting
Policy in the Development Banks: The Case of Chile*, 99th Cong., 1st Sess., December 5,
1985, 6. U.S. officials were more enthused by the reports of the UN Special Rapporteur
for Chile, Fernando Volio, which put the best possible face on the regime's depredations
against the civilian population, including a preparedness "to accept at face value the
regime's claim that terrorism was impeding democratization." Ensalaco, *Chile under
Pinochet*, 172. In a November memo to the USUN mission in New York, the Secretary
of State's office praised the "balanced approach" of Volio's latest assessment, which
"avoids the rhetorical excesses of past reports." Telegram, Shultz (Whitehead) to USUN
Mission, New York, November 20, 1985, DOS/FOIAe, III.
[88] Interview with Elliott Abrams.
[89] Interview with Langhorne Motley.
[90] Note, "PDC Party in PP Era," February 1985, "January–March 1985, Vol. 1, 1985,"
Box 24, JDT Collection.

that would not "get through the legalistic hurdles and strictures that Pinochet and his team had assembled."[91]

Most recently, Valdés had provoked Washington's ire by initially resisting the State Department's strategy of meeting with the Chilean political opposition as a group. Most AD leaders held Valdés personally responsible for the disarray within that loose network of opposition parties as well as for the earlier collapse of the negotiations with Jarpa. Indeed, wrote Theberge, he was "widely distrusted by all sectors, even in the PDC, not least due to his insistence that communists be allowed to participate in any transition process."[92]

These judgments concerning Valdés's personality and political flaws conveniently overlooked a number of salient facts: Pinochet himself was ultimately responsible for scuttling the Jarpa-AD dialogue; and the Communist Party's historic commitment to, and participation in, Chile's pre-1973 democratic polity. It helped create the Popular Front coalition that won the 1938 presidential election; in 1946, party members were allocated three portfolios in the first cabinet of Gabriel González Videla's Radical Party government; and it was a senior partner in the democratically elected Unidad Popular that governed Chile from 1970 to 1973. In addition, Valdés's reelection as PDC President by a wide margin cast great doubt on the alleged significant opposition his actions had generated among his own party colleagues. American perceptions, to put it simply, did not necessarily reflect Chilean ones on the issue.

Nonetheless, Washington's problems with the Chilean opposition went beyond one man or even one party. Secretary of State Shultz had already exhibited his frustration over the inability of the democratic opposition to transform itself into a structured and coherent movement and sever all ties with the Communists.[93] In a June communiqué, the Santiago Embassy put it in more erudite language: the relationship between the so-called democratic parties and the radical left was both "the litmus test and the Gordian knot of Chilean politics." Until the knot was severed or undone, "it is difficult to see significant progress in the democratic transition in Chile." It was unclear if, or when, this might happen given the reluctance on the part of the acceptable opposition "to burn their bridges" to the left social movements because of the latter's key role in keeping pressure on the regime.[94]

[91] Interview with Robert Gelbard.
[92] Handwritten notes, "AD & Gabriel Valdés," March 1985.
[93] U.S. Congress, House, *Foreign Assistance and Related Programs Appropriations for 1986, Part 3,* 285.
[94] Telegram, Theberge to Shultz, June 27, 1985, DOS/FOIAe, III.

For all the professed concern about the radical left, few U.S. officials believed it posed an immediate or significant threat. At most, remembered Motley, there was less a "concern" with the reemergence of the left than merely "awareness" of that possibility.[95] DCM George Jones felt "there wasn't much of a far left on the scene" at all when he arrived in Santiago in early 1985. The majority of their traditional leaders "were either dead or in exile," and the latter had lost all influence because they had been out of the country for so long. Those who had remained "turned out to be very moderate."[96] Nor did soon-to-be-appointed Ambassador Harry Barnes recall being excessively preoccupied with the need "to ward off something like a threat from the left."[97]

The neoconservatives held similar views. Elliott Abrams, in dismissing any serious threat from the radical left, took as further evidence the AFL-CIO's preparedness to vouch for the union movement: "If George Meany says to you 'We're working with this group of trade unions in Chile and they're our kind of people' the notion that they are all communist becomes ludicrous."[98] Likewise, the Assistant Secretary for Human Rights, Richard Schifter, saw no evidence that the Communist Party had reemerged as a "major or significant" political presence to the extent that it posed any kind of new and fundamental challenge to U.S. interests.[99]

Even Robert Gelbard, whose constant theme in meetings with Chilean politicians was the imperative to sever all ties with the Communists and the radical left, dismissed as sheer nonsense the argument of NSC staffers that the Communists presented a serious threat to the interests of the United States and its allies inside Chile. At best, the threat was "marginal"; the real concern was that Pinochet's obdurate behavior risked making it less so over time.[100] State's more pressing concern lay elsewhere: if the moderate political parties did not see more progress toward democracy relatively soon, they might "line themselves up with the more radical" elements in ways that might present a serious problem down the track.[101]

---

[95] Interview with Langhorne Motley. At its 1984 National Conference, the Communist Party reaffirmed its commitment to all forms of struggle. See "PCCH Holds National Meeting, Issues Conclusions," *FBIS: DR: LA*, June 14, 1984, E6.
[96] Interview with George F. Jones.
[97] Interview with Harry G. Barnes.
[98] Interview with Elliott Abrams.
[99] Interview with Richard Schifter.
[100] Interview with Robert Gelbard.
[101] Confidential telephone interview 2. Strengthening this perception was the nature of the 1983–1984 popular mobilizations. Aside from its ideological aversion to "Marxists" and "Marxism" – which explained much of the regime's targeted repression – the junta

These U.S. perceptions of the Chilean political landscape struck many opposition leaders as misguided because they took little account of Chile's historic political culture, which was closer to the European experience of social democracy, with its multiplicity of parties ranging from right to left, making and unmaking tactical alliances to achieve their ends, than it was to the American model of a stable two-party electoral system operating within a much narrower spectrum of ideological and class differences. Washington "didn't understand the Latin American culture which is highly ideological and collective," said Gabriel Valdés, because its own political culture is "more individualistic."[102] The Socialist Party's Ricardo Núñez echoed this view: U.S. officials simply "didn't have the conceptual tools to understand the process" being played out in Chile and were particularly hostile to the idea of social transformation through democratic means (e.g., what Eurocommunism was offering) as a legitimate and responsible expression of a left-wing politics.[103]

While opposition party leaders abhorred violence, were mindful of protecting their largely middle-class interests, and sought to maintain control over any mass-based, lower-class challenge to the regime, they nonetheless remained convinced that popular mobilization was the strongest means available for bringing pressure to bear on Pinochet to implement reforms. They were fully aware that Chilean politics were being conducted in the abnormal circumstances of a repressive regime, which necessitated a range of tactics beyond the kind of roundtable negotiations that had so far proven fruitless. Beyond that, opposition leaders remained highly suspicious of Pinochet's intentions and of the practical, long-term consequences of the 1980 Constitution. Given the Reagan administration's sharp break with Jimmy Carter's approach to the Chilean junta, its early

had implemented a development strategy based on creating the optimal conditions for private domestic and foreign capital to flourish. A key prerequisite for the success of this economic model was a compliant and disciplined labor force. Another plank of the strategy was the sort of economic restructuring that produced a large pool of displaced workers and peasants in the burgeoning urban fringes or *poblaciónes*, and their demands, voiced in large measure by disgruntled youths, were more far-reaching than those of employed Chilean workers. The participation of these angry unemployed young men in the 1983–1984 street demonstrations created a growing momentum for socioeconomic change well beyond the limited electoral demands of the professional political class – threatening much more than the protected democracy that the Pinochet leadership was intent on entrenching in Chile. See Pollack, *New Right in Chile*, 86; James Petras, "State Terror and Social Movements in Latin America," *International Journal of Politics, Culture and Society* 2, no. 3 (1989): 203–204.

[102] Interview with Gabriel Valdés.
[103] Interview with Ricardo Núñez.

embrace of Pinochet, and its ongoing willingness to deal with the regime on various levels, they were just as uncertain about Washington's new-found commitment to democratic change. The effect was to further isolate U.S. officials from the key opposition political players inside Chile. The emergence of the National Accord in mid-1985 showed just how wide that gulf had become.

The National Accord

In July, State Department officials were still mulling over what lessons could be drawn from the Motley visit to Santiago. In a memo to newly appointed Assistant Secretary for Inter-American Affairs Elliott Abrams, the Director of the Southern Cone Office, Michael Durkee, conceded that the visit "was probably a net plus for Pinochet," bemoaned the political parties' failure to take "constructive advantage [of the] opening created" by the June lifting of the state of siege, and proposed a series of actions designed to accelerate the redemocratization process. The first order of business, he suggested, should be to take advantage of the arrival of a new Ambassador – Harry Barnes – to bolster the pro-transition political parties and to send a clear signal to the armed forces that the Department was determined to promote a return to civilian rule, which, it was hoped, would increase institutional pressure on Pinochet. The message must be that it is no longer "business as usual." Above all, "we need to avoid allowing the GOC to set our agenda for us in the way Pinochet maneuvered the Motley visit." Durkee advised Abrams to consult with key European allies and encourage them to apply pressure on the moderate political parties to overcome their disunity or risk financial sanctions, and to get their own left-wing parties to put pressure on the Chilean Communist Party to eschew terrorism, "i.e., to put the onus of Communist violence on the Europeans." Abrams's agenda should include a visit to the Vatican "to review the situation and seek Church support." This could provide a "backdoor" attempt to energize Fresno (elevated to a Cardinal in May), who clearly required "further motivation and direction." Lastly, there needed to be a more aggressive effort to cultivate support among conservative legislators on Capitol Hill.[104]

Much of the sentiment in Durkee's memo echoed a discouraging report on the situation in Chile prepared by Theberge earlier that month, in which the outgoing Ambassador highlighted the disunity plaguing the

---

[104] Memo, Durkee to Abrams, July 23, 1985, DOS/FOIAe, III.

moderate opposition sectors – ranging from personal conflicts to flawed leadership to incompatible ideological outlooks to the absence of consensus on relations with the Communists and their allies. Only the Church appeared capable of wielding any political influence, wrote Theberge, but "it moves cautiously and its influence is limited."[105] This repeated an April assessment of the Church as an unlikely agent for democratic change and compounded an earlier Embassy report that Fresno felt divisions between dissident and moderate bishops within the Catholic hierarchy meant that the Church "cannot afford to lead the kind of anti-government crusade that was carried out under Cardinal [Jaime] Sin of the Philippines." A further constraint on an activist clergy was the influential role played by the fervently anticommunist Papal Nuncio, Archbishop Angelo Sodano, who was instrumental in shifting the balance of power within the Church in favor of the conservative bishops.

Despite these assessments, following a series of compromises thrashed out among Chilean opposition leaders and brokered by Cardinal Fresno, eleven parties from the center-right to the center-left signed an Acuerdo Nacional (National Accord for a Transition to Full Democracy) – an initiative that caught the Embassy, and thus Washington, completely unaware. The participation of the pro-government Renovación Nacional (National Union), and other conservatives who supported democratization but were more flexible than most opposition parties regarding the transition timetable, gave the accord a more conservative flavor than its AD counterpart. The document essentially incorporated General Matthei's earlier preconditions for a renewal of a dialogue between the government and the political opposition: it excluded any role for the radical left; did not demand Pinochet's immediate resignation; accepted the need for a transition government; ruled out bringing military officers to account for political crimes; and agreed to the basic parameters of the authoritarian 1980 Constitution. The accord stopped short of accepting all of the key components of Pinochet's staggered and carefully controlled transition plan, insisting on direct presidential elections and calling for a stronger, elected Congress. It also papered over unresolved tactical divisions among its signatories. Some Socialist Party members together with left-leaning Christian Democrats, argued that street protests had made the accord possible and must continue to keep pressure on the regime to fulfill its end of the transition bargain; conservatives and moderate

---

[105] Telegram, Theberge to Shultz, "Ambassador Meets with Cardinal," July 11, 1985, LAAD, NSC, Chile-1985 (5), Box 91713, RRL.

Christian Democrats argued that further demonstrations and protests would only cause the regime to become more defensive.[106] While the accord constituted a shaky coalition, and was viewed in some quarters as little more than a statement of principles, it potentially constituted the most encouraging force for change since the 1973 coup and, if nothing else, revealed how politically isolated Pinochet was becoming. At the same time, it represented an important, albeit tentative, sign that the moderate opposition had resigned itself to work with the junta's own road map back to a protected democracy.

The Reagan administration greeted the accord initiative as a positive step forward. Although it could take little credit for the breakthrough, meetings with leaders of six center-right parties buoyed State Department officials, who described the agreement as a laudable and "pragmatic" step. "We've been hammering at the opposition for months to get their act together," observed one U.S. diplomat. "It's nice to have something positive to talk about for a change."[107] Another praised this "new political voice on the scene," providing a "time-limited" opportunity to accelerate the transition process. In a broader sense, the National Accord "changed the political dynamic" in Washington, said Chile Desk Officer James Swigert. No longer did officials say, "'Oh the opposition just can't get their act together: they just can't agree, so who is it that we should support?'"[108] Elliott Abrams responded with a mixture of optimism and cautiousness. Although Pinochet remained "very much in control," the momentum had shifted to the democratic opposition with the lifting of the state of siege, the decision by conservative groups to support the center-right transition movement, and "growing military interest in reaching a consensus with civilians." Chile was now either "on the verge of a new opening or poised for another political crackdown." The important point was that, no matter what the outcome, the "gridlock which previously paralyzed any effective action by moderates has been broken."[109]

In a memo to the White House, Shultz was mildly optimistic that the accord might ease Pinochet's "intransigent" stance over the political transition issue and thus arrest the further polarization of Chilean society. The document's main virtue was an acceptance of the junta's key

---

[106] Constable and Valenzuela, *A Nation of Enemies*, 292.
[107] Quoted in Pamela Constable, "Thaw Seen in Relations between US, Chile Diplomats," *BG*, September 17, 1985, 3.
[108] Interview with James Swigert.
[109] Memo, Abrams to Shultz, September 1, 1985, DOS/FOIAe, III.

demands: excluding a role for the Communist Party; supporting a "legitimate" post-transition role for the armed forces; affirming a commitment to private property; and approving the 1980 Constitution.[110] Chilean Ambassador Errázuriz was sufficiently disturbed by what he perceived as a "new, sharper tone" in Washington's pronouncements on Chile and increased support of the opposition that he warned Abrams this shift "could jeopardize the 'new dynamic' unfolding in Chile since the lifting of the state of siege." Although the administration considered the accord "a major advance," Abrams assured Errázuriz, this did not imply a closer embrace of the opposition viewpoint.[111]

Excluded from the agreement, the Communist Party reaffirmed its call for nationwide demonstrations against the regime to mark the fifteenth anniversary of Allende's election on September 4, 1970. Demands for a return to civilian rule, together with protests over high-level unemployment and underemployment, declining wage levels, and falling living standards, combined to produce the largest antiregime protests since fall 1984. Pinochet responded in his usual heavy-handed fashion, and hundreds of demonstrators were arrested as a result of violent clashes with police in Santiago, Antofagasta, and other major cities.[112] The dictator renewed the state's emergency powers for six months and then further aggravated the situation by dismissing the National Accord signatories out of hand. "We are separated by irreconcilable differences," he declared, which "cannot be reconciled through mutual concessions or through giving our complete trust to those who seek to deceive us."[113] A government communiqué did concede that the accord included one "very significant" provision that excluded "Marxism and its dissociating actions," with the caveat that it did not consider this exclusion "totally clear."[114] Pinochet himself later acknowledged that some of the accord partners might have contributions to make to the nation's institutional development if they could demonstrate that they were interested in more

[110] Memo, Shultz to President, September 3, 1985, ibid.
[111] Telegram, Shultz to AmEmb Santiago, "Errázuriz's Sept Call on Abrams," September 27, 1985, LAAD, NSC, Chile-1985 (5), Box 91713, RRL.
[112] See James L. Rowe Jr., "6 Killed, 567 Arrested in Chilean Protests," *WP*, September 6, 1985, A25; "6 Die, 577 Arrested in Protest Demonstrations," *FBIS: DR: LA*, September 6, 1985, E1; "Demonstrations in Antofagasta," *FBIS: DR: LA*, September 1985, E4.
[113] "Pinochet Comments on National Accord Document," *FBIS: DR: LA*, August 29, 1985, E1.
[114] "Government Communiqué Replies to National Accord," *FBIS: DR: LA*, September 5, 1985, E5.

than "just the mere conquest of power."[115] Overall, however, it was clear that the National Accord had made little impression on Pinochet, much less on his transition plans. According to the Embassy's George Jones, the Chilean leader told Cardinal Fresno that "'we have turned a page,' meaning [the accord] was a closed book and he had no intention of doing anything about it."[116]

Architects of Washington's "New Policy"

By mid-1985, Secretary of State George Shultz was coming around to the view that a democratic Chile was within reach. Both he and Reagan were of one mind that "foreign policy had to start in your neighborhood," and Chile was one backyard Shultz knew particularly well. For years he had been President of the Bechtel Corporation, an engineering, construction, and management services company with numerous interests in Chile, and a University of Chicago professor, where he contributed his expertise to the U.S. Agency for International Development (AID) program for Chile and trained a cohort of Chilean PhD economics candidates (the so-called Chicago Boys), who returned to take up positions in the Pinochet government. Shultz's passionate belief in the notion that "economic openness tends to bring about political change" gave him an ongoing interest in Chile's economic development and an ever-increasing sense of frustration that, under Pinochet, the nation's political development was lagging behind its economic reforms.[117] As the Secretary now began to formulate the new direction in Chile policy, a principal concern was to maintain the economic policy set in train by the 'Chicago Boys' because of a fear that "those economic policies would become discredited and it would be impossible to salvage them and maintain them, deepen and broaden them" the longer Pinochet remained in office.[118]

Elliott Abrams's focus on political change complemented Shultz's focus on economic enlargement. Abrams had been a vocal critic of the Carter administration for pursuing a human rights policy at the expense of a

[115] Quoted in Martin Andersen, "Pinochet Hits Opposition, Does Not Reject Its Plan," *WP*, September 12, 1985, A39.
[116] George F. Jones interview, FAOHC. Harry Barnes confirmed Pinochet's blunt message to Fresno. See "Text Used as Basis for Talks at Committee on Foreign Relations, Minnesota, October 6, 1986; Chicago, October 8, 1986; Notre Dame, October 9, 1986." "Speeches and Statements 1978–1986," Box 1, Papers of Harry G. Barnes.
[117] Telephone interview with George P. Shultz.
[118] Interview with Robert Gelbard.

"democracy policy" and dismissive of Carter's Chile policy as fundamentally flawed because it failed to advocate "institutional change" as a long-term solution to the human rights problem.[119] A common assumption among some U.S. officials at the time was that his commitment to democracy in Chile was somehow a trade-off for his leading role in prosecuting the administration's ideologically driven Cold War policies in Central America – that you had to "throw" the Democrats and those on the political left "a bone" to "stave off" attacks on White House support for the Nicaraguan contras and "what we were doing in Central America." Because the latter was of greater importance, "you could dump on Chile a little to protect your flank in Central America."[120]

Yet, in a very real sense, Abrams's thinking had remained fundamentally consistent. In both Chile and Central America, he was determined to resist the kinds of radical changes sought by nationalist movements and/or governments and champion instead right-wing or centrist electoral democracies or military regimes that might be encouraged to preside over acceptable transitions to civilian rule. In Central America, that meant rolling back the political gains of the left; in Chile, it meant short-circuiting the left's ability to make gains by preventing a repressive military regime from polarizing the nation in a manner conducive to a radical outcome. Whatever his motives, Abrams's strong anti-Pinochet sentiment created a "major problem" for those diplomats in Santiago fearful that too much pressure might be counterproductive.[121]

Because of Abrams's preoccupation with the Central American crises, much of the responsibility for implementing Chile policy was delegated to his key aide, Deputy Assistant Secretary Robert Gelbard, who acknowledged being given "extraordinary latitude" when it came to dealing with this Southern Cone nation.[122] The other diplomat who would soon become an integral part of this democracy-promotion team – the newly appointed U.S. Ambassador Harry Barnes – credited Gelbard as "the most important individual" in devising a new policy approach toward Chile during 1985 and 1986.[123]

---

[119] Interview with Elliott Abrams.
[120] Wade Matthews interview, FAOHC. Robert Gelbard emphatically denied that Abrams was playing Chile policy off against Central American policy. Interview with Robert Gelbard.
[121] Wade Matthews interview, FAOHC.
[122] Interview with Robert Gelbard.
[123] Interview with Harry G. Barnes.

If Shultz was going to relocate Chile policy along a different track, his choice of Ambassador to replace James Theberge was of crucial importance. The stonewall and cold shoulder treatment that Motley experienced during his February 1985 visit to Santiago reinforced the Secretary's growing conviction that Chile policy was "at a dead end" and that something had to be done to get the regime to move in the direction of democracy, however slowly. "We'd get promises [from the government] and nothing would happen," said George Jones. "So all these things influenced Shultz's decision that we've got to bring somebody in who will follow a different course."[124] Shultz "persuaded" Reagan to send Barnes, a career Foreign Service Officer and currently Ambassador to India. He was impressed by Barnes's ability to develop contacts with "people in all walks of Indian life" during his four years in the post, at times risking the Delhi government's censure in the process. This quality Shultz considered a "sterling recommendation" for the kind of diplomatic skills that would be required to deal with the complicated Chilean environment.[125] Gelbard was equally convinced of Barnes's talents, lauding him as "one of the very best, and maybe the very best person in the foreign service."[126]

At first, Barnes was reluctant to accept a less important diplomatic posting than the one he held but eventually was persuaded to accept the Santiago assignment for three years.[127] Conservative legislators, led by North Carolina Republican Jesse Helms, held up the nomination, reportedly because he and others suspected that in appointing Barnes, the White House was preparing a campaign to force Pinochet from power. As well, they viewed Barnes himself as too much of a liberal and desired to substitute a nominee more ideologically compatible with their (and Pinochet's) agenda. Shultz insisted on Barnes and wanted to send a clear message to

---

[124] Interview with George F. Jones.

[125] Shultz, *Turmoil and Triumph*, 971.

[126] Ibid. Two other Department officials played significant roles in implementing the new policy approach. One was DCM George Jones, in charge of the Embassy during the interregnum between Theberge's departure and Barnes's arrival, who continued to write astute assessments of the internal political situation in Chile. The other was recently appointed Assistant Secretary for Human Rights Richard Schifter, a neoconservative and formerly the U.S. representative at the UNHRC, who saw the political challenge in "exactly the same way" as Abrams and worked closely with Barnes during this period. Interview with Richard Schifter.

[127] Shultz had become "increasingly irritated at some of the idiotic ambassadors that the Reagan administration saddled him with" and eventually convinced the President to approve a policy limiting these appointments to a three-year tour of duty. Interview with George F. Jones.

Santiago that the U.S. Ambassador enjoyed his full confidence.[128] Awaiting confirmation, Barnes honed his language skills and consulted widely with Reagan officials and "everybody he could on the Hill" to get as accurate a sounding as possible on the expectations and limitations of policy toward Chile and "what parameters he could operate in."[129] Barnes's confirmation hearing before the SFRC gave no real indication of just how policy would change beyond the Ambassador-designate's vague commitment to "encouraging [a] transition back to democracy in Chile" based primarily on a continued emphasis on "private diplomacy."[130] What Barnes meant by "private diplomacy" was not necessarily identical with Motley's interpretation of the term. Gelbard identified the new thrust of Shultz's democracy strategy as all about "working with the legitimate opposition while delivering a message that we continued to support the economic policy [of the regime] and thought it was the only way to go."[131]

It soon became clear that any effort to reroute policy could not avoid a certain amount of bureaucratic resistance. Not even all of State's diplomats agreed with the proposed new policy direction, among them IO Bureau officials and the Southern Cone's Kim Flower. More formidable resistance, remembered Gelbard, came from the NSC Latin American specialists who opposed State's abstention or no vote strategy on Chile loans in the MDBs. This, in turn, created "a great deal of difficulty" in making sure that Treasury voted in accordance with the State Department's wishes in these institutions.[132] The Defense Department had its own reservations about the Shultz strategy. Initially at least, Abrams had occasion to complain about certain Pentagon officials, such as Inter-American Defense Board Chairman Lieutenant General Robert Schweitzer, who visited Chile in October 1985, where he "presented Pinochet with a sword and gave a speech clearly indicating his support for Pinochet in Chile's current internal disputes." In a letter to Assistant Secretary of Defense Richard Armitage, Abrams wrote that this kind of behavior was "inconsistent" with U.S. policy and only added unnecessarily to the administration's difficulty in "walking a tightrope by trying to maintain normal

---

[128] John M. Goshko and Don Oberdorfer, "House Panel Endorses Sanctions against Chile 'Deterioration' in Human Rights Cited," *WP*, March 21, 1985, A29.

[129] George Jones interview, FAOHC; interview with Robert Gelbard.

[130] U.S. Congress, Senate, Committee on Foreign Relations, *Official Transcript to Hear Testimony on Nomination of Harry G. Barnes to Be Ambassador to Chile*, June 17, 1985.

[131] Interview with Robert Gelbard.

[132] Ibid.

relations with the [Chilean] government while pressing it to hold elections and permit establishment of a civilian, democratic government."[133] Finally, the policy shift advocates had "serious difficulties" with UN Ambassador and Pinochet's close friend Vernon Walters. This lack of an interagency consensus fueled doubts among Chilean opposition leaders and a number of European governments about how "serious" the Reagan White House was about a change of policy and, more generally said Gelbard, "about what we were doing."[134] From the Embassy, George Jones cabled that "the appearance of a divided U.S. Government, speaking with contradictory voices plays right into [Pinochet's] hands" as he searched for "any straw of support" to justify remaining in power beyond 1989.[135]

The Chilean opposition received Harry Barnes's appointment with great enthusiasm. "When he arrived in Chile [in November 1985] everything changed," said Gabriel Valdés, who was one of the first prominent figures to meet with him.[136] Barnes himself described a more polarized reaction to his appointment: "I don't think I exaggerate if I say that there are some who feared that my mission was to 'boot out' the Government, especially after the fall of Marcos and Duvalier, and others who hoped it was."[137] Whereas Theberge had cultivated and socialized with a number of cabinet ministers, Barnes had a very different view of an ambassador's role and responsibilities, believing that the Embassy should communicate with representatives of all major political parties and organizations. Pursuing that approach, the Embassy political officer described Barnes's visit to the office of the Socialist Party leader as "sen[ding] shockwaves throughout the Pinochet government."[138] No one was quicker to appreciate the shift in Embassy strategy than Pinochet. Heraldo Múñoz described the junta leader interrupting the new Ambassador during the presentation of his credentials – the only time Pinochet met Barnes on a one-to-one basis – when the latter began talking about the need for democracy in Chile. "Don't come over here to interfere in our internal affairs," was

[133] Letter, Abrams to Armitage, October 26, 1985, DOS/FOIAe, III.
[134] Interview with Robert Gelbard. One official who found dealing with Walters particularly difficult was Richard Schifter: "Walters really hated me for my position on Chile because he felt that Pinochet was a good friend." Interview with Richard Schifter.
[135] Telegram, AmEmb Santiago (Jones) to Shultz, "General Schweitzer's Speech," October 24, 1985, LAAD, NSC, Chile-1985 (3), Box 91713, RRL.
[136] Interview with Gabriel Valdés.
[137] Keynote address, Florida State University, Miami, March 20, 1987, "Speeches and Statements, 1987–88," Box 1, Papers of Harry G. Barnes.
[138] Charlotte Row interview, FAOHC.

his vehement response.[139] This warning fell on deaf ears, according to Chile's Ambassador to Washington, Hernán Erráruriz, who subsequently accused Barnes of acting in a totally partisan manner throughout his tour of duty.[140]

Meanwhile, Pinochet had more pressing challenges to overcome. Back in September 1984, the junta had introduced a bill to establish the Tribunal Calificador de Elecciones (TRICEL), a special electoral court that would be responsible for the organization and oversight of future elections, especially the plebiscite on the presidency mandated by the 1980 Constitution. Over the vociferous objections of air force General Matthei in particular, Pinochet included a transitory article in the bill stating that the electoral court would be constituted a mere thirty days prior to any plebiscite. Despite continuing protest from the air force and the navy, this transitory article was replaced in July 1985 with a final article again severely restricting the operations of TRICEL.

Two months later, however, Chile's Constitutional Tribunal brought down a decision that would significantly alter the course of events over the next four years, ruling by a 4–3 majority that the first transitory article was unconstitutional and that the government had to enact further legislation to assure the constitutionality of the future plebiscite. In other words, TRICEL had to be fully in place, as did the passage of other laws on voter registration and voting counts, well in advance of the actual date to ensure the plebiscite's constitutionality. When the junta met to consider the ruling, Matthei insisted that it must be respected and later said so publicly. After a series of discussions, the other members finally agreed. To have rejected Matthei's defense of the Tribunal's ruling would have been to risk the integrity of the 1980 Constitution and, therefore, the legitimacy on which the junta now based its claim to authority.[141] On this tenuous basis, Chile's Constitutional Tribunal had assumed a major role in restricting Pinochet's ability to act with impunity in the conduct of the transition and in determining the legal framework of the proposed 1988 presidential plebiscite. While the Tribunal's decision significantly increased the possibility of a free and fair vote, Pinochet, of course, could use other legal – and illegal – devices to prolong his rule. But the stakes were now much higher and went to the heart of the junta's claim to

---

[139] Telephone interview with Heraldo Múñoz. The account of the meeting was given to Múñoz by a Chilean general. Ibid.

[140] Interview with Hernán Errázuriz.

[141] For a discussion, see Barros, *Constitutionalism and Dictatorship*, 293–302.

legitimacy. Again, the Reagan administration could take no credit for this decision, even though it now provided a clearer framework for devising measures to deter Pinochet and those around him from any temptation to thwart the transition process.

During late October and early November, junta members met with Pinochet to discuss the erosion of popular support for the regime. To stem the slide, they argued, he should not be a candidate in the 1988 plebiscite, there must be no reinstitution of a state of siege, and his "methods of operation and governing would have to change." Other proposals included amendments to the 1980 Constitution, an open presidential election, and a renewed engagement with the moderate opposition groups. The discussion produced "somewhat heated" exchanges without making much of an impression on Pinochet himself.[142] His response to criticism by the Church was just as combative, accompanied by increasingly terse verbal responses. Barnes described a document issued by the Chilean Bishops' conference denouncing "state-supported violence" (as well as the regime's economic program and foot dragging on redemocratization) as "bound to hit a nerve in a government which is already paranoid about what it considers to be the Church's opposition stance." A twenty-page letter from Cardinal Fresno in early November urging dialogue with the moderate opposition was reportedly "answered with a curt one-liner" from Pinochet dismissing the suggestion.[143]

In a November assessment of the prospects for a democratic transition, the Embassy's DCM George Jones spelled out the significance of these recent developments. Although Pinochet harbored ambitions to rule beyond 1989 and continued efforts "to divide and discredit" the National Accord, it appeared increasingly unlikely that he would succeed because he had "lost the political initiative to the Catholic Church, the courts which are investigating human rights abuses by the security forces, and an opposition which is invigorated by newfound realism, unity and the incorporation of part of the political right." The armed forces were still loyal to Pinochet partly because they could discern "no acceptable alternative to continued military rule." If that were to change, Jones wrote, it could well have significant consequences because of an emerging new reality: socioeconomic unrest and repeated human rights abuses were "eroding

[142] Telegram, Theberge to Shultz, "General Matthei Confirms That Junta," October 29, 1985, LAAD, NSC, Chile-1985 (1), Box 91713, RRL. Also see Telegram, AmEmb Santiago (Jones) to Shultz, "Junta Members to Ask Pino," November 7, 1985, LAAD, NSC, Chile-1985 (3), Box 91713, RRL.
[143] Telegram, Barnes to Shultz, November 21, 1985, DOS/FOIAe, III.

[the] military zest for governance." What the Accord potentially offered was "an honorable exit" from power, notwithstanding questions over the "durability" of the agreement given the "precarious commitments of some of its signatories to non-violence and no pacts with Communists" and their merely "tacit" acceptance of the 1980 Constitution.

Jones predicted an ever-widening gap between Pinochet and his three junta colleagues "over the issues of the pace of transition progress and the presidential succession" and thought it likely that "increasing disenchantment" with the head of state's plans would spread within the army itself.[144] He described Matthei as a "sharp guy" who wanted to acquire the most up-to-date air force equipment, "and it was absolutely clear to him that he wasn't going to get it unless Chile moved back to democracy."[145] Exploiting junta frictions was one of Barnes's major objectives, and whenever the opportunity arose, he would "try to divide the military commanders," in particular isolate Matthei and Stange, with whom he met "very frequently."[146] Assuming success in this endeavor, what they could contribute to Washington's objectives was problematic. Matthei himself acknowledged that he had "very limited influence on political matters [and] no idea what the President [was] thinking." Nor did he have any sense of the discussions taking place among or between other branches of the armed forces. "Communication among the services," he told Barnes, "is practically non-existent."[147]

The DCM reported that Embassy officials "would not be surprised" if Pinochet entered negotiations with the opposition for purely tactical reasons – to divide the opposition parties and diffuse popular discontent. While the Country Team "expect[ed] the government to continue its tactics of sequential hardening and relaxation of controls," they thought it unlikely that the regime would reinstitute a state of siege unless it perceived its "political survival" to be at stake. Above all, what most in the Chilean military now wanted was to create a stable and acceptable democratic government and then "withdraw but with [their] prerogatives intact," an amnesty from prosecution over human rights abuses, and "guarantees that Communists or Marxists will not exercise significant power in government again." The officer corps was aware that the

---

[144] Interview with George F. Jones.
[145] Telegram, AmEmb Santiago (Jones) to Shultz, November 8, 1985, DOS/FOIAe, III; interview with George F. Jones.
[146] Interview with Harry G. Barnes.
[147] Telegram, AmEmb Santiago (Jones) to Shultz, December 24, 1985, LAAD, NSC, Chile (09/25/1985–12/30/1985), Box 91713, RRL.

majority of Chileans desired a return to civilian rule and that "the prestige of their services is damaged by their association with government
performance." Until now, they saw no "acceptable alternative [although]
divergent opinions have begun to re-emerge privately" within a broader
consensus that, whatever the outcome, "institutional cohesion" must be
preserved.[148]

For a change, this was a generally encouraging Embassy assessment
after three years of relatively gloomy reports. But given the limited influence Washington had over events in Chile, the levers available to those
in the State Department eager to exploit these openings were restricted
to public and private diplomacy, decisions with respect to Chilean loan
requests in the MDBs, and efforts to enlist America's European allies
in support of democracy promotion. Even so, by the end of 1985, a
more consistent notion was emerging, at least within State, about how
to achieve a democratic Chile in which the center-right governed and
the radical left was marginalized from the centers of political power.
Shultz's instructions to Barnes provided a concise summary of the new
approach: relations with the Pinochet government, these read, were "correct and should be maintained." Nonetheless, U.S. interests would be
"best served" by a rapid and stable return to democracy accompanied
by the political exclusion of the Communist Party. Washington could
further these interests by working with the regime to facilitate its access
to World Bank, IMF, and private commercial bank funds, supporting
the adoption of structural adjustment loans (SALs) and "cooperating on
regional security to the extent practicable." Shultz then enumerated the
administration's principal objectives: to convince Pinochet of the depth
of Washington's commitment to democratization, which could only be
achieved through "political dialogue"; to make the same argument with
the democratic opposition, which required "non-violent and responsible
behavior on their part"; to reaffirm U.S. support for Chile's foreign debt
and domestic economic program, while retaining the option of applying
"economic influence to press the political process forward"; to actively
press the regime to improve its human rights record; and to expand and
deepen U.S. ties to Chile's military leadership.[149]

For the moment, American policy makers remained frustrated over
Pinochet's attitude and the opposition's erratic behavior: the former

---

[148] Telegram, AmEmb Santiago (Jones) to Shultz, November 8, 1985.
[149] Telegram, Shultz to Barnes, December 4 1985, DOS/FOIAe, III. Also see Letter, Shultz
to Barnes, December 3, 1985, ibid.

appeared as reluctant as ever to implement practical measures to hasten the transition process; the political parties seemed unable to devise a consistent strategy for negotiating with the military regime. During a November 27 meeting at the State Department with Abrams, PDC President Valdés "painted a bleak picture" of Chile's prospects and reported party rank-and-file "pressures" to continue participation in mass mobilization politics. In the circumstances, the PDC and the rest of the democratic opposition were effectively left with only one option: "to play various cards, including both mobilization and dialogue." The PDC, Valdés insisted, "could not concede the streets to others," which accounted for its decision to sponsor an upcoming protest rally to "preempt" a planned major demonstration by the left. Moreover, Valdés insisted that the PDC would not reconsider its support for the eventual legalization of the Communist Party.[150]

Pinochet's refusal to reconsider his transition timetable not only fed the reluctance of moderate antiregime leaders to jettison social mobilization politics; it also ran the risk of bolstering support for the radical groups and insurrectionist movements of the left at the expense of an acceptable opposition that had nothing to show for its willingness to compromise and dialogue with the dictatorship. U.S. concerns about this dynamic received short shrift from Chilean officials. In what the U.S. Ambassador to Colombia Charles Gillespie described as a "long emotional, finger-pointing monologue" during a bilateral meeting with Elliott Abrams at Cartagena in early December, Chilean Foreign Minister Del Valle objected to Washington's resort to pressure tactics to accelerate the transition to civilian rule. These were "worthless [and] counterproductive" because they would only harden Pinochet's stance. Del Valle particularly complained about Ambassador Barnes's decision to contact senior democratic opposition leaders and human rights activists soon after his arrival in Santiago and prior to meeting with junta leaders. Abrams responded that Barnes was simply following instructions and countered del Valle's unhappiness about U.S. transition pressures by noting that military regimes in Uruguay, Argentina, and Brazil had recently presided over "successful transition[s] to democracy."[151]

For all of that, there were still limits beyond which the United States was not prepared to go in pressuring Pinochet – some arising from the administration's desire to support the Chilean economy, others less

[150] Telegram, Shultz to AmEmb, Santiago, December 7, 1985, ibid.
[151] Telegram, AmEmb Bogota (Gillespie) to Shultz, December 6, 1985, ibid.

easily explained. Washington had shown its reluctance to vote against, or actively lobby to block, MDB loans to Chile; U.S. government credit guarantees for exporters to Chile were increasing (up from $31 million in 1983 to $110 million in 1985); and Eximbank exposure in 1984 (almost $115 million) represented a sevenfold increase in direct credits over 1982.[152] Politically, the White House registered limited enthusiasm for supporting the 1985 UN General Assembly resolution (drafted by Mexico) critical of Chile's human rights record because, "in tone and content," it made little allowance for the positive developments that had taken place inside the country.[153]

Conversely, the previous 12 months had deepened Washington's frustration over its seeming inability to influence or change Chile's internal political dynamics with the objective of getting Pinochet to take concrete steps toward a transition. But the combined impact of the National Accord, the Church's more active embrace of the need for change, the growing confidence of the Constitutional Tribunal, and the armed forces' declining enthusiasm for governing had given rise to new opportunities and possibilities. Frustration had gelled into a determination among key U.S. officials to relocate U.S. policy along a new track in ways that would have been inconceivable four years earlier. Washington's decisive, if for the moment subtle, break with Pinochet had begun.

---

[152] "Chile: Banking on Pinochet," *The Nation*, October 26, 1985, 400.
[153] Telegram, Shultz to USUN Mission, New York, December 6, 1985, DOS/FOIAe, III.

4

Changing Tack

By 1986, the Chilean dictatorship seemed out of step with a transformed regional political landscape, and the nation was led by what Secretary of State George Shultz now pointedly called "the odd men out."[1] Within the State Department, the debate over Chile policy had decisively shifted in favor of a more activist effort to prod the ruling generals to improve the human rights situation and accelerate the democracy transition process. Driving this new approach were Shultz, Assistant Secretary of State for Inter-American Affairs Elliott Abrams, his deputy Robert Gelbard, Ambassador Harry Barnes, and their bureaucratic allies, who were, in turn, being continuously pressured by Congress where dwindling support for the autocratic regime was evidenced by the defection of previously uncommitted legislators more and more annoyed by "Pinochet's continued intransigence and [the] persistence of severe human rights violations." Yet making Pinochet and his more conservative advisers appreciate Washington's commitment to this policy shift remained an uphill battle given a strong belief in Santiago that the regime still had the unstinting support of senior Defense and White House officials. This necessitated repeated messages to the regime leaders, often via Chilean Ambassador Hernán Errázuriz, that "there [were] no significant divergences within the administration on Chile policy" and that Ambassador Barnes had the President's unqualified support.[2]

---

[1] Quoted in Joanne Omang, "Shultz Puts Chile on List of Latin 'Dictatorships,'" WP, March 30, 1986, A18.
[2] DOS, Briefing Paper for Meeting with Chilean Ambassador, February 5, 1986, DOS/FOIAe, III.

Pinochet's refusal to deal with the National Accord in a way that might advance the transition to democracy had a number of significant implications. First, it provided further evidence – if any was needed – of his total refusal to compromise or bend to opinions other than his own. The Accord was not a perfect arrangement from the military's point of view: many of its signatories were divided by "old feuds and rivalries" and disagreed over some of the concessions the regime would have to make to warrant the opposition's full cooperation.[3] Nonetheless, those who signed the multiparty document had come close to accepting Pinochet's transition plan in full. They represented a broad coalition of Chileans, enjoyed the backing of the Catholic Church, and had the support of the United States and its allies in Europe and Latin America. Pinochet's rejection of the Accord made light of all of this and seemed to confirm suspicions that he was intent on ruling indefinitely. His response undermined the argument of conservative opposition leaders that further acts of popular protest against the regime were unnecessary, although recourse to the streets still threatened to create conflicts between the accord members and strengthen the case of those among them urging a tactical alliance with the leftist MDP, which was influential in precisely those sectors of the population – student organizations, trade unions, and the urban poor – that would need to be drawn on for popular mobilization.[4]

Although Pinochet's response to the National Accord came as no great surprise to those U.S. officials most involved in Chile policy, it was a disappointment and something of a reality check on the assessment made publicly by Abrams in December 1985 that Chile was "moving in the right direction."[5] The State Department had hoped that the Accord would offer a way of opening negotiations on a transition with those military officers keen to isolate the left by doing business with the political opposition and, ultimately, accelerate the military's return to barracks.[6] Senior Reagan policy makers repeatedly warned their Chilean counterparts that the regime's "failure to pick up the offer of dialogue with the democratic opposition in the National Accord... only plays into the hands of the extreme left."[7] If those warnings were heard, they could not be

---

[3] Constable and Valenzuela, *A Nation of Enemies*, 291.
[4] See Memo, INR Abramowitz to Platt and Rodman, February 14, 1986, DOS/FOIAe, III; *Newsweek*, January 10, 1986.
[5] Interview with Robert Gelbard; quoted by AP, February 3, 1986.
[6] See Cynthia Brown, "The U.S. Options Narrow in Chile," *The Nation*, September 20, 1986, 242–244.
[7] DOS, Briefing Paper for Meeting with Chilean Ambassador.

heeded without Pinochet's acquiescence. During an end-of-March meeting with a close political adviser to air force General Fernando Matthei, the Embassy's political counselor asked if the junta would agree to meet with Accord members "if they divorce themselves from the left and present a proposal that has clear legislative implications, appealing to the junta's legislative responsibilities." Reflecting Pinochet's viselike grip on the transition process, the adviser, a senior air force General himself, simply "had no answer." The only point he emphasized was how "essential [it was] that the U.S. position be crystal clear regarding an orderly transition to democratic rule and that [administration officials were] not planning to try to precipitate a crisis, as in the Philippines."[8] That was certainly not on Washington's agenda. Rather, U.S. officials would continue to try to mediate between the junta and the opposition – a decidedly different approach – but as the Embassy again pointed out, Pinochet would "continue to stonewall unless the opposition [was able] to undermine his vital armed forces constituency."[9]

A Difficult Year

Discussing the reluctance of the Reagan administration to "beat up" on pro-U.S. allies in the Third World because "you can end up with a lot worse," a senior official dismissed the likelihood of any dramatic shift in Chile policy. In contrast to the Philippines, where there was an acceptable national leader in waiting, "I don't think anybody has any idea what will follow [in Chile]."[10] In the midst of Shultz's spring offensive, some officials in ARA continued to advise caution in how the administration dealt with Pinochet. "This will be a difficult year, and we need to keep our powder dry for the right moment," Michael Durkee suggested to Abrams. It was hoped that over the next few months, a collaboration between democratic opposition leaders and Chile's Cardinal Juan Fresno would produce another negotiation proposal. "This will be the moment when we shall need all the influence available to us to push for GOC concessions, especially on electoral machinery and acceptance of a plebiscite to permit open presidential elections."[11]

[8] Telegram, Barnes to Shultz, March 11, 1986, DOS/FOIAe, III.
[9] Report, AmEmb, Santiago to DOS, April 1, 1986, ibid.
[10] Quoted in David K. Shipler, "U.S. Tries to Dampen Speculation over Ousters of Friendly Despots," *NYT*, April 20, 1986, 20.
[11] Memo, Durkee to Abrams, March 5, 1986, DOS/FOIAe, III.

Above all, Reagan and his senior advisers were determined to avoid any premature political upheaval that might force Pinochet from office without an acceptable alternative ready to step in and assume the reins of government. Chile was not comparable to the Philippines in the dying days of the Marcos regime when, in the face of massive opposition to the continuation of autocratic rule, Washington threw its support behind the popular (and elite middle-class) opposition leader Corazon Aquino in February 1986; nor was it comparable with Haiti where, that same month, the White House offered to facilitate the departure of Jean-Claude ("Baby Doc") Duvalier, who fled in the face of a sustained popular revolt that eventually prompted a military coup. Both of those regimes were on the verge of collapse when the United States acted. Pinochet's dictatorship, by contrast, remained firmly in control of the nation; had a substantial support base, particularly among the middle class; and had proved to be a reasonably competent manager of the Chilean economy. "Jabbing Pinochet with comparisons to Duvalier and Marcos," wrote Durkee, "may have less effect on him than on the opposition leaders, who are only too ready to believe that we can pull the plug [and see Pinochet fall]. If we want to point to lessons from Manila, we might explain the importance of a united democratic center which could attract military support as a credible alternative."[12] Although comparisons with the Philippines and Haiti were popular at the time, these transitions had no "operational" impact on U.S. policy toward Chile, insisted Elliott Abrams, because the country presented a different situation altogether.[13]

Taking no action that might precipitate an ill-timed transition in Chile, however, did not imply simply ignoring Pinochet's foot dragging on a return to civilian rule. During spring 1986, Shultz led a small team of State Department officials in what he described as "an unpublicized but tough fight within the administration to develop a dramatically different position toward Chile," the first fruit of which was the decision to sponsor a resolution critical of Chile's human rights record at the UNHRC March meeting in Geneva.[14] The final draft resolution, which hewed closely to the initial U.S. submission, calling for a halt to abuses by the Chilean police and security forces and the reestablishment of democratic institutions, was adopted by all forty-three UNHRC members. This was a major achievement. Yet there was no consensus within State as to whether

[12] Ibid.
[13] Interview with Elliott Abrams.
[14] Shultz, *Turmoil and Triumph*, 971.

this initiative represented a break with past policy. Assistant Secretary Richard Schifter described the final draft as "a significant step forward" and used few words to explain the U.S. decision to support a public condemnation of Chile, telling a Geneva press conference that the regime simply rebuffed efforts at quiet diplomacy.[15] Conversely, Executive Secretary Nicholas Platt reassured NSC Adviser Admiral John Poindexter (appointed December 1985) that this success in getting the UNHRC to vote for "a reasonable alternative" to the December 1985 UNGA resolution tabled by Mexico, Cuba, and Algeria "does not mean a policy shift or abandonment of private diplomacy."[16]

In preparation for a discussion of Chile policy with Reagan, and in light of the still less than enthusiastic White House embrace of any policy shift, Shultz was briefed by his department officials to stress to the President that "our objective was to preempt the harsh Mexican-Cuban resolution which normally passes, obtain consensus on a more moderate draft, avoid another U.S. negative vote with the minority and send a careful signal to Pinochet." If necessary, the Secretary could seek to ease whatever concerns Reagan might harbor about the UNHRC outcome by noting that "the political background behind our Chile strategy changed significantly over the last six months with the fall of the Duvalier and Marcos governments [and] what seemed like a cautious, careful policy in January now looks like [but should not be taken to be] a 'hit list' policy."[17] None of this, of course, related to the impact of the UNHRC vote. Abrams claimed that while it "caught the attention of Chilean authorities," Pinochet cried "Yankee intervention" and responded to Washington's criticism by ordering the junta "to hold up long-awaited action to legalize political parties."[18]

Convinced that the March UNHRC vote had sent a powerful message to the Chileans, the State Department now "became more insistent about the importance of democratic reform as well as economic performance." An extremely "upset" Pinochet government sought to counter this effort by exploiting perceived differences within the executive branch

---

[15] Quoted in Thomas W. Netter, "U.N. Panel Accuses Chile of Abuses," *NYT*, March 15, 1986, 5. Also see Bernard Gwertzman, "U.S. in Reversal, Faults Chileans over Rights Issue," *NYT*, March 13, 1986, 1, 5.

[16] Memo, DOS, Platt, to Poindexter, White House, March 13, 1986, DOS/FOIAe, III.

[17] Talking Points/Briefing Paper for Shultz, March 13, 1986, ibid.

[18] Memo, Abrams to Shultz, "Keeping Chile Policy on Track," undated, LAAD, NSC Chile (03/02/1986–03/18/1986), Box 91713, RRL.

and "appeal[ing] to their friends in the White House."[19] It was in this
context that the transitions in the Philippines and Haiti had relevance for
Chile policy – less as guides to what action the United States should take
and as reassurances that occasionally dictatorships can be replaced by a
more preferable arrangement. In Chile, "there was an alternative and it
was a moderate alternative," said Abrams. "This was an excellent case
for us of where we did not have that risk of a communist take-over."
Referring to those NSC staffers who were especially prone to downplay
the extent of human rights abuses in Chile, Abrams observed that "we
never really won them over, we never persuaded them. Dick Walters, José
Sorzano, Jackie Tillman kept to what you might call the Kissinger view:
'This is nuts, we're going to have another Nicaragua.' But, they were not
in control of the policy, Shultz was."[20]

Shultz himself insisted that Reagan "was blessing what I was doing."[21]
One example of the President's apparent support was a March 19 letter
to Pinochet explaining the administration's policy toward Chile. The
letter began by complementing Pinochet on his "historic achievement" in
preventing "the consolidation of a permanent communist beachhead in
South America" and ended by insisting that Washington's approach "will
remain fully consistent with the noble goals" announced by the junta in
September 1973. Later reports confirmed that these comments, together
with the overall tone of the letter, had pleased Pinochet. But there was no
mistaking the substance of Reagan's message, which noted "continued
indications of deep divisions within Chilean society regarding the pace
and nature of the transition" and defended U.S. calls for dialogue and
reconciliation on the grounds that they were intended to promote the
most rapid transition to democracy and were not about siding with either
the opposition or the government.[22]

Despite such instances of White House support for Shultz, other officials told a slightly different story. "All too often issues were covered
over and not raised to the President, and the President was not forced
to make decisions giving clear policy guidance," said Abrams of Reagan's foreign policy management style. "Reagan did give what I would

[19] Shultz, *Turmoil and Triumph*, 972.
[20] Interview with Elliott Abrams.
[21] Telephone interview with George P. Shultz.
[22] Presidential Message to President Pinochet, LAAD, NSC, Chile (03/19/1986–
04/04/1986), Box 91713, RRL. For Pinochet's response to Reagan's letter, see Telegram,
Barnes to DOS, "Conversation with General [Julio] Canessa," April 14, 1986, LAAD,
NSC, Chile (04/07/1986–04/16/1986), Box 91713, RRL.

call ideology or political guidance, which conditioned many of the wars that took place within the administration at lower levels. [This] meant that on an issue like Chile, you had to be careful how hard you pushed because you had the sense that the President wasn't fully with you. On Central America, however, you could push hard because you knew the President was with you."[23] Harry Barnes attended an NSC meeting on Chile during one of his recalls to Washington and was appalled by the quality of the discussion on Chile. "It revolted every professional fiber in him," said DCM George Jones. "Reagan was telling jokes and telling a long story about Mexico that had absolutely nothing to do with Chile." Jones was convinced that Reagan's "heart was not in pushing for reforms in Chile but the pro-democracy scene had become so solidly established that the apparatchiks were able to get things into Reagan's statements, and things he signed off on that were very pro-democracy and we tried to make every possible use of them in Chile. I don't think it fooled Pinochet at all, the wily scoundrel that he was: he knew perfectly well there were saboteurs who were damaging the true Reagan position."[24] Yet, as the Chile Desk Officer observed, "at the end of the day Reagan supported us and Ronald Reagan was as anti-communist as you could find."[25]

The other unresolved interdepartmental conflict over Chile policy concerned the U.S. position in the MDBs. Since 1981, the Reagan administration had resisted congressional pressures for a fixed voting position against Chilean loan applications in the absence of human rights improvements, preferring to make decisions on a case-by-case basis "so as to maintain the maximum tactical flexibility" for promoting U.S. policy goals.[26] In early January 1986, Assistant Treasury Secretary David Mulford, under pressure from Capitol Hill, requested that State review the existing policy on Chile loan requests, citing recent critical reports on the human rights situation and the regime's negative response to the National Accord as a missed opportunity to engage the democratic opposition.[27] Abrams reacted angrily to Treasury's request, suspecting that it was prepared to sacrifice policy flexibility on Chile to appease Congress and so

---

[23] "Transcript of interview with Elliott Abrams," 116.
[24] Interview with George F. Jones.
[25] Interview with James Swigert.
[26] DOS, Talking Points for call to Deputy Secretary of the Treasury, Richard Darman, February 2, 1986, DOS/FOIAe, III.
[27] Memo, Mulford, DOT, to Abrams and Schifter, DOS, "Human Rights in Chile," January 10, 1986, LAAD, NSC, Chile 1987 [January–February 1986], Box 91172, RRL.

secure future appropriations for U.S. contributions to the MDBs. "Blanket opposition to MDB loans to Chile," he charged in a memo to Shultz, "makes sense neither on domestic political nor on foreign policy grounds. But Treasury sees this issue only in terms of buying Congressional support for replenishment and ignores the fact that its actions are limiting our maneuvering room." Abrams also denounced the actions of other economic agencies for "complicat[ing] our efforts to carry out [a] policy of carefully calibrated steps to encourage a democratic transition in Chile."[28] Undeterred by these sentiments, the Treasury representative on the Interagency Working Group on Human Rights and Foreign Assistance raised the issue again at a meeting a few days later, asking for another review of the U.S. position on two upcoming World Bank loans because Mulford was "uncomfortable" in dealing with congressional criticism.[29] Such pleading left State Department officials unmoved. On the contrary, they proceeded to lobby the NSC's Admiral Poindexter that "Treasury needs to be told firmly now to stop their unilateral efforts to manage a foreign policy issue; otherwise, we may find ourselves on the defensive and less able to use our loan votes as carrots rather than sticks."[30] Abrams was emphatic that the administration "will continue to review MDB loans to Chile on a case-by-case basis."[31] Appearing before a House subcommittee following a request from two of its members urging action on Mulford's appeal, Chairperson Stanley Lundine (D-NY) described Abrams's demeanor as "very arrogant and very difficult."[32]

The NSC had adopted an equally inflexible position on Chilean loan requests – one of almost automatic support. This became clear after the SFRC passed 16–1 what the Council's Jacqueline Tillman described as a "fairly harmless" resolution supporting the National Accord and the renewal of a dialogue between the government and its moderate protagonists, only to have Jesse Helms (R-NC) cast a negative vote and insist on a full Senate vote with the apparent intent of resorting to a filibuster. "This is *SO* counterproductive," wrote Tillman in mid-March.

---

[28] Memo, Abrams to Deputy Secretary of State, January 10, 1986, DOS/FOIAe, III; Memo, Abrams to Deputy Secretary of State, March 19, 1986, ibid. In a memo to Shultz the same month, Abrams accused Treasury of "deliberate leaks to Congress of inter-agency memoranda on the loan issue." Abrams to Shultz, "Keeping Chile Policy on Track," RRL

[29] Letter, Durkee to Barnes, January 16, 1986, DOS/FOIAe, III.

[30] DOS, Talking Points for call to Admiral Poindexter, February 10, 1986, ibid.

[31] Letter, Abrams to Representative Doug Bereuter, February 11, 1986, ibid.

[32] Quoted in Mary McGrory, "Dollars and Dictators," *WP*, March 16, 1986, D5.

"The last thing we need is a full fledged debate on Chile." She was particularly concerned that a filibuster could end up in the passage of legislation "we have managed to stave off" to date that would force the United States to oppose MDB loans to Chile, thereby playing right into the hands of Treasury's David Mulford, "who would love to have [such] legislation [become law]." A filibuster could only add to the "difficult time" the administration was already having in "keeping everyone on the reservation on Chile."[33]

State officials knew they were up against vocal anti-Pinochet hardliners in Congress, many of whom "consider that we long ago reached the point where we should play our last card, put maximum pressure on Pinochet, and damn the consequences." But the Department and the Embassy continued to view blanket economic pressure as "the tool of last resort,"[34] insisting that automatic opposition to Chilean loan requests in the MDBs was too blunt a policy instrument and one that could prove highly risky to Chile's ability to service its international debt repayments (and thus the larger U.S. interest in discouraging a generalized Third World default). Durkee's advice to Abrams prior to an April 4 meeting with Susan Segal, the Chairperson of Chilean and Philippines advisory committees for a consortium of private banks, underlined this point: "stress our opposition to a policy of economic warfare against Chile" but emphasize that if Pinochet refuses to take "concrete steps" to facilitate an eventual regime change, "we can't rule out the possibility of a symbolic abstention [on MDB loan applications from Chile] later this year." More indicative of State's unwillingness to put serious pressure on the dictatorship was Durkee's comment that if forced to abstain, "we would choose a loan that we are confident would be approved anyway."[35] As long as the loans actually kept flowing, along with foreign investment and some disguised military assistance, Pinochet could live with such ineffectual quiet diplomacy. For the moment, and despite "new signs of unease in the White House about 'the direction of our Chile policy,'"[36] no one in the State Department was prepared to push for, or take, any step that could mean abandoning Chile to an uncertain future and, with it, U.S. interests in the country. Factored into this reluctance was the need to consider how

---

[33] Note, NSC, Tillman to Reilly, March 18, 1986, LAAD, Chile 1987 [May–December 1985], Box 91172, RRL (emphasis original).
[34] Letter, Durkee to Barnes, April 10, 1986, DOS/FOIAe, III
[35] Memo, Durkee to Abrams, April 3, 1986, ibid.
[36] Letter, Durkee to Barnes, April 4, 1986, ibid.

best to deal with the country's debt problem as well as the equally thorny human rights and democracy progress issues.

While the tug-of-war with Treasury continued over how to deal with the MDB loans, the outcome of a broader reconsideration of Chile policy by ARA in conjunction with Ambassador Barnes was a statement of "goals and objectives" approved by Secretary Shultz in mid-April. In a single cogent sentence, it stated what the United States hoped to achieve in Chile: "a peaceful, orderly process of transition to democracy as quickly as possible [mindful of] the effects and timing of our efforts toward that goal on our longer range goal of a successor government that is friendly to the U.S. and supportive of major U.S. interests." Anticipating the possibility of "sharply increased political unrest and instability and growing support for the extreme left" if Pinochet continued to tough it out, the challenge was obvious: "to make clear to the armed forces and to Pinochet that concrete steps in advancing the transition, such as legalization of the political parties and political activity, are in Chile's interest as well as our own." The statement then turned to the critical policy issue of "how to bring our influence to bear." In striking contrast to Nixon and Kissinger's ability to destabilize the Allende government with the active support of multiple forces in the state and civil society, with Pinochet, there were few internal instruments or levers at Reagan policy makers' disposal. Externally, the opportunities were just as limited, confined to votes at the UN critical of the regime's human rights performance together with U.S. formal and informal power within the MDBs. A decision to abstain or vote against Chilean loan submissions would likely have a major "psychological impact." However, this was a road the Secretary was exceedingly reluctant to go down: "economic pressure is our last, strongest and most risky card. Once played, if Pinochet trumps it by toughing it out and appealing to nationalist sentiment, particularly in the military, we will have nothing left in our hand. Timing will be crucial." Such considerations further reinforced the cautious approach to applying sustained pressure on the regime.

Amid this "bleak picture," Shultz singled out the National Accord as one positive political development. Not only did it include "a broad spectrum of the democratic opposition," it also signaled to the armed forces that it was possible to undertake a genuine transition dialogue so long as Accord leaders demonstrated "more concrete evidence" of a responsible commitment to negotiations. The United States had the opportunity to play a role in promoting this dialogue while, at the same time, having a strategy in hand "to maintain influence with the democratic opposition if Pinochet does not initiate a meaningful transition process." Included among the specific U.S. policy goals for 1986 was a wish list that left little to chance: getting Pinochet and the military to dialogue with moderate opposition leaders; reinstating limited military aid programs for Chile as a means of increasing Pentagon contact with the nation's armed forces; devising a strategy that linked the U.S. voting stance in the MDBs to the broader effort to advance the transition; maintaining support for the National Accord; encouraging Cardinal Fresno and the Vatican to actively push the transition process and exploiting the papal visit to Chile in early 1987 to this end; making clear to the democratic opposition "the importance of staying united, avoiding violence, remaining open to dialogue with the government, eschewing alliances with nondemocratic left, and widening their direct contacts with the military"; and eliciting European and hemispheric support for a return to civilian government in Chile.[37]

Another Challenge from the Streets

Unlike the National Accord, the formation of the Asamblea de la Civilidad (Civic Assembly, AC) in April by more than two hundred social organizations was not a development that generated much enthusiasm in Washington. The AC was a response to growing popular frustration over the lack of results achieved by those political leaders who had signed on to the National Accord, and it reflected a consensus that only mass mobilization politics involving cooperation among all political groupings could force the regime to make serious concessions – if not, in fact, to withdraw from power.[38] This gave rise to new challenges for the regime – and U.S. policy makers. It posed the biggest direct threat to Pinochet since 1973 by subsuming antiregime forces (political party leaders) into a much broader and far more radical antisystem front – and given his likely response, the possibility of plunging Chile into a new round of bloodletting, possibly even civil war. For another, among the ranks of the AC's grassroots sympathizers were hundreds of thousands of slum dwellers (*pobladores*) with

---

[37] Telegram, Shultz (Armacost) to AmEmb Santiago, April 26, 1986, ibid. Weeks later, Robert Gelbard made the same point during a discussion with Socialist Party International Secretary Heraldo Múñoz: "Sanctions are like a gun with one bullet; if you fire it then you don't have anything else to use." Quoted in Múñoz, *The Dictator's Shadow*, 158.

[38] James Petras and Fernando Ignacio Leiva, "Chile: The Electoral Transition to Authoritarian Politics," *Latin American Perspectives* 15, no. 3 (1988): 112.

an agenda for radical, class-based change.[39] A secret Embassy cable to the State Department reported that the democratic opposition was being forced to resort to more militant actions and, "in an increasing number of instances," was participating with the left social movements in antiregime protests, in the apparent belief that "strikes and demonstrations combined with foreign pressure will force Pinochet to relinquish power." Embassy officials were skeptical about any such outcome, contending that Pinochet was not vulnerable to this sort of pressure at least so long as his support within the military "remains solid," and even if he was persuaded to adopt a more flexible posture, the opposition lacked "the kind of clearly defined program that would allow it to take advantage of the situation." This was the nub of the problem: unless the opposition "demonstrates an ability to mobilize broadly-based anti-Pinochet sentiment and, thereby begin to undermine his vital armed forces constituency," Pinochet would continue to stall or obstruct all efforts to induce him to make the changes Washington desired.[40]

The prospect that the struggle against Pinochet might head in an increasingly radical direction appeared all the more alarming given the Communist Party's refusal to disavow the use of force and its declaration that 1986 would be the "decisive year" in which widespread acts of protest and sabotage would make Chile ungovernable and force the military from power.[41] In response to these developments, the State Department struggled to maintain what pressure it could on the dictator to take concrete steps toward a transition as private U.S. urgings to this effect continued to be ignored. Abrams cautioned Shultz that "keeping Chile policy on track during the period ahead will require careful calibration of actions and statements," especially in regard to MDB loan votes.[42]

In a typically forthright admission, Ambassador Barnes told visiting Congressman Bruce Morrison (D-CT) that "neither we nor anyone is certain how to influence Pinochet in the desired direction." This included the democratic opposition given its inability to reach a consensus on relations with the Communist Party and its increased protests that lacked "any clear purpose."[43] The State Department continued to exhort Embassy officials to apply pressure on the center-right parties to ease their demands as the price for cooperating with Pinochet's transition scenario, hoping

---

[39] See Petras, "State Terror and Social Movements in Latin America," 187.
[40] Report, AmEmb Santiago to DOS, April 1, 1986, DOS/FOIAe, III.
[41] See Constable and Valenzuela, *A Nation of Enemies*, 292–293.
[42] Memo, Abrams to Shultz, April 7, 1986, DOS/FOIAe, III.
[43] Telegram, Barnes to Shultz, April 10, 1986, ibid.

that this would induce the military to begin the necessary preparations for its return to barracks. What State had in mind were steps such as legalizing political parties, ending press restrictions, and reducing human rights abuses, together with the maintenance of a unified opposition that had broken all ties with the radical left social movements and parties,[44] expanded its links to the armed forces, and was open to any possible regime initiatives to dialogue.

Rejecting ties with the radical left applied, first and foremost, to the Communists. In briefing notes for a May meeting between Shultz and General Matthei, Abrams wrote that the Communist Party's strategy was to keep Pinochet in office as long as possible in the hope that "polarization continues and prevents military-civilian agreement," thus increasing its own chances of seizing power. This, said Abrams, was the basis for the administration's repeated warnings that the democratic opposition should not cooperate with the radical left.[45] To further limit this possibility, the NSC was "working on ideas to . . . isolate the members of the Christian Democratic Party who want to work with the Communists."[46] Reassuring the U.S.-Chile Chamber of Commerce that the administration was not blind to the interests of its members, Deputy Assistant Secretary Robert Gelbard informed them that the AD leaders had been told in no uncertain terms that Washington would withdraw all support for the National Accord "if Communists were brought into it."[47]

In his meeting with Shultz, Abrams, and Armacost, General Matthei gave a candid assessment of several leading Chilean officials most closely involved with, or members of, the junta. He portrayed Merino and Stange as men who generally agreed with him "but were reluctant to face up to Pinochet," offered a more scathing assessment of Foreign Minister del Valle ("a man with no influence on policy"), and labeled both Justice Minister Hugo Rosende and Government Minister Francisco Cuadra as "fascists." The only cabinet minister to escape criticism was Interior

---

[44] The idea of a "unified" opposition excluding sectors of the left was absurd, reflecting a limited understanding of Chilean politics and history. Furthermore, the idea of isolating PDC members who desired to work with the moderate, or even the radical, left was simply unrealistic. The parties of the right, the center, and the left all had deep roots in the democratic polity that existed in Chile prior to 1973. The radical left parties included the Communist Party, the MIR, and fractions of the Moviemento de Acción Popular Unitario (MAPU) and the Socialist Party.

[45] Briefing memo, Abrams to Shultz, May 13, 1986, DOS/FOIAe, III.

[46] Memo, NSC, Tillman to Poindexter. "Close Hold Luncheon with Chilean Air Force Chief," May 16, 1986, LAAD, NSC, Chile 1986 (1), Box 91181, RRL.

[47] Telegram, Shultz to AmEmb, Santiago, May 9, 1986, DOS/FOIAe, III.

Minister Ricardo Garcia, described as "intelligent and sincere in his attempts to get Pinochet to approve forward steps." As for Pinochet himself, Matthei expressed "grave concerns" about his "intransigence" and urged the United States to "keep up quiet pressure" to bring about a transition to civilian rule as this policy approach "seemed to be on exactly the right track."[48] This advice was significant because it demonstrated the contradictory nature of what U.S. officials were hearing from junta members with Merino, for instance, insisting that Pinochet would abide by the 1980 Constitution.

Back in Santiago, Pinochet was making it difficult for U.S. officials not to share Matthei's concerns by cracking down harder on his opponents. Beginning in late April, he dispatched police and army units to conduct massive sweeps in Santiago's shantytowns, ostensibly in a hunt for criminals, in reality to flush out "political agitators." In one such typical sweep of three shantytowns, all male residents were arrested and held in a gymnasium until their police and political records were checked and while security forces raided each of their homes. Although the head of the Carabineros, General Rodolfo Stange, insisted that the sweeps were being conducted without violence, the Catholic Church and the Chilean Human Rights Commission denounced them as an abuse of human rights that were contributing to a "warlike atmosphere" fueling violence throughout the country.[49] Such acts of mass intimidation deepened fears among centrist Christian Democrats and moderate Socialists that if they did not align in some way with those Chileans engaged in active resistance to the government, they might lose members and supporters to the more radical left. Officially, the Christian Democrats continued to publicly disavow any connections with the Communist Party and stand by the National Accord.[50] In practice, however, they were unwilling to decisively break all ties with the radical left forces, and party members continued to

---

[48] Telegram, Shultz, (Armacost) to Barnes, "Meetings with General Matthei," LAAD, NSC Chile (05/02/1986–05/23/1986), Box 91713, RRL.

[49] Quoted in "Police, Military Raid Santiago Shantytowns," *FBIS: DR: LA*, May 5, 1986, E1. Amnesty International estimated that from April 20 to May 25, fifteen thousand Chileans were arrested and held in short-term detention. See Jim Anderson, "Administration Disputes Helms on Rojas Case," UPI, July 14, 1986. Matthei described the raids to Barnes as another example of Pinochet's "craziness" that had produced "trifling results." See Telegram, Barnes to Shultz, Meeting with General Matthei, LAAD, NSC Chile (05/27/1986–06/02/1986), Box 91713, RRL.

[50] Christian Democratic Party Vice Chairman Gutenberg Martínez denied suggestions that the Party had formed a pact with the Communists, insisting that it had no political ties with any nonmembers of the AD and the National Accord. See "PDC's Martínez Denies Pact with Communists," *FBIS: DR: LA*, April 24, 1986, E3.

participate in organizing antiregime street protests and strikes by university students.

Similarly, the newly elected Secretary General of the Socialist Party, Ricardo Núñez, while careful to distinguish his party faction from the Almeyda Socialists whom he characterized as more orthodox Marxists and closer to the Communist Party, saw no inconsistency between his faction's membership of the National Accord and support for the Civic Assembly "because both are making a great effort toward unity, which does not have to be achieved under a single organization."[51] The same balancing act (being seen to be politically "responsible" as well as "representative" of opposition to the regime) posed a challenge to the AD. Although Ambassador Barnes was in no doubt that the AD had "changed its tone significantly" and was no longer seeking the "political rupture and ungovernability sought by the communist-led [MDP]," some AD leaders, frustrated over Pinochet's refusal to engage in transition negotiations, were openly speculating about a common strategy with sectors of the Marxist left as they searched for ways to exert pressure on Pinochet and the junta.[52]

After a May 27 meeting with Cardinal Fresno, the Embassy's George Jones cabled Washington that the head of the Chilean Church was "discouraged" and unlikely for the time being to want to try again to bring the government and opposition together.[53] What particularly concerned the bishops, said the Church's Vicar General for Pastoral Affairs Christian Precht, was "the growing frustration and desperation among youth in the shanty-towns leaving them open to recruitment to the far left."[54] Meanwhile, Abrams reported to Shultz that Pinochet's response to the earlier letter from Reagan expressing concern about human rights and democracy in Chile indicated that the General had not shifted from his "reluctan[ce] to allow a genuine transition to democracy" or take any significant steps toward compromise and negotiation despite "the signs of increasing polarization."[55] On the contrary, he "has become even

---

[51] See "Socialist Secretary Calls for 'Bloc for Changes,'" *FBIS: DR: LA*, June 11, 1986, E1.
[52] Telegram, Barnes to Shultz, June 26, 1986, DOS/FOIAe, III; Shirley Christian, "Pinochet Foes Weigh Link with Left," *NYT*, April 25, 1986, 3.
[53] Telegram, AmEmb Santiago (Jones) to Shultz, June 2, 1986, DOS/FOIAe, III.
[54] Telegram, Jones to Shultz, June 18, 1986, ibid.
[55] Memo Abrams to Shultz, June 4, 1986, ibid. That same month, 129 House Democrats wrote to Secretary of State Shultz urging him to sack Assistant Secretary Elliott Abrams after he lied to Congress that no third-party funds had been channeled to the Nicaraguan contras. Shultz refused to accommodate the request, even though Abrams's reputation on Capitol Hill had been badly damaged.

more open about his real intention to stay in office indefinitely [and will] continue to hammer away in public that the choice in 1989 is between his government and the Marxists, while doing his best to deliver a self-fulfilling prophecy." The most that can be expected are "some limited gestures" to give the appearance of a democratic process. This strategy, Abrams predicted, would almost certainly force the Chilean dictator to increase pressure on his military and government supporters "to fall into line... We will need to watch carefully for any signs that significant cracks may be developing in the army." If the past was any indication, Pinochet was unlikely "to blink first," which would probably render Matthei's effort to promote the idea of a "consensus civilian candidate" in 1989 a dead letter.[56] Abrams was now convinced that there was little the Reagan administration could do about Pinochet's ambition to hold on to power, with the possible exception of using MDB votes as pressure "and lobby[ing] others to follow the U.S. lead" in these organizations.[57] Pinochet's refusal to have virtually any contact with Ambassador Barnes added to Washington's frustration.

Barnes himself remained "pessimistic" about the ability of the domestic opposition to devise a strategy that could at one and the same time force Pinochet to the negotiating table and gain the support of the armed forces leadership. The Chilean leader's short fuse when provoked "and the opposition's ability to delude itself with protests alone," he told a June meeting of the Council on Foreign Relations in New York, would likely result in greater violence and a more polarized society.[58] At mid-month, Barnes had flown to Washington for a series of consultations which State's Michael Durkee later described as "extremely useful in keeping Chile 'on the screen' for Shultz and Poindexter." The Secretary now finally seems to have "woken up to Chile," Durkee wrote in a letter to the Ambassador. In answer to Barnes's question as to what "specific [transition] steps" the Embassy should encourage the Chileans to take as a quid pro quo for positive U.S. votes in the MDBs, Durkee was in no doubt that the critical factor was the "succession question," which now demanded private lobbying for a "constitutional change to allow open elections in 1989." This was more of a longer-term goal than "the 'key'

---

[56] Memo, Abrams to Shultz, June 18, 1986, ibid. Also see Briefing Memo, Abrams to Armacost, for meeting with Barnes, June 11, 1986, ibid.
[57] Ibid.
[58] "Notes for a Talk to the Council on Foreign Relations," New York, June 3, 1986, Speeches and Statements 1978–1986, Box 1, Papers of Harry G. Barnes.

to the MDB issue, [but] it would be helpful to lay down a marker now, even should we settle for less."[59]

With violence escalating, the regime digging in its heels, and the middle ground of Chilean politics shrinking rapidly, the AD attempted to seize the political initiative in late June by calling for free elections and the military's return to barracks. The AD reaffirmed its opposition to the 1980 Constitution as undemocratic and insisted that "an irrevocable decision must be made now to subject the country to the verdict of the will of the people first by re-establishing public freedom and individual guarantees and by introducing the necessary institutional changes." This did not mean any backing away from an agreement with the armed forces to achieve an effective transition to democracy.[60] Rather, it signaled a reluctance to completely jettison its two-track strategy of seeking negotiations while actively supporting the AC's efforts to mobilize mass opposition to the regime. Less than two weeks later, Chile was virtually paralyzed by a forty-eight-hour nationwide strike, accompanied by mass street protests which resulted in the arrest of several prominent AC leaders and more shantytown raids by the security forces.[61]

Assessing the Damage

This nationwide challenge to the regime raised the political temperature significantly and forced the Junta to reassess its hold over the pace and timing of any transition process. In the aftermath of the strike and street protests, the attention of many Chileans, as well as U.S. diplomats, was focused on Los Quemados (The Burned Ones): Rodrigo Rojas, an exiled Chilean photographer, resident in the United States, and Carmen Gloria Quintana, a local student and community organizer. Seized by an army patrol while constructing a barricade with other anti-Pinochet demonstrators on the first day of the July protests, they were doused with gasoline and set alight. The soldiers wrapped the burned bodies in blankets and dumped them on the outskirts of Santiago. Quintana, although

---

[59] Letter, Durkee to Barnes, June 26, 1986, DOS/FOIAe, III.

[60] In fact, Assembly leaders sent letters to various vice commanders of the army, navy, air force and Carabineros on June 27, urging them to open a dialogue with the opposition. See Telegram, AmEmb Santiago to Shultz, "General Strike (July 2–3) Review and Wrapup," July 8, 1986, LAAD, NSC, Chile (07/02/1986–07/13/1986), Box 91713, RRL.

[61] "9 Civic Assembly Leaders Sent to Prison," *FBIS: DR: LA*, July 14, 1986, E5; "Combined Forces Raid Santiago Slum 12 July," *FBIS: DR: LA*, July 14, 1986, E6.

badly disfigured, survived to allege that she and Rojas had been beaten, intentionally burned, and left to die by their captors.[62] In Washington, Abrams immediately called in the Chilean Chargé and emphasized the priority the United States attached "to a swift, thorough and impartial investigation" of Rojas's death (as well as the subsequent police/security forces disruption of the photographer's funeral). He reminded the Chargé that how the government conducted the Rojas investigation would have a major impact on U.S. policy toward Chile in the MDBs. On leaving Abrams's office, the Chilean diplomat told Desk Officer James Swigert he doubted there would be a rapid investigation of the deaths.[63] This prediction proved accurate. After three officers and twenty-two soldiers were arrested in connection with the incident and brought before a civil court, the judge declared that he lacked jurisdiction in the matter and handed the case over to a military court, where it was allowed to lapse until 1991.[64]

Against the background of the July upheaval and the Rojas killing, Ambassador Barnes cabled Secretary Shultz that a requested Chile strategy paper – one more comprehensive than his earlier statement of "goals and objectives" – had now been completed and reviewed with Elliott Abrams and Robert Gelbard, both of whom concurred with its conclusions and suggested approach. This paper, once adopted, would essentially become the blueprint for Washington's policy toward Chile over the next two years. It was based on several key assumptions: first, that Pinochet was "determined to stay in office beyond 1989"; second, his strategy was "to force his own people (and us) to choose between him and the Communists by eliminating the democratic center"; third, U.S. strategy must therefore be "to do what we can to preserve and strengthen the democratic element and convince Pinochet to leave office by 1989"; fourth, that the Communists' actions "reinforce Pinochet's strategy by seeking short term alliances with the democratic opposition while using terrorism and violence to sabotage prospects for successful negotiations on a transition"; fifth, that time "is increasingly on the side of those

---

[62] See *Report of the Chilean National Commission on Truth and Reconciliation* [Rettig Report], vol. 2 (Notre Dame: Center for Civil and Human Rights, 1993), 745; Mary Helen Spooner, *Soldiers in a Narrow Land* (Berkeley: University of California Press, 1994), 209–213.

[63] Telegram, Shultz to AmEmb Santiago, July 15, 1986, DOS/FOIAe, III.

[64] See "Military Brought Before Court for Alleged Torching," *FBIS: DR: LA*, July 21, 1986, E1; "Judge Turns Burns Case Over to the Military," *FBIS: DR: LA*, July 24, 1986, E1.

working for polarization and an undemocratic outcome"; sixth, that U.S. influence "is exaggerated greatly in Chile [but] our support or withholding of support is perceived as extremely important and therefore is important"; and seventh, that Pinochet "has been exceptionally able in resisting pressures domestic and foreign [but] has shown he can compromise, if only at the last minute."

According to Barnes, the United States had an interest in promoting regime change, but not in any circumstances. If the alternative was Pinochet or the Communists, he wrote, reflecting a general perception among administration officials, *we have no choice but to prefer Pinochet.* He proposed a two-track strategy designed to "a) bring pressure on [Pinochet] to cooperate in an effective democratic transition and, b) to strengthen the democratic center as an alternative while weakening and dividing the communists." The key to achieving the first objective was separating the President from his coercive base of support. As the primary roadblock to a satisfactory outcome, "he must be persuaded to change or be removed," which could only be achieved by convincing the armed forces "that its institutional interests are jeopardized by continued unconditional support for Pinochet." This was not beyond the bounds of possibility, said Barnes, recalling "General Matthei's mood of deep depression when he returned to Chile and got the full effect of Pinochet's 'crazy' handling of demos in May." Such behavior might well "accelerate army concerns" about his open-ended determination to hold on to power. U.S. efforts to capitalize on this mood of growing anxiety needed to be accompanied by "public actions in the UN, OAS and the MDBs...that Pinochet cannot exploit...to claim continued U.S. support." As for the democratic opposition, it must be "encourage[d]...to offer a realistic alternative by agreeing on moderate proposals for a transition in 1989." The other message to them needs to be particularly blunt: "Any alliances with the Communists, no U.S. support."

The paper echoed Shultz's earlier comment about "playing the economic card wisely," especially in light of almost certain growing congressional pressure to vote against MDB loans to Chile. Barnes suggested this could be best achieved by using economic sanctions as a psychological tool in preference to any immediate threat to wield the big foreign debt–refinancing stick. Washington could threaten to delay projects or change voting patterns to induce Pinochet to take "concrete liberalization steps toward democracy." Although measures of this kind would not pose a short-term danger to the regime, they "could further undermine [Pinochet's] ability to retain backing by the military as they saw him becoming an increasing liability." U.S. efforts could be further bolstered by "greater coordination" between the White House and its European and Latin American allies, no matter how limited their influence might be. To implement the action plan, Treasury and the NSC should participate in discussing MDB tactics, and the administration must maintain constant contact with key legislators "so as to keep control of the process." Finally, Barnes proposed that a special presidential envoy visit Chile "to emphasize U.S. concerns still more forcefully to Pinochet."[65]

In a memo to Shultz commenting on the strategy paper, Abrams described a "worsening situation in Chile" that would require "more than verbal volleys" to force Pinochet to give up power or to convince the army to take matters into its own hands. If further evidence was needed, Pinochet provided it some twenty-four hours prior to Abrams's memo, when he "almost entirely cropped the veil" with a speech indicating a determination to remain in the Moneda Palace until the late 1990s. The timing, against a background of growing agitation over the Rojas death, wrote Abrams, "suggests that he intends to ignore international criticism and tough it out at home with more repression."[66]

Barnes's decision to attend Rojas's funeral prior to informing Washington was a highly symbolic gesture that provoked the wrath of some junta members and their sympathizers in the U.S. Congress. Admiral Merino suggested that Washington would be better informed about events in Chile if Barnes were replaced, forcing the Embassy to respond that the Ambassador spoke and acted with the full authority of the White House.[67] Paradoxically, instead of raising questions about Barnes's performance, Merino's disquiet may have demonstrated to Shultz and senior State Department officials that Barnes had proved to be a wise choice to replace Theberge. The behavior of right-wing Senator Jesse Helms almost certainly reinforced this view.

---

[65] Strategy Paper, Barnes to Shultz, July 8, 1986, DOS/FOIAe, III (our emphasis). Weeks later, Jaime Guzman, Secretary-General of the pro-government Independent Democratic Union Party (UDI) and a principal drafter of the 1980 Constitution, told Barnes that Pinochet was "dangerously isolated," producing considerable unease among the armed forces. Barnes agreed but found even more "interesting" Guzman's unsolicited statement "that a U.S. threat of credit sanctions was a valuable pressure tool." Telegram, Barnes to Shultz, "UDI Leader Guzman on Pinochet and Right," August 21, 1986, LAAD, NSC, Chile 1986 (6), Box 91181, RRL.

[66] Memo, Abrams to Shultz, July 11, 1986, DOS/FOIAe, III.

[67] "Merino Advises U.S. to Change Ambassadors," *FBIS: DR: LA*, July 15, 1986, E1; "U.S. Ambassador Replies," ibid. Barnes confirmed the decision to attend the Rojas funeral on his own initiative during an "Interview with Mike Wallace of '60 *Minutes*,'" October 28, 1986, "Speeches and Statements 1978–1986," Box 1, Papers of Harry G. Barnes.

Accompanied by three staff aides, Helms, who rarely traveled abroad, visited Santiago in the second week of July, formally at the invitation of a Chilean agricultural organization but actually at the specific request of Augusto Pinochet. Neither State nor the Embassy was informed of the trip in advance.[68] Helms was enamored of the Chilean leader, believing he "had done a service to mankind" in ousting Allende, could not be faulted in the economic sphere, and "was being pilloried by the U.S. Government for the minor defect of not holding elections."[69] He accepted Pinochet's explanation of the Rojas case (that Molotov cocktails the two protesters were carrying accidentally broke when they were arrested and set them alight) and urged Washington to do the same.[70]

During a meeting with Barnes at the Embassy, the Senator launched a savage attack on the Ambassador's competence in dealing with the Rojas affair. Helms was incensed that Barnes had attended the funeral and "planted the American flag in the midst of a Communist activity"[71] and criticized another Embassy official for having condemned the regime for not seriously investigating the killings. Going further, he denounced the administration over its insistent pressure on Pinochet to carry out an independent inquiry into the Rojas and Quintana cases. "You have screwed it up," the Senator exploded at Barnes, "you and the people in Washington."[72] George Jones described Helms's group arriving at the Embassy "with their minds made up that Barnes was a left-wing Ambassador who was trying to undermine this noble government which was doing so much good for Chile. It was one of the two or three occasions when I can remember Barnes being visibly angry and visibly upset when he came back from that meeting."[73] Abrams and Shultz countered with a ringing endorsement of Barnes's actions and repeated, for good measure, that he was carrying out the policy approved by the White House.[74] Shultz later accused the regime of cultivating congressional right-wingers such as Helms, who "were viscerally opposed to what Barnes and I were doing in Chile."[75]

[68] Interview with Robert Gelbard.
[69] George F. Jones interview, FAOHC.
[70] See William A. Link, *Righteous Warrior: Jesse Helms and the Rise of Modern Conservatism* (New York: St. Martin's Press, 2008), 330.
[71] Quoted in Shirley Christian, "Helms, in Chile, Denounces U.S. Envoy," *NYT*, July 14, 1986, 3.
[72] Memo of Conversation, from Barnes, July 15, 1986, DOS/FOIAe, III.
[73] George F. Jones interview, FAOHC.
[74] See Christian, "Helms, in Chile, Denounces U.S. Envoy."
[75] Shultz, *Turmoil and Triumph*, 973.

The Ambassador sent his own report to Washington on what had tran-spired in his meeting with Helms. Parroting the junta critics of Barnes, the Senator had claimed that the diplomat was sent to Chile to "undermine" Pinochet and that the Embassy was sending unreliable information back to Washington. Helms gave as an example the possibility that Rojas's burns "did not come from his being set afire, and in any case, the girl who suffered burns at the same time is a Communist."[76]

On his return from Santiago, Helms telephoned Abrams and resumed his attack on the Ambassador for allegedly failing to implement Reagan's policy, and he requested that State drop its "sanctimonious attitude" and arrange for a White House meeting between Pinochet and the President. Exasperated and furious in equal measure, Abrams responded that he "had felt blindsided" by Helms's trip and by the suggestion that Barnes was going off the rails: the reality, insisted Abrams, was that he "does nothing of significance without checking with Washington."[77] When the dust had settled on the dispute, Barnes concluded that Helms's visit "prob-ably helped" the administration's strategy because the Senator overplayed his hand and was shown in an exaggerated light.[78]

Within hours of Helms's departure from Santiago, Deputy Assistant Secretary of State Gelbard flew into the Chilean capital on July 14.[79] Dur-ing a six-day visit, Gelbard delivered what were by now well-rehearsed messages to both sides of the Chilean political divide, warning the regime that a failure to promptly restore full democratic rule would only result in increased turmoil and the opposition that it needed to be pragmatic and responsible, and keep the Communist Party and other extremist groups at arm's length. The increasingly radicalized and polarized nature of Chilean politics, he told reporters, "is a problem that worries us."[80]

---

[76] Telegram, Barnes to Shultz, for Abrams and Kalb, July 13, 1987, DOS/FOIAe, III.

[77] Telegram, for Ambassador from Abrams, July 16, 1986. Also see Jon Elliston, "Deadly Alliance," *Independent Weekly*, May 23, 2001, http://www.indyweek.com.

[78] Interview with Harry G. Barnes.

[79] While Gelbard postponed an earlier planned trip due to pressing personal matters and the timing of this rescheduled visit was purely coincidental, it gave rise to the impression that the latter was some kind of emergency damage-control mission to "try to reassure everybody what our policy was." What was not in dispute was the ongoing rancor between Gelbard and Helms's office, which was in the habit of leaking information about the administration's internal policy debates on Chile to Pinochet. The animosity resurfaced in March 1988 when Helms attempted, unsuccessfully, to block Gelbard's nomination to be U.S. Ambassador to Bolivia. Interview with Robert Gelbard.

[80] Quoted in "U.S. Official Says Failure to Restore Democracy Could Spark More Unrest," AP, July 18, 1986. Also see Shirley Christian, "U.S. Envoy Urges Compromise in Chile," *NYT*, July 18, 1986, 3.

In a detailed report to State on the visit, Ambassador Barnes could hardly have been more downbeat in his assessment of Gelbard's reception at the hands of both the regime and the National Accord party leaders. Pinochet refused to see the Assistant Secretary on the grounds of his lesser rank, while, of the other service chiefs, Gelbard found Admiral Merino "frigid" and concluded that only Generals Matthei and Stange understood the importance of implementing major political changes. To make matters worse, Gelbard was deliberately prevented from "reaching out to the army below the very top level."[81] Barnes managed to arrange a meeting between Gelbard and the Director of Chilean Intelligence, General Humberto Gordon, who "apparently had some sort of license from Pinochet to go a little further" than other senior army officers – even though Barnes described his responsiveness to U.S. views as "nil." Gelbard's overall impression was of a political and military leadership "with blinders on."[82] Meetings with civilian cabinet ministers were equally unproductive. Foreign Minister del Valle characterized the U.S. response to the Rojas killing as "an overreaction," while Finance Minister Büchi, when asked by Gelbard to intercede with Pinochet to take measures that would avoid a U.S. no vote on MDB loans, explained that "outside the economic sphere, he had little influence with the junta." Gelbard told del Valle that while Washington "expected a full and prompt investigation" of the Rojas matter, this was nonetheless a second-tier issue that would not be allowed "to infect the overall relationship or other broader issues."[83]

If Gelbard found the government "rigid in its position [and] without the will to engage its own population, much less the opposition," his discussions with the center-right opposition revealed the absence of a pragmatic approach that "was only slightly less stark." Although the major

[81] Telegram, Barnes to Shultz, "Visit of DAS Robert Gelbard – July 13–18: Overview of Visit Results," July 21, 1986, DOS/FOIAe, III. Getting to meet with army generals was generally impossible, and if access was granted, "it was usually to discuss some military visit, some exchange program, and just that and nothing more." George F. Jones interview, FAOHC.

[82] Telegram, Barnes to Shultz, "Visit of DAS Robert Gelbard – July 13–18," DOS/FOIAe, III. Pinochet had originally scheduled to host a lunch for Gelbard as long as Barnes was not present. Eventually a compromise was reached. The lunch was abandoned, and Barnes could attend a thirty-minute conversation between Pinochet and Gelbard. See Mimi Whitefield, "U.S. Has Little Leverage as Chile Faces Turmoil," *MH*, September 29, 1986, 4A.

[83] Telegram, Barnes to Shultz, "DAS Gelbard's Meeting with Finance Minister Buchi," July 21, 1986, DOS/FOIAe, III; Telegram, Barnes to Shultz, "Visit of DAS Robert Gelbard: Meeting with Foreign Minister del Valle," July 21, 1986, ibid.

democratic party leaders participating in the National Accord acknowledged the need to provide a set of assurances to the military to move the
transition process forward, there were sharp divisions over how to proceed. Gelbard lobbied hard to dissuade them from engaging in social
mobilizations that merely "play[ed] into the hands of the extremes"
but could not overcome the hopes of the majority that "such pressure
will erode military zest for governance enough to remove Pinochet and
begin bargaining."[84] In a follow-up cable, Barnes described the tenor of
Gelbard's meetings with the Accord representatives. On each occasion,
Gelbard stressed to them the importance of persuading the military that
it was in their self-interest to negotiate with the moderate opposition on
the transition formula and conveyed Washington's strong opposition to
any links with the Communists. Their response was not totally in accord
with Gelbard's hopes: though opposed to formal political pacts with the
radical left, "the center-left party leaders could not rule out the possibility of working with MDP activists in the social arena." Socialist Party
General-Secretary Ricardo Núñez said that cooperation with the MDP
parties in strikes and other protests was critical to his party maintaining its popular base, while PDC President Gabriel Valdés argued that
noncooperation with the social movements on the left "which can bring
pressure on the regime would destroy those organizations." Most participants in these discussions, said Barnes, "hemmed and hawed," leaving
the question basically "unresolved."

The Ambassador did not consider the Gelbard visit totally unproductive. He partly attributed the PDC directorate's subsequent attack on the
prominent Socialist Party leader, Ricardo Lagos, for proposing a dual
strategy of militant struggle and social mobilization, and the decision
by the Christian Democrats to withdraw from an informal coordinating committee that included the MDP and AD parties, to the "positive
impact" of Gelbard's meetings with the party. While the PDC had not
yet reached a consensus over "tactical cooperation" with the Communist
Party and the radical left, Barnes thought this represented "the closest
the Christian Democrats have come in recent years toward completely
breaking all links with the Communists."[85]

If the visit proved fruitless in prodding either side to move forward with
Chile's transition back to democracy, it nonetheless had an important

---

[84] Telegram, Barnes to Shultz, "Visit of DAS Robert Gelbard, July 13–18," ibid.
[85] Telegram, Barnes to Shultz, July 22, 1986, ibid.

impact in concentrating Gelbard's thinking about the political dynamics inside the country and how Washington could make a difference. Although he came away with no illusions about the possibility of persuading Pinochet of anything, he nonetheless sensed that there was an opportunity "to create fissures or fractures" within the junta that would allow Washington to "work with people who clearly were showing a lot of understanding that times were changing." Unlike Admiral Merino, whom Gelbard found "erratic, sometimes he'd be friendly, sometimes he'd be hostile," he had "developed very close relationships" with Matthei and Stange, who themselves enjoyed a unique bond by dint of the fact that they were from the same small village and spoke German, a language in which they often conversed during junta meetings so that other members did not know what they were discussing.[86]

The democratic opposition presented another, and in some respects more difficult, problem. What the United States sought here was a root-and-branch reassessment of its strategy and tactics vis-à-vis the left social movements and the military. Foremost among Gelbard's concerns was avoiding the distinct possibility of the anti-Pinochet movement being overtaken by Communist Party "radicals":

The Communist Party in many ways was the best off of the opposition because a lot of them had been protected and given asylum over the years by Cuba, by the Soviet Union, by some of the other Eastern Europeans, and some of them had gone to Western Europe too. We didn't have any evidence of a serious moderation of their views. To the contrary, we saw that they had become, if anything, more radicalized, and we were afraid that if the moderate opposition – and this is moderate writ quite broadly – began to move in that direction, moving leftward, this would guarantee that they would lose. It had less to do with maintaining the economic policy, which was important, but it didn't mean much if the junta was staying in power because over the time it was going to deteriorate due to a lack of popular support. But we felt that the future of Chile really had to be in a hands-off the center-left to center-right. Now if the Communists wanted to moderate their behavior and wanted to figure out the reality that it wasn't 1973 anymore, fine, but that was indeed my message. And it was a strong message.[87]

Gelbard was merely articulating "a key tenet of U.S. policy," said a Department colleague: the Communists were perceived "as supporting violence as a tool and they had not participated in the National Accord,

---

[86] Interview with Robert Gelbard.
[87] Ibid.

and so I think that was a clear red line for Washington."[88] Shultz was similarly convinced that 'extremist' politics prefigured violence, which could only benefit Pinochet "because it would give him the excuse to call off the election or crack down or whatever and so we constantly counseled people 'No violence.'"[89]

Gelbard himself implied a more nuanced understanding of his message to the opposition about the dangers of flirting with the Communists: "The majority of the business community were clear supporters of the junta and were concerned about what might happen in the future. We spent a great deal of time talking through our view with them, that if they were going to salvage what they liked about what the junta had done that the time had come to look elsewhere and try to work with the opposition to bring about the kind of government that would be supportive."[90] This required the opposition not to spook the business community by entertaining alliances with forces that threatened private capital in general or Pinochet's economic reforms in particular. "It seemed to us useful," said Abrams, "to get the Christian Democrats to say to us, and to say publicly, some things on the economy" so that any domestic capitalist-class anxieties about the nature of economic reforms in a postmilitary government could be put to rest.[91] Gelbard insisted that he wasn't dismissive of the moderate opposition's argument that they needed the pressure of the street protests to get any traction with the regime. "I think it was possible, to a degree, to have it both ways. You could be involved with the left in the social mobilization on the one hand versus working the politics on a very different level."[92] He did not elaborate on how the opposition might manage this juggling act. For his part, George Jones was doubtful that Gelbard's message was getting through because the image of invincibility that Pinochet had cultivated was very much in the minds of his opponents: "It was all very well for us to tell the opposition that they should participate [in the government's transition scenario] but Pinochet was going to come out of this the victor in any event, either through manipulation of public opinion or by outright stealing the election. He had always won and he was going to win again, he was going to set the rules of the game."[93]

[88] Interview with James Swigert.
[89] Telephone interview with George P. Shultz.
[90] Interview with Robert Gelbard.
[91] Interview with Elliott Abrams.
[92] Interview with Robert Gelbard.
[93] Interview with George F. Jones.

The Crisis Deepens

Preparing for a July 24 meeting with Ambassador Hernán Errázuriz, Elliott Abrams received a memo from the Office of Southern Cone's Acting Director suggesting the issues he might raise with the Chilean diplomat. The starting point should be a reminder that the Pinochet government's response to the Helms visit, the Rojas case, and statements about the transition were responsible for "let[ting] the genie out of the bottle" and that, when combined with the army sweeps through the shantytowns, prosecution of the Catholic Church's Vicariate of Solidarity staff, restrictions on freedom to assemble, and new instances of state-authored torture, the regime's "balance sheet . . . does not look very good." Above all, Abrams was advised to make it clear to Errázuriz that the United States expected "fast, effective action" on the Rojas case and to leave him in no doubt that congressional pressure regarding MDB votes "will be intense [and that] this is not a threat, this is reality."[94] A few weeks later, Undersecretary of State for Economic Affairs Allen Wallis warned Errázuriz that societal pressures could "grow so strong that they explode some day and . . . drive the Chilean people into the hands of the Communists."[95] If that happened, the consequences would be dire not only for Chile but also for the U.S. presence throughout the region. Testifying before Congress at the end of the month, Abrams restated his concern that "failure to return to democracy will be accompanied by increasing polarization and violence." Such an outcome, in turn, could have potentially far-reaching implications for Santiago *and* Washington: "The strengthening of the far left in Chile resulting from this can have a negative impact on some still fragile democracies elsewhere in the region and would jeopardize U.S. interests."[96]

The navy and air force commanders may have expressed a cautious interest in considering revisions to the 1980 Constitution, but Pinochet continued to stymie U.S. efforts to break the impasse in Chile or to foster doubts within the army about his leadership credentials. A report by State's Bureau of Intelligence and Research explained why: "He has been adept at manipulating the Army's promotion and retirement

---

[94] Memo, Cox to Abrams, July 22, 1986, DOS/FOIAe, III.
[95] Telegram, Shultz to AmEmb Santiago, August 8, 1986, ibid.
[96] U.S. Congress, House, Committee on Banking, Finance and Urban Affairs, Subcommittee on International Development Institutions and Finance, *Human Rights Abuses in Chile: Time for United States Action*, 99th Cong., 2d Sess., July 30, 1986, 23.

system to ensure absolute loyalty and control."[97] A three-day visit by the head of U.S. Southern Command in Panama, General John Galvin, in early August 1986 highlighted Washington's dilemma. Galvin's visit had a dual purpose: to convince Chilean military officials that the Pentagon shared administration concerns over human rights and the lack of progress toward a political transition and to persuade the officer corps that Pinochet did not offer the best guarantee of the institution's future. Recalling General Schweitzer's embarrassing 1985 visit when he showered praise on Pinochet during a military ceremony, a U.S. official declared that "there will be no presentation of swords this time."[98] Robert Gelbard described Galvin as a real "diplomat soldier" who "followed the talking points, and the message, the State Department wanted him to follow one hundred percent."[99] When Galvin suggested that greater clarity about the transition scenario would be in Chile's interest, Pinochet rejected the very idea "because the Communists would take whatever Chile said, 'wrap it up,' and distort it." The dictator's icy response to Galvin's request for human rights improvements was "that he, Pinochet, will set Chile's course without advice from anyone else."[100] This latest failure to move Pinochet off dead center led Ambassador Barnes to express some astonishment that for a person of senior political and military standing, Pinochet "is surprisingly unsophisticated in his world views [and] sounded strangely like a Chilean Archie Bunker."[101] What in fact the exchange with Galvin demonstrated was how confident Pinochet was in his own position and how little he cared for U.S. advice or pressure. In dismissing Galvin's proposals out of hand, Pinochet did so with no risk of fracturing his key support base and little concern for what his rejection might mean for U.S.-Chilean relations.

In one of his regular discussions with Barnes, Foreign Minister del Valle conveyed Pinochet's annoyance at the "U.S.'s inability to understand

---

[97] Intelligence Research Report, INR, "Chile: Pinochet's Future Dependent on Military Loyalty," July 23, 1986, DOS/FOIAe, III.

[98] Quoted in Pamela Constable, "U.S. General Begins Talks with Chile," *BG*, August 7, 1986, 39.

[99] Interview with Robert Gelbard.

[100] Telegram, Shultz to USDEL, from Barnes, "Gen Galvin's Call on President Pinochet," August 8, 1986, LAAD, NSC, Chile 1986 (5), Box 91181, RRL; U.S. official quoted in "Chile Loans Facing Close U.S. Scrutiny," *WT*, August 19, 1986, 6A; Chilean official quoted in Bernard Weinraub, "Chile's Leader Reported to Reject U.S. Calls for Democratic Change," *NYT*, August 18, 1986, 1.

[101] Telegram, Barnes to Shultz, August 7, 1986. Bunker was a bigoted and reactionary character in a popular 1970s American television sitcom.

what was going on in Chile" and its failure to take into account what del Valle claimed was the anti-Chile effort being mounted by the Soviets and Pinochet's "firm promises" to return the country to democracy.[102] The Embassy's annual report on bilateral ties later that month concluded that Pinochet "appears to have become increasingly dogmatic, trumpeting the view that the choice in Chile is between order (Pinochet) and chaos (the Communists)." By subsuming all of the opposition forces as "part of the Communist plan to take over Chile," he had created the paradoxical situation of "the ardent anti-communist [being] in numerous ways the inadvertent ally of the Communists."[103]

The August discovery of a huge arsenal of Cuban and Soviet-origin weapons stockpiled for future use by leftist guerillas only increased Pinochet's confidence in the absolute certainty of his own convictions.[104] So too did the call from the outlawed MIR for a popular uprising across Chile.[105] In a speech eviscerating politicians and opposition leaders, Pinochet "shrilly announced that he could not be removed [and] further accused a vast array of labor, religious, and social organizations of trying to overthrow the GOC."[106] By month's end, he was boasting that the armed forces were prepared to fight to the last drop of their blood in defense of Chile against efforts to destabilize the country through violence.[107]

The rhetoric on both sides of the political divide in Chile was getting more and more bellicose. Barnes reported that there was little more that the United States could do to help defuse the situation by working on the democratic opposition. Repeated demarches by Embassy officials seemed not to have clearly gotten through to them the message that "U.S. pressure on Pinochet is contingent on their responsible behavior, i.e., no flirtation with the Communists. The argument that an acceptable alternative to Pinochet exists must be plausible to the military." This meant terminating all links with Communist Party and its members and refusing to participate in street demonstrations and strikes that could provide any leverage to these more radical forces.[108] Pinochet, the Ambassador

[102] Telegram, Barnes to Shultz, "Conversation with Del Valle: Part 1," August 19, 1986, LAAD, NSC Chile (07/30/1986–09/16/1986), Box 91713, RRL.

[103] Airgram, AmEmb Santiago to Shultz, August 28, 1986, DOS/FOIAe, III.

[104] "Pinochet Scores Subversive on Arsenal," *FBIS: DR: LA*, August 19, 1986, E1.

[105] "MIR's Andres Pascal Allende Returns Secretly," *FBIS: DR: LA*, August 12, 1986, E5.

[106] Telegram, Barnes to Shultz, August 25, 1986, DOS/FOIAe, III.

[107] "Pinochet: Armed Forces Willing to Shed Blood," *FBIS: DR: LA*, August 20, 1986, E2.

[108] Telegram, Barnes to Shultz, August 29, 1986, DOS/FOIAe, III.

wrote some days later, while publicly supporting a transition based on the plebiscite formula, was "keeping open his options," and few doubted that he would attempt to use whatever means were required to maintain his hold on political power. This was the only realistic conclusion that could be drawn from his multitrack strategy of dividing the opposition, combining limited political openings with repression, "delay[ing] transition steps which appear to close options [and] unleash[ing] forces that are difficult to control" to avoid the risk of lame duck status.[109]

Within days of Barnes's warning, members of the FPMR attempted to assassinate Pinochet in an attack on his motorcade outside Santiago. Pinochet emerged unscathed, although several of his bodyguards were killed.[110] To Gelbard, the attack emphasized how fractured Chilean society had become, for which he largely blamed the dictatorship: "What deeply concerns us is that the lack of communication, the lack of consensus, the lack of clarity and the lack of credibility on the part of the Government is enhancing the extreme left."[111] Pinochet declared the attack further confirmation of a communist plot to overthrow the regime and announced restoration of a state of siege and a rigid adherence to the transition timetable, which allowed him to run for the presidency in 1989.[112] What he didn't do, perhaps surprisingly, was use the assassination attempt as an excuse to abrogate the 1980 Constitution or suspend the transition – options he might have been able to defend to the other junta members had he seriously harbored ambitions to rule indefinitely, as many U.S. officials then assumed.

In his annual September 11 address to the nation, Pinochet denounced the National Accord, alleging that its "moderate appearance hid serious contradictions and ambiguities," and attacked the Civic Assembly as "a front whose real aims are to conduct pointless protests and attempted strikes to disguise its ties with all Marxist political groups." He insisted that the regime was abiding by its transition timetable – despite a

---

[109] Telegram, Barnes (Keane) to Shultz, September 2, 1986, ibid. Shultz himself would later write that the unrest of early July only "seemed to stiffen the regime's resistance to change." Shultz, *Turmoil and Triumph*, 973.

[110] See "Attack on Pinochet, State of Siege Declared," *FBIS: DR: LA*, September 8, 1986, E1; "Pinochet Describes Attack," *FBIS: DR: LA*, September 8, 1986, E2; "Death Toll at Seven," *FBIS: DR: LA*, September 8, 1986, E3: "Pinochet: Situation Grave," *FBIS: DR: LA*, September 9, 1986, E2.

[111] Quoted in "Ex-Envoy Says Pinochet Faked Attack to Win US Support," *SMH*, September 11, 1986, 8.

[112] See Bradley Graham, "Arms Caches in Chile Prompt Reassessment of Rebel Might," *WP*, May 17, 1986, A1, A28.

"mistaken interpretation by certain U.S. sectors" – and justified the declaration of a state of siege in terms of the immediate threat from extremists with a "totalitarian objective."[113] After the failed assassination plot, the military closed ranks behind Pinochet, thus further bolstering his position, and weakened any inclination to begin the process of political reform. It had a similar negative impact on Washington's perceptions of the Chilean situation, especially given the "fragmented" nature of the democratic opposition and its lack of a "strong, coherent leadership." An apparently dejected Shultz telegrammed the Madrid Embassy that the attempt to kill Pinochet, the discovery of the arms cache, the reimposition of a state of siege, increased activities of "rightist terrorists," and the continuation of "credible reports" of torture by security forces had combined "to reinforce and accelerate an already existing trend toward deepening polarization."[114] The Santiago Embassy added to the Secretary's gloom, reporting that not only was Pinochet "in [the] ascendancy" but that the FPMR had emerged from this episode with its position enhanced. Though its actions may have caused frictions with its closest political ally, the Communist Party, "it will probably also be considered a political plus as it has demonstrated the Front's resiliency and reaction power."[115]

The democratic opposition parties and trade unions were quick to condemn the FPMR's action even while they held the regime partially responsible for creating an environment in which extremism flourished. The PDC condemned both the attack on Pinochet and all acts of political violence and highlighted the atmosphere of uncertainty created by "fanatic forces able to resort to any foolish act or crime."[116] The Radical Party declared its "energetic rejection and condemnation" of terrorism, blaming the government for its refusal to dialogue with the opposition about Chile's future. The CNT likewise denounced the escalation of violence and held the regime culpable in its disregard for human rights and abuses against the democratic opposition.[117] The Núñez Socialists issued a statement rejecting armed confrontation with the regime, adding that

[113] "Pinochet's Address to the Nation on Anniversary," *FBIS: DR: LA*, September 12, 1986, E1.
[114] Telegram, Shultz to AmEmb, Madrid, September 16, 1986, NARA/FOIAe, III.
[115] Telegram, AmEmb Santiago (Jones) to Shultz, September 19, 1986, DOS/FOIAe, III. On the relationship between the Communist Party and the FPMR, see Constable and Valenzuela, *A Nation of Enemies*, 293; Múñoz, *Dictator's Shadow*, 160–181.
[116] Quoted in Aylwin, *El Reencuentro de los Demócratas*, 317.
[117] See "Leaders React to Attack," *FBIS: DR: LA*, September 10, 1986, E2.

the reimposition of a state of siege did "not contribute" to the solution to Chile's current political problems.[118]

Inadvertently, the attempt on Pinochet's life would eventually prompt a further refinement of tactics by the political opposition. In its aftermath, several prominent PDC leaders warned that violence only made the regime stronger, emboldened the most radical members of the opposition, and damaged the entire transition prospects.[119] Ricardo Núñez, who, along with other prominent Party members, was forced to go into hiding, said the attack more clearly differentiated the political opposition from terrorists who wanted to defeat the regime by force and so "made it easier to reach an understanding between forces of left democratic socialism and some supporters of Pinochet."[120] Growing support for a political settlement as the only viable option, observed the Socialist Party's Enrique Correa, now strengthened around the belief that "if your only strategy was to apply strong pressure to overthrow the dictatorship so that Pinochet fell the same way as Somoza and Stroessner fell, for instance, then the only outcome was going to be the death of thousands of people."[121]

Nonetheless, a general acceptance of working within the constraints of the regime's transition plan, keeping the Communist Party and other radical leftists at arm's length, and abandoning social mobilization tactics was still some way short of a consensus view among the opposition forces. While the PDC's Edgardo Boeninger wrote to all national and provincial party leaders in October advocating the "political isolation" of a Communist Party that refused to jettison its commitment to armed struggle, for instance, the Socialist Party stance was not as straightforward. The Núñez faction supported Boeninger's view insofar as they "thought it was necessary to mark its difference" with the Communist Party but advocated ongoing "dialogue and confrontation" in an effort to bring them into the democratic fold. Ricardo Lagos agreed that the Communist Party, if willing to dump its belief in "all forms of struggle," had a legitimate role to play in Chilean politics, especially given its "central" role in reviving mass political consciousness and challenging the legitimacy of the military regime. The problem of how to deal with the Communist Party, however, paled into insignificance as compared with

---

[118] "Socialist Party on Attack," *FBIS: DR: LA*, September 10, 1986, E3.
[119] Aylwin, *El Reencuentro de los Democratas*, 317–318.
[120] Interview with Ricardo Núñez.
[121] Interview with Enrique Correa.

Pinochet's entrenched hold on power and their limited options available to change that state of affairs, except for taking the struggle back to the streets if the need should arise again.[122]

Earlier in the year, Washington's most important junta contact, air force General Matthei, had advised State and NSC officials that any likely "credible" challenge to Pinochet would almost certainly come from inside the army itself, where questions about his leadership were already being discussed.[123] Keen to encourage this potential cleavage, the administration looked more to Pentagon generals than to diplomats. Apart from the obvious *simpatico* between military officials, Washington had become more and more reconciled to the reality that "no one believes any longer that [civilians or presidential envoys] going down there and making a rational argument will have any effect [on Pinochet]."[124]

Throughout 1986, U.S. policy makers continued to target the armed forces leadership as the most likely solution to its "Pinochet problem." In a communiqué to Secretary Shultz on September 2, Ambassador Barnes spelled out the military's basic demands for participation in a political transition process that essentially mirrored Washington's own goals for a post-Pinochet Chile: "a stable 'protected democracy' where traditional interests, particularly the economic model and property rights are respected"; firm guarantees "that Marxists will not reach power again"; and a commitment on the part of any new government "to preserve the prestige and cohesion of their institutions."[125] To date, though, "several initiatives to enhance military-to-military relationships,"[126] including visits by high-ranking Pentagon officials Deputy Secretary Nestor Sánchez and General John Wickham Jr., had failed to drive any kind of wedge between the army generals and their commander in chief. The army would not abandon Pinochet, wrote the NSC's Jacqueline Tillman, unless it was convinced, first and foremost, that a civilian government "can successfully

---

[122] Quoted in Aylwin, *El Reencuentro de los Democratas*, 318–320, 322.

[123] Memo, NSC, Tillman to Poindexter, "Close Hold Luncheon with Chilean Air Force Chief," May 16, 1986, LAAD, NSC, Chile 1986 (1), Box 91181, RRL.

[124] Quoted in Shirley Christian, "3 Chilean Services, but Not Army, Backing an Open Election in 1989," *NYT*, April 28, 1986, p. 9.

[125] Telegram, Barnes (Keane) to Shultz, "Prospects for Chile's Political Transition," September 2, 1986, DOS/FOIAe, III.

[126] "Background Paper on US Policy Goals in Chile," attached to Memo, Platt to Poindexter, for Shultz, November 10, 1986, ibid. When Army Chief of Staff General John A. Wickham Jr. met with Pinochet in November 1985, according to a Pentagon official, "he was the first visitor whom Pinochet did not lecture to." Quoted in Christian, "3 Chilean Services."

meet the threats to Chile's security posed by well-armed Soviet/Cuban supported terrorists and that there would be no witch hunts against the Army, such as human rights trials."[127]

Even though the Department went out of its way to reassure the NSC that the non-army junta members – Admiral José Merino, air force General Fernando Matthei, and Carabinero Commander Rodolfo Stange – "maintain a close dialog with the USG [U.S. government] and to a large degree (especially Matthei) share USG views," and were all opposed to a Pinochet plebiscite candidacy, there was no sign of these service chiefs attempting to leverage Pinochet out of power, at least in the absence of strong backing from the Army High Command. Their reluctance to press more forcefully for political reforms was not unrelated to a perception that the moderate opposition "has been unable to mobilize significant support or present a credible alternative."[128] This concern resonated in State, where officials were convinced that a civilian governing alternative that posed no essential threat either to the interests of the military or to the gains of its 1973 coup was the most important factor that might incline Chile's armed forces to abandon Pinochet.

Momentarily, developments within the opposition gave Washington a glimmer of hope that the groups it supported might be about to turn away from social mobilization and mass protests in favor of institutional/electoral struggle. When the Civic Assembly called for a national strike on September 4–5, the AD refused to participate, urging instead a national "day of reflection." The State Department response was one of cautious encouragement. Secretary Shultz welcomed the refusal of the democratic opposition to support the Communists and their allies, terming their action "a significant development with a positive effect on prospects for a peaceful democratic transition."[129] Undersecretary Michael Armacost instructed the Embassy to praise the AD for withholding its support for these antigovernment protests while simultaneously urging "intensified efforts in Santiago, with Chilean visitors in Washington, and through like-minded third countries to encourage a firm rejection by democratic forces of any cooperation with communists or communist-dominated groups."[130]

---

[127] Memo, from Poindexter, prepared by Tillman for "Meeting with the NSC on Chile," November 17, 1986, LAAD, NSC, NSC Meeting on Chile 11/18/1986, Box 91172, RRL.

[128] Telegram, Barnes (Keane) to Shultz, "Prospects for Chile's Political Transition," September 2, 1986, DOS/FOIAe, III.

[129] Telegram, Shultz to AmEmb Santiago, October 23, 1986, ibid.

[130] Telegram, Shultz (Armacost) to AmEmb Santiago, October 15, 1986, ibid.

Nonetheless, concerns persisted about the depth of the political opposition's commitment to a new "pragmatic" approach. Shultz remained uneasy "about the serious and increasing polarization... which the Chilean Communists, actively supported by Cuba and the Soviet Union, are using to worsen the situation."[131] Ambassador Barnes recalled a June conversation with Shultz who was already convinced that "Pinochet's game was to make sure that there was no choice save between himself and the communists. This is, if possible, even more his game now," Barnes cabled the Secretary, "[and as you] told me [then] our job was [and remains] to avoid falling into that trap."[132] In October, Shultz sought to avoid the "trap" by calling on the political parties to demonstrate "a greater sense of realism" and a willingness to risk tactical setbacks by not entering into alliances with communist groups when it came to issues such as university elections.[133] Barnes kept urging the opposition to adopt a more realistic negotiating posture by dropping its preconditions for entering into talks with the armed forces. He was especially critical of the "disingenuous" PDC leadership for requesting the army's position on amending the Constitution before it would agree to negotiations: "[Gabriel] Valdés knows that the Army's opinion is Pinochet's alone, and yet he and the PDC refuse to talk to Pinochet's representatives." While Pinochet might have been determined to prevent an alternative to his extended rule, the opposition had not helped its case by an "apparently incorrigible tendency" to bungle opportunities, preferring to engage in internecine conflicts and eschew dialogue "with the willing junta members." Their thrashing around, the Ambassador wrote, was the equivalent of "political epilepsy: lots of motion but no movement." He added that many opposition politicians "have shared the illusion since 1983 that Pinochet would be forced out of office by a combination of demonstrations at home and pressure from abroad," followed by new military leaders who would outline an election timetable and confine their activities to administration of the country until the transfer of power. "This is a comfortable hope, for it lets them turn away from difficult decisions."

Compounding U.S. frustration at getting the opposition to play ball, a substantial number of Christian Democrat, moderate Socialist, and Radical Party members remained "extremely reluctant to break with leftist parties who share similar social goals." The reasons were not hard to

---

[131] Telegram, USDEL, New York, to Shultz and AmEmb Santiago, September 30, 1986, ibid.
[132] Telegram, Barnes to Shultz, October 31, 1986, LAAD, NSC, Chile (10/30/1986–10/31/1986), Box 91713, RRL.
[133] Telegram, Shultz to AmEmb, Santiago, October 23, 1986, ibid.

find. Vote counters, argued Barnes, were "averse to permanently burning their bridges to the far left," which could cost them "influence over 20 or more percent of the electorate." Furthermore, a negotiated settlement would undoubtedly include the banning of the Communist Party, an amnesty for human rights abusers, a permanent role for the armed forces in national security affairs, and "other unpalatable military impositions," unless the opposition managed to increase its influence vis-à-vis the coercive institution. To that end, Barnes claimed, "the principal purpose of the National Accord and Civic Assembly was to broaden opposition unity, first to the right with the accord and then to the left with the Civic Assembly, while simultaneously projecting and sustaining an image of being willing to negotiate."[134]

Interagency Conflict: State Under Pressure

If anything, the discovery of the arms cache and the botched effort to kill Pinochet only deepened the conviction among State Department pragmatists who had gained the upper hand in Chile policy making that their new approach was the correct one. "We were sympathetic to the government of course about this because of the fear of terrorism," explained Robert Gelbard. "But much more so these events strongly reinforced our views that *the longer the junta stayed in power the more they were going to radicalize the population.* We had crystal-clear evidence that Cuba and the Soviet Union supplied arms to the group that tried the assassination attempt. It just buttressed our views and this is what we said to the opposition."[135] Getting the same message across to other parts of the foreign policy bureaucracy was another matter.

George Jones dismissed any notion that "everybody in Washington or even everybody in the State Department or in ARA was a supporter of the Barnes approach to Chile." Some policy makers were concerned on ideological grounds that "Pinochet might turn out to be right after all and a return to democracy would be a return to someone like Allende." Others felt "as a matter of style" that an Ambassador "ought to be a quiet observer of events and not be trying as openly and vigorously to influence

---

[134] Telegram, Barnes to Shultz, October 29, 1986, ibid. In speeches delivered earlier that month, Barnes asserted that the tactics of social mobilization had achieved little in terms of extracting concessions from the junta. See text used as basis for talks at Committee on Foreign Relations, Minnesota, October 6, 1986, et al., "Speeches and Statements 1978–86," Box 1, Papers of Harry G. Barnes.

[135] Interview with Robert Gelbard (our emphasis).

events as Harry was."[136] The dramatic events of August and September gave fresh argument to these minority views and perspectives. However, no officials argued that Washington should draw closer to Pinochet as a result. That case, said Chile Desk Officer James Swigert, had been lost: "Of course, there were people who said that it would be wrong to push too hard, we would make it harder for the Chilean government, we'd end up encouraging the violent groups." Beyond the confines of State, the Defense Department still "wanted military to military relations to be robust which was a good in and of itself" irrespective of the government in power, Treasury "didn't want to politicize the MDB process," the CIA's bureaucratic instinct was to predict the worst so it wouldn't be wrong, and UN Ambassador Vernon Waters generally opposed a tough approach. So, holding to a firm and consistent policy line was always a challenge. "The question," said Swigert, "was always how much did such and such an issue matter to Shultz – and usually it did."[137]

Yet not even Shultz could win every fight as the ongoing saga of MDB loan strategy was about to make clear. Appearing before a House subcommittee at the end of July, Abrams lauded the junta's economic policies and their "solid free market orientation," which itself justified voting in support of most junta MDB loan proposals. That said, Abrams acknowledged that the economic model could not be isolated from the regime's human rights performance. The latter would primarily dictate U.S. voting behavior, allowing the administration to retain maximum flexibility regarding implementation of the law relating to MDB loans. Under questioning, Abrams conceded that, in current circumstances, he would recommend a no vote on any non–BHN loan to Chile. He then proceeded to remind the legislators of the Carter administration failure to defeat a single MDB loan to Chile despite a consistent policy of voting against such loans. The message Santiago took from those U.S. setbacks was "that it didn't need to pay attention to Washington, and I don't want to get us into that box."[138] Therefore he would oppose legislation under discussion that obligated the United States to vote against all Chile MDB loan requests for twelve months. "It would not be good policy to remove our flexibility," Abrams said. "If they see we will vote no, no matter what they do . . . they will say, 'To hell with the Americans.'"[139] Whether

---

[136] Interview with George F. Jones.
[137] Interview with James Swigert.
[138] U.S. Congress, House, "Human Rights Abuses in Chile," 24, 26, 34.
[139] Quoted in "U.S., in Shift, May Oppose Loans to Chile, State Dept. Officials Say," *NYT*, July 31, 1986, 1, 12.

this stance would satisfy Congress was highly questionable. In response to Pinochet's foot dragging on human rights and democracy, Congress had increasingly narrowed administration options, and there was every indication that the pressure to increase sanctions would grow unless the Chilean regime exhibited a greater commitment to reforms.

The trigger for this renewed loans debate was Secretary Shultz's decision to finally wield a big stick by announcing that the United States would vote against a $250 million World Bank structural adjustment loan (SAL-II) for Chile, despite President Reagan's reservations and the strong opposition of NSC Adviser John Poindexter and members of the White House staff.[140] The Executive Board failure to approve this loan would not only endanger dispersal of the last $49 million tranche of the 1985 SAL-I but "almost certainly" ensure that the foreign private commercial banks would not provide new, and urgently needed, loans to Chile in 1987. Lacking a majority of voting shares to block a loan, and unable to postpone loans temporarily without the support of other countries or to get Bank President Barber Conable "to sit" on loans for long – and with Congress "sniff[ing] blood" in the absence of significant junta reforms – the Office of Southern Cone's Kim Flower advised Abrams that the United States "probably cannot sustain a yes vote" and that abstaining would serve little purpose. Under those circumstances, Shultz's threat "provided the only real economic leverage we have."[141]

In a follow-up memo to Shultz prior to his meeting with British Foreign Minister Sir Geoffrey Howe, Abrams urged him to take up the issue of MDB lending to Chile, keeping in mind that the U.K. government was reluctant to apply "pressure" on Pinochet "given their strategic interests in the Falklands." The primary objective should be to solicit Whitehall's support "in persuading [the] GOC to postpone loans" until such time as the democratization process has accelerated and the human rights situation has improved. To buttress this request, Shultz should emphasize the "deepening polarization" that was occurring due largely to "Pinochet's intransigence," the opposition's disarray, and the congressional legislation on human rights abuses.[142]

Ambassador Barnes also raised the issue of MDB leverage with Shultz, distinguishing between a "threat" to block loans, which he considered "a useful tool," and the actual decision to do so, which he cautioned

---

[140] Shultz, *Turmoil and Triumph*, 974.
[141] Memo, Flower to Abrams, September 4, 1986, DOS/FOIAe, III.
[142] Briefing Memo, Abrams to Shultz, September 5, 1986, ibid.

"could do serious damage, force Pinochet to revert to economic autarky and populism, complicate problems even more for [a post-Pinochet government] and ultimately benefit the extreme left." Barnes considered that whatever action was taken would be "much more effective" if coordinated with key Latin American and European allies as it would diffuse the inevitable nationalist "backlash" against U.S. pressure. This would be no easy task because of other governments' reluctance to politicize the MDBs. Among Country Team officials, Barnes informed the Secretary, there was a consensus that the most effective approach "would be gradually escalating pressures starting with postponement of loans, and moving on as necessary to abstention, negative votes and affirmative action to block loans."[143]

Redirecting Chile policy along these lines was anathema to a number of White House officials and NSC Adviser Poindexter, whose relations with Shultz "were enormously strained at the time."[144] Determined to prevent a no vote, they sought to gain the ascendancy in the bureaucratic debate – with unexpected help from the attempt on Pinochet's life. A Department memo to Shultz written four days after the assassination plot indicated that "we will almost certainly have to abstain at a minimum [but] our best course of action is to try and get the loan votes postponed." A decision to oppose the loans without blocking their passage "will gain credit on the Hill for showing concern over the rights situation" and bolster MDB replenishment funding prospects – but it "would not lead to any improvement in Chile, and would be used by Pinochet against us." A negative vote that failed to block passage of the loan had an obvious "downside" to it: "we could lose our little remaining leverage over the Pinochet regime, and give him a visible target . . . with which to drum up nationalistic support."[145] As Shultz prepared for a meeting with the Chilean Foreign Minister, Jaime del Valle, ARA's James Michel suggested he deliver a strong recommendation that because the White House was constrained by legislation, and subject to intense congressional pressure over the twin issues of human rights and a political transition, the upcoming MDB loan votes be postponed pending movement in these two areas. The message should be: "Don't box us in a corner. We will not be put in position of pursuing [the] sterile approach on MDB loan votes for Chile of [the] last Administration," which voted no on loans

---

[143] Telegram, Barnes to Shultz, August 29, 1986, ibid.
[144] Shultz, *Turmoil and Triumph*, 974.
[145] Briefing Memo, McMinn to Shultz, September 11, 1986, DOS/FOIAe, III.

that were regularly passed.[146] Abrams delivered the same message to Ambassador Errázuriz: while the United States desired to vote in favor of loan requests, in the absence of any progress toward democracy and an end to state-authored repression, it "would have no choice" but to oppose them.[147]

By late September, most State, Treasury, and NSC officials were in agreement that "under current conditions a yes vote in these institutions could not be sustained" and that they would support an abstention.[148] Treasury had shifted from its earlier position and no longer believed that an abstention would put at risk congressional support for MDB replenishment. In the absence of significant movement on the human rights and democratic transition issues, legal constraints and congressional pressures would make it virtually impossible to vote favorably on upcoming loan requests.

On October 2, Abrams, Barnes, and Deputy Assistant Secretary of the Treasury for Developing Nations James Conrow met, in executive session, with the House Subcommittee on International Development Institutions and Finance to brief its members on the interagency debate over U.S. policy toward Chile in the MDBs, and especially the difficulties in mobilizing support among allies in Europe and Latin America who exhibited a great reluctance to oppose loans on political grounds. Part of the explanation derived from the fact that in most European countries, these decisions were made by finance ministries where human rights were not considered. Washington's dilemma, Abrams told the subcommittee, was twofold: on one hand, Pinochet seemed utterly resistant to taking measures that would allow the United States to vote yes; on the other, even assuming the United States could round up sufficient votes to reject a loan, "Pinochet could whip up a kind of nationalistic fervor," and, worse still, if a U.S. no vote is unsuccessful, it will give the appearance of U.S. weakness, thereby "reduc[ing] our ability to move [him] in the future." Exasperated by what seemed like an insoluble problem, Abrams was at a loss as to what the next step should be: "What is missing in all of this [is] we don't know how to get from here to there. We know what is wrong, but we don't know how to fix it." Conrow highlighted the inevitable consequences of an Executive Board vote to reject the SAL-II loan in mid-November: the commercial bank package and the debt rescheduling

---

[146] Briefing Memo, Michel to Shultz, September 25, 1986, ibid.
[147] Telegram, Shultz to AmEmb Santiago, September 27, 1986, ibid.
[148] Report, DOS, Report to Files, September 25, 1986, ibid.

effort will come to an abrupt halt "precipitat[ing] a financial crisis." He then posed the question as to whether that was a desirable outcome: "I think the answer in all of our minds is that is a hell of a roll of the dice."[149]

The U.S. private banks, who were owed $6.6 billion (by end 1985), or just over one-third of Chile's total foreign debt, could not have agreed more. The Santiago branches uniformly opposed a U.S. vote based on human rights grounds and "enlisted the help of their headquarters to lobby in Washington." The banks' argument was straightforward: the military regime had an exemplary record when it came to implementing SAL programs, and any U.S. attempt to "put the knife in Chile's back" would send a powerful negative signal to other debtor countries.[150] The Executive Regional Vice President of Manufacturers Hanover Trust, which had the largest exposure in Chile, praised the regime's economic policy, which had made it "a pioneer internationally in reshaping its external liabilities."[151] The banks feared that a no vote would lead the Pinochet government to "demand concessions" during upcoming negotiations on debt rescheduling and new funds. Manufacturers Hanover Trust and other leaders of the twelve-bank steering committee repeated Conroy's warning that if the SAL-II were voted down, there would be no release in December of the remaining $49 million in the 1985 economic package for Chile, and the private banks would advance no new funds or reschedule existing debts in 1987.[152] The debtor banks found an unlikely supporter in Cardinal Juan Fresno, who, at all costs, wanted to avoid any economic crisis that might interfere with the Pope's visit in the new year.[153]

Not that there was a clear bureaucratic consensus in Washington about what stance to take. On October 9, Embassy DCM Jones cabled Shultz that "our Chile MDB strategy is not working. The [regime] perception is

[149] U.S. Congress, House, Committee on Banking, Finance and Urban Affairs, Subcommittee on International Development Institutions and Finance, Transcript, *Briefing on Chile*, Executive Session, October 2, 1986, 10, 31, 35.

[150] Telegram, AmEmb Santiago (Jones) to Shultz, October 8, 1986, DOS/FOIAe, III.

[151] See Portales, "De 1985 a 1986: Estados Unidos y la Transición a la Democracia en Chile," 4.

[152] Telegram, AmEmb Santiago (Jones) to Shultz, October 8, 1986. According to Conrow, Chile's total outstanding debt stood at $19.3 billion, of which around $800 million was owed to U.S. government agencies (principally Eximbank) and approximately $12 billion to European and other foreign creditors (plus the $6.6 billion owed to U.S. private banks as of 1985). U.S. Congress, House, *Briefing on Chile*, 29.

[153] Telegram, AmEmb Santiago (Jones) to Shultz, October 2, 1986, DOS/FOIAe, III.

that we lack the leverage to stop the [SAL]," thus eliminating any "strong incentive to accelerate political change."[154] Five days later, Matthei told Barnes that Pinochet had expressed his wrath at U.S. statements about the World Bank SAL and had no intention of caving to any American pressure. If the United States successfully blocked the loan "or otherwise upset Chile's economy for political reasons [Pinochet] would overturn the transition plans by throwing out the 1980 Constitution, end all talk of a transition and rule by fiat indefinitely."[155]

Poindexter and NSC staffers continued to indicate significant concerns with an SAL no vote, less so with an abstention. Kim Flower summarized the outcome of a pre-NSC interagency meeting the day prior to Jones's cable. There was a unanimous view that the United States will probably cast an abstention vote "as the least bad alternative." Congress would not countenance a favorable vote, "and an outright no vote has little support [within the administration]."[156]

Reagan officials repeatedly told Chilean diplomats that the U.S. government wanted to support the MDB requests and resented being forced into "a position in which we have to oppose these loans" because of the regime's failure to improve its human rights record. The blame for this "difficult dilemma" was laid squarely at the doorstep of Pinochet, who "has not been helpful."[157] Undersecretary of State for Economic Affairs Allen Wallis experienced the regime's inflexible position firsthand when he suggested to Finance Minister Hernán Büchi that the SAL vote be postponed until early 1987 in the hope that some progress on human rights and redemocratization would diffuse congressional opposition to MDB lending to Chile. Büchi brushed the possibility aside, "insist[ing] that delay was not feasible" because the scheduled vote on, and passage of, the SAL in late November was a precondition for new commercial banks' funds over the coming year and thus critical to economic recovery.[158]

The Chilean government's refusal to postpone the $250 million World Bank loan vote forced the issue. Shultz's preferred no vote lost out to those administration officials urging a more cautious abstention position on this and future non-BHN loans, to be complemented by ongoing efforts to mobilize international support for that stance. The latter was

[154] Telegram, AmEmb Santiago (Jones) to Shultz, October 9, 1986, ibid.
[155] Telegram, AmEmb Santiago (Jones) to Shultz, "Air Force Chief Matthei," October 14, 1986, LAAD, NSC, Chile (10/11/1986–10/15/1986), Box 91713, RRL.
[156] Memo, Flower to Abrams, October 8, 1986, ibid.
[157] Briefing Memo, Abrams to Shultz, October 24, 1986, ibid.
[158] Telegram, Shultz to AmEmb Santiago, October 6, 1986, ibid.

intended to minimize the possibility of Pinochet exploiting Washington's lack of allies "to rally the troops around him."[159] Undersecretary of State Michael Armacost sought to put the proposed abstention in the best possible light vis-à-vis the bilateral relationship. The U.S. was seeking to accommodate "GOC concerns that too much public criticism would hinder efforts to make progress on human rights and political issues."[160] Although the administration "could sustain that kind of position up to a point," Shultz warned that they "needed more evidence of responsiveness by the GOC than the limited steps [it had] made to date."[161]

On November 17, Admiral Poindexter forwarded a memo prepared by Tillman to the White House for an NSC meeting the following day to discuss, as Reagan wrote in his diary, "how we can persuade Pinochet to move toward a democratic form of government."[162] For background, it provided the President with a brief assessment of the problems Washington confronted in devising an effective policy approach: Pinochet appeared intent on holding on to power for as long as possible by polarizing the country and taking actions to ensure that the democratic opposition remained "weak and divided," with the ultimate objective of making the 1988 plebiscite a choice between himself and Communists, in the process "forcing" his three reluctant junta colleagues to support his candidacy; the latter were "meeting discreetly with opposition leaders" and were reluctant to see Pinochet run for office, but the army would not "abandon" its leader without assurances that a civilian government will meet national security and other concerns and not prosecute officers for human rights abuses; and the democratic opposition continued to act in "undisciplined and unpragmatic ways."[163]

When Poindexter opened the NSC meeting, he was in receipt of an earlier Tillman memo: a broadside against what she considered State's failure to achieve its objectives over the past year. Chile policy, she wrote, was biased against Pinochet and "champion[ed]" the democratic opposition, which had the effect of offering no incentives to either the army to align with the pro-transition junta members or to the opposition

---

[159] Telegram, Shultz to AmEmb, London et al., October 25, 1986, ibid.
[160] Telegram, Shultz to AmEmb, Santiago, November 20, 1986, ibid. The abstention vote sent a clear message to Santiago that "a shot was being fired across the Pinochet bow." Interview with George F. Jones.
[161] Telegram, Shultz to AmEmb Santiago, November 20, 1986.
[162] Douglas Brinkley, *The Reagan Diaries* (New York: HarperCollins, 2007), 451.
[163] Memo, Poindexter to President, prepared by Tillman, November 17, 1986, Executive Secretariat, NSC, Meeting Files, NSC 139, Nov 18, 1986 [1], Box 91304, RRL.

to adopt a "hard-headed, pragmatic [approach] required to outmaneuver Pinochet." Tillman accused State of making recent policy by "self-fulfilling prophesy," advocating specific actions (e.g., in the UNGA or World Bank) only to respond to bureaucratic opposition by falling back on the argument that U.S. "credibility" was at stake if its decisions were rejected.[164]

Apart from specific issues, such as the Chile SAL vote and whether to certify to Congress that Chile should keep its duty-free access to U.S. markets under the GSP,[165] the NSC Adviser explained that the primary objective of the meeting was to integrate these and other decisions within "the context of an effectively constructed and carefully calibrated policy." This larger universe was defined by support of Pinochet's junta colleagues, accommodating the army's security and institutional concerns; making the democratic opposition more credible partners of, and eventually an alternative to, the army; applying "effective pressure" on Pinochet; and taking congressional concerns seriously. CIA Director Robert Gates focused his remarks on how the arms caches and assassination episodes had added to the difficulties of promoting a transition to civilian rule. Admiral Merino, the strongest junta advocate of the dialogue and the transition, had already spelled out the set-in-concrete preconditions for any deal with the military: no prosecution of military officials for human rights abuses; maintenance of the free market economic model; no rollback of other basic programs implemented by the regime; and a commitment that a future government will ban the Communist Party. One positive development since the attempt on Pinochet's life was the decision by the moderate opposition leaders to cease cooperating "with Communists and their radical allies" and to begin private meetings with junta members Matthei, Merino, and Stange. Nonetheless, Gates concluded, Pinochet's reluctance to give up the presidency after 1989 and the inability of the moderate opposition to agree on a transition scenario acceptable

---

[164] Memo, Tillman to Poindexter, "NSC Meeting on Chile, November 14," November 10, 1986, DDRS (2008: 0304).

[165] Interoffice Memo, Sullivan to Tillman, "GSP Eligibility for Chile," November 3, 1986, LAAD, NSC, Chile 1987 [November 1986], Box 91172, RRL. The 1984 Trade and Tariff Act gave the President authority to deny GSP eligibility to countries "that fail to meet internationally-accepted labor standards." Complaints filed against Chile, wrote Sullivan, were "not markedly worse than the others"; the problem was a much stronger perception that the regime was "less committed to reform." State's position was that the withdrawal of GSP eligibility would have only a limited impact on Chile trade with the United States, whereas the NSC contended that it would affect the nation's "attempts to diversify its exports," could weaken its creditworthy status, and may result in a loss of access to OPIC's insurance program. Ibid.

to the armed forces still constituted significant obstacles to Chile's return to democracy.

At this point, President Reagan intervened in the discussion, apparently not totally convinced that the democratic opposition had severed all its ties with the Communists, and signaled his reluctance to unnecessarily antagonize an important regional ally. The Secretary of State disagreed, siding with Gates's view that the United States had been "reasonably successful in carving them ['democrats'] away from the Communists." The Department was more concerned about "stem[ming] the radicalization" of the youth and student sectors of the population, who "don't have the inoculation the older crowd has. Instead they have the repression, the aspects of Pinochet that are terrible [and] simply indefensible." Hence the importance of publicly, as well as privately, supporting the transition. Shultz concluded his mini-lecture to Reagan on the following note: "That's why our actions, like going to the [Rojas] funeral, have given us credibility. If we only do things that are agreeable to Pinochet, we won't get anywhere. We need to be willing to rock him a little." Convincing Reagan to let go of a foreign head of state with whom he had close political, ideological, and/or personal ties, if his extreme reluctance to acknowledge the end of the Marcos regime in the Philippines the previous year was any indication, would not be easy. Nonetheless, Shultz remained firm, addressing Reagan "in a way you don't talk to a President." His impatience boiled over when the President suggested a state visit to the United States by Pinochet:

Reagan: If there was some way we could appear as not being opposed to him, to indicate that we respect what he has accomplished, yet say we want to help Chile...

Shultz: But I don't think we can just try persuasion. We have to use some muscle, or he won't change. Pinochet's bottom line is to stay in power, to create a Pinochet or communist choice.

Reagan: Maybe though it makes him dig his heels in. There should be someway we could get to him. Well, I guess there would be screaming and hollering from the Congress but maybe we should think about a state visit.

Shultz: No way. This man has blood all over his hands. He has done monstrous things.[166]

---

[166] Telegram, Barnes to Shultz, 'Private Junta Contacts with Opposition," October 23, 1986, LAAD, NSC, Chile (10/23/1986–10/24/1986), Box 91713, RRL; interview with Elliott Abrams; Minutes of Meeting, Cabinet Room, "Chile," November 18, 1986, LAAD, NSC, NSC Meeting on Chile 11/18/1986, Box 91172, RRL.

The meeting ended on a calmer note: all were agreed that, however difficult the task might be, "we must try" to get Pinochet to support a return to democracy.[167] Gelbard recalled the Secretary's characterization of Pinochet as "an extraordinary moment," a forthright declaration that he was in charge of Chile policy. From then onward, it was "much easier" in dealing with those officials who opposed the Shultz strategy.[168]

At a high-level meeting in the Cabinet Room to discuss Chile, the list of agenda items included the joint decision by Shultz and Treasury Secretary James Baker to abstain, rather than vote against, the World Bank SAL-II for Chile. The explanation for this decision was irrefutable, according to a senior State Department official: "the worse possible signal to send Pinochet" was if the loan passed despite a U.S. no vote, in which case "we [would] look impotent."[169] Shultz provided a more detailed and revealing commentary on the thinking behind the decision. Given Chile's "outstanding" economic policies, the "real problem" was how to force Pinochet to accelerate the transition process without endangering the economic program. A complicating factor was the "tremendous pressure" being applied by Congress to vote against the World Bank loan, which could not be ignored. No doubt, Shultz observed, "we'll [still] get our rear end kicked" by the legislators for deciding to abstain. Underlining the limits of the policy shift that Shultz, Abrams, Gelbard, and Barnes had initiated, the Secretary indicated that the United States would not actively lobby Executive Board members to vote against the loan: "We're not trying to block the loan. We're abstaining with others and hope that the yeses plus the abstentions will pull it through."[170]

As the vote neared, a positive outcome for Chile seemed assured. Most Latin American and West European governments had already cited a "reluctance to 'politicize'" the Bank's loan process.[171] German officials added that to evaluate Chilean loans other than on the basis of "normal aid criteria . . . would create a precedent which the FRG [Federal Republic

[167] Brinkley, *The Reagan Diaries*, 451.
[168] Interview with Robert Gelbard.
[169] Quoted in Clara Germani, "Washington Softens Position on Key World Bank Loan to Chile," *CSM*, November 7, 1986, 11.
[170] Minutes of Meeting, Cabinet Room, "Chile," November 18, 1986.
[171] Memo, Tillman to Poindexter, "Meeting Request from US Ambassador to Chile; Possible Meeting with Chilean Junta Member," September 29, 1986, WHORM: Subject File, C0033 Chile (420000–429999), RRL. On British reluctance to use political criteria, see Telegram, AmEmb London (Price) to Shultz, September 30, 1986, DOS/FOIAe, III.

of Germany] might not wish to follow for other countries."[172] This concern influenced the British decision to support the loan. Elliott Abrams reported that "strategic interests in the Falklands" further reinforced Whitehall's stance. Close ties between the two countries also dictated Spain's vote: "Chile is very big in Spain. They don't like to vote against loans. They hate it."[173] Even Asian members balked at shifting away from traditional economic criteria in determining MDB votes. When requested by a U.S. Embassy officer to abstain on the SAL vote, Japanese foreign affairs officials "cited [the] World Bank principle to assess loans based on economic rather than political criteria and thought it might be 'difficult' for the GOJ [Government of Japan] to abstain."[174]

In the aftermath of the Executive Board vote to grant the loan, unhappy conservatives in State and the White House compared the U.S. decision to abstain with the Carter administration that "voted no [on Chile loans] eight times, and the things passed eight times; they stood alone and what good did it do them?"[175] Secretary Shultz sought to downplay any polarizing impact the final decision might have by characterizing the message it projected "as ambiguous at best."[176]

After the extremely mild rebuke Washington had delivered Chile in the World Bank, the Secretary now sought to craft a "balanced" resolution ahead of the annual UNGA vote to maintain "the credibility of U.S. policy of strong encouragement for movement toward a peaceful democratic transition and improved respect for human rights." To allay any objections from the NSC, State's Nicholas Platt lobbied Admiral Poindexter to support the Shultz initiative because it would "enhance our standing with Chile's democratic opposition" and bolster efforts to "drive an effective wedge" between it and the Communists. The objective was similar to the

---

[172] Telegram, AmEmb Bonn (Dobbins) to Shultz, "Germans Share US-Chile Assessment; Hesitant on Use of Loans," September 24, 1986, LAAD, NSC, Chile 1986 (3), Box 91181, RRL.

[173] Briefing Memo, Abrams to Shultz, September 9, 1986, DOS/FOIAe, III; U.S. Congress, House, *Briefing on Chile*, 34.

[174] Telegram, Shultz (Whitehead), Info AmEmb Montevideo, November 1, 1986, DS/FOIAe, III. The final vote was 51 percent in favor, 41 percent abstentions, and 5 percent against. To U.S. officials, the closeness of the vote signaled to Pinochet "our continued concern for human rights and for democratic transition in Chile." Paper, "Chile World Bank Loan," LAAD, NSC, Chile (11/14/1986–11/20/1986), Box 91713, RRL.

[175] Administration official quoted in Joanne Omang, "U.S. Said to Be Planning Abstention on Chile Loan," *WP*, November 20, 1986, A36. Two weeks later, the U.S. also abstained on a $319 million loan for a hydroelectric plant approved by the IADB.

[176] Shultz, *Turmoil and Triumph*, 974.

U.S.-drafted "balanced resolution" passed by the UNHRC in March. The Secretary wanted to counter any Cuban-Mexican proposal that would "play into the hands of both extremes within Chile." Finally, it would forestall congressional criticism of the World Bank vote that it amounted to a policy shift more accommodating of Pinochet.[177]

NSC staffers posed the strongest bureaucratic challenge to Shultz's strategy, ably supported by UN Ambassador Vernon Walters. Jacqueline Tillman attacked State's justification for a U.S.-authored resolution as additional evidence of why American policy toward Chile was "veering off course" and in need of "a mid-course correction." She was especially critical of the lack of any reference in Platt's memo to the military, its failure to take into account that three of the junta members did not support a Pinochet candidacy in the 1988 plebiscite and had "publicly called for dialogue with the opposition," and how this proposed resolution would impact on U.S. ties with these dissenting commanders.[178] Whether Poindexter felt likewise was not immediately evident, leading Elliott Abrams to conclude that the NSC "seems paralyzed on the subject."[179]

In a revised version of his earlier memo to the NSC Adviser, Platt pointed out that in light of the earlier UNHRC effort, "our passivity will be misrepresented as a shift... in favor of Pinochet" and a willingness to overlook the regime's human rights abuses during the past six months. Furthermore, it would almost certainly have a negative impact, coinciding as it did with the U.S. abstention vote on the World Bank SAL loan to Chile. This proposal, he argued, "is critical to maintaining the credibility of our policy, in Chile and with Congress."[180] Managing the impact of the World Bank SAL abstention vote on Capitol Hill also dominated Abrams's thinking. "Congressional sentiment on Chile is so strong," he wrote, "that we really must say something in [the] UNGA." Given the inevitable resentment among liberals in the House and Senate over the proposed abstention vote, a U.S. decision to authorize this kind

---

177 Memo, Platt to Poindexter, October 21, 1986, DS/FOIAe, III. Shultz told former Chilean finance minister Sergio de Castro a week later that the administration "was prepared to stand up for Chile before the U.S. Congress or in the United Nations but that we needed to have a solid moral basis for doing so." Telegram (Whitehead) to AmEmb Santiago, "Secretary's Meeting Oct. 28 with Former Chilean MINFIN De Castro," S/S to AmEmb, LAAD, NSC, Chile (11/05/1986–11/07/1986), Box 91713, RRL.
178 Draft Memo, Tillman to Poindexter, "Chile," undated, LAAD, Chile 1986 (1), Box 91181, RRL.
179 Telegram, Shultz (Whitehead) from Abrams, Info USDEL, "UNGA Resolution on Human Rights in Chile," November 1, DOS/FOIAe, III.
180 Memo, Platt to Poindexter, October 31, 1986, ibid.

of resolution would "enable us to head off Congress from running away with the issue."[181]

The NSC staffers opposed the resolution on ideological grounds as well: the discovery of the arms cache and the attempt to kill Pinochet signaled "communist intentions to greatly raise the level of government repression and violence – by possibly moving from terrorism to insurgency – and to most likely move strongly against a presumably weaker post-Pinochet government." For this reason, there was need to "evaluate whether our current high visibility, activist policy should be recast and refocused to a more carefully calibrated strategy."[182] Harry Barnes gave this argument short shrift, warning that if the United States failed to submit its own UN resolution, "we would gain absolutely nothing with the opposition who are vital to a successful transition and would lose most, if not all, of what we have gained this year." The Ambassador made an unusually impassioned plea to Shultz to hold firm:

In your remarks at my swearing in you spoke of my having to focus on the fact that Chile had deviated sharply from the democratic path. To me an essential ingredient of my mission has therefore had to be in the area of human rights. I do not see how I can perform that mission effectively without a continuation of the support I have been receiving from Washington. Hence I am prepared to come back to Washington to make the case in person if that is what it takes.[183]

In the end, Shultz could not overcome the objections of his bureaucratic protagonists. Instead, the United States joined with a small minority (Chile, Paraguay, Indonesia, Lebanon) in voting against a Mexican-Cuban resolution (supported by eighty-four member states with forty-six abstentions) critical of human rights violations in Chile. In a cable to the Santiago Embassy, Shultz rationalized this decision, like an earlier one not to support a resolution critical of Chile at a recent (November) OAS General Assembly meeting, to "concerns that too much public criticism [including the SAL vote] would hinder efforts to make progress."[184]

---

[181] Telegram, Shultz (Whitehead) from Abrams, Info USDEL, ibid.
[182] Memo, from Poindexter, prepared by Tillman, November 17, 1986, "Meeting with the NSC, November 18 on Chile," LAAD, NSC, NSC Meeting on Chile 11/18/1987, Box 91172, RRL.
[183] Telegram, AmEmb (Barnes) to Shultz, November 4, 1986, DOS/FOIAe, III.
[184] Telegram, Shultz to AmEmb Santiago, November 20, 1986, ibid. Following the adoption of the Mexican-Cuban document by the UN Third (Social) Committee on November 28, Walters cabled State complaining that the resolution ignored the activities of terrorist groups and failed to acknowledge "the positive steps taken by the [regime]" to limit state-authored abuses. Telegram, USUN Mission, New York (Walters) to Shultz, December 3, 1986, ibid.

Following an interagency meeting on Chile that same month, the NSC began preparing a draft National Security Study Directive (NSSD) that laid out the basic U.S. objectives. Above all, it was imperative to transform the democratic opposition into a "more disciplined and pragmatic" movement, thereby creating a more "credible" alternative in the eyes of the armed forces; to ensure that the former continue to distance themselves from the Communists; to avoid actions that would allow Pinochet to exploit nationalist sentiments in the army; to expand U.S. ties and influence with the army; to apply "effective pressure" on Pinochet; and to take no actions that might be "counterproductive." Indicative of the White House reluctance to precipitate an open rupture with Pinochet himself, President Reagan issued instructions that "private diplomatic pressure" remained a preferred means for pursuing Chile policy goals.[185]

Reflecting on events during the second half of 1986, Harry Barnes could see little evidence of progress toward democracy. Pinochet had, month by month, consolidated his authority and power while the democratic opposition wallowed in "considerable turmoil." Efforts to replicate the social mobilization and street protest tactics of 1983–1984 had failed to attract significant support, thus allowing a gloating Chilean dictator to say "I told you so."[186]

In mid-December, senior State Department officials met to discuss U.S. strategy for a February 1987 UNHRC meeting and agreed that a U.S.-sponsored resolution on Chile would "help us to fend off congressional meddling" and revive the administration's "credibility" with the moderate opposition which had eroded in the wake of "our [recent] UNGA indecisiveness." To send a message of U.S. intent at this early stage, opined Assistant Secretary for Human Rights Richard Schifter, would increase support for the resolution. Elliott Abrams was not so sure: "I doubt it," he wrote in a handwritten note on the memo of the conversation.[187]

The Department's report on achievements in Chile policy over the past year and how to proceed during 1987 began by acknowledging that moderate gains in the period under review could not conceal the reality that "no breakthrough" on a democratic transition or human rights was in sight. Pinochet and his advisers remained in control of the process and made little secret of their ultimate objective: a transition from military rule

---

[185] Memo, NSC, Rodney McDaniel to Donald P. Gregg, "NSDD on Chile," November 26, 1986, Ludlow "Kim" Flower, Chile: NSDD, Box 91528, RRL.

[186] Quoted in "Basis for Council on Foreign Relations Talk in New York," February 18, 1987, "Speeches and Statements 1987–88," Box 1, Papers of Harry G. Barnes.

[187] Memo, Flower to Abrams, December 19, 1986, DOS/FOIAe, III.

to a "protected democracy most likely with Pinochet still at the helm." The centrist opposition parties, wrote the authors of the report, were not part of Pinochet's "scenario," and they had not helped their case by a failure to provide a "credible alternative [due to] competing personal ambitions and strategies." In response to pressure from the United States and the Vatican in particular, Pinochet had taken limited steps toward the political openness required by his 1980 Constitution (initiating a slow process of electoral registration, providing for the legalization of political parties, improving media access for the non-radical opposition), but not enough that would ensure a democratic outcome. It was evident that he had "not been deflected from his goal of emulating [Spanish dictator General Francisco] Franco's lifelong tenure."

The report proposed a series of measures to be implemented over the next twelve months: increased contacts between senior U.S. military officers and Chilean civilian leaders in the government and opposition; more regular meetings between the U.S. Ambassador and senior regime officials; greater encouragement to Chilean officials to dialogue with their U.S. counterparts in Washington; private support for the "pragmatists" among the democratic opposition and constant opposition toward "tactical alliances" with the Communists; utilizing "the only muscle [economic] we have" intelligently in an effort to promote desired changes in the regime's domestic policies; and enlisting Harry Barnes to play a central role in "targeted lobbying" of conservative and moderate Republicans in Congress to oppose sanctions legislation. Essentially, this amounted to a continuation of the approach that had evolved over the previous twelve months, constrained, as always, by the fear of creating a situation where the only alternatives were Pinochet or the Communists, which, as Barnes had earlier observed, "[would leave us with] no choice but to back Pinochet."[188]

By year's end, the Reagan administration was encouraged by two developments: the withdrawal of the Socialist Party faction (and its replacement by the Liberal Party) from the AD, with whom Washington hoped the junta would negotiate; and the AD's decision to surrender any ambitions to move Chile beyond Pinochet's favored protected democracy model. These moves were the first fruits of a decisive shift within the Chilean opposition toward accepting the parameters laid down by Pinochet on the transfer of political power. Working the military side of

[188] Report, DOS, drafted J. Swigert ARA/SC, "US Policy toward Chile: Strategy for 1987," December 1, 1986, ibid.

the equation would pose a more difficult challenge for U.S. officials. As the State Department's 1987 policy paper realistically concluded, any new initiatives had to be based on the assumption that Pinochet would stand down before he was ready "only if somehow convinced to do so by his military colleagues[,] who are unlikely to force his hand."[189] Efforts by the administration to encourage this outcome undoubtedly influenced the leadership of the antiregime forces, although much less than the growing realization that social mobilization tactics had served a purpose but had failed to induce the junta to respond with other than brute force, which was unlikely to change if this form of challenge to the dictatorship were to continue.

[189] Ibid.

5

Abandoning Pinochet

Entering 1987, the Reagan administration faced a major challenge to restore a degree of coherence and credibility to its foreign policy-making processes in the wake of the Iran-Contra scandal involving illegal arms transfers to the Nicaraguan rebels. White House intervention in Nicaragua and elsewhere in Central America did not touch directly on Chile policy, but it did change the cast of characters previously involved in the debate and eventually altered the balance of influence between the various foreign policy agencies, damaging the reputation of the NSC and the CIA and restoring a leading role to George Shultz and the State Department in the overall conduct of foreign policy.

Although not at the top of the Reagan foreign policy agenda, Chile would rise to prominence at regular intervals – surrounding deliberations of the UNHRC and annual UNGA meetings, when the Pinochet regime's human rights record came under scrutiny and when Chilean loan requests came before the MDBs. As well, Chile was fast becoming a standout concern in Latin America as other military regimes passed power back to democratically elected governments, and it was regarded by many within the administration as the sole major example the White House could cite to demonstrate that its professed commitment to democracy included targeting right-wing dictatorships in the region.

In contrast to the difficulties Reagan and his senior foreign policy officials now confronted domestically, Pinochet was in as strong a position as ever. He had ridden out the most sustained period of popular mobilization against the regime since it seized power in 1973 and had done so without making any substantive concessions either to the political opposition or to the court of world opinion. His control over the army, the junta, and the various state instrumentalities remained essentially unchallenged, and the events of August–September 1986 – the discovery of an arms cache destined for use by radical leftists to fuel a violent challenge to the dictatorship and the failed assassination attempt – had breathed new life into his assertion that Chile needed the strong hand of a military government if it was not to descend into civil war. According to a mid-February assessment prepared by U.S. Ambassador Harry Barnes, "the period from June [1986] to January [1987] was one of considerable reinforcement for Pinochet and one of considerable 'soul searching' for the democratic opposition. If last June the equation 'tilted' toward Pinochet it had moved decisively in his favour over the past six months." The reason was twofold: during 1986, demonstrations no longer attracted large numbers of participants in comparison with the 1983–1984 protests; and Pinochet was able to exploit anti-communism to maintain his grip on power.[1]

Pinochet's renewed strength was accompanied by the absence of any imperative or pressure to engage with his opponents, whom he now disparagingly called "'pilgrims of power' who travelled around the world seeking foreign support."[2] Although most opposition leaders were resigned to playing by the military's rules and timetable if they ever hoped to see it return to barracks, they were still divided on key tactical issues, distrustful of Pinochet himself and of his entire transition plan, and skeptical about the extent to which they could count on the support of a vehemently anticommunist White House. As a result, they posed no serious threat to Pinochet and presented no credible alternative in the eyes of his supporters.

The Chilean economy's encouraging prospects after the dark days of the early 1980s further bolstered the regime's position. Declining international oil prices and rising copper prices not only improved the nation's balance of payments; they made less likely any external debt default and thus increased vulnerability to outside pressures. While other members of the junta may have held reservations about Pinochet's ultimate intentions and their long-term consequences for Chile, none was prepared to break openly with him while the chances of an orderly return to an acceptable civilian government remained uncertain. In a New Year's speech, Pinochet had announced that a two-year-old predawn curfew in Santiago

---

[1] Notes for Talk, Council on Foreign Relations, New York, February 18, 1987, Container No. 1, "Speeches and Statements, 1987–88," Box 1, Papers of Harry G. Barnes.

[2] "Keynote Address: Journalists and Editors Workshop on Latin America," Florida International University, Miami, Florida, March 20, 1987, ibid.

would be lifted and that most of the regime's political opponents still in exile would be allowed to return home. Shortly thereafter, he promised to introduce a new law that would legalize non-Marxist political parties. These "concessions" were as much a sign of Pinochet's confidence that he had a firm grip over events inside Chile as they were attempts to appease critics of his rule.

Policy Skeptics

Writing in the *Los Angeles Times* in early January, Senator Edward Kennedy launched a scathing attack on the Reagan administration's approach toward Chile. He noted that the Inter-American Human Rights Commission, the UN's Special Rapporteur, and the State Department were in agreement that the human rights situation had deteriorated in Chile over the previous twelve months. Why, he then asked, had the United States decided merely to abstain on a $240 million World Bank SAL to Chile in November, voted against a resolution critical of Chile's human rights record in the UNGA in December, and failed, that same month, to speak out in open session during IADB deliberations on a $350 million loan request for a hydroelectric project – preferring instead to abstain behind closed doors after the loan had been approved? These actions, Kennedy charged, "exposed the Reagan administration's look-the-other-way policy on human rights in Chile."[3]

The day Kennedy's article appeared, U.S. Trade Representative Clayton Yeutter announced that Chile would not be deleted from the list of nations whose exports to the United States were duty free because of its failure to abide by legislation requiring the beneficiaries to maintain internationally recognized standards of workers' rights. A senior State Department official rationalized this decision on the grounds that, notwithstanding "'some problems' regarding harassment and repression by Chile's security forces against certain union figures," the situation of organized labor "isn't that bad" compared to other countries in the region. Hence the dictatorship would remain on probationary status for the time being. This decision raised further concerns among Chile policy critics, who perceived an executive branch a little too eager to defend Pinochet's regime.[4]

---

[3] Edward M. Kennedy, "America Sides with Pinochet's Atrocities," *LAT*, January 2, 1987, 5.

[4] Quoted in Paul Glickman, "Critics Say US Is Easing Pressure on Chile for Political Reform," *CSM*, January 22, 1987, 5.

Publicly, Department officials were quick to vindicate the administration's UN record on Chile, conveniently overlooking the NSC's success in persuading Reagan to override a Department recommendation to abstain on the recent UNGA resolution.[5] Deputy Assistant Secretary for Inter-American Affairs Robert Gelbard told reporters that U.S. officials had held an "agonizing debate" over the resolution and only voted against it "with regret" because it failed to endorse the report of the UN's own human rights envoy on Chile. Irrespective of that decision, Washington "continu[es] at all levels to press Chile for change and they are definitely getting the message," he added.[6] Whereas the first claim was accurate, the second clearly was not.

Abrams was more candid about his attitude toward Kennedy's criticism during a private meeting with Chile's Ambassador, describing it as a "declaration of war" and the prelude to a campaign in the Democrat-controlled Congress to make the Latin nation the "next South Africa."[7] In hindsight, though, he acknowledged that "a certain amount of congressional pressure was useful" and described Kennedy's comments as mostly "grandstanding" because the Senator and his aides "thought of us as the good guys." With the exception of Jesse Helms and his staff, "who really thought as General [Vernon] Walters did that we were promoting communism, and were really tough on us," the White House and Congress "had the same goal on Chile."[8]

Abrams's interpretation aside, Kennedy's critique tapped into the thinking of some State Department officials. The day after the Senator's broadside, the SCA Director Kim Flower received a memo drafted by the Chile Desk Officer, James Swigert, who wrote that "the credibility of our Chile policy has been questioned by the Chilean democratic opposition" precisely owing to our failure to sponsor (unlike 1985) a successful human rights resolution in the UNHRC and as a result of the no vote on the Mexican text of the UNGA resolution critical of the regime's human rights abuses. Chile's opposition parties began to suspect that these decisions

[5] See Memo, Tillman to Powell, January 6, 1987, Ludlow "Kim" Flower, Chile: NSDD, Box 91528, RRL.

[6] Quoted in Pamela Constable, "US Appears to Be Taking a Softer Line on Chile's Pinochet," *BG*, January 4, 1987, 3. Dismissing assertions of any shift in U.S. policy, executive branch officials maintained that abstention votes in the MDBs "technically fulfilled Congress' requirement that the U.S. oppose multilateral loans to human rights violators." Glickman, "Critics Say US Is Easing Pressure on Chile for Political Reform," 5.

[7] Telegram, Shultz to AmEmb Santiago, January 24, 1987, DOS/FOIAe, III.

[8] Interview with Elliott Abrams.

might constitute the beginning of "a major policy shift toward Pinochet." An attached background paper noted a "growing tension between our national interest and an orderly and peaceful democratic transition in Chile, and President Pinochet's apparent desire to maintain himself in office indefinitely." The paper suggested that one possibility for a peaceful transition lay in the "increasingly open" resistance to Pinochet's ambitions from the non-army members of the junta, although only if "increasing polarization does not prevent development of the necessary civilian-military cooperation." This outcome necessitated increased U.S. efforts to bolster the center-right antiregime groups while simultaneously strengthening ties to, and influence with, the Chilean armed forces. It was unclear how these broad objectives could be achieved, although Admiral Jose Merino, and Generals Fernando Matthei and Rodolfo Stange at least, had already established "a close dialogue with the USG [U.S. government]."[9] This was in stark contrast to Pinochet's deliberately limited contact with Embassy and Washington officials, highlighted by his refusal to hold a single meeting with Ambassador Harry Barnes, except for the presentation of credentials ceremony in November 1985.[10]

Kennedy and some State Department officials were not alone in suggesting that U.S. policy had gone soft on Chile. Before a group of businessmen in Valparaiso, Pinochet's Foreign Minister Jaime del Valle actually praised Shultz's moderate approach to Chile, attributing problems that arose in the bilateral relationship to the actions of mid-level foreign policy officials in Washington. An acerbic Ambassador Barnes commented that del Valle was simply repeating "the Chilean myth that President Reagan is a friend of Pinochet but that 'Chile-bashers' within the bureaucracy have circumvented the President's wishes."[11] While acknowledging that the international community had failed to sufficiently recognize the "positive" political steps taken by the regime, Secretary of State Shultz conceded that there was still "a widespread perception in the U.S. and elsewhere that these steps were not part of a broader program of liberalization."[12]

The disagreement between State and the NSC over how best to achieve the consensus goal of a political transition compatible with U.S.

[9] Memo, DOS, ARA/SC-Ludlow Flower III to S/PPR-William Harrop, January 5, 1987, and attachment "Chile/US Bilateral Relations and Issues," Ludlow "Kim" Flower, Chile; Democratic Opposition Political Parties, Box 91528, RRL.
[10] See Múñoz, *The Dictator's Shadow*, 157.
[11] Telegram, Barnes to Shultz, January 13, 1987, DOS/FOIAe, III.
[12] Telegram, Shultz to AmEmb Santiago, January 24, 1987.

interests remained a complicating factor in efforts to settle on a coherent policy approach. In November 1986, the NSC had convened an interagency meeting for the purpose of drawing up a National Security Decision Directive (NSDD) on Chile. When a final draft was circulated in December, it began by acknowledging that Pinochet's "resistance to a full democratic transition and his apparent strategy of polarization are major problems which themselves increase the prospects for the Communists and future instability in Chile and in the region, and put at risk Chile's future chances of preventing a Communist takeover." The democratic opposition was taken to task over its failure to "develop an effective and comprehensive strategy to challenge and maximize the openings which the implementing steps of the Constitution may afford them." Severing all ties with the Communists and radical left was at the top of the list. Economic developments required close attention as well: while stability and continued growth would provide a "positive climate for a transition and improve the prospects for moderate solutions," any downturn in Chile's economic performance would have the opposite effect of "weaken[ing] the moderate center and enhancing the opportunities for the Communists and terrorists to sabotage a democratic transition." For these reasons, U.S. objectives must be to "sustain the positive role" of pro-transition junta members, to seek "broader contacts and influence with the Army," to maintain pressure on Pinochet while avoiding actions that might prove counterproductive, to push and prod the democratic opposition to adopt "a more disciplined and pragmatic posture so it gains credibility with the Army," and to ensure there is no backsliding in "its present course of distancing from the Communists." Implementing these steps, the draft repeated at several points, required an "interagency consensus."[13]

If the NSDD illustrated the challenges and potential pitfalls facing U.S. policy makers in their attempts to encourage a return to civilian rule in Chile, its reception again highlighted the difficulty of reaching an interagency consensus. State Department officials, angered over the authors' failure to insert key suggested changes, or to modify parts of the document, charged that this simply reflected "the poor job done by [the] NSC on NSDDs in general." In a memo to Abrams, the Southern Cone Office's David Cox spelled out some of the objections. While the NSDD rightly drew attention to the Communist threat in Chile, it did not make sufficiently clear that "Pinochet's opposition to a genuine transition in 1989 is the fundamental problem." At the operational level, the draft

---

[13] Memo, NSC, Flower to Powell, attached "NSDD on Chile," January 8, 1987, Ludlow "Kim" Flower, Chile: NSDD, Box 91528, RRL.

would make it "impossible to achieve full interagency consensus in response to fast-breaking issues" because it allowed each involved agency to be its own judge of what constituted appropriate pressure on Chile instead of letting the State Department make the final determination. "The result is such serious problems of substance and bureaucratics," Cox concluded, "that *no* NSDD would be better than the 'final draft' as presently written."[14]

Cox's assessment was echoed by Shultz's Executive Secretary Nicholas Pratt. In its current form, he wrote to NSC Adviser Frank Carlucci (who had succeeded Admiral John Poindexter in December 1986) the draft does not sufficiently emphasize the fundamental obstacle confronting U.S. policy makers: Pinochet's "lack of commitment to a genuine democratic transition." As the November 17 NSC meeting indicated a "broad interagency consensus" to this effect, any "ambiguity" on this key point "distorts the meaning of the document." An additional and "potentially unmanageable" problem with this draft could emerge when it came time to implement the policy because it would "require even routine matters to be subject to interagency consensus." Imposing a constraint of this kind on the Secretary of State's role as the President's senior foreign policy adviser "would open the way for confusion, interagency discord, and indecisiveness" when U.S. policy toward Chile demands precisely the opposite approach, based on "continued close interagency coordination of policies [rather than] micromanagement of foreign policy by individuals not in a position to be up-to-the-minute on the situation in Chile."[15] The CIA was critical of the draft for different reasons, accusing its authors of a tendency "to exaggerate the degree of U.S. influence" over the major protagonists in Chile and to excessively stress the threat arising from Pinochet's determination to hold on to power. The Agency did not question the accuracy of this latter appraisal; rather, it bemoaned the absence of virtually any attention "to the feasibility or practicality" of Pinochet's ambitions given the steady erosion of support for his candidacy in the 1988 plebiscite.[16]

The Office of Management and Budget (OMB) was reasonably comfortable with the draft NSSD, except for an explicit assumption it

---

[14] Memo, ARA, David Cox to Abrams, January 2, 1987, ibid. (emphasis original).

[15] Memo, DS, Nicholas Platt to WH, Frank Carlucci, "Draft NSDD on Chile," attachment to Memo, DS, ARA David Cox to Abrams, January 2, 1987, ibid. Also see Memo, Platt to Frank Carlucci, February 11, 1987, and attached "State Department Revisions to Draft NSDD on Chile," ibid.

[16] Memo, CIA, Standall, to Green Jr., Executive Secretary NSC, "CIA Comments on Second Draft of NSDD on Chile," January 5, 1987, ibid.

contained, namely, that "continued economic stability and growth in Chile will improve the prospects for moderate political solutions." In the short term, a buoyant economy could just as easily "strengthen Pinochet's hand considerably and work against our stated [redemocratization] goal." Imperative as it was to reject implementing trade, credit, or other sanctions that could undermine the market-based economy, OMB concluded that Washington's best interests would be served by avoiding the perception of an administration "too supportive" of the dictator.[17]

As the debate proceeded, it soon became clear that those NSC staffers who had qualms about the NSSD were in no mood to make any significant concession, singling out the State Department's failure to press its "activist approach" on a number of measures, most recently concerning the UNGA resolution on human rights in Chile, which had gone all the way to the White House, where Reagan gave it the thumbs-down. The NSC's more cautious line on Chile seemed to resonate more with the President. Not that the staffers were committed to dumping the NSSD altogether. "The fact that there still are remaining disagreements with State does not mean that we should kill the NSDD," José Sorzano advised his superior NSC Deputy Adviser Colin Powell. The focus should be on achieving a consensus with State because it was critical to "get all our ducks in a row."[18] The debate dragged on for some months before an acceptable consensus was reached that "had no impact on diluting support for the policy of injecting human rights and democracy concerns into US-Chile relations" but did not fully resolve the interagency differences.[19]

Constraining the Tactical Shift

If officials in State were pursuing a more "activist" approach toward Chile than other parts of the foreign policy bureaucracy, it was nevertheless one that featured both contradictions and limits. In an attempt to court

---

[17] Memo, Executive Office of the President, Office of Management and Budget, Arny to Green, January 6, 1987, ibid. Senior Interagency Groups, the NSC Adviser or NSC staff members could request a policy study on major security issues. The President would then issue an NSSD calling for the study, and if it involved economic development or an aid issue, an OMB member would usually be part of the study group. See, for example, NSSD Number 2-85, January 9, 1985, "Economic Development for Central America," National Security Study Directives, 1981–1989, http://www.reagan.utexas.edu/archives/reference/NSSDs.html.

[18] Memo, Sorzano to Powell, January 6, 1987, ibid. Also see Memo, Tillman to Powell, January 6, 1987, ibid.

[19] Interview with James Swigert.

greater influence with the Chilean armed forces – and despite its professed concern over the human rights situation – the administration refused to give up on the possibility of getting Congress to renew military aid to Chile, which was an essential part of the Shultz-Barnes strategy. A March 1987 request triggered a sharply worded letter to Shultz from nineteen House members, reminding him that the Letelier-Moffitt case was still unresolved, that human rights conditions were getting worse rather than better, and that the aid spigots could only be turned on by a legislative waiver or presidential certification that the level of abuses in Chile had declined.[20]

That same month, Senators Kennedy and Tom Harkin (D-IA) and Representatives Edward Feighan (D-OH) and Bruce Morrison (D-CT) introduced into Congress bills to impose further sanctions on Chile unless the President could certify that the military regime had made substantial improvements in human and labor rights, demonstrated progress in the transition to democracy, and was working toward a resolution of both the Letelier and Rodrigo Rojas cases. The sanctions included mandatory no votes in the MDBs, the end of tariff exemptions for Chile under the GSP, the termination of insurance cover for investments in Chile under OPIC, a ban on copper imports (which had topped more than $250 million in 1986), and the withdrawal of landing rights for the state-owned Lan Chile airline. State Department officials estimated that if these sanctions were imposed, Chile stood to lose more than $1 billion in MDB loans, almost $60 million in tariff exemptions, and as much as $750 million in OPIC coverage, threatening more than $1 billion in foreign investment projects. The United States, in turn, would lose a major market for aircraft and aircraft spare parts (Lan Chile accounted for $121 million in U.S. exports during 1986). The Department called the proposed changes to existing policy in relation to the MDBs, the GSP, OPIC, and Chilean imports contrary to "the spirit of free and fair trade practices." And any move to abrogate Lan Chile's landing rights was equally objectionable unless Chilean authorities first implemented a similar discriminatory measure against U.S. airlines.[21] But in view of this attempt to strengthen sanctions, it was little wonder, wrote ARA's Richard Howard, that "our current relations with Chile ... are cool and difficult."[22]

[20] Letter, House of Representatives, Ted Weiss, Joe Moakley plus sixteen others to Shultz, March 23, 1987, DOS/FOIAe, III.
[21] DOS, Talking Points/Briefing Paper, January 8, 1987, ibid.
[22] Memo, Howard to S/PPR-ARA Inspectors, March 10, 1987, ibid.

The challenge posed by the Kennedy-Harkin initiative and the State Department response embodied two sharply differing views of U.S. policy toward Chile. Whereas congressional critics desired a forceful, get-tough approach in dealing with Pinochet's institutionalized repression, State preferred a more nuanced response based on encouraging, and even rewarding, the regime in return for concessions – while limiting pressure to actions that did not pose a fundamental challenge to U.S. economic interests in particular. Elliott Abrams told Chilean Ambassador Hernán Errázuriz that recent actions by Pinochet constituted "the most important advance in Chile toward 'normalization' since the approval of the 1980 Constitution."[23] To Errázuriz, such praise indicated Washington's greater understanding of how to maximize its interests in Chile: "If you push, what you get is, you unite the people – they don't like a foreign country to push their country around. The wise thing was to be very subtle with this."[24]

The Department's hostility toward congressional pressure for new sanctions was another part of its "subtle" approach. In a letter to Harry Barnes, the ARA's Southern Cone Director Richard Howard informed him that "the Administration will strongly oppose this [Kennedy-Harkin] measure." State's level of concern eased after speaking with the senators' aides, who agreed that their sanctions bill "was unlikely to prosper." Diplomats in Washington and Santiago would still need to remain vigilant to "keep this legislation on the back-burner." Close monitoring of the Chilean opposition political parties should be a priority in case they decided to "opt for short-term (perceived) political benefits by backing the sanctions bill."[25] To Abrams, sanctions were simply counterproductive; they only hurt the Chilean populace and could "spur a kind of nationalistic backlash that would help the [regime] rather than helping the opposition."[26] Ambassador Barnes agreed. Notwithstanding the slow progress on human rights and democracy promotion, he told a group of editors and journalists in Miami, there was no evidence that past sanctions on Chile had "brought about changes of the sort intended."[27]

"Talking Points" briefing papers set out State's objections to further sanctions legislation more comprehensively. The administration, one

[23] Telegram, Shultz to AmEmb Santiago, January 24, 1987, ibid.
[24] Interview with Hernán Errázuriz.
[25] Letter, Howard to Barnes, March 13, 1987, DOS/FOIAe, III.
[26] Telegram, Shultz to AmEmb Santiago, March 19, 1987, ibid.
[27] Telegram, AmEmb Santiago (Jones) to Shultz, "Ambassador's Keynote Speech, Miami, Fl," March 17, 1987, ibid.

explained, opposed suspending OPIC insurance coverage and mandating U.S. negative votes on non-BHN loans to Chile in the MDBs for a number of reasons: first, to avoid a possible rise in anti-U.S. sentiment, "which extremists on both sides would exploit to their advantage"; second, such measures would undercut Chile's "excellent economic program, which promotes free market policies and responsible management of debt"; third, sanctions exposed American exports to Chile, valued at around $1 billion annually, to retaliatory measures; fourth, they "would remove the leverage that present legislation provides to encourage constructive change"; and finally, legislated sanctions would eliminate administration "flexibility" in the MDBs.[28] A follow-up paper made the obvious point that further "punitive economic sanctions" would not force the Pinochet regime from power because the United States does "not have that kind of leverage." Terminating OPIC programs, currently under review by Congress because of the workers' rights situation in Chile, was doubly troubling because it was likely to backfire, "undermin[ing] the authority of that review" and producing a "negative impact on sensitive discussions with other countries."[29] On Capitol Hill, however, these kinds of arguments carried little weight.

The State Department's caution in devising a Chile strategy characterized its approach to the country's human rights performance before the UNHRC. Since late January, ARA had been pushing for the United States to table a resolution at the forthcoming March meeting of the UNHRC that was "more forthright in its praise of the Chilean Government actions, less tough on the abuses which exist and stronger in targeting Cuba and the Eastern Bloc for meddling in the nation's internal affairs"[30] – partly an allusion to the arms cache uncovered the previous year. The result was a concerted two-track campaign to garner support for a U.S. resolution that would recognize improvements and "end the practice of singling Chile out" by considering it under a separate agenda item before the UNHRC. Track 1 investigated the possibility of encouraging the Europeans to formulate their own resolution on Chile that would be acceptable to the democratic opposition and could "persuade Mexico not to proceed with its resolution."[31] Track 2 involved directing U.S. embassies to approach the foreign ministries of West European and Latin American governments

---

[28] DOS, Talking Points/Briefing Paper, drafted by ARA/SC Swigert, April 1, 1987, ibid.
[29] DOS, Talking Points/Briefing Papers, April 6, 1987, ibid.
[30] Memo, Cox to Gelbard, January 23, 1987, ibid.
[31] Telegram, AmEmb London (Price) to Shultz, February 4, 1987, ibid.

in particular to persuade their Geneva delegations to fall into line behind a Washington resolution rather than the blunter, more critical one being proposed by Mexico and Cuba – which made no reference to either the terrorist problem or the Pinochet assassination attempt and left unaltered Chile's status as a country singled out for special consideration over the level of human rights abuses.[32] The process of developing an alternative text, wrote State's Richard Howard, turned out to be "much more onerous than we had anticipated."[33]

The British government gave in-principle approval to the "balanced" nature of the eventual U.S. draft but was critical of its failure to cite specific human rights abuses perpetrated by the Pinochet regime. David Gordon-McCloud, the Foreign and Commonwealth Office's (FCO) senior Chile Desk Officer, commended the U.S. draft "with the qualification that it would have to be more 'hard-hitting' to win British support."[34] The Western Hemisphere governments presented a different problem. Because State was particularly disappointed with the initial level of regional support for its efforts to end Chile's special treatment, Elliott Abrams determined that the Track 2 approach also be channeled through the Latin embassies in Washington.[35] Delivering the message personally to the Argentine Ambassador, Abrams stressed that the time had come "to stop treating Chile as the worst human rights offender on earth" by moving it from a special to a general agenda item.[36]

In the course of recent informal discussions with Chilean opposition leaders, however, Argentina's Vice Minister of Foreign Relations and Defense, Raúl Alconada, discovered their strong opposition to any change in Chile's special status on the grounds that it "would cut the political ground out from under them." Sufficiently impressed by this argument, he recommended that his own government's UNHRC delegation be instructed to oppose efforts to move Chile to a general agenda item. Alconada also challenged the timing of the UNHRC meeting as unfortunate precisely because it coincided with a nationwide spotlight on the prosecution of Argentine military officials for human rights abuses during the 1970s Dirty War as well as passage of the controversial *punto*

---

[32] Telegram, Shultz (Whitehead) to U.S. Mission, Geneva, February 22, 1987, ibid.
[33] Letter, Howard to Jones, AmEmb Santiago, February 19, 1987, ibid.
[34] Telegram, AmEmb London (Price) to Shultz, February 26, 1987, ibid.
[35] Telegram, Shultz (Armacost) to AmEmb Brasilia et al., February 28, 1987, ibid.
[36] Telegram, Shultz (Whitehead) to AmEmb Buenos Aires, February 26, 1987, ibid.

final legislation, which limited further trials of the perpetrators of the state-authored violence.[37]

On March 5, Deputy Assistant Secretary of State John Whitehead cabled the Santiago Embassy that the effort to move consideration of Chile to a general agenda item was getting nowhere. Vigorous lobbying for revisions of the Mexican resolution had only partially incorporated American concerns, support for a separate U.S. resolution was almost nonexistent, and to continue pursuing this option "could critically damage whatever possibility remains to get the needed votes" for passage of a sharply worded resolution on Cuba. The consensus among delegations contacted by the U.S. mission was that "victory is doable" but getting the numbers remains "an uphill battle." Whitehead reported that these same delegations were generally underwhelmed by the Chilean regime's human rights improvements. The typical comment was that "it has not been much." To most, the language in the U.S. text was seen as markedly "imbalanced [and] over-generous" to the regime. Numerous delegations told their U.S. colleagues that it was imperative to "keep the pressure on [and not] send the wrong signal." Eliminating consideration of Chile under a special agenda item would unquestionably send that message. Whitehead expressed dismay that the Vatican delegate was "strongly opposed" to deleting Chile as a special agenda item, equally committed to supporting the revised Mexican draft, and had been urging delegations "to keep the pressure on the Chile Government leading up to the pending trip of the Pope to Chile [in April]." The USUN delegation should therefore mount a full court press to encourage the Latin American and the West European and Others Group (WEOG) delegations to support the American formulation.[38]

After considering the lack of success of this effort, State's Seventh Floor cabled instructions to its UN diplomats to inform Mexico and the WEOG delegations that Washington was prepared to support their compromise resolution provided the U.S. delegation was "reasonably convinced that WEOG has given [a] firm commitment to make a good faith effort" to

---

[37] John Bushnell, at the time DCM in the Buenos Aires Embassy, was unimpressed with this argument, accusing the Argentines of "blowing domestic political smoke to cover positions taken to protect perceived foreign policy interests." Telegram, Bushnell to Shultz, March 3, 1987, ibid.

[38] Telegram, Shultz (Whitehead) to U.S. Mission, Geneva, March 4, 1987, ibid. The WEOG composed the Western European states, Turkey, New Zealand, Australia, Japan, Canada, and the United States.

eliminate the consideration of Chile as a separate agenda item in the next UNHRC session and that the American diplomats judged the likelihood of a positive outcome as "reasonable." In that circumstance, Shultz instructed the delegation "to join consensus on Mexican text without revision and to vote yes."[39] There remained one minor obstacle the Secretary and his allies had to overcome. State's IO Bureau had "serious problems" with a paragraph in the draft text related to the 1986 attempt on Pinochet's life that did not "adequately" ensure the submission of a comprehensively balanced resolution. ARA eventually convinced its IO colleagues that, granted their argument had substance, "we do not feel the Mexican formulation . . . should prevent our voting for the resolution."[40] Meanwhile, Abrams and Gelbard were instrumental in overcoming NSC doubts about the decision. The threat of further sanctions legislation enacted by Congress "apparently was what brought the NSC around."[41]

Writing to Harry Barnes in early April, ARA's Richard Howard was pessimistic regarding likely developments on Chile in the months to come. He expressed a "sinking feeling" about the continuing ability of the executive branch to contain hostile congressional actions. OPIC and the GSP were already under the spotlight, and both appeared "vulnerable because of the controversy over the worker rights review." At the UN, the situation was just as bleak. The failure to submit a U.S. resolution in the UNGA the previous year had undermined the administration's "negotiating position" achieved at Geneva in 1985. Compounding this setback, the delay in reaching an interagency agreement on a text for consideration by the UNHRC this year had allowed Mexico to secure its resolution as the point of reference.

The U.S. delegation might have regained the initiative if the administration's priority had not been gaining (ultimately insufficient) support for a harsh resolution criticizing Cuba's human rights record. The decision to support the Mexican resolution on Chile as a trade-off for passage of one critical of Cuba only promised to harden the stance of some U.S. officials in their approach to both countries at the upcoming UNGA meeting. Then "we can expect both problems in spades," wrote Howard. It would be "another knockdown fight over Cuba." As well, embarrassed by the failed attempt to condemn Cuba, USUN Ambassador Walters was "unlikely to be enthusiastic about our supporting any Chile resolution,

[39] Telegram, Shultz to U.S. Mission, Geneva, March 11, 1987, ibid.
[40] Memo, Howard to Michel, March 16, 1987, ibid.
[41] Letter, Howard to Barnes, March 13, 1987, ibid.

let alone introducing one;" nor under any circumstances would he support one cosponsored by Cuba. And given the U.S. decision to sign on to the "extremely detailed and relatively harsh" Mexican resolution on Chile, the NSC would "almost certainly be reluctant" to undertake new initiatives to mediate between Walters and the State Department. For all these reasons, a "more balanced" Chile resolution at the next UNGA meeting in New York would be that much "more difficult to secure."[42]

Chile's former Foreign Minister Miguel Schweitzer was urging an altogether different tack. During a visit with Assistant Secretary for Human Rights Richard Schifter, he complained that because "the U.S. had not given sufficient attention to the possibility" that Pinochet might be replaced by "a weak democratic government," which could "buckle under Communist pressure," there was an urgent need for Washington to reassess its entire policy approach. Pinochet would not step down of his own accord and would "never allow any member of the army to be prosecuted for a human rights abuse," Schweitzer added. Knowing this, the army "will support [him] to the end." In short, U.S. officials were being urged to recognize the obvious: Pinochet intended to cling to power "whether fairly or unfairly elected."[43]

The situation inside Chile offered little reason to question this conclusion. Although Pinochet was taking steps to implement his own transition plan, he did so only haltingly and in ways that kept alive suspicions about his commitment to the process. Robert Gelbard perceived a "symbiotic relationship" between Pinochet and the radical left, with both sharing the same medium goal of "trying to destroy the possibility of a democratic alternative." To make matters worse, Gelbard wrote, Pinochet appeared tempted to use the considerable means at his disposal to "meddle with the economy and produce a temporary boom in time for an election" irrespective of the impact this might have on Chile's longer-term economic welfare. On the other side of the political divide, no credible alternative leader or leaders had emerged as "rallying points" for the opposition.[44]

Washington's disappointment over the leadership problems among the opposition political parties was accentuated by their endless debate over whether to participate in Pinochet's plebiscite plans. No political party wanted to be seen as legitimizing the dictator's transition blueprint by being the first to inscribe under the new political parties law and the voter

[42] Letter, Howard to Barnes, April 8, 1987, ibid.
[43] Telegram, Shultz to AmEmb Santiago, April 10, 1987, ibid.
[44] Telegram, Shultz to AmEmb Lima, March 18, 1987, ibid.

registration process – which was proceeding at a snail's pace. This failure to resolve internal disagreements actually benefited the regime insofar as it diverted the opposition's energies away from organizing street protests and demonstrations that the Embassy reported were now more "limited in size and appeal." Of course, part of this reluctance to revert to mass mobilization politics was the violent state response this tactic had earlier provoked. There was also a desire to avoid any major public challenge to Pinochet in the weeks leading up to the Pope's visit for fear that it would be exploited by the regime "to discredit these parties."[45] For this reason, the Church hierarchy distanced itself from a statement by one of its bishops that the regime was "marked by an immense immorality."[46]

Pinochet versus the Pope

In the course of a visit to Chile in late March, Southern Cone Director Richard Howard consulted with the leaders of most of the key participants in the Chilean drama: senior government and Church officials, Chilean and U.S. businessmen, and political opposition, human rights, and labor leaders. Summing up the meetings, Harry Barnes cabled Washington that Chilean officials were most anxious about the proposed Kennedy-Harkin economic sanctions bill and were told that the best response to the threat of such legislation was "to remove the grounds for legitimate external criticism" of the state's repressive behavior. The regime would continue to come under "heavy fire unless a genuine 'political opening' accompanied the promulgation of political laws." This brought a sharp retort from Foreign Minister del Valle that the United States had adopted a "'tutorial' attitude toward Chile and that nothing the GOC does seems to be enough."[47]

Although the message delivered by Howard had little impact on Pinochet himself, the Southern Cone Office Director's bleak reflections on the week-long visit and its implications for U.S. policy were taken far more seriously in Washington. Reporting to Abrams, Howard confirmed that Pinochet would almost certainly be a candidate in the 1988 plebiscite and observed that there was little evidence to suggest that the junta, and especially the army, would stand in his way and risk fracturing

---

45 Telegram, Barnes to Shultz, March 13, 1987, ibid.
46 Bishop Carlos Camus, quoted in Shirley Christian, "Harsh Criticism of Pinochet Softened by Chilean Bishop," *NYT*, March 14, 1987, 3.
47 Telegram, Barnes to Shultz, April 7, 1987, DOS/FOIAe, III.

its unity. The Chilean military was just as "unlikely to accept any formula which allows the [Christian Democrats] and/or left of center parties to regain significant power and influence." The new electoral registration and political parties laws had put the regime "in a strong position to set and enforce the rules of the game in its controlled political opening." While most democratic parties – including the PDC – had serious reservations about these laws, they were "likely sooner or later to sign up for the only game in town." Howard's critique of the major opposition parties echoed that of Gelbard: "[they] are not united and have no obvious leader who could serve as a rallying point." An anti-Pinochet alliance across the political spectrum from the Núñez Socialists on the moderate left to the right-wing National Party was "fragile [because] neither end of the ideological spectrum trusts the other." While the PDC remained the most formidable force within the antiregime movement, it was also the "most divided [and] internally fragmented." The ties between Pinochet and the armed forces were further strengthened by their hostility toward PDC President Gabriel Valdés – a politician, Howard said, they "cannot abide" – and his continuing leadership role virtually ensured that the military would "remain united in their opposition to any formula which might give the PDC real power." Howard's assessment of the Núñez Socialists, if not as sweeping, was equally cutting: they "talk a democratic political game and may for their own ends be willing to play [but] they don't strike me as friends of the U.S. or necessarily democratic." In contrast, left-leaning Christian Democrats appeared to "understand the U.S. and our domestic political levers." The greater certainty was that "for the foreseeable future, democratic politics as we know it will not be allowed to threaten Pinochet's version of the New Chile."[48]

One hope of breaking this impasse resided with Pope John Paul II, although expectations among U.S. officials that his visit to Chile might somehow spur the transition process were not high. "I don't think anybody thought he was coming to Chile for that reason," recalled the Embassy's George Jones, who downplayed the significance of the previsit dialogue between U.S. and Vatican officials. "There was a lot of to-ing and fro-ing with the Vatican because they have a very good diplomatic service. You always want to make sure that the Vatican understands your policy. You know it's not going to say anything publicly to endorse it but you don't want it to say anything privately to undermine it either. So you want to keep the Vatican informed and particularly in the Chilean

---

[48] Memo, Howard to Abrams, April 15, 1987, ibid.

context we didn't want the Vatican to put any restraints on Fresno because the Cardinal was one of the most effective allies we had."[49] To Elliott Abrams, "it wasn't as though Church officials were asking us to do anything or vice versa but we were parallel" in seeking an end to military rule.[50]

The expectations of the visit among at least some of the Chilean organizers were another matter. So, too, were the Pope's own intentions. Ahead of the visit, he told reporters that he considered the Pinochet regime to be "dictatorial" and that the Church's pastoral mission was to replicate the actions of the Church in the Philippines, whose clergy played a key role in the demise of the Marcos regime and the restoration of democracy. "I think [a transition] is not only possible but necessary," John Paul declared.[51] On his arrival in Chile, the Pope's message became more restrained. This may have been because Pinochet still enjoyed considerable support among those Chileans who had benefited from the "economic miracle" and/or were convinced that he had saved the country from the turmoil of the Allende years. As well, the local Church hierarchy was itself divided between dissident bishops who desired the Church to be at "the cutting edge for change" and moderates who felt the institution "cannot afford to lead the kind of anti-government crusade that was carried out under Cardinal [Jaime] Sin in the Philippines." Opposed to both was a small, influential group of "pro-government" bishops who "staunchly oppose[d] the notion that the Church should intervene in social and political issues" – a position shared by the Papal Nuncio, Cardinal Angelo Sodano. U.S. Embassy officials described Sodano as preoccupied with the danger posed by "communist infiltration" of the Church, a viewpoint he was able to propagate through his close ties to the predominantly conservative mass media.[52] Sodano "certainly was not a Pinochet critic," wrote Barnes.[53] Indeed, he had a reputation for his fawning attitude toward the Chilean leader, and it was he who had played a

[49] Interview with George F. Jones.
[50] Interview with Elliott Abrams.
[51] Quoted in Don A. Schanche, "Pope Critical of Pinochet Regime at Outset of South American Tour," WP, April 1, 1987, A17; Roberto Suro, "Pope, on Latin Trip, Attacks Pinochet Regime," NYT, April 1, 1987, 1. The Pope's statement "perplexed" many Chilean priests, who remembered his lukewarm support for the Philippine bishops' anti-Marcos campaign. Dawn Gibeau, "Pope, Pinochet Face Off as Chile Trip Unfolds," NCR, April 10, 1987, 18.
[52] Telegram, AmEmb (Jones) to Shultz, March 20, 1987, DOS/FOIAe, III.
[53] Interview with Harry G. Barnes.

major role in choreographing the Pope's entire visit.[54] One further reason for the Pope's caution may have been that Pinochet received the backing of powerful right-wing Catholic organizations such as Opus Dei, which, in turn, enjoyed the support of John Paul.

Regime attempts to manipulate the Pope's presence in Chile for political ends on occasion made it difficult to judge John Paul's own position with respect to the dictatorship. On one occasion, Pinochet's entourage managed to maneuver him onto the balcony of the presidential palace in a tableau that seemed to indicate the Pope's acceptance of the General's rule. Other efforts to lure the pontiff into public endorsements of Pinochet were less successful. These included an attempt to have him offer a personal blessing to the dictator and his wife in a private chapel in the presidential palace: the Pope on that occasion merely blessed the two from a distance as he passed by the chapel.[55] For Christian Precht, a key leader of the Vicariate of Solidarity and deputy to Cardinal Fresno, the five-day visit was carefully planned to emphasize the Church's role as a defender of human rights and promoter of reconciliation. In the Chilean context, this meant combining statements on behalf of victims of repression with admonitions to the government and opposition to work together to ensure a nonviolent transition to the kind of inclusive, law-abiding democracy envisaged in the National Accord. The Pope's thirty addresses emphasized this message, as did his numerous public appearances (including one with Carmen Quintana, the burn victim), which were also intended to allow Chileans the opportunity to demonstrate their support for a transition from military rule. Encouraging attendance at these public gatherings, said Precht, helped rebuild civil society by "reconquering the streets" as places of peaceful intermingling rather than repression or violent confrontation. The regime understood this kind of symbolism as well: at a papal Mass held in Santiago's Bernardo O'Higgins Park to beatify a Chilean nun, six hundred attendees and police were injured when a riot broke out. No explanation was ever given as to how some

---

54 See John L. Allen, "These Paths Lead to Rome," *NCR*, August 22, 2003, http://natcath .org/NCR. A group of priests and lay theologians organized an unsuccessful campaign to get Sodano recalled to Rome, arguing that he had shown "a clear affinity with the military dictatorship." Quoted in "Recall Move against Nuncio in Chile," *NCR*, May 8, 1987, 4. Pinochet had numerous influential supporters in the Vatican. See Hugh O'Shaughnessy, "The Cardinal Who Stood Up to Pinochet," *The Tablet*, February 27, 1999, http://www.thetablet.co.uk/article /6703.
55 See Mario I. Aguilar, *A Social History of the Catholic Church in Chile: Volume III. The Second Period of the Pinochet Government, 1980–1990* (Lewiston: Edwin Mellen Press, 2004), 194.

of the participants managed to smuggle rubber tires and gasoline into the venue, why the police took so long to intervene, or why so few agitators were ever arrested in connection with a disturbance of this magnitude. Church officials strongly suspected the regime of orchestrating the riot to bolster its claim that Chile remained a dangerous and violent nation that required a continuation of authoritarian rule.[56]

Christian Precht's assessment of the Pope's visit – that it "helped the country to mobilize itself, and to encounter ourselves as a people"[57] – did not feature in the Embassy cable traffic. Indeed, U.S. officials held a much narrower (and arguably far less sophisticated) assessment of the visit, which was largely focused on consideration of its impact on the fortunes of Cardinal Fresno. In a communiqué to Shultz, Ambassador Barnes concluded that the Pope's "warning against excessive politicization," together with his wholehearted support of the Church's social mission, undoubtedly provided a boost to Fresno, who had been subjected to relentless criticism by dissident bishops and clergy over his perceived failure to sufficiently defend the Vicariate of Solidarity.[58]

Not that the Chilean government itself was disappointed with the results of the visit. Chilean Air Force Colonel Enzo Dio Nocera García confided to the U.S. Embassy's political officer that the Pope had maintained "a 'very strict line' which was well received by the military."[59] Harry Barnes more or less agreed in observing that the visit had "very little" impact on the Chile's political dynamic.[60] Some opposition leaders concurred. "Pinochet didn't listen to Reagan," said Heraldo Múñoz, "so why would he listen to the Pope?"[61]

[56] Quote and interpretation of events in George Weigel, *Witness to Hope: The Biography of Pope John Paul II* (New York: Cliff Street Books/HarperCollins, 1999), 531–536.

[57] Quoted in Jeffrey Klaiber, *The Church, Dictatorships, and Democracy in Latin America* (New York: Orbis Books, 1988), 62.

[58] Telegram, Barnes to Shultz, April 6, 1987, DOS/FOIAe, III. Pinochet merely added to the pressure on Fresno by "undercut[ting]" him in refusing to renew a dialogue on the transition to democracy. Ibid. That said, the Pope was personally exposed to the internal divisions within the Church when a reference to Fresno during a meeting with poor Chileans "brought jeering hisses." The Pope came under some subtle criticism himself over the role of the Nuncio in convincing the Vatican to choose conservative bishops to fill openings in the Chilean hierarchy. Quotes in Dawn Gibeau, "Papal Visit Symbols Grip Chileans," *NCR*, April 17, 1987, 22.

[59] Memo of Conversation between Embassy Political Officer Charlotte Roe and Air Force Colonel Enzo Di Nocera, May 8, 1987, DOS/FOIAe, III.

[60] Interview with Harry G. Barnes.

[61] Telephone interview with Heraldo Múñoz.

Taking a longer view, however, the Pope was able to demonstrate that there were possibilities in Chile not allowed for in the regime's depiction of the country as dangerously poised for a return to chaos without the firm hand of the military. He conferred with a range of opposition leaders, including Christian Democrats, Rightists, Socialists, and Communist Party officials, at a meeting hosted, somewhat ironically, by Sodano in the Vatican Nunciature – the first time such a range of Chilean politicians had gathered under the same roof since September 1973.[62] The Pope's visit provided further ammunition to those in the junta seeking to advance an orderly transition. Within days of his departure, General Matthei publicly urged a degree of political reform, warning that "otherwise the country's future is bleak indeed." Admiral Merino called for a dialogue to advance the transition. Barnes interpreted these statements as a "respon[se] to the Papal visit in a way that could encourage a political opening," even if neither junta member was offering guarantees that a "genuine dialogue" would take place and both continued to insist that the Chilean government (for all practical purposes, Pinochet himself) "must define the moment and framework for any talks."[63] At a cabinet meeting ten days after the Pope's return to Rome, even Pinochet spoke of the visit in positive terms and, coincidentally or not, began planning in earnest for the 1988 plebiscite.[64] The Pope later confided that he had suggested to Pinochet that he begin preparations to step down from power.[65]

Working on the Opposition

In early May, Barnes forwarded a comprehensive assessment on current developments surrounding the plebiscite and the transition prospects to Shultz. Aware that the administration was still equivocating over whether

---

[62] See Carl Bernstein and Marco Politi, *His Holiness: John Paul II and the Hidden History of Our Time* (London: Bantam Books, 1997), 516.

[63] Telegram, Barnes to Shultz, April 13, 1987, DOS/FOIAe, III.

[64] See Aguilar, *A Social History of the Catholic Church in Chile, Volume III*, 205. Cardinal Fresno's behavior in the wake of the Papal visit – accepting a medal from Pinochet and being photographed with the Chilean dictator, and giving communion to former CNI head General Humberto Gordon "during a televised ceremony" – appeared to confirm the view of those within the Church uneasy over his refusal to take a more independent stance toward the regime. See Tim Frasca, "Chilean Prelate Is Center of Refired Debate," *NCR*, May 8, 1987, 4.

[65] See Bernstein and Politi, *His Holiness*, 517.

to accept Pinochet's transition scenario, he urged Washington not to reject the plebiscite in favor of transparently free and fair elections because it "would not advance our interest... if the U.S. too flatly opposes a mechanism which many moderate Chileans consider a viable means to end Pinochet's rule." As well, to make such opposition public would further "complicate" problems for the moderates, who were being forced to defend even the idea of registering as official parties against the "attacks of the communist-led parties of the MDP and the leftist-oriented segments of their own constituencies." Pinochet himself would surely exploit U.S. rejection of his plans "to stir a nationalistic backlash that would pressure the junta members into joining him in defying U.S. interference." Last, but not least, Barnes warned that there was unlikely to be any transition at all in the near future unless the military was able to wrest an iron-clad agreement from the democratic opposition guaranteeing that the former's "vital interests are beyond risk."[66] Securing such a deal now became a White House priority.

Days after receiving Barnes's memo, Gabriel Valdés arrived in the U.S. capital for a round of meetings. State Department officials were determined (on the advice of the Ambassador) to convey a twofold message: the Communists needed to be completely isolated from the political opposition; and democratic leaders should resist the temptation to lend support to the more punitive sanctions against Chile being proposed by the anti-Pinochet elements in Congress. Responding to claims from Valdés that Washington regarded "the Right as the easy solution to the problem" in Chile, HA's Richard Schifter was at pains to insist that the U.S. government was "committed to working with the entire democratic opposition [but] that democracy can be built only by democrats." When Valdés indicated his reluctance to sever links completely with the Communists, Schifter condescendingly suggested that he read Lenin, where he would find "proof that Leninists could not possibly be trusted as partners in building democracy."[67]

Valdés's meeting with Abrams and Gelbard focused on the issue of MDB loans to Chile. The PDC leader argued that the United States should take a "very hard" line on loan submissions, especially those, such as SALs, that didn't directly benefit the populace because economic pressure was "the only way to convince the Army to break with Pinochet."

---

[66] Telegram, Barnes (Whitehead) to DOS, May 8, 1987, DOS/FOIAe, III.
[67] Telegram, Shultz to AmEmb Santiago, May 12, 1987, ibid.

Neither U.S. official was convinced this proposed tactic would work and suggested Valdés drop it. Gelbard asserted that sanctions would be "ineffective" in achieving the opposition's goals: they were more likely to have a "boomerang" effect, mobilizing the middle class behind, rather than against, Pinochet. And he reminded Valdés that the decision to abstain rather than vote no on the SAL-II the previous November was for one reason only: there was no possibility of getting a majority of World Bank Executive Directors to block the loan. PDC leaders, including Valdés, created their own problems for State with their enthusiastic support for sanctions. Undersecretary Michael Armacost cabled the Santiago Embassy that this "will complicate efforts to hold off adoption of counter-productive legislation toward Chile." Other responsible opposition leaders proposing to visit Washington in the near future should be encouraged or persuaded "to think through seriously the full implications of punitive [legislation currently before the Congress]." State's opposition to additional sanctions continued to be rationalized on the grounds that they were more likely to entrench, rather than weaken, Pinochet's hold on power.[68]

Sergio Molina, the Christian Democrat coordinator of the National Accord, received the same message from Armacost when he visited Washington in mid-June. An ARA briefing memo stated that the White House had "quietly encouraged" NED funding for Molina's efforts to bolster the antiregime moderates and the democracy program but was waiting until the opposition movement demonstrates "greater national dynamism and grassroots strength" before publicly supporting open elections in Chile. Armacost was advised to point out as forcefully as possible that the democratic opposition parties had failed to present a coherent and realistic challenge to the military regime; that they continued to exhibit a "lack of pragmatism [which] helps Pinochet"; that they remained "plagued by divisions over strategy and leadership," particularly the Christian Democrats, "whose support is essential for [an] effective campaign"; and that the result of these weaknesses had been "no discernible progress" in developing a civilian alternative acceptable to the military. The ARA memo did not understate the difficulties of the task confronting U.S. policy makers: Washington's influence was limited, Pinochet "ignores the USG views, and the Chilean Army remains virtually unreachable." While the administration was working to improve the lines of communication

---

[68] Telegram, Shultz (Armacost) to AmEmb Santiago, May 14, 1987, ibid.

with the armed forces, chances were "slim" for a breakthrough on a transition, and the sentiment on Capitol Hill about imposing new sanctions had undoubtedly "reduced our maneuvering room."[69]

Accompanied by Abrams and Gelbard, Armacost began the meeting with Molina by referring to the democratic transition in the Philippines where Marcos "was able to stimulate and exploit fights within the opposition parties, so that eventually it became the weakness of the opposition, rather than Marcos's own strength, that was the source of his longevity." Marcos was finally toppled once he confronted a united opposition headed by a credible and popular leader. Gelbard then addressed the Chilean opposition's call for harsher sanctions, repeating earlier warnings that further punitive action "could boomerang to give a boost to Pinochet in this critical period."[70] On this issue, Molina was not easily convinced (or what U.S. officials termed "less than forthright"), and he left Washington after reportedly persuading "at least one Congressional office" that he actually supported additional sanctions against Chile.[71]

Another opposition political figure to visit Washington at this time was Carlos Lazo, the exiled Executive Board member of the Almeyda Socialist Party (PSCH/A) faction, who complained to ARA officials that they were too ready to couple his group with the Communist Party. Insisting on a sharp distinction between the two, he claimed that his faction was "adamantly opposed to violence and [had] said so publicly" and that it wished to enter into an "open dialogue" with the State Department. This request produced a "very wary" response from the Seventh Floor because "it could send the wrong signal to the democratic opposition about alliances with the PCCH." Shultz was particularly worried about the impact of opening such a dialogue on the PDC, which was soon to elect a new leader – one Washington hoped it could support and work with much more effectively than was the case with Valdés. The other concern was that dealing with the Almeyda Socialists could weaken the more moderate Núñez Socialists. "We do not wish to rebuff this approach out of hand," Shultz cabled the Santiago Embassy, "since there may be opportunities to encourage non-totalitarian tendencies within the [Almeyda faction]." Nonetheless, Lazo's professed acceptance of democratic precepts and rejection of violence was treated with "considerable scepticism"

---

[69] Briefing Memo, Bushby to Armacost, June 15, 1987, ibid.
[70] Telegram, Shultz (Armacost) to AmEmb Santiago, June 21, 1987, ibid.
[71] Letter, Cox to Barnes, June 25, 1987, ibid.

because State was determined to avoid giving Pinochet "[an] easy means with which to try to discredit U.S. pressure for democratization."[72]

Responding to Shultz's request for a more detailed assessment of the Almeyda Socialists, the Embassy praised their recent tactical decision to support the voter registration drive but characterized their attitude toward the presidential elections as "ambiguous" and more about "keeping lines open" than an unequivocal commitment. The Embassy generally concurred with Shultz's own view that they should be kept at arm's length: "Their current emphasis is on a political struggle, but they continue to hold that [they] must be prepared for an eventual armed struggle."[73] In any event, by now, Washington was not particularly concerned about the radical left playing any leading role if Chile were to revert to civilian rule. U.S. contacts with Socialist Party leaders were "kind of secondary," explained Abrams, because the feeling in Washington was that if the transition did happen, the new civilian government would return the Christian Democrats to political power.[74] The bigger question, of course, was whether the transition was going to take place at all.

Penetrating the Military

U.S. officials remained committed to expanding what lines of communication they could with the Chilean armed forces despite considerable opposition on Capitol Hill. When the administration, back in March, proposed renewing military aid to Chile, this triggered a strong reaction from twenty congressmen, who signed a letter to Shultz expressing "grave concern" that such a move was even being considered. They reminded the Secretary that military aid could not be provided without a waiver of Section 726 of the FAA or a presidential certification that the human rights provisions written into legislation had been met. Acting precipitously on military aid "would profoundly set back the cause of human rights in Chile."[75] This did not preclude the Executive Branch from occasionally taking advantage of loopholes in the legislation. During 1987, for instance, it secretly agreed to the Chilean Army purchase of fifteen transport helicopters on the grounds that they had not been outfitted for

---

72 Telegram, Shultz to AmEmb Santiago, July 24, 1987, ibid.
73 Telegram, AmEmb Santiago (Jones) to Shultz, August 7, 1987, Ludlow "Kim" Flower, [Chile] [2], Box 91528, RRL.
74 Interview with Elliott Abrams.
75 Letter, House of Representatives, Ted Weiss, Joe Moakley plus sixteen others to Shultz, March 23, 1987, DOS/FOIAe, III.

offensive use, had nonmilitary applications, and were therefore not on the list of munitions subject to human rights conditions.[76]

Personal liaisons were an important part of White House efforts to cultivate and deepen ties with the Chilean officer corp. Following a May 1987 meeting in Santiago with high-ranking military personnel, U.S. Southern Command head General John Galvin regaled Ambassador Barnes with the "very alarming symptoms of isolation apparent in senior Chilean military officers [and their] heightened sense of both mission and threat." There were indications, Barnes reported, that younger generations of officers are "more and not less hardline," and given the armed forces' "pivotal role" in a successful transition to civilian rule, both he and Galvin considered it "vitally important to use every measure available to expand contacts between the U.S. and the Chilean military." Priority should be given to establishing a program of regular Chilean "civilian/military" visits to the United States.[77] This recommendation was quickly adopted by the State Department, which began working on training programs that would include a civilian component to make it more "politically saleable" to Congress.[78] Within forty-eight hours of the Barnes memo, the NSC Deputy Director for Latin American Affairs had transmitted a request to the U.S. Embassy for "a list of our initiatives for expanding our contracts and strengthening our relationship with the Chilean armed forces."[79]

On Capitol Hill, selling any proposal that looked like a concession to the Chilean military was always going to be difficult. It wasn't made easier by reports such as the one Barnes filed in early June on how the security forces continued to engage in torture, threats, and harassment of regime opponents with the active support of "unidentified groups." While there had been some progress toward a democratic transition in the first five months of 1987, including a lifting of the state of siege in Santiago and a lessening of restrictions on opposition political activity, the Ambassador could not say for certain whether these improvements were "genuine" or mere "window dressing" to ease international pressure and facilitate

[76] See "Overview of Human Rights Developments 1989: Chile," Human Rights Watch, http://www.hrw.org. The helicopters were not delivered until after the 1988 plebiscite.
[77] Telegram, Barnes to Shultz, "Proposal for Visits by Chilean Military Officers to the US," May 29, 1987, Ludlow "Kim" Flower, [Chile] [2], Box 91258, RRL.
[78] Letter, Howard to Barnes, June 11, 1987, DOS/FOIAe, III.
[79] Letter, Jones, AmEmb Santiago, to Flower, Deputy Director for Latin American Affairs, NSC, June 1, 1987, Ludlow "Kim" Flower, [Chile] [2], Box 91528, RRL.

the best possible climate for Pinochet's election scenario. "Positive steps taken by the GOC to create a more propitious climate for the visits of the Pope and the UNHRC Special Rapporteur were taken by one person, the President, and he can reverse any or all of these actions at will."[80]

Yet Barnes's comments could not disguise the momentum for change that was growing inside Chile. In June, the AD created the Political Parties Committee for Free Elections (COPPEL), whose members were drawn from eight parties, including the PDC, the Radical Party, and the Popular Socialist Union Party. A few days later, confusing the issue of who stood for what, a rival Left Committee for Free Elections was created by several Chilean cultural leaders and headed by the Socialist Party's Ricardo Lagos (a former President of the AD).[81] Both groups demanded constitutional reforms and free elections that were anathema to Pinochet but at the same time redirected social mobilization tactics toward purely political ends by urging Chileans to register to vote.[82]

Whereas a major concern for U.S. officials was that ongoing civil disobedience and antiregime mobilizations would radicalize political conflict, this was not a key factor in the decision of the moderate political opposition to move the struggle from the streets to the negotiating table. The PDC's Edgardo Boeninger elaborated: at first "the force and emotion of the popular protests generated a sense among the parties that the regime could not last" and the efforts of the opposition were "concentrated on bringing down the regime quickly, as was reflected in slogans like 'this is the decisive year.'" Over time, many moderate leaders "began to see clearly that social upheaval would not defeat a military force which still had significant, if minority, popular support."[83] The Socialist Party leadership had drawn a similar conclusion. According to Heraldo Múñoz, even during the coordinated mass protests of 1983–1984 with the left, the moderate opposition "never thought that we would lose control of the situation." We were convinced that, eventually, "the regime would fall through the protests until we realized that Pinochet was willing to shed a lot more blood to stay in power."[84] The moderate political antiregime leaders were being driven toward an electoral democracy model less by a

[80] Telegram, Barnes to Shultz, June 4, 1987, DOS/FOIAc, III.

[81] See Aylwin, *El Reencuentro de los Democratas*, 323.

[82] Interview with Ricardo Núñez.

[83] Quotes in Paul H. Boeker, *Lost Illusions: Latin America's Struggle for Democracy, as Recounted by Its Leaders* (New York: Markus Wiener, 1990), 37.

[84] Múñoz, *The Dictator's Shadow*, 179; telephone interview with Heraldo Múñoz.

further shift to the right than by a realization that maintaining the rage had reached a point of diminishing returns, that they were never going to achieve a return to civilian rule by staying on the streets, and that to do so would simply result in more bloodletting. There was also a strategic factor to consider: the street protests were beginning to weaken popular opposition to the regime by dividing it: "When the Communists came out to join the protests, the middle class went home," said Boeninger. "The protests waned not because politicians failed to seize the initiative, but because the middle class did not want to be seen in the streets with the Communists."[85] The Socialist Party's Enrique Correa dismissed any suggestion that U.S. pressure had played a role: "We had to create a big gap between us and the extreme left. Otherwise, we were never going to be in government."[86]

Whatever Pinochet's interest in some future return to civilian rule, his consistently violent response to the threat from the streets dramatically exposed the key dilemma confronting the left social movements and their political allies: although the extraparliamentary struggle had proved the only means of bringing significant pressure to bear on the junta, it could not effect a regime change so long as the armed forces remained united and retained a monopoly of coercive power. It was primarily this fear of Pinochet's capacity for violence, his determination not to compromise, and, to a lesser extent, a concern that they were losing control of the antiregime leadership to those forces making demands that went beyond their own political and social boundaries that explained the decision of the center-right parties to break with the unacceptable or radical left and negotiate with the military high command and their elite supporters. Although such an outcome meshed perfectly with U.S. efforts to broker an acceptable transition, internal factors rather than external pressures played a more decisive role.

The anti-Pinochet AD and COPPEL coalitions, it must be remembered, had no interest in "radically altering" the military's economic model if only because to do so would be to threaten "a transition to democracy that would be stable and that would succeed." To the Múñoz Socialists, this meant not alienating the most conservative opponents of Pinochet, for whom the economic reforms were a red line not to be crossed. To radically challenge the market-based model, and thus its capitalist-class supporters (as well as the military), would make it impossible for a new civilian

---

[85] Quoted in Boeker, *Lost Illusions*, 37.
[86] Interview with Enrique Correa.

government to achieve its primary goals of changing the Constitution and tackling the human rights problem.[87]

Although viewed in positive terms by the executive branch, this decision by the acceptable anti-Pinochet forces had no impact on congressional resistance to any major change in the military aid status quo nor to legislators' demands for the imposition of further economic sanctions on the regime. The latter took the form of growing pressure on the White House to campaign more aggressively against MDB lending to Chile and to strip the country of its GSP benefits and OPIC coverage. In July, at the invitation of Chairman Walter Fauntroy, Elliott Abrams appeared before the House Subcommittee on International Development Institutions and Finance to allay concerns that the November 1986 abstention by the U.S. representative on a World Bank SAL loan to Chile could be interpreted as an "endorsement" of Pinochet and to clarify U.S. policy on future MDB loans.[88] Abrams testified that the decision to abstain was based on his recommendation and that it was influenced by the manifest lack of support for a negative vote among the European and Latin representatives on the bank's board. "So we came to the conclusion that if we voted 'no' we would be isolated, but that we could get a group together which would abstain, and there was in fact a substantial group of countries which abstained on the SAL, for the first time on human rights grounds." Joining with allied democracies "was the most effective means of using our voice and vote in the IFIs to express our human rights concerns regarding Chile," and it had the further advantage of not "strengthening hardliners in Chile opposed to carrying out a genuine transition to civilian rule."

On purely economic grounds, of course, the case for supporting Pinochet's Chile was irresistible as far as the administration was concerned. Testifying alongside Abrams, Treasury's Deputy Assistant Secretary James Conrow effusively praised the Pinochet government's economic performance, calling its free market approach a "model" for the rest of Latin America to emulate.[89] Paradoxically, though, bowing to White House pressure, his Department had earlier instructed the U.S. executive directors to abstain on two new World Bank loan requests ($95 million for power generation; $21 million for an irrigation project)

---

[87] Telephone interview with Heraldo Múñoz.

[88] Letter, Walter E. Fauntroy to Abrams, July 7, 1987, DOS/FOIAe, III.

[89] U.S. Congress, House, Committee on Banking, Finance and Urban Affairs, Subcommittee on International Development Institutions and Finance, *Current Directions for US Policy toward Chile*, 100th Cong., 1st Sess., July 21, 1987, 23, 25, 79, 87.

and on an application to restructure a loan to the Cape Horn Methanol Company for a project in Chile's petroleum- and gas-producing region north of Punta Arenas, which awaited a decision by the Bank's International Finance Corporation.[90]

If the State Department had few qualms about urging an abstention vote on Chile MDB loan submissions, it was less enthusiastic about eliminating the country's access to GSP and OPIC benefits. In late May, Barnes received a letter from Richard Howard indicating that the Department was resigned to Chile losing both benefits, the result of an interagency meeting on the subject where the "sentiment" of those present was "heavily weighted against Chile."[91] In the House of Representatives, Douglas Bereuter (R-NE) had already introduced a resolution highly critical of Chile's worker's rights situation – the passage of which threatened to preempt the ongoing review of GSP eligibility ordered by Reagan in January. While officials in the Department of Labor and the U.S. Trade Representative scored the regime for "not taking steps to meet internationally recognized standards of worker rights" – which legally required its exclusion from both OPIC and GSP programs – the State Department, with strong support from Treasury and the NSC, maintained that the United States had "important economic and political stakes in Chile," which militated against any move to terminate these programs.[92] For the moment, that seemed enough to hold the line.

Meanwhile, State had changed its stance on bailing Chile out of its ongoing problems with commercial bank lenders. In January 1987, the Chilean Ambassador had complained to Abrams about Citibank decisions to twice veto a request from Santiago to restructure Chile's commercial bank loans, which accounted for just under $15 billion of a total $21.4 billion foreign debt.[93] The Chileans had requested modest interest rate reductions and a retiming of interest payments that would result in a one-off savings of several hundred million dollars in 1987–1988. Ambassador Errázuriz denounced Citibank, one of twelve creditor banks negotiating with Chile in the so-called Bank Advisory Committee (BAC), which represented all 350 private bank lenders to the

---

[90] Letter, Howard to Barnes, May 28, 1987, DOS/FOIAe, III.

[91] Ibid.

[92] Letter, Howard to Barnes, August 14, 1987, ibid.

[93] John Whitelaw, "Hard Line at Citibank Irks Third-World Debtors and Other US Banks," *CSM*, January 27, 1987, 11; Peter Truell, "Commercial Banks to Raise at Least $400 Million to Meet Chile's '87 Needs," *WSJ*, February 6, 1987, 22.

Latin nation, for "acting unreasonably" to block any agreement being reached. Abrams, however, took no action other than to sympathize with Chile's plight.[94]

By February, the negotiations had reached an "impasse." The commercial banks were prepared to reschedule maturities but reluctant to provide new funds. Instead, they settled on a strategy that would see them shift part of their debt burden to the World Bank and, indirectly, to the creditor/donor governments. The BAC Chair, Manufacturers Hanover, proposed that the World Bank cofinance $20 million of the $400–430 million proposed package for Chile with cross-default clauses. Although the administration had supported a move to have the World Bank guarantee some commercial bank loans to Chile in 1986, this time Abrams and his EB colleague Doug McMinn advised Secretary Shultz that the commercial banks were simply "playing politics" and further accused them of falsely telling the Chileans that the United States was "blocking the solution on 'political grounds.'" Chile's economic performance now made a cofinancing arrangement unnecessary, they said, and, given the mood for tougher sanctions in Congress, entering into such a scheme would place at risk future MDB funding at adequate levels. The response of the World Bank itself was revealing: although Vice President Ernest Stern initially endorsed the cofinancing scheme, his superior Barber Conable quickly "backed away from the idea," reportedly after being informed that the United States opposed such a move.[95]

Treasury Secretary James Baker vetoed the cofinancing proposal, apparently to avoid giving the banks "an easy way out" in view of Chile's excellent record on debt renegotiation and IMF relations, which could justify a normal bank loan.[96] Additionally, this decision was part of a

---

[94] Telegram, Shultz to AmEmb Santiago, "Abrams-Errázuriz Meeting," January 24, 1987, DOS/FOIAe, III.

[95] Memo, McMinn-Abrams to Shultz, "The Case against IBRD Cofinancing for Chile," February 5, 1987, ibid. Two factors largely explained the Abrams-Minn reaction. One was the upturn in the Chilean economy. The other was the February 1987 announcement that Brazil was suspending its debt service payments on the more than $100 billion owed to commercial banks, which triggered no negative reaction from the market for bank stocks because by now such news carried little shock value. See George C. Philippatos and K. G. Viswanathan, "Third World Debt Default Announcements and Market Learning: Effects of Sequential Debt Defaults on U.S. Banks," *Managerial Finance* 22, no. 7 (1996): 75–76.

[96] Quoted in James L. Rowe Jr., "U.S. Vetoes World Bank Role in Chile Loan," WP, February 17, 1987, D4.

broader effort to redirect pressure back on the commercial banks to take a more accommodating line on Third World debt negotiations generally. Under "strong pressure" from Washington and other BAC members, Citibank agreed to moderate its stance, and the BAC eventually agreed to reschedule Chile's interest payments, saving more than $400 million over the next twelve months, to restructure most of the country's debt and to reduce interest rates payable to all creditors. Finally, in an unprecedented concession, Chile was permitted to repay interest on its debt once a year for four years beginning in 1988, instead of the normal six monthly payments.[97] In contrast to the difficulties experienced with its commercial creditors, the restructuring of Chile's debt to official (Paris Club) creditors concluded without a hitch. At a club meeting in April, an agreement was reached with the IMF, the World Bank, and individual governments to reschedule debts maturing over the next twenty months.

In late July, ARA's Richard Howard informed the U.S. Embassy in Santiago that a new UNGA strategy was being developed based on the idea of collaborating with European, and perhaps selected Latin, governments to produce a "balanced resolution" on Chile's human rights performance. The reasons for not proceeding at this point with an exclusively American-authored draft were twofold: the difficulty in reaching an interagency consensus and the limited possibility of "producing a text with a realistic chance of passage." Cosponsoring a resolution proposed by another government was one option "provided, of course, that we can overcome International Organization's (IO) opposition to any action other than voting no." The other problem to be gotten around was UN Ambassador Walters, who remained "adamantly opposed to what he sees as an unfairly singling out of the Chileans."[98] In a letter to Walters, Abrams attempted to overcome the Ambassador's objections. While he "fully shared" the Ambassador's frustration with the "hypocrisy of those quick to criticize Chile, but silent concerning horrendous human rights abuses in Cuba," persuading Latin American democracies to join the United States in condemning Cuba required a "consistently even-handed" approach in speaking out against human rights abuses wherever they occurred.[99] Walters was not the only hurdle to overcome. The IO Bureau was just as reluctant to support the UNGA resolution strategy.

---

[97] "U.S. Banks Recognize Chile's Financial Responsibility," *News from Chile*, March 3, 1987.
[98] Letter, Howard to Jones, AmEmb, July 23, 1987, DOS/FOIAe, III.
[99] Letter, Abrams to Vernon Walters, June 15, 1987, ibid.

Despite approaches by other Department officials to IO, brokering a consensus was proving "far from easy."[100]

Assessing the Transition Prospects

At the end of July, Abrams summed up the challenges facing U.S. policy in a detailed communique to Shultz. The next twelve months would be critical in determining Chile's future. Pinochet was "consciously diminishing possibilities for an orderly transition," and his insistence on being nominated as a candidate in the plebiscite would "dangerously polarize" the nation. There was no doubt that he would "pull out all stops to win, including fraud," making it all the more incumbent on the opposition and the Church to focus their efforts on a major voter registration drive. The task for U.S. policy makers was "to intensify efforts to identify the USG with democracy and to avoid mixed signals." Above all, Washington must "find ways to promote a political atmosphere – and electoral procedures" that ensured the legitimacy of the plebiscite, thereby confronting Pinochet with "a narrowing band of choices." Almost as important was ensuring that Congress took no policy initiative, such as economic sanctions, leaving the administration "trapped into powerlessness."

The Assistant Secretary identified the "fragmentation of the democratic opposition [as] perhaps Pinochet's greatest asset." Both State and Embassy officials expressed continuing frustration with the "debilitating divisions over personal rivalries and tactics" and the interparty ideological and political struggles that were "slow[ing] the process of developing a common platform" and selecting a leader. On the plus side of the ledger, though, State was encouraged by the decision of these parties to further "distance themselves from the communist, totalitarian left" and the early August election of center-right candidate Patricio Aylwin to replace the "left-leaning, ineffective" Gabriel Valdés as PDC President, which, Abrams insisted, had clearly boosted the odds of achieving "an orderly transition" to civilian rule. The one caveat was some uncertainty as to "how effective a leader" Aylwin would be. Abrams assured Shultz

---

[100] Letter, Howard to Barnes, August 28, 1987, ibid. Another challenge to administration policy was the establishment of a Committee to Support Free Elections in Chile. The brainchild of Senators Edward Kennedy and Richard Lugar (R-IND), the Committee included former Presidents Jimmy Carter and Gerald Ford. State's Robert Gelbard personally told Kennedy that the group risked propelling U.S. supporters of democracy in Chile "out ahead of Chilean democrats." See Letter, Howard to Barnes, June 11, 1987, ibid.

that Aylwin at least offered "the possibility of a [post-Pinochet political] soft-landing."

The core obstacle remained as immovable as ever. Abrams had no doubt that Pinochet "fully understands" Washington's commitment to a "genuine transition." Yet, he "continue[s] to ignore us," and as long as his key support base remains firm, there is little prospect of getting him to change his mind:

[He] is buttressed by a generally loyal Chilean army that is virtually unreachable. (General Galvin commented that the Chilean armed forces seemed like they inhabit a different solar system). Our efforts to enhance service-to-service contacts will not convert them to democracy, but do help to keep open importance lines of communication. Chile's dependency on MDB loans provides our only real leverage.

With the executive branch's "maneuvering room" further narrowed by persistent demands from Capitol Hill to impose new economic sanctions, the "central dilemma," wrote Abrams, "is how to use our limited influence effectively, while avoiding counterproductive congressional action... which would spark Chilean nationalism and perversely aid Pinochet's election campaign."[101]

An NIE prepared by the CIA reached essentially the same conclusions while claiming to discern rising unease within the Chilean armed forces over the dictator's election plans (especially his determination to stay in power beyond 1989) and noting that "he appears to be less confident about how to control the military than in the past." Pinochet's relations with non-army members of the junta – Matthei and Stange in particular – had worsened in recent months over his refusal to stand aside for a civilian candidate. But the most serious threat would always be the possible erosion of his army support. Pinochet might ignore external diplomatic pressure and feel only "slightly more vulnerable" to threats of economic sanctions and cutbacks in foreign lending or debt rescheduling. A similar response was untenable when it came to dealing with a significant number of the officer corps increasingly worried about their country's international pariah status and concerned that the institution's image would "suffer permanent damage" if Pinochet remained in power. This group within the military should now be the principal target of U.S. efforts.

---

[101] Memo, Abrams to Shultz, July 29, 1987, ibid.; Memo, Abrams to Shultz, August 10, 1987, ibid.; Telegram, AmEmb (Jones) to Shultz, October 15, 1987, ibid.

Discussing the likely plebiscite outcome, the NIE reasoned that Pinochet could not win a clear majority in an "honest" vote and would probably seek to manipulate the result if he stood as a candidate. His determination to hold on to power indefinitely could only "jeopardize" the possibility of a genuine and comprehensive democratization of the Chilean polity. On a more optimistic note, the intelligence community agreed with Abrams that Aylwin's election to head the PDC could only help U.S. policy objectives, describing the new PDC President as "a respected moderate willing to try to gain the trust of the armed forces." The other positive news was that the "the main subversive force in Chile," the Communists, had still not recovered from the setback occasioned by the discovery of the arms cache and the botched assassination attempt on Pinochet. In the absence of "very dramatic actions," they were unlikely to lend the dictator "any lasting advantage from raising the specter of Communist violence."[102] Abrams complemented the NIE authors in a memo to Shultz, adding that "our own analysis" in the Department and in the Embassy agreed with "virtually all of their major conclusions."[103]

Prior to the release of the NIE, Shultz had already cabled U.S. diplomatic posts that "more than ever before, the administration is courting the armed forces rather than the civilian opposition, as the key to a controlled 'democratic transition' [because] only the military can upset General Pinochet's plan to become the sole candidate in a presidential plebiscite."[104] One early initiative was a funded visit to the United States by four senior Chilean Army officers "in what is hoped will serve as a prototype for a broader program of visits."[105]

Going to the Source

The unresolved Letelier investigation remained another complicating factor in U.S.-Chilean relations throughout the latter half of Reagan's second term in office. "We were pressing hard on this issue because in terms of the policy, it would show the opposition we were serious," explained

---

[102] NIE, CIA, "Chilean Prospects for Democratic Transition," August 1, 1987, CIA/FOIAe, III.
[103] Memo, Abrams to Shultz, October 13, 1987, DOS/FOIAe, III.
[104] Telegram, Shultz (Whitehead) to All American Republic Diplomatic Posts, August 15, 1987, ibid.
[105] Bradley Graham, "Administration Seeks Improved Ties with Chile's Military," WP, October 11, 1987, A37.

Robert Gelbard. "We were doing all kinds of things, very quietly."[106]
When Armando Fernández Larios – the DINA agent accused of organizing the assassination – surrendered voluntarily to U.S. authorities in
February 1987, the case was catapulted back into the political limelight,
and the White House once more declared that achieving a satisfactory
outcome was critical to any improvement in bilateral ties. Larios denied
playing any direct role in the killings, limiting his statements to a confes-
sion of involvement in gathering information on the former Chilean foreign minister's movements in Washington, D.C., and implicating senior
DINA agents in the terrorist act – both of which constituted a significant breakthrough in the investigation, nonetheless. However, much to
the frustration of State and Justice Department officials, the response
from the Chilean authorities was negligible and remained so over the
next twelve months. Despite repeated diplomatic initiatives and meetings
with Ambassador Errázuriz, the Pinochet regime continued to stonewall
attempts to have those responsible for authorizing the killings – DINA's
head Manuel Contreras and his deputy Pedro Espinosa Bravo – prosecuted in a court of law. All it required, a frustrated Gelbard insisted
during one of his meetings with Errázuriz, was "political will," which the
government in Santiago evidently lacked.[107]

Gelbard returned to Santiago in August 1987 for another round of
discussions with key military leaders, government officials, and members of the political opposition. Two items were high on his agenda: the
Letelier case and the upcoming plebiscite. Gelbard told newly appointed
Foreign Minister Ricardo García that Washington wanted the former
resolved and expressed the administration's "deep disappointment at the
Government of Chile's evident and continuing unwillingness to cooperate in bringing the culprits to justice."[108] On the plebiscite, Gelbard
said publicly that Washington favored competitive presidential elections
but would support a single-candidate plebiscite if the vote was free and
transparent, and there was no fraud.[109] Earlier, in a report to Shultz,
Barnes opined that Pinochet was planning "to cast the plebiscite as a
vote of popular confidence in military rule" and to interpret a favorable
outcome as legitimating his continued hold on power. "In other words,"

---

[106] Interview with Robert Gelbard.
[107] Telegram, Shultz to AmEmb Santiago, June 5, 1987, DOS/FOIAe, III. Also see
  Telegram, Shultz (Armacost) to AmEmb Santiago, May 13, 1987, ibid.
[108] Telegram, Barnes to Shultz, August 24, 1987, ibid.
[109] Bradley Graham, "Pinochet Balks at U.S. Nudges; After 14 Years in Power, Chilean
  Runs for Office," WP, August 25, 1987, A12.

the Ambassador wrote, "it is another attempt to polarize the electorate, to recreate the conditions of the 1980 victory [in the tainted referendum on a new Constitution]."[110]

In a subsequent telegram, Barnes described Gelbard's exceptionally chilly reception by the Chilean government, which "made its displeasure towards the visit clear by limiting the number of official calls, which covered only those ministers directly involved in aspects of American policy." Although Pinochet's refusal to see the Deputy Assistant Secretary was predictable (Chileans, he declared, "don't accept anyone coming here to impose foreign doctrines or ideas"), Gelbard was "very upset" over being snubbed by Interior Minister Sergio Fernández and the failure of the Foreign Affairs Ministry to pass on to junta members his request for appointments.[111] It was left to the Ambassador to arrange meetings with Generals Matthei and Stange and with army General Humberto Gordon (a member of Pinochet's inner circle and Chief of Intelligence). Matthei "went out of his way" to welcome Gelbard. By contrast, Admiral Merino denounced the American diplomat as an "intruder"[112] and refused to meet with him:

> Merino blew up and said he wouldn't meet with me – I did have an appointment set with him – because I was interfering in their internal affairs, because I'd visited the national election center. But what he didn't realize – or maybe didn't like – was that the Foreign Minister had invited me to visit because his own brother, a career civil servant, was the head of it, and they wanted to show me that this was an honest, legitimate center and organization. The second interesting thing that happened there was that Pinochet announced that he refused to meet with me even though I'd never requested a meeting since I knew he wouldn't meet with me. And I didn't think there was anything to be gained by meeting with him anyway.[113]

Hernán Errázuriz declared that the only outcome of the visit was to elevate Gelbard to the status of the Chilean government's "enemy number one."[114]

Amid this sea of official hostility, Gelbard's encounter with General Matthei was clearly a relief. Having originally scheduled the meeting

---

[110] Telegram, Barnes to Shultz, August 21, 1987, DOS/FOIAe, III.

[111] Telegram, Barnes to Shultz, August 28, 1987, ibid.

[112] Quotes in "Chile Military Chief Snubs Senior U.S. Official," *RNS*, August 19, 1987; Pamela Constable, "As Relations Cool, US Role in Chile Wanes," *BG*, August 27, 1987, 3; Telegram, Barnes to Shultz, August 26, 1987, DOS/FOIAe, III; interview with Robert Gelbard.

[113] Ibid.

[114] Interview with Hernán Errázuriz.

"outside of the junta building," the General changed the venue to his office. On arriving there, the senior U.S. diplomat found the outside hallway "jammed with television crews and print journalists. Matthei strode out, put his arm around my shoulders, and walked me into his office. And he said 'I'm here to welcome my good friend Ambassador Gelbard.' That was fascinating, because it was a powerful, highly unsubtle signal both to Pinochet and, of course, to Merino, but most importantly to Pinochet."[115]

Reporting on Gelbard's visit, Barnes noted, approvingly, that the "opposition did less ideological posturing than during previous visits [and] demonstrated a greater sense of pragmatism," especially when it came to addressing the problems that needed to be resolved if Chile was to return to democracy. The Aylwin-led PDC had a much better understanding of "what U.S. policy is attempting to achieve, and why." The U.S. Ambassador was equally impressed by the opposition parties' more realistic approach toward key political and economic issues. Although the PDC and the Núñez Socialists challenged Gelbard's unqualified admiration for the military's free market economic program, their disagreements did not extend to political issues. Notably absent from the discussions was the traditional attitude that Chile's problems, "both political and economic, stemmed mainly from U.S. mistakes in the past."[116]

Another cable from Barnes that day focused exclusively on Gelbard's meeting with the Christian Democrats, who, differences aside, "appear to share our basic goals and have a similar perception of the Chilean political equation." For Barnes, the PDC leadership was now "more realistic and pragmatic." It nonetheless remained to be seen whether Aylwin had "the backbone to lead a difficult party in which challenges occur often." Another concern was the arrangement between the PDC and the left-wing MDP in elections for one of the biggest unions in the country – the one-hundred-thousand-strong Teachers Union – which resulted "in joint PDC-Communist control." Aylwin insisted that the PDC would "reject alliances with the far left," except for the teachers' union, which was "a special situation." Barnes was troubled by this argument because it had the potential to "open a cavernous loophole for all the other PDC leftists to jump through."[117] More importantly, though, he stressed that

[115] Interview with Robert Gelbard.
[116] Telegram, Barnes to Shultz, "Atmosphere and Themes," August 26, 1987, DOS/ FOIAe, III.
[117] Telegram, Barnes to Shultz, "Gelbard Meeting," August 26, 1987, ibid.

Aylwin was "very aware that the PDC has to achieve credibility with the military," even though other PDC leaders seemed less persuaded to that reality. Andrés Zaldívar, for example, had challenged the idea that the PDC should "disown" a call by the CNT for a nationwide, twenty-four-hour work stoppage in October because "it is not appropriate to oppose a legitimate right of the workers to strike for better working conditions [and] the PDC does not want to cause disaffection in labor ranks." Another senior party official, Edgardo Boeninger, had expressed solidarity with the union movement, reportedly pointing out that the political opposition was going to need labor leaders to work on the voter registration drive.

Barnes nevertheless assured Washington that whatever lingering doubts the administration might have, Aylwin and the new party leadership were like "a breath of fresh air." The PDC was not only "more realistic about the obstacles it faces [but also] basically centrist in orientation." It generally preferred "no bargaining with the radical left and wants to avoid tactical alliances with them, even in the so-called social field." This was in marked contrast to Gabriel Valdés, who pursued such alliances for long-term tactical reasons, "was always holding something back, was insincere, and [his] objectives were not the ones he wanted us to believe."[118] In hindsight, Barnes described Aylwin as someone who had "more equilibrium and less passion than Valdés but overall was very thoughtful, very reasonable and at the same time very skilful."[119] To Elliott Abrams, "Aylwin was a different kettle of fish" compared with his "unfriendly" predecessor.[120] Gelbard agreed wholeheartedly: Valdés lived in "in a time warp" and, like a number of opposition politicians, was "immensely frustrating" to deal with because he "didn't understand that it was not 1972 [anymore]." Aylwin may have been "less colorful but he was more pragmatic, more of a serious politician, more of an American-type politician [in contrast to Valdés's more European outlook]." His election to the PDC presidency demonstrated that the party finally comprehended that now "it was a different kind of politics and a different kind was definitely needed at this point to get through the legalistic hurdles and strictures that Pinochet and his team had assembled."[121]

---

[118] Telegram, Barnes to Shultz, August 26, 1987, ibid.
[119] Interview with Harry G. Barnes.
[120] Interview with Elliott Abrams.
[121] Interview with Robert Gelbard.

Keen to counter any notion inside Chile itself that U.S. policy toward the regime was the product of a small State Department clique, the Seventh Floor approved an August visit to Chile by four Republican legislators. At a meeting with government officials, including Pinochet, the delegation leader, Senator Robert Lagomarsino (R-CA), highlighted Washington's support of the 1973 coup and its consistent lauding of the post-coup economic reforms before addressing the principal message the group wanted to convey to the Chilean leader: continued White House support was dependent on a democratic transition, as was the effort to ward off the passage of further economic sanctions legislation through Congress. This was also a subtle reminder to Pinochet that the administration's Chile policy enjoyed widespread support at both ends of Pennsylvania Avenue.

Still, it remained a policy adept at issuing mixed signals that were not lost on Chilean opposition leaders. The Reagan administration "cannot get too close to a Chilean regime that violates human rights and resists moving toward a democracy," the Socialist Party's Heraldo Múñoz perceptively observed. "Yet it also cannot afford falling too far into confrontation with a military government whose anticommunism and pro-free market policies coincide with those of Washington."[122] Such contradictory interests continued to fuel residual differences of opinion, priorities, and agendas among Reagan officials that frustrated efforts to reach interagency agreement over how best to advance a return to democracy in Chile. Pinochet was well aware of the limits to what he had to fear from Washington, and thus his ambitions remained undiminished. It would take a determined effort by those senior State Department officials in charge of Chile policy, together with the President's unequivocal public support, to ultimately draw the line under the General's dictatorship.

---

[122] Quoted in Graham, "Pinochet Balks at U.S. Nudges," A12.

6

Toward Endgame

A number of assumptions concerning the situation in Chile had become fixed in the minds of Secretary of State George Shultz, other high-ranking Department officials, and Ambassador Harry Barnes by summer 1987. Chief among these was that the slowness of the regime to take concrete steps to advance the transition process (principally those measures needed to genuinely open up opportunities for antiregime forces to mobilize and campaign) raised more than suspicions about the military's ultimate commitment to return the country to democratic rule. Most policy makers were convinced that Pinochet intended to stay in power. Shultz, in particular, worried that the General's determination to do so had seen him "consciously diminishing possibilities for an orderly transition" and, were he to put himself forward as a candidate in the presidential plebiscite in 1988, the effect would be to "dangerously polarize Chile."[1] As to the opposition, it failed to inspire confidence in Washington, let alone among the regime leadership, as a potential alternative government: it was too divided for the comfort of either; too reluctant to fully embrace the plebiscite route for the transition from military to civilian government as laid down by Pinochet; and too far away from presenting a credible – and acceptable – policy platform. Most infuriating of all, Washington had very little influence over events in Chile and Pinochet had made it repeatedly clear that, ultimately, he cared little for how it was exercised.

---

[1] Draft Cable, Shultz to AmEmb London, Bonn, Paris et al., "Consideration of Chile at UNGA," July 31, 1987, Ludlow "Kim" Flower, Chile: UNHRC Human Rights Resolution, Box 91528, RRL.

Shultz and those advisers responsible for overseeing Chile policy were determined to use what little influence they had carefully and imaginatively to encourage the transition to a pro-U.S. center-right civilian government that would retain the fundamentals of the military's neoliberal economic model. To achieve this outcome was difficult enough without having to contend with interagency conflicts over policy implementation as well as resistance from influential legislators eager to see not only the end of military rule but also an accounting for the overthrow of Salvador Allende, the litany of human rights abuses, and, of course, the Letelier-Moffitt murders. On the latter issue, at least, the State Department and Congress were in total agreement. At a luncheon hosted by Elliott Abrams, Robert Gelbard, and Richard Howard for Chile's three most senior foreign policy officials (Foreign Minister Ricardo García, Ambassador Hernán Errázuriz, and Foreign Office Director General Gastón Illanes) in September 1987, the American diplomats once again forcefully criticized Chile's failure to prosecute those responsible for this act of terrorism perpetrated on U.S. soil, only to be fobbed off with the usual "evasive response." A frustrated Shultz cabled the Santiago Embassy that a resolution of this problem "continues to poison our relations," and he could see no likelihood of any greater cooperation on the part of the Chilean government in the future.[2]

A Two-Pronged Approach

Ahead of the UNGA meeting in December, American diplomatic posts were instructed to lobby host country governments to support a human rights resolution acceptable to the United States that put maximum pressure on General Pinochet. An early Seventh Floor draft of a cable in July requested Embassy staffs to ensure that "senior officials [of these governments] understand the importance we place on their actively working with [the] U.S. in advance of the UNGA to bring about a resolution which [the] U.S. could support."[3] A second draft warned that there must be no repeat

---

[2] Telegram, Shultz to AmEmb, Santiago, October 7, 1987, DOS/FOIAe, III. The previous month, prior to a meeting with the U.S. Ambassador at Large, Richard Kennedy, to discuss Chile's vote on expelling South Africa from the International Atomic Energy Agency, Ambassador Errázuriz commented to another State official that visiting the Department "was like entering a 'torture chamber.'" Letter, Howard to Jones, September 11, 1987, ibid.

[3] Draft Cable, Shultz to AmEmb London, Bonn Paris, et al., RRL.

of the 1986 vote on an "unbalanced" Cuban resolution, which forced the United States to abstain in a way that was "misinterpreted by democrats in Chile as a sign of our on-going support for the Pinochet regime – which it is not." Any recurrence of that outcome would "send unhelpful mixed signals" concerning the administration's "strong commitment" to democracy promotion. Only an "early, forceful, and consistent" U.S. role in shaping the human rights resolution on Chile would encourage others to work toward the kind of "balanced" document that Washington could "support and work with." Convincing foreign governments, especially European Union members and the Holy See, to line up behind such a resolution was one objective. The other was to reach agreement on a "game-plan so that Cuba and hard line members of the [Non-Aligned Movement] cannot easily maneuver the process on the floor in order to paint all of us into a corner which makes the only choices appear to be either voting for an unbalanced resolution, or seeming to accept the policies of Pinochet." Summarizing the overall approach in dealing with Chile's human rights practices, the draft was emphatic about the administration's preference for mobilizing international criticism as an alternative to more draconian measures, such as economic sanctions that would allow Pinochet to play the "aggrieved nationalist card against the opposition" and likely damage U.S. commercial interests. Creating economic chaos through sanctions would also strengthen the extremists and create "very difficult problems for [a] successor democratic government."[4] As in the past, persuading State's IO Bureau to support a new resolution would not be easy but was imperative "to avoid the negative mixed signals and bureaucratic bad blood" that occurred in 1986.[5]

Despite this reluctance to apply economic pressures, the possibility of limited initiatives complementing public diplomacy could not be dismissed out of hand. In early September, Richard Howard requested advice from the Santiago Embassy on how the United States should respond to future Chilean SAL submissions to the World Bank, already aware of Treasury's conclusion that an abstention vote would not affect Executive Board decisions either way.[6] Embassy officials, it turned out, were of a similar mind: "Even a massive abstention clearly orchestrated by the U.S. gains nothing in terms of political change within Chile and runs the

---

[4] Draft Cable, DOS, "Consideration of Chile at UNGA," August 27, 1986, DOS/FOIAe, III.
[5] Letter, Howard to Jones, September 11, 1987, ibid.
[6] Letter, Howard to Barnes, August 14, 1987, ibid.

risk that a dissatisfied U.S. Congress might impose serious sanctions in response to perceived administration weakness."

With Pinochet seemingly determined to hold on to power beyond 1989, the key challenge was to identify available and appropriate levers that could be used to ensure as fair an electoral process as possible. Ambassador Harry Barnes suggested that the upcoming World Bank vote on the SAL-III for Chile presented just such an opportunity to be exploited, either through seeking a postponement or casting a negative vote. Utilizing one of these options would not have a "crippl[ing]" effect on any part of the regime's economic program, thus avoiding the possibility of "uncontrollable radical political conditions [or] hav[ing] the perverse effect of consolidating the military, business and middle class behind Pinochet." The Country Team's preferred option was to seek postponement of the scheduled November vote, based on its "moderate economic importance" in terms of the amount involved ($250 million in two tranches between December 1987 and mid-1988), Chile's successful debt rescheduling, and the positive impact of the latter on the country's balance of payments. The Embassy was fairly certain that Chile was now in a "relatively comfortable" position to meet its foreign exchange requirements and obligations during 1988, even should the SAL-III be withheld or voted down. Not surprisingly, comments minimizing the importance of the SAL-III did not impress the Chilean government. Pinochet's economic officials insisted that the loan was critical to future financial planning and worried about the negative impact of a World Bank no vote on potential new donors and investors. Given these sentiments, the United States had a certain amount of leverage to wrest concessions from Santiago in return for ultimately supporting the SAL-III.

The United States could vote no, abstain, or seek a postponement of any decision on the loan. Of the three alternatives, Barnes and his fellow diplomats agreed that anything less than an abstention would probably be interpreted in Chile and on Capitol Hill as a win for Pinochet. Tactically, they advocated postponement as the best option because it would allow some countries that normally objected to politically determined voting to align with the United States and had the added benefit of the lack of a specific time frame for consideration of the loan request, which would "amplify" the economic impact inside Chile.[7] The Embassy recommended lobbying other World Bank members to support postponement. In the

[7] Telegram, Barnes to Shultz, September 4, 1987, ibid.

event this was not possible, the United States should cast a no vote on the SAL-III "with no attempt to lobby other votes." According to George Jones,

we in the Embassy saw this as being one of the rare occasions when we actually had some leverage that might affect the situation in Chile. There's so much that went on day to day that we had no effect on. But here was an instance of a large loan very much desired by Chile, and it seemed like a perfect opportunity and a rare opportunity to actually have some leverage other than just endless talking, which is mostly what we did.[8]

ARA officials "fully" agreed with the Embassy that "a solution must be found which packs enough punch and yet avoids real damage to the Chilean economy." Otherwise, further progress in Chile "may never come about." The postponement strategy held out the possibility of "maximum advantage to us," but ARA did not underestimate the difficulty of the task at hand: "Clearly this will be a tough nut to crack unless Treasury, NSC and World Bank officials and their governments are thoroughly convinced of the wisdom of our policy."[9]

The bureaucratic debate over the next two months was dominated by the World Bank vote on Chile's SAL request. State was convinced that if Pinochet obtained the loan, he would redirect it into a "war chest" to prime the economy to bolster his chances of winning the plebiscite. By late September, the administration was still undecided as to whether to abstain, vote against, or seek a postponement.[10] That same week, the Southern Cone Director Richard Howard cabled DCM George Jones that a memo was being prepared for Secretary Shultz supporting the postponement option despite the long odds of "lining up bureaucratic and World Bank support." He also briefly referred to a "curious" luncheon with Hernán Errázuriz, when the Chilean Ambassador "suddenly mused that we would look back on the lunch as a memory of the last moments of decent relations between the U.S. and Chile since the administration is out to get rid of Pinochet, regardless of whatever positive steps the GOC takes." The already "damaged state" of bilateral ties was "bound to deteriorate" further, Errázuriz gloomily concluded.[11]

---

[8] Interview with George F. Jones.

[9] Letter, Howard to Jones, September 11, 1987, DOS/FOIAe, III; Memo, Howard to Gelbard, September 18, 1987, ibid.

[10] Telegram, Shultz (Whitehead) to All American Republic Diplomatic Posts, September 23, 1987, ibid.

[11] Letter, Howard to Jones, AmEmb, Santiago, September 25, 1987, ibid.

Shultz's Gambit

During October, NSC Adviser Frank Carlucci entered the debate over Chile's SAL-III loan. In a memo to President Reagan, he argued against postponement on the grounds that the administration unequivocally supported Pinochet's economic program and that there was "no reason to oppose the loan on grounds of economic conditionality." To take State's advice would be interpreted as a decision made on the basis of political, not technical, criteria and, additionally, would undermine the Baker Plan devised by Treasury Secretary James Baker to relieve Third World debt through a combination of deferred interest payments and large-scale lending by the IMF, the MDBs, and private commercial banks contingent on debtors undertaking liberalizing economic reforms. Finally, Carlucci reminded the White House that IO and the USUN Mission had previously rejected the ARA/HA strategy of working with allies to achieve a balanced resolution as "an unrealistic goal." Domestic politics would make it impossible for the Europeans to reach agreement on such a resolution, and in the highly unlikely circumstance they did, "it would ultimately be disfigured by amendments from the floor" or be forced to compete with a cosponsored Mexican-Cuban alternative.[12]

Meanwhile, Treasury further complicated matters by requesting an interagency meeting to try to reach a consensus decision on the U.S. position toward the loan. ARA questioned this initiative, characterizing Treasury's stance as "entirely unclear." It was grappling with its own problem involving State's EB Bureau, which "appears to share ARA's position but urges a multilateral approach which will not be easy to execute."[13] Whatever the outcome of the debate, Abrams was convinced that this was "possibly [the] last major opportunity to use our economic leverage to influence [the] climate for [the] plebiscite."[14]

In late October, Shultz received a memo prepared by Abrams and the EB's Douglas McMinn outlining the case for a "conditioned-postponement" of the SAL loan for Chile. This strategy, the authors wrote, offered two main advantages: it was one of the few pressure points that Washington could exploit to encourage Pinochet to preside over "a free and fair electoral process" and, in the absence of some White

---

[12] Memo, Carlucci to President, "Chile," undated, Ludlow "Kim" Flower, Chile: Policy (2), Box 91528, RRL.

[13] Letter, Howard to Barnes, October 23, 1987, DOS/FOIAe, III.

[14] Briefing Memo, Abrams to Acting Secretary, October 15, 1987, ibid.

House action, the danger of expanded congressional sanctions would likely grow. "Congress could take the initiative out of our hands and pass sanctions against Chile or block MDB replenishments," which would inevitably create "divisions within the [U.S. government], limit Executive Branch flexibility, and hurt us in Chile." By contrast, "bottl[ing]-up" the loan via a conditioned postponement would not "do long term harm to Chile's economy" while simultaneously allowing the United States to exert greater pressure on the regime to terminate the state of emergency, lift restrictions on freedom of assembly, and give the opposition increased television coverage. Any alternative option that involved a more extensive delay should not be considered because it would negatively impact on Chile's ability to meet its "short-term IMF loan obligations and have a strong psychological effect in both domestic and international financial circles [and] discourage commercial bankers from providing new funds." Treasury, the memo concluded, had been talked around to the conditioned postponement strategy, but the NSC was refusing to budge in its opposition.[15]

The SAL debate was not the only issue exercising the minds of Chile policy makers. What position to adopt in the UNGA on Chile's human rights situation had begun to generate quite heated discussion among State Department officials. NSC Adviser Carlucci received a letter from Ambassador Vernon Walters decrying the overall tenor of the General Assembly debate, which largely focused on the "negative comments" and ignored the "good and balanced" points in the reports on Chile submitted by the Special Rapporteur, Fernando Volio. "I do not want to see the U.S. involved in needless Chile-bashing," Walters complained.[16] In State, IO strongly agreed, refusing to support a U.S. strategy jointly drafted by ARA and HA, arguing instead that the American delegates "should simply not show up to vote on any UNGA resolution on human rights in Chile."[17]

The strategy advocated by ARA and HA started from the premise that Washington "had few levers" with which to influence Pinochet's calculations. Among the few was its potential ability to mobilize support in the UNGA. The two bureaus preferred a "cautious, but active" approach that included a "demarche campaign to [European and other] capitals to secure a human rights resolution on Chile that the U.S. can vote for." What especially concerned them was the potential impact of

[15] Action Memo, Abrams, McMinn to Shultz, October 27, 1987, ibid.
[16] Letter, Walters, USUN to Carlucci, NSC, October 2, 1987, ibid.
[17] Letter, Howard to Jones, AmEmb, Santiago, October 8, 1987, ibid.

Pinochet's plebiscite candidacy on Capitol Hill, as this possibility had already increased pressure from congressional elements for "new punitive legislation." Although the United States had not voted for a resolution critical of Chile in the UNGA for the past seven years, on this occasion, it was imperative "to avoid allowing Congress to lead policy" and thereby reduce executive branch flexibility. ARA and HA wanted to see a "ratcheting down [of] the criteria for an acceptable UNGA resolution". IO and the USUN Mission disagreed, insisting that it would be "impossible" to gain passage of a "balanced" UNGA resolution on Chile largely because of the voting strength of the Eastern Bloc countries and members of the Non-Aligned Movement. Instead, U.S. efforts to achieve a "balanced text" should be pursued in the more manageable UNHRC which was also responsible for deciding whether or not to renew the Special Rapporteur's mandate. The resolute HA/ARA commitment to lobbying for a more "reactive approach" presented the Seventh Floor with a tough choice.[18]

With the UNGA situation at an impasse, Secretary Shultz approved the SAL-III postponement strategy. Treasury concurred despite its anxiety about the impact on broader U.S. economic and Third World debt management interests. With a final decision pending, NSC officials continued to "tacit[ly] resist" State's decision, citing concerns over the "economic risks" and Pinochet's likely reaction. The NSC's José Sorzano reportedly posed the question: what would the United States do if the Chilean leader simply refused to comply with the U.S. preconditions? In a communiqué to the Embassy, Southern Cone Director Howard wrote that "the ball is still in play." At Washington's request, the World Bank agreed that no paperwork on the loan would begin prior to President Barber Conable's return to headquarters in mid-November. State and Treasury officials now embarked on a delicate mission: lobbying donor governments to support the postponement option, while simultaneously avoiding the perception that the Bank, and especially its President, was "doing [the] bidding of the U.S."[19]

With little evidence that a significant majority of Bank members favored the U.S. proposal, and after consulting with senior management officials, Conable decided that Chile's loan submission "must go forward." In the meantime, Sorzano had informed Carlucci's deputy, Colin

---

[18] Action Memo, Abrams, Smith, Schifter to Shultz, October 8, 1987, ibid.

[19] Letter, Howard to Barnes, November 6, 1987, ibid.; Briefing Memo, Larson to Shultz, November 10, 1987, ibid.

Powell, that Treasury was having second thoughts and "now is inclined not to support State's position." Further discussions among Treasury officials convinced Sorzano that the decision had been taken to withdraw support for the postponement strategy. The reasons offered by Deputy Assistant Secretary James Conrow were twofold: State's desire that American embassies approach host country governments "on the basis of a written record" would almost certainly become public, thereby exposing the United States to attack for "overtly politicizing" the Bank; and Treasury's calculation that the required Executive Board majority vote for postponement was simply unattainable.[20] Sorzano's memo was dated November 19. That same evening, Conrow dined with six World Bank Executive Directors, where he "sounded them out on State's proposal." He discovered a "positive interest" in the postponement strategy and a belief that their governments would support this initiative so long as Washington took the lead. The next day, Sorzano reported to Powell that "Treasury has reversed itself again."[21]

As the interagency debate awaited a definitive resolution, the Chilean regime sought to bring its own influence to bear on the outcome. In the lead-up to the December 15 vote, a succession of Chilean officials employed what ARA's Howard characterized as a "scare tactic" to achieve a positive result.[22] In Santiago, Finance Minister Hernán Büchi advised Ambassador Barnes that if his government did not get the SAL-III loan, "it will have real trouble meeting its obligations to the IMF" and, by extension, to the commercial banks as well. Barnes replied that the United States was fully aware of the regime's economic situation but reminded Büchi "of the narrow limits within which we would have to make our decision about how to vote." Supporting the loan was not an option, and Büchi must appreciate that whatever position was chosen would be very closely scrutinized by Congress.[23] Chile's Foreign Minister, Ricardo García, complained to Barnes that the United States was "taking a purely 'political' approach" on the loan issue. The Ambassador's response was succinct and pointed: "of course, there were 'political' matters" that could not be avoided, just as there were concerns about human rights and democracy issues. Barnes cabled Shultz that for "the second

---

[20] Memo, Sorzano to Powell, November 19, 1987, Ludlow "Kim" Flower, Chile: Economic Policy SAL-III, Box 91258, RRL.

[21] Memo, Sorzano to Powell, November 20, 1987, ibid.

[22] Letter, Howard to Barnes, December 4, 1987, DOS/FOIAe, III.

[23] Telegram, Barnes to Shultz, November 27, 1987, Ludlow "Kim" Flower, Chile: Economic Policy SAL-III, Box 91258, RRL.

time in several months García has sought to convey a plea for supporting the 'good guys' by taking it easy on some of our 'concerns.' What he has yet to do is talk about what the quids and quos would be."[24]

At the beginning of December, Büchi made an unscheduled visit to Washington "exclusively to make *demarches* to get the SAL approved." His reception by Treasury officials was no more positive than the one he received from the U.S. Embassy. At a meeting with Conrow, David Mulford, and other senior Department officials, he repeated the same warning given to Barnes that a postponed SAL would make it impossible for Chile to meet its IMF commitments and added, for good measure, that no one could predict "what Pinochet might do when faced with difficulty in meeting debt obligations." His audience was completely unmoved, and its response was just as blunt: the United States could "no longer separate the economic from the political where Chile is concerned and given the lack of a tangible progress by the GOC in the area of civil and human rights, there is a 'substantial chance that the loan will not go through.'" That said, the Americans were aware that West Germany (FRG) was yet to sign on to State's strategy, and Britain's support was uncertain.[25] Nor had this fact escaped the notice of NSC Adviser Colin Powell (appointed to the post in November 1987) and his staff, who refused to budge from their opposition to the whole postponement idea. Suddenly, Treasury was having another bout of second thoughts. "The worm seems to have turned again," Sorzano informed Powell's deputy, John Negroponte. "Treasury now predicts that our initiative to indefinitely postpone Chile's SAL loan will fall flat." Conrow's recent meeting with World Bank Executive Directors revealed that there had been a "great deal of hand wringing and lack of instructions from [their] Capitals." The United Kingdom and Japan seemed less enthused about postponing the vote, while Canada, France, and the FRG remained undecided. State Department officials viewed FRG support as particularly vital if the "momentum" were to shift in favor of postponement. Sorzano predicted that if this option were rejected, Chile's SAL would almost certainly "be approved no matter how we vote."[26]

In Santiago, this "escalation" of U.S. pressures was generating "serious worries," which Barnes interpreted as "giving voice to the contradictions

[24] Telegram, Barnes to Shultz, December 4, 1987, DOS/FOIAe, III.
[25] Letter, Howard to Barnes, December 4, 1987, ibid.
[26] Memo, Sorzano and Danzansky to Powell and Negroponte, December 8, 1987, Ludlow "Kim" Flower, Chile: Economic Policy SAL-III, Box 91258, RRL.

in Pinochet himself who will compromise when he has to but ably seeks always to avoid having to."[27] On December 9, Büchi's chief of staff Christian Larroulet began a conversation with an American Embassy official by bluntly asserting that the United States was "finally going to put the lid on Chile." Irrespective, his government would not back down on its demand for a December 15 vote, and "if the loan were blocked, the GOC would unleash an already-prepared anti-U.S. campaign."[28]

Two days later, Sorzano updated Negroponte on the interagency impasse regarding the SAL vote. No one disputed that the loan itself met all the requisite economic and technical criteria. However, State believed that a negative vote (that is, a no or abstention) would serve three important purposes: it would send a "political signal to Pinochet; [act] as a gesture of solidarity with the democratic opposition; and ... preclude Congress from seizing control of our policy toward Chile as it has with South Africa." Treasury was ambivalent and uncomfortable about how to proceed. As the executive branch department most closely linked to the private corporate world and the MDBs, it viewed Chile as a "model debtor country" and praised its free market economy. At the same time, Treasury officials fretted over any action that might undermine MDB replenishment goals and feared that relations with Congress would be damaged if the Department became identified with a pro-Pinochet outlook. The NSC, conversely, was adamantly opposed to any talk of economic sanctions against Chile because they could only bode ill for the nation's "laudable economic performance" and undermine U.S. efforts "to facilitate a transition to democracy."[29]

Prior to the scheduled World Bank vote, the Junta's Fernando Matthei met with Barnes during a visit to Santiago by U.S. General Frederick Woerner, who had succeeded Galvin as head of the United States Southern Command. When the conversation moved to the SAL, "Matthei turned accusingly to the Ambassador and asked what the State Department was up to with regard to 'boycotting' the SAL-III World Bank loan." When told that he should be aware that the United States "couldn't block the loan by ourselves since we didn't have the votes, even if we wanted to," Matthei agreed it was perhaps better to wait for the outcome of the December 15 vote but accompanied that comment with a sting in the

[27] Telegram, Barnes to Shultz, November 25, 1987, DOS/FOIAe, III.
[28] Telegram, Barnes to Shultz, December 10, 1987, ibid.
[29] Memo, Sorzano to Negroponte, "Chile World Bank Loan," December 11, 1987, Ludlow "Kim" Flower, Chile: Economic Policy SAL-III, Box 91258, RRL.

tail: he intended to halt all future visits by U.S. Air Force officers if perchance Washington were successful in halting the loan.[30]

State's hard line on the SAL vote was explained in part by Abrams's growing concern that Pinochet was determined to "perpetuate himself in power," and it was not beyond the realms of possibility that he would resort to fixing the plebiscite to ensure victory. "We would be less concerned about Chile's future," he cabled the Santiago Embassy, if the regime had made good on its promises to improve civil and human rights well before the vote took place. "Instead, we see no progress [but] rather backsliding" on these issues. Abrams feared that an open-ended Pinochet rule would only benefit the "violent Marxist left" to the detriment of foreign investment, the country's foreign debt strategy, and the free market economic model.[31]

Nevertheless, this was not a battle Shultz was destined to win. On December 15, the executive directors approved the SAL loan: Britain, Canada, and the major Latin American countries voted in favor; France, Belgium, Spain, the Netherlands, and the United States abstained; while Italy and the Scandinavian countries caste no votes.[32] "We were hardly surprised by the final outcome," Southern Cone Director Richard Howard wrote to Barnes, "given the lack of effective support for the postponement initiative from the Bank, Treasury, Commerce, the NSC, and even within the [State] Department. Carrying out our strategy would have been difficult enough even with greater backing, but being restricted to telephone *demarches* practically doomed the effort."[33]

Winning over Reagan

With IO still resisting what Vernon Walters had termed "unnecessary Chile-bashing" at the UN, Shultz cabled New York that the first priority was to "facilitate passage of a fair and balanced resolution" in the General Assembly "that would not be anathema to the United States."

---

[30] Telegram, Barnes to Shultz, December 14, 1987, DOS/FOIAe, III.
[31] Telegram, Shultz (Whitehead) to AmEmb Buenos Aires et al., for Ambassador and DCM from Abrams, November 26, 1987, ibid. International companies invested a record $1.17 billion in Chile in 1987. Richard Waddington, "Chile's Economic Policies Succeed in Luring Record Foreign Investment," *TGM*, March 21, 1988, B11.
[32] "World Bank Lends Chile $250 Million; U.S. Delegate Abstains from Vote," AP, December 15, 1987; Pamela Constable, "$250m Loan Approved for Chile," *BG*, December 16, 1987, 3.
[33] Letter, Howard to Barnes, December 18, 1987, DOS/FOIAe, III.

If this proved impossible, an abstention together with a statement of U.S. policy toward Chile would be an "acceptable outcome," provided a number of key moderate Europeans and Latin countries adopted a similar course.[34] Another three weeks of discussion and negotiations moved Washington no closer to achieving its primary objective. The Mexican draft still "[did] not fill the bill" in the absence of any reference to human rights advances, praise for the Special Rapporteur's "balanced" report, or a denunciation of violence "from all quarters."[35] Having for these reasons deemed the Mexican document "inadequate" and lacking "balance," Shultz instructed the USUN Mission to "abstain [in order] to send the proper signal to the GOC during this crucial pre-election period."[36] With a balanced resolution no longer a realistic goal, State's Howard initiated an aggressive lobbying effort "to bring IO on board our abstention strategy." Abrams enlisted Walters to make "a final pitch," which "helped quite a bit" to get IO's agreement.[37]

On December 8, the Mexican resolution condemning Chile's human rights record passed by a vote of 83–5 with fifty-three abstentions. The White House decision represented the first time the Reagan administration had not opposed such a resolution in the UNGA. This outcome "clearly pleased" the Chilean Human Rights Commission's Vice President, Maximo Pacheco. Pinochet, he told the American delegation, would certainly be surprised as well as angry because he had always been convinced that the United States "would never change its negative vote in the General Assembly and that the U.S. would support him until he died."[38]

Nine days later, and after much urging, State finally convinced President Reagan to agree to issue a joint statement with Secretary Shultz on democracy in Chile. Invoking the Latin nation's historic "democratic tradition," it declared America's support for the complete restoration of democracy based on "the observance of basic human and civil rights in the period leading up to and during the election" to ensure the "legitimacy" of the result:

This atmosphere would be marked by easy and equitable access to the mass media, especially television, by unrestricted discussion of political issues, broad

[34] Telegram, Shultz to USUN Mission, New York, November 4, 1987, ibid.
[35] Telegram, Shultz (Whitehead) to AmEmb Ankara, November 25, 1987, ibid.
[36] Telegram, Shultz to USUN Mission, New York, November 26, 1987, ibid.
[37] Letter, Howard to Barnes, December 4, 1987, ibid.
[38] Telegram, Walters, USUN Mission to Shultz, December 3, 1987, DOS/FOIAe, III.

freedom of assembly, early announcement of the rule of any electoral proceeding, facilitation of registration by prospective voters, and freedom for citizens and political groups to campaign peacefully in favor of their ideas. States of exception which limit freedom of assembly, association, and expression are not compatible with a legitimate electoral process.[39]

This statement had its origins in an Abrams memo to Shultz that Chile was approaching a "political watershed" and that Pinochet's continuation in office "not only jeopardizes [our transition objective] but also threatens our security interests, since his regime is rapidly polarizing Chilean society." A major beneficiary of "the prolongation of authoritarian rule" would be the Communist Party, and for all these reasons, the opposition's campaign "needs and deserves our support."[40] Shultz remained silent on who drafted the document, conceding only that it "originated in my Department" and that the critical achievement was convincing Reagan to sign it.[41] The final draft reversed the original sequence of paragraphs to place greater emphasis on the administration's commitment to a democratic transition.[42] The joint statement laid down clear markers for judging what constituted "respect for basic guarantees and freedoms." Arguably, the most important was the call for "easy and equitable access to the mass media, especially television," even though, as one involved State Department official put it, getting Pinochet to give ground on "the holy grail of mind control" was the last concession Washington thought he would make. Nevertheless, the United States was adamant; this request was nonnegotiable: "We said 'if no TV, no legitimacy in our eyes.'" The Embassy in Santiago reported that Pinochet hit the roof when he read the statement.[43]

The document was significant as well for having been made public over the vociferous objections of NSC staffers who thought it "unprecedented" that the White House should "issue a statement about an individual country when there is no real crisis or situation that warrants it." They pounced on Shultz for not making it on his own, describing his success in enlisting the President as a "Barnes-Gelbard bullshit ploy

[39] "U.S. Statement on Support for Democracy in Chile," attached to Memo, Green to Levitisky, November 18, 1987, Ludlow "Kim" Flower, Chile: Statement of Support for Democracy, Box 91528, RRL.
[40] Action Memo, Abrams to Shultz, November 7, 1987, DOS/FOIAe, III.
[41] Telephone interview with George Shultz.
[42] See Memo, Green to Levitsky, November 18, 1987, Ludlow "Kim" Flower, Chile: Statement of Support for Democracy, Box 91528, RRL.
[43] Confidential telephone interview 1.

to keep pushing for more." NSC officials also vented their anger at the alleged role played by Abrams. "This is Elliott's way of trying to use the symbol of R[onald] R[eagan] to give political force to yet another ratchet upward in a ceaseless campaign to destabilize Pinochet," Council staffer Kim Flower complained in a note to José Sorzano. "But it won't work. Not a single vote in the plebiscite will be affected by the statement; and Pinochet may well use it to his advantage by pointing to it as yet another example of the gringo's silly interventionism." State Department officials could have put their energy and time to much better use by finding a way "to galvanize the Center-Right opposition into formulating a program and fielding a candidate acceptable to the military and the people." The Chilean middle class perceived no viable alternative to Pinochet, Flower wrote, and absent any change in that situation, the dictator would maintain his capacity "to divide and rule; and better him than many others who come to mind."[44]

But the pendulum had clearly shifted in State's direction on Chile policy, as was soon evident in the debate over whether to suspend Chile's trade benefits under the GSP – a move that would automatically trigger the withdrawal of OPIC insurance protection for U.S. investors in the country. Initially, this was not a step State had been keen to take. In 1985, the AFL-CIO had filed a petition to deny Chile trade benefits under the GSP on the grounds of its draconian labor practices. Subsequently, an interagency Trade Policy Review Group (TPRG) decided that Chile had failed to take adequate "steps" to afford its workers internationally recognized rights. Under the 1974 Trade Act (as amended), this dictated removal from, or suspension of, the GSP program. Initially, the TPRG recommended keeping the situation under review for a further twelve months, which, at the time, represented a major victory for the State Department over a number of other agencies "who wished to remove Chile from the program entirely at an earlier date." A key factor in Chile's favor was the regime's written commitment to pass legislative amendments "within a reasonable time" and to guarantee organized labor's right to assemble, organize, and engage in collective bargaining.[45]

To Washington's disappointment, the promised amendments never saw the light of day. A strike called by the CNT in October was

---

44 Note, Flower to Sorzano, February 1, 1988, Ludlow "Kim" Flower, Chile: Statement of Support for Democracy, Box 91528, RRL; Note, NSC, from Tillman, undated, ibid.
45 Memo, Larson, Walker, Schifter, Freeman to Shultz, December 10, 1987, Ludlow "Kim" Flower, Chile: NSDD, ibid.

ruthlessly crushed with the arrest of more than three hundred participants. State revisited and revised its position on the GSP. Ambassador
Barnes told senior Chilean government officials that the regime's failure to
take any action to improve workers' rights over the previous nine months
had put the GSP "in jeopardy" of being terminated. Their response was
almost contemptuous. Barnes left the meeting convinced that the government had "little if any intention to make further revisions of the labor
laws or practices, even to avoid losing GSP benefits." On December 9,
the TPRG unanimously recommended that the benefits be suspended.
Although unlikely to have a major impact on U.S. trade and direct investment, Shultz approved the recommendation after receiving a joint memo
from four of his bureaus that to do otherwise "would damage Administration credibility" with Chile and other GSP beneficiaries and risk
congressional action to eliminate our "flexibility on worker rights and
other trade issues." Furthermore, given the likely failure of U.S. efforts
to postpone the World Bank SAL loan to Chile, backsliding on the GSP
would be interpreted "as a strong signal that the U.S. is weakening its
policy of support for human and civil rights in Chile [and] put at risk
our efforts to . . . discourage Congress from legislating strident economic
sanctions against Chile." Shultz recommended to the President that he
suspend Chile's GSP benefits, and before year's end, Reagan announced
the decision.[46]

The GSP suspension may only have cost Chile several million dollars
in duties it was now required to pay on exports to the United States, but
its symbolic significance as an indicator of Washington's attitude toward
the Pinochet regime was far greater.[47] Shultz suggested that it might be
useful for an OPIC representative to travel to Santiago and explain to
business community leaders why the GSP had been terminated and what
was required "to prevent the loss of the OPIC agreement" on the chance

[46] Ibid. Stuart Auerbach, "Reagan Strips Chile of Right to Duty-Free Imports, Citing
Worker Policies," *WP*, December 25, 1987, B6. Also see Memo, Risquet, White House,
to President, December 22, 1987, Economic Policy Council, General System of Preferences (GSP): Chile (2), Box 1321, RRL.
[47] Clyde H. Farnsworth, "U.S., Citing Worker Rights, Revokes Chile Trade Benefit," *NYT*,
December 25, 1987, D1, D2. In May 1988, William Doherty, Executive Director of the
American Institute for Free Labor Development (AIFLD), told a House subcommittee
that the elimination of Chile's status under the GSP had affected, in total, $87 million
in preferential trade to the United States. U.S. Congress, House, Committee on Foreign
Affairs, Subcommittee on Human Rights and International Organizations and on Western Hemisphere Affairs, *U.S. Policy, Human Rights, and the Prospects for Democracy
in Chile*, 100th Cong., 2d Sess., May 17, 1988, 152.

that this would "encourage" the regime to moderate its behavior.[48] Once again, Chilean officials exhibited a dismissive attitude, with Ambassador Errázuriz pontificating that the loss of GSP benefits (and subsequently OPIC coverage) were punishments that "didn't matter."[49] Although their impact was "not terribly great," said Embassy DCM George Jones, the message it sent was not lost on the Chileans: "The question was how much publicity do you get from it, how much impact do you have on people's thinking. That was what really counted and the little economic pressures were just another grain of sand building up in a pile of saying, 'We're serious about this: the plebiscite has got to go forward.'"[50] In Washington, Abrams concluded that Chile and the United States were now "moving toward the endgame," which made it doubly incumbent on the administration to "push harder to get something done."[51]

Jones ascribed much of this shift to a tougher approach to Harry Barnes's effort "to move our policy forward, to bring pressure to bear" on the regime, combined with an ongoing fear among U.S. officials that Pinochet might be having second thoughts about holding a plebiscite. Therefore "we were looking for ways in which we could ratchet up the pressure to make sure that Pinochet kept his word to let the plebiscite go forward on a fair basis or something approaching a fair basis."[52] Chilean Foreign Ministry officials' attacks on Barnes, accusing him of repeatedly communicating to State that the plebiscite "is not going to happen or there is a high probability that this is not going to happen," seemed to confirm this assessment.[53]

Public diplomacy along the lines of the UNGA vote, the Shultz-Reagan statement, and GSP/OPIC-type economic pressures might momentarily keep the Chilean regime focused on adhering to the transition timetable, but these policy instruments were unlikely to influence the outcome of the plebiscite. To do that, the State Department would need to intervene more directly. Ironically, it was Congress that facilitated a shift to this track, approving a $1 million grant to the NED to promote democracy-building projects that would ensure a free and fair election campaign. Out of a total of $4 million provided since 1985 to fund voter registration drives, training of poll watchers, public opinion polling, focus

---

[48] Telegram, Shultz to Barnes from Abrams, January 25, 1988, DOS/FOIAe, III.
[49] Interview with Hernán Errázuriz.
[50] Interview with George F. Jones.
[51] Interview with Elliott Abrams.
[52] Interview with George F. Jones.
[53] Interview with Hernán Errázuriz.

groups, publishing and media activities, community organizations, trade unions, anticommunist groups, and a variety of seminars and training programs, this was the largest single NED grant in support of the democratic opposition.[54] The White House augmented the NED funds when it agreed to indirectly help finance another "large-scale voter registration and civil education campaign" under the direction of a Catholic Church–related organization, Fundación Civitas, amounting to $1.3 million, provided by the U.S. Agency for International Development (AID).[55] Only AID registered objections to the NED allocation – on the grounds that to do otherwise would be tantamount to condoning Congress "earmarking its funding for anything" – which State officials attributed to an ongoing turf battle between NED and AID.[56]

Pinochet officials were incensed by the scarcely disguised intent behind this series of recent U.S. measures. Ambassador Errázuriz protested to State Department officials that his government considered them "hostile and/or interference" in the nation's internal affairs, which had pushed bilateral ties to "a dangerous and difficult point." The Ambassador ticked off each of the negative "episodes" in turn: the U.S. abstentions in the UNGA and World Bank; Reagan's provocative statement supporting a return to democracy in Chile; the suspension of GSP (and OPIC) privileges; and the allocation of $1 million via the NED to support a free and fair election campaign. He concluded with a warning that if U.S. policy were to continue down this road, relations would be "bound to deteriorate further." Unmoved and unimpressed by this presentation, the American diplomats upbraided Errázuriz for sidelining or ignoring Washington's priority concern: that the regime was "not moving fast enough to ensure stability" because of continuing high levels of repression that had undermined efforts "to put a lid on a kettle where steam is building and

[54] Alan Angell, "International Support for the Chilean Opposition, 1973–1989: Political Parties and the Role of Exiles," in Laurence Whitehead, ed., *The International Dimensions of Democratization* (New York: Oxford University Press, 2001), 194. Also see Jeffrey M. Puryear, *Building Democracy: Foreign Donors and Chile*, Conference Paper 57 (New York: Columbia University, December 6, 1991), 11, 14–16.

[55] Telegram, Shultz to AmEmb Paris et al., "Coordinating Support for Democracy in Chile," January 16, 1988. Also see Puryear, *Building Democracy*, 5, 15, 16. The voter registration drive was highly successful. Between January and May 1988, the number of registered eligible voters climbed from fewer than 4 million to 6 million. See Cynthia Brown, "Democracy vs. Fear and Propaganda," *The Nation*, October 3, 1988, 257, 275–277.

[56] Letter, Howard to Barnes, December 18, 1987, DS/FOIAe, III; interview with James Swigert.

could erupt and destabilize society." Whether future ties remained tense or improved, said Elliott Abrams, "will hinge on the conditions surrounding the plebiscite."[57] This reading of the riot act added to the regime's conviction that U.S. policy had fundamentally shifted: the Chilean government "no longer saw the United States as a strong supporter who was mainly focused on their economic record," recalled a State Department official. "Previously, it assumed that strong economic performance was such an important calling card, so to speak, that all they had to do was bring in someone to talk about what they were doing and everyone would basically say, 'That's great.' Now, however, the Chileans knew there had been a shift and they took it seriously."[58]

As the Pinochet dictatorship entered its fifteenth year, Washington's fundamental problem was how to thwart the Chilean President's apparent determination to hold on to power by running in and winning the upcoming plebiscite. In a memo to the White House, Shultz left no doubt that the consequences of a Pinochet victory "would be highly dangerous for Chile and the region as a whole."[59] Another involved U.S. official expanded on Shultz's remark: not only would the impact of a Pinochet victory be highly destabilizing inside Chile, the regional consequences would be equally, if not more, dire in the form of a "significant spillover into Peru and Argentina which would likely serve as transit points for Cuban arms."[60] Within the foreign policy bureaucracy, there was a consensus that a post-1989 Pinochet-led regime was undesirable but a difference of opinion between officials advocating the immediate adoption of "an assertive policy aimed at thwarting Pinochet's intentions" and others who preferred a more cautious approach on the grounds that it was "not at all certain that Pinochet will prevail" in the plebiscite.[61]

What was not in dispute were the advantages Pinochet held over the opposition based on access to state coffers and government resources and

[57] Briefing Memo, Abrams to Kampelman, December 28, 1987, DOS/FOIAe, III; Telegram, Shultz to AmEmb Santiago, January 7, 1988, ibid. In hindsight, Errázuriz was dismissive of NED funding, even though he had criticized it as a form of intervention during this meeting with U.S. officials: "We didn't care because much more money was coming from Germany, Russia, and many countries. So these funds didn't make much difference." Interview with Hernán Errázuriz.

[58] Interview with James Swigert.

[59] Memo, Shultz to President, "Pinochet and the Letelier-Moffitt Murders," October 15, 1987, Ludlow "Kim" Flower, Chile: Policy (2), Box 91528, RRL.

[60] Quoted in Wayne, "US Looks at Chile as the Next Place to Promote Democracy," 6.

[61] Memo, Frank Carlucci to President, "Chile," undated, Ludlow "Kim" Flower, Chile: Policy (2), Box 91258, RRL.

his domination of the mass media (radio, newspapers, and television). The junta leader could also draw on a nationwide municipal political network of handpicked mayors who were instructed to "neutralize" local opposition groups and use resources and personnel to encourage their local constituents to vote yes on the day of the plebiscite.[62] Finally, he had presided over three consecutive years (1986–1988) of economic growth, low inflation and unemployment, and increased real wages that would likely build on the not insignificant electoral support he was thought to already enjoy.[63]

As the countdown to the plebiscite began, U.S. policy makers set about impressing upon Pinochet the need for a transparently fair vote and encouraging the political opposition to present a credible alternative that would be acceptable to the armed forces leadership. This strategy presumed that without sustained pressure, Pinochet would, as Shultz contended, seek to cling to power at all costs, thus polarizing the country, playing into the hands of the Communist Party, and placing at significant risk American interests in Chile and throughout South America. Despite having "very few 'carrots and sticks'" to wield, there was now a clearer sense of U.S. purpose and a greater willingness to enlist the support of allies to guarantee its success.[64]

Keeping up the pressure through public diplomacy was a first priority. Shultz instructed the U.S. delegation to the UNHRC in Geneva "to seek a balanced resolution we can support and, to that end, to circulate . . . the same language of the draft resolution that ARA and HA had prepared for us to introduce as a U.S. resolution." ARA's Peter DeShazo foresaw two problems that might arise: most concerning was the prospect that the Cuban delegation would seek a tougher resolution; the other was related to the difficulty in convincing the head of the U.S. delegation, Armando Valladares, who had rejected every nominee for membership of the delegation that HA had put forward, "crossed bureaucratic swords" with Assistant Secretary Richard Schifter, and joined with Ambassador Walters and NSC staffer Jose Sorzano in "firm opposition" to any U.S.-authored resolution.[65] In January, Shultz cabled U.S. embassies in Europe, Latin America, Canada, and Japan that with Chile "rapidly approaching

[62] Quoted in Chris Hedges, "Pinochet's Push: Chilean Leader, in Office for 14 Years, Aims to Extend Rule a Decade More, Observers Say," *DMN*, December 27, 1987, 1A.

[63] See ECLAC, *Economic Survey of Latin America and the Caribbean 1990*, vol. II (Santiago: United Nations, 1992), 147, Table 1.

[64] Speech, Harry Barnes, San Francisco, Phoenix et al., January–February 1988, "Speeches and Statements, 1987–88," Box 1, Papers of Harry G. Barnes.

[65] Memo, DeShazo to Barnes, January 1, 1988, DOS/FOIAe, III.

a political watershed," the time had come to accelerate efforts "to coordinate our activities" with host country governments, political parties, and foundations to the "greatest extent possible" in support of democracy in Chile.[66]

The outlook for mobilizing this kind of support was not very encouraging. True, the European Community had provided around $1.2 million to Chile in 1987 via the Church's social welfare agency, Caritas, and other nongovernmental organizations (NGOs). Yet this kind of funding could not mask a noticeable reluctance on the part of Western governments to become directly involved in State's political strategy.[67] U.S. Embassy officials in London reported that the United Kingdom was forcefully pressing Pinochet on human rights and a democratic transition but felt that the "megaphone diplomacy" favored by Washington was inappropriate. The British Foreign Office considered "irrelevant" the idea of "throwing money" at the democratic opposition and remained highly skeptical "about the usefulness of the USAID and NED [sponsored] programs."[68] It was a similar story in Bonn, where the German Foreign Office took "a predictably cautious" view of how active a role the government should play in promoting democracy in Chile that partly reflected "differing views" within Chancellor Helmut Kohl's governing coalition and within his Christian Democratic Union (CDU). As the latter was less constrained in providing advice to Chile's opposition leaders, the Bonn Embassy was directed to expand its contacts with the CDU as well as like-minded organizations and NGOs that had close ties to Chile's PDC.[69]

Between 1984 and 1988, four West German foundations provided $26 million in support of the PDC and the transition process. The most prominent of these was the Konrad Adenauer Foundation, which had been a key financial supporter of the PDC for more than two decades. During the mid-1980s, it was directly involved in coordinating eight ostensibly nonpolitical projects with the PDC, ranging from agricultural enterprises to research institutes and a slum dwellers' self-help project.[70]

---

[66] Telegram, Shultz to AmEmb Paris et al., January 16, 1988, DOS/FOIAe, III.

[67] Telegram, AmEmb Brussels (Kingon) to Shultz, January 22, 1988, Ludlow "Kim" Flower, Chile: Democratic Transition, Box 91528, RRL.

[68] Telegram, AmEmb London (Price) to Shultz, January 29, 1988, DOS/FOIAe, III.

[69] Telegram, AmEmb Bonn (Dobbins) to Shultz, January 29, 1988, ibid.

[70] Michael Pinto-Duschinsky, "Foreign Political Aid: The German Political Foundations and Their US Counterparts," *International Affairs* (UK) 67, no. 1 (1991): 40, 41. On the role of the German Foundations and their links to the PDC, see Telegram, AmEmb (Jones) to Shultz, October 18, 1985, DOS/FOIAe, III; Michael Pinto-Duschinsky, "International Political Finance: The Konrad Adenauer Foundation and Latin America," in Whitehead, *International Dimensions of Democratization*, 244–245.

In February 1988, the U.S. Ambassador to Germany, Richard Burt, conferred with the head of the Adenauer Foundation's International Programs section, Josef Thesing. Discussing Pinochet's chances of victory in the forthcoming plebiscite, and the consequences for Chile of such an outcome, they were both convinced that it would result in "a serious radicalization" and that the opposition's discord remained the biggest single obstacle to a successful anti-Pinochet campaign. Thesing promised that the institute would "work hard" to support democratic groups in Chile and reminded Burt that it opposed the Kohl government's decision the previous December to vote for Chile's World Bank SAL, which had "undermined" statements by senior government and CDU officials highly critical of the dictator's rule.[71] U.S. representations to the Vatican likewise revealed reservations about the ability of the opposition parties to subordinate their "partisan quarrels" to a common democracy objective. Meanwhile, the Holy See assured the Rome Embassy political officer that it "fully supports the efforts of the Chilean Bishops' Conference to help forge a non-violent transition to democracy."[72]

Diplomatic Maneuvering

In early 1988, Assistant Secretary of State for Human Rights Richard Schifter began a curious, informal, back-channel dialogue with Chile's Ambassador Errázuriz on the details of the forthcoming plebiscite. Meeting on at least a fortnightly basis over several months, the latter's intent was "to create a situation where the United States would be satisfied that the referendum had been run fairly and that, from then on, we would stop bothering Pinochet." Errázuriz assumed the task of making sure that every detail of the unfolding plebiscite process was acceptable to Washington. Schifter recalled how their dialogue proceeded:

These very frequent meetings were devoted to his asking me about specific issues and my telling him what it is that we expected. My first concern was that they were going to have a referendum, and only the army would vote. So the one

[71] Telegram, AmEmb Bonn (Burt) to Shultz, February 4, 1988, DOS/FOIAe, III.
[72] Telegram, AmEmb Rome (Shakespeare) to Shultz, February 2, 1988, ibid.
        The December 1987 election of a progressive Bishop, Carlos González of Talca, to the presidency of the Episcopal Conference was interpreted by Harry Barnes as a "correction to a conservative drift in the Chilean Catholic Church hierarchy" since the papal visit earlier that year. Although this did not foreshadow a more confrontational Church, it did put the institution in a stronger position to campaign "forcefully on the need for a fair and clean plebiscite." Telegram, Barnes to Shultz, January 20, 1988, ibid.

thing I wanted to be sure of, and we really began to focus on this, was a voter registration system that we could approve. We went into incredible detail, such as my telling him that for people who were working during the day, there were to be registration opportunities in the evening, there should be registration opportunities on weekends. So that was the first thing and he would come back to me with figures that would indicate that indeed they didn't just have the army registered. The next question was what it is that could be done to allow a free press. I kept emphasizing that particular point. My impression is that he really played a very important role in guiding people [in the junta] along in Santiago. Then I went on to talk to him about electronic media. When I look back on it, it was incredible as to how much I was able to work out with him.[73]

The Ambassador had a somewhat different memory of the meetings. They were "very open conversations" whose purpose was limited to simply "informing Schifter of what we had in Chile" – a long democratic tradition untainted by accusations of fraud or corruption. State's principal motivation in pursuing this back-channel strategy was to compare Chilean government reports on the plebiscite preparations with those provided by the U.S. Embassy.[74]

Whatever Errázuriz's true motives might have been, a number of critical decisions governing the conduct of the plebiscite were being taken out of the hands of the regime. As part of the junta's claim to legitimacy, some institutions, such as the Tribunal Constitucional (Constitutional Tribunal), which had been set up under the 1980 Constitution, had been allowed to operate with relative independence, and their decisions were often defended on the grounds of the need to adhere to the approved constitutional framework, especially by the air force and the navy, whose leaders insisted that the plebiscite in particular had to be above international reproach.[75] Beginning with its landmark ruling in September 1985 that a Tribunal Calificador de Eleciónes (Electoral Court) must be set up in advance of the rules and regulations under which the plebiscite was to be held (in order that it might actually serve its oversight function), the Constitutional Tribunal "compelled the military government to structure legal political party formation and the circumstances of the plebiscite in ways that ultimately provided opponents of the regime and its constitution with incentives to play according to the rules of the military's own game and to win according to them." In April 1988, for instance, another Tribunal ruling – concerning political campaigning during the run-up to

---

[73] Interview with Richard Schifter.
[74] Interview with Hernán Errázuriz.
[75] See, e.g., Barros, *Constitutionalism and Dictatorship*, 295, 301.

the plebiscite – eventually forced the junta to enact legislation providing equal and free television time to both sides in line with the Constitution's "fairness test."[76]

By February, the issue of a Chile human rights resolution that the United States could support in the 1988 UNHRC session had assumed the status of "the current hot [interagency] issue."[77] The involved State Bureaus – ARA, HA, and IO – saw a balanced document as having the benefit of "undercut[ting] the efforts of the far left to take the initiative on Chile" and possibly assisting U.S. efforts to pass a critical resolution on Cuba.[78] The other participating agencies, perhaps surprisingly in lieu of past actions, quickly reached agreement with State over how to proceed. Key UNHRC members would be informed of the "essential criteria" allowing the United States "to join a consensus on this issue." Interagency agreement was to no small degree the result of the friendly relationship between Shultz and NSC Adviser Colin Powell. Once achieved, U.S. officials began to work behind the scenes with other UNHRC members to compose a resolution that would not do "unnecessary damage to our bilateral relationship."[79] Once again, Cuba and Mexico complicated Washington's objective by jointly sponsoring (with other members) a resolution that Ambassador Walters (with IO backing) denounced as "highly biased" and nothing more than another instance of "unmitigated Chile bashing."[80]

ARA and HA proposed presenting Mexico (the principal author) with a set of amendments to the text referring to incidents of leftist terrorism, progress toward democracy, removing Chile's status as a special agenda item, and recognition of Special Rapporteur Volvio's report on a take-it-or-leave-it basis. The idea was to place the onus squarely on Mexico: if it balked at making its resolution more balanced, the United States would

---

[76] Ibid., 257, 305.

[77] Memo, Sorzano to Negroponte, "Meeting with Harry Barnes," February 19, 1988, Ludlow "Kim" Flower, Chile: U.S. Ambassador, Embassy, Box 91528, RRL.

[78] Action Memo, Abrams, Schifter, Smith to Shultz, February 6, 1988, DOS/FOIAe, III.

[79] Memo, NSC, Sorzano to Negroponte, February 19, 1988, Ludlow "Kim" Flower, Chile: U.S. Ambassador, Embassy, Box 91528, RRL.

[80] Telegram, U.S. Mission Geneva (Petrone) to Shultz, for Powell from Walters, March 8, 1988, DOS/FOIAe, III; Action Memo, Abrams, Schifter, Shaw to Shultz, March 8, 1988, ibid. In light of Walters's "reputation as a trouble shooter" and Pinochet supporter, Barnes was aghast at a proposal that he visit Chile in mid-April with the plebiscite campaign in full swing. At a time when it was imperative for the United States to maintain as low a profile as possible, an appearance by the controversial diplomat would almost certainly have "damage[d] our interests." Telegram, Barnes to Shultz, March 29, 1988, Robert Pastorino, Chile-1987 (03/29/1988–08/31/1988) [Subject File], Box 92348, RRL.

resubmit these amendments for debate by the entire UNHRC. Endorsing the "seriously flawed" Mexican text, said Abrams and Schifter, would be to participate in "an intellectually dishonest enterprise [by] heaping criticism on one of the lesser human rights offenders and ignoring the steps forward which Chile has taken during the last year." IO and Ambassador Walters predictably took a more hard-line stance, opposing the Mexican text with or without amendments. The two State officials countered that a balanced Chile resolution would embolden the opposition, whereas to reject a proposal supported by a majority of UNHRC members would be interpreted by the military regime as "a victory for Pinochet."[81] In the end, a satisfactory compromise proved unattainable, and the United States abstained on the vote. Chilean officials were later told that they should take little comfort from the vote because Washington remained extremely concerned about the level of human rights abuses.[82]

Shortly after the UNHRC vote, Barnes sent Washington a bleak assessment of the likely consequences of a Pinochet victory in the plebiscite: "Human rights violations will continue as long as he rules Chile, the judiciary will remain a farce, the Letelier case will not be resolved, the U.S. will not resume military or economic assistance and Chile's odd-man-out status in regional and world affairs will continue."[83] The prevailing sentiment in State was that there could be no letup in utilizing all available levers or access points to improve the prospects for a democratic transition. When Chile's Finance Minister Büchi approached the U.S. Trade Representative with a proposal that his government agree to trade concessions in return for reciprocity on Chilean agricultural exports and the elimination of tariffs on previous GSP-eligible items, for instance, ARA suggested that Santiago was probing for a loophole to circumvent the GSP suspension penalty without having to take any measures to improve workers' rights. The worry was that such a deal could be "trumpeted by Pinochet as a sign of U.S. support in the critical period leading up the plebiscite." Any such negotiations, Shultz instructed, required "a full and careful vetting within State," and any decision must be formally cleared by ARA.[84]

In April, Assistant Secretary Abrams traveled to Rome to discuss U.S. Latin America policy with Vatican officials, and Chile was high on the agenda. Abrams told Foreign Minister Archbishop Achille Silvestrini that

---

[81] Memo, Abrams, Schifter, Smith to Shultz, March 8, 1988, DOS/FOIAe, III.
[82] Telegram, Barnes to Shultz, May 2, 1988, ibid.
[83] Telegram, Barnes to Shultz, April 11, 1988, ibid.
[84] Telegram, Shultz (Grant/Hopper) to AmEmb Rome, April 14, 1988, ibid.

Washington had let the Chilean regime know "that it must hold an honest plebiscite, and that the worst possible outcome would be a vote that is perceived as crooked." The administration preferred a candidate other than Pinochet to contest the vote. Unfortunately, "there were few in the military who would dare oppose him" if he decided to put his name forward. Abrams and Silvestrini showered praise on PDC leader Patricio Aylwin, implicitly anointing him as an acceptable head of state in a post-Pinochet Chile.[85] On a visit to Washington in May, Shultz complimented Aylwin on the "positive steps" the PDC had taken since he took over the party leadership in July 1987, above all the moves to "distance itself" from the Communist Party and embrace the Pinochet economic model. Political, not economic, "management," Shultz never tired of repeating to Chilean officials, was the regime's major problem as well as the principal U.S. concern.[86] He delivered a similar message to the junta's General Matthei that another eight-year term by the seventy-two-year-old Pinochet would "polarize Chile and greatly augment the influence of the anti-American and anti-military left."[87]

The State Department publicly expressed deep regret over the decision to renew the state of emergency, which had expired on May 31, for another ninety days. Robert Gelbard dismissed Errázuriz's objections to the statement, reminding him that actions of this kind contradicted his government's professed commitment "to create an atmosphere of fair play before the plebiscite," allowing it to maintain "tremendous advantages . . . over its opponents by limiting civil rights." Taken aback by the tenor of Gelbard's response, Errázuriz countered that anti-Americanism in Chile was "reaching levels never seen before," even moving Pinochet to ask him, "Why do the Americans hate me so much?"[88]

Barnes interpreted the latest extension of the state of emergency as a signal that the United States needed to strengthen its efforts in "keeping the pressure on Pinochet," most immediately to ensure a "fraud-free plebiscite." This could be achieved by increased military exchange programs, expanding contacts with prominent business leaders, approaching

---

[85] Telegram, AmbEmb Rome to Shultz, April 18, 1988, ibid.
[86] Telegram, Shultz to AmEmb Santiago, May 6, 1988, ibid. While Shultz complimented the PDC on its economic outlook, this was apparently not a consensus view within the junta. General Fernando Matthei seemed to believe that the opposition was still wedded to "old statist [economic] solutions." Briefing Memo, Abrams to Shultz for May 6, 1988, meeting with Matthei, ibid.
[87] Telegram, AmEmb (Jones) to Shultz, April 20, 1988, ibid.
[88] Telegram, Shultz to AmEmb Santiago, June 16, 1988, ibid.

European governments to participate in making sure the vote was trouble-free, and encouraging opposition "pragmatism and unity." In the likely event that the military junta nominated Pinochet as the single candidate, in the yes-no plebiscite stipulated in the 1980 Constitution, and then lost the vote, the Department should be prepared, above all, to act in "concert with our allies to convince the Chilean military to resist the coup temptation and hold competitive presidential elections."[89] What should not be lost sight of was that the Constitution further stipulated that Pinochet stay in office until 1990, even if he were to lose the plebiscite.

Electoral Intervention: Supporting the No Vote

The decision by sixteen political parties – including both the Núñez and Almeyda Socialist Party factions – to form the National Command of the No (NCN) in February 1988 signaled that the opposition intended to wage a coordinated campaign in the upcoming plebiscite. Over the next five months, the NCN built up sufficiently rapid momentum that even the Communist Party called for a no vote after having initially advocated a boycott of the plebiscite – and a revival of mass mobilization politics and armed struggle to oust Pinochet.[90] With the plebiscite campaign in full swing, the Reagan administration had established an interagency Chile Working Group providing logistical and organizational support to the no campaign to counter the overwhelming advantages available to Pinochet. The NED was particularly active, distributing $600,000 to the NCN alliance and other groups advocating a no vote.[91] The Socialist Party's Heraldo Munoz described U.S. intervention as nothing short of "open collaboration" in the effort to defeat Pinochet.[92] For all that, Barnes continued to report that the good news could not overcome the bad news: the ongoing failure of the regime to provide "the conditions, the propitious atmosphere, for a free and fair vote."[93]

In a report to Shultz at the end of June, Abrams attempted to strike a more optimistic chord: while the regime still enjoyed a wide

---

[89] Telegram, Barnes to Shultz, June 14, 1988, ibid.

[90] See Report by the International Commission of the Latin American Studies Association, "The Chilean Plebiscite: A First Step toward Redemocratization," *LASA Forum* XIX, no. 4 (1989): 22.

[91] Shirley Christian, "Group Is Channeling U.S. Funds to Parties Opposing Pinochet," *NYT*, June 15, 1988, 1, 14.

[92] Telephone interview with Heraldo Múñoz.

[93] Telegram, Barnes to Shultz, June 27, 1988, DOS/FOIAe, III.

advantage in terms of resources and media access, and maintained a relentless "harass[ment]" of opposition members, the outcome was not a foregone conclusion. The activities of the NED and the USAID had produced "some significant gains" in the areas of voter registration, civic education seminars, and improvement in the opposition's polling and publicity technique skills. AID had established an office in the Embassy and was funding an observer group to monitor the plebiscite process. The White House continued to press America's allies to lend their support to its democracy-promotion efforts, although several European governments, notably the United Kingdom and West Germany, had essentially capitulated to pressure from pro-Pinochet lobbies within their ranks, claimed Abrams, "by watering-down and delaying [European Community] initiatives [to help ensure a free and fair vote] in the planning stage."[94]

Not only had the Europeans displayed a reluctance to support Washington's political strategy; its Atlantic allies and other economic competitors had filled the vacuum created by recent U.S. sanctions against Chile. Suspension of OPIC's coverage, its President Craig Nelson told a congressional hearing, had affected American investments totaling between $400 million and $500 million that were "sitting on the sidelines," poised to enter Chile. "Many of those projects have withdrawn, and guess who has those projects now?" asked Craig. "The Japanese, the Germans, and the Italians."[95] State Department officials were just as critical of the Europeans for refusing to sufficiently support the U.S. ban on arms sales to Chile "when the United States was in the trenches in favor of democracy."[96] Other than the United Kingdom, Abrams could not recall much substantive assistance from these governments.[97]

Relations with London were certainly not trouble-free regarding Chile policy. In late June, a Chilean diplomat brought to the attention of Washington's London Embassy a recent meeting between one of his government's senior Foreign Ministry officials, Jaime Lagos, and high-ranking British officials. The diplomat surmised that the reason for the visit was Santiago's desire to get "an independent assessment of whether the British were becoming more hardnosed on Chile" based on its concern over

[94] Memo, Abrams to Acting Secretary of State, June 30, 1988, ibid.
[95] U.S. Congress, House, Committee on Foreign Affairs, Subcommittee on International Economic Policy and Trade, *Reauthorization of the Overseas Private Investment Corporation*, 100th Cong., 2d Sess., March 15, 1985, 84.
[96] Confidential telephone interview 1.
[97] Interview with Elliott Abrams.

Embassy cable traffic indicating "a stiffening UK view" toward the dictatorship. If such "friends" of the Pinochet regime as Prime Minister Margaret Thatcher and Foreign Minister Geoffrey Howe had indeed adopted a more critical posture, the Chilean informant was convinced that U.S. pressure must have played a part. In its telegram to Washington, the U.S. Embassy noted that "both the [well-informed] Chilean Embassy [in London] and FCO officials have an interest in our perceiving that HMG [Her Majesty's Government] is getting tougher on Chile and that the Chileans know it." Lagos apparently "was given a polite but strong message of HMG disapproval regarding the political and human rights situation" as well as a "polite but stronger-than-expected" warning of British concern over the conduct of the plebiscite. Whitehall was "well aware that a universally-condemned Pinochet 'victory' could put considerable additional and unwanted strain on UK-Chilean ties."[98] Two weeks later, the London Embassy reported one British Foreign Office official reacting with "mild irritation" to what he called "the implication that 'all virtue on this [the democracy promotion] issue resides in Washington.'" While the British government might have shared "exactly the same aims" as the White House and State Department, and "entirely endorse[d]" U.S. concerns regarding the unfairness of the plebiscite campaign,[99] Whitehall's sensibilities were further ruffled in September when the Foreign Office expressed its "annoyance" over newspaper reports that State, in the person of Robert Gelbard, had warned London that sales of warships to Chile could endanger the balance of power between Santiago and Buenos Aires, and boost Pinochet's plebiscite prospects. British diplomats accused the Americans of overreacting to the amount of funds involved, of exaggerating the "regionally destabilizing" impact of the arms sales, and of failing to appreciate the "comparative effectiveness" of British efforts to promote a democratic transition. "What clearly does irk them," the Embassy telegrammed State, "is what they see as an unjustified self-righteous tone in USG pronouncements on Chile."[100]

If Chilean officials were having limited success defending the regime's preparations for the plebiscite, a U.S. Embassy review of the human rights situation during the first six months of 1988 did not make their task any easier. Although incidents of extrajudicial killings and torture

[98] Telegram, AmEmb London (Price) to Shultz, July 1, 1988, DOS/FOIAe, III.

[99] Telegram, AmEmb London (Price) to Shultz, July 15, 1988, ibid.

[100] Telegram, AmEmb London (Price) to Shultz, September 7, 1988, ibid.; Hugh O'Shaughnessy, "Britain Told to Stop Aid to Chile," *The Observer* (UK), September 4, 1988, 23.

were decreasing, the regime and its rightist paramilitary allies continued to practice both methods of intimidation and had "increasingly used the legal system to contain political dissent and to punish or harass the opposition," especially targeting the leaders of political parties, human rights organizations, and trade unions.[101] Appearing before a congressional subcommittee, Gelbard praised the reduced exile lists, the legalization of political parties, and the improved treatment of arrested protesters but conceded that these positive developments were "lamentably counterbalanced by continuing grave violations of other civil and human rights." In other words, there had been too little change in the overall situation. Torture, arbitrary arrests, harassment of journalists and human rights workers, and severe limits on freedoms remained a feature of the political landscape, Gelbard testified, as well as "disappearances, kidnappings, and unauthorized searches."[102]

The regime's intransigent stance on the Letelier-Moffitt murders still cast a long shadow over U.S.-Chilean relations. The case remained "a source of permanent tensions in our bilateral relations," Assistant Secretary of State Schifter told legislators in May, and would remain so in the absence of a satisfactory resolution.[103] His testimony came hard on the heels of a Chilean Supreme Court decision to refuse U.S. officials access to a general who had investigated the murders.[104] Robert Gelbard drew attention to "insulting language" contained in the latest diplomatic note rebuffing the U.S. extradition request, which finally convinced the administration that Santiago had "no desire whatsoever to reach a just settlement in the matter and is hiding those responsible for the murders." Ambassador Errázuriz lamely replied that the United States was "politicizing the Letelier case . . . for political ends."[105] A frustrated Elliott Abrams wrote to Undersecretary Armacost that Santiago "flatly rejected all our requests for cooperation often couching their replies in obstructionist and insulting language." Their position was that "future discussion of the case would be a waste of time." The latest evidence of

[101] Telegram, AmEmb Santiago (Jones) to Shultz, August 1, 1988, DOS/FOIAe, III.
[102] Prepared statement of Robert E. Gelbard before U.S. Congress, House Subcommittees of Human Rights and International Organizations, and Western Hemispheric Affairs, May 1, 1988, DOS/FOIAe, III.
[103] U.S. Congress, House, "U.S. Policy, Human Rights, and the Prospects for Democracy in Chile," 142, 143.
[104] Bradley Graham, "U.S. Hope of Exposing Letelier's Killers Dims," WP, May 7, 1988, A17.
[105] Telegram, Shultz to AmEmb Santiago, June 16, 1988, DOS/FOIAe, III.

stonewalling was a July 14 Chilean Supreme Court ruling that denied a Letelier family appeal to reopen the case "on the basis of fresh evidence presented by a participant in the crime."[106] Congressional pressure was not taken seriously in Santiago because Ambassador Errázuriz kept reporting that interest in the case on Capitol Hill was confined to only a handful of individuals: "You see in the Congress there were only three, four, or five among five hundred" campaigning on the issue.[107] By now, Washington had virtually exhausted all legal avenues, and despite the importance the White House and State supposedly attached to the case, they had long since forgone the effective use of political or economic sanctions as a means of forcing Pinochet's hand.

U.S. officials continued to praise the government's economic record – in August, Chile won approval of a $75 million IMF loan, the first Fund loan in three years[108] – while just as consistently expressing strong misgivings about the country's political evolution. During a meeting with Chile's Foreign Minister Ricardo García, Shultz lauded the regime's "impressive economic program" and was favorably impressed by the limited human rights improvements, but they were no substitute for the failure to lift the state of emergency. The other bone of contention was the slow pace of legislation to provide the opposition with equal access to television during the plebiscite campaign, which did not add to the perception, said Shultz, that an "honest and legitimate" process was taking place.[109] At the end of the month, in the hope of parrying some of Washington's criticism, the regime lifted the state of emergency and, in a minor and grudging concession, provided the opposition with a daily fifteen-minute slot on all television channels and gave its leaders access to political talk shows.[110]

To help effect an orderly transfer of power should the no faction win the plebiscite, Ambassador Barnes had already turned his attention to encouraging a dialogue between the political opposition and moderate

[106] Briefing Memo, Abrams to Armacost, July 19, 1988, ibid.
[107] Interview with Hernán Errázuriz.
[108] Catherine Gwin, "U.S. Relations with the World Bank, 1945–1992," in *The World Bank: Vol. 2. Perspectives*, ed. Devesh Kapur, John P. Lewis, and Richard Webb (Washington, DC: Brookings Institution Press, 1997), 402.
[109] Telegram, AmEmb Quito (Holwill) to Shultz, August 15, 1988, DOS/FOIAe, III.
[110] "We mainly wanted to show singing, music, the sky and happiness, all images that showed the meaning of our slogan: 'Democracy is happiness and happiness is coming,'" said Gabriel Valdés of the opposition's television campaign. "We wanted to send a message that told people that happiness could defeat terror." Interview with Gabriel Valdés.

Pinochet supporters.[111] Furthermore, he looked to the Church to perform a similar stabilizing role to that it played in the Philippines, where the Bishops' Episcopal Conference issued a declaration immediately after the February 1986 elections to limit unrest as much as possible following Corazón Aquino's victory over Ferdinand Marcos. He cautioned, though, that the United States must not dismiss a possible Communist Party attempt to deliberately instigate violent protests on election day or soon after with the objective of producing a junta "overreaction" that would set back the transition process.[112]

As the plebiscite date neared, Abrams and Errázuriz remained in close contact. When they met in late September, the Chilean appeared to have reached the conclusion that there was no good outcome to the plebiscite whichever side won: a win for the yes campaign would likely doom the democratic transition; a no vote would "trigger extremism." Trying to interpret this statement, Abrams asked if the government might "try too hard to win." To counter any such thinking on the part of the generals, Abrams indicated "that a 'narrow' win by the GOC might be called into questions if conditions were not clearly fair."[113] To a skeptical Michael Skol, who replaced Gelbard as Deputy Assistant Secretary of State for South America in mid-1988, the difficulties in getting through to the regime leadership when it came to political issues had never changed: "We always had to go through a kind of contortions whenever we talked about the political situation with the Chileans."[114]

Before another meeting between Shultz and Errázuriz, Abrams briefed the Secretary that the regime had to be deterred from taking "violent and illicit steps" to cancel or nullify the outcome of the plebiscite,[115] and to this end, he had called the British Embassy to lobby Whitehall to "weigh-in with their contacts in Chile as well" and had instructed Barnes and Southern Command's General Frederick Woerner "to use similar points with their key contacts."[116] The same day (October 1), Barnes wrote to Abrams that Pinochet's plan was simple: "A) if the 'yes' is winning, fine;

---

[111] Briefing Memo, Abrams to Armacost, July 25, 1988, DOS/FOIAe, III.
[112] Telegram, Barnes to Shultz, August 29, 1988, ibid.
[113] Telegram, Shultz to AmEmb Santiago, September 23, 1988, ibid.
[114] Telephone interview with Michael Skol.
[115] In mid-August, Barnes reported a conversation with a Church official who suggested the military was planning a coup should the opposition win the plebiscite. Telegram, Barnes to Shultz, August 18, 1988, DOS/FOIAe, III.
[116] Briefing Memo, Abrams to Acting Secretary, October 1, 1988, ibid.

B) if the race is very close rely on fraud and coercion; C) if the 'no' is likely to win clearly then use violence and terror to stop the process." With Pinochet's closest advisers predicting his election defeat, "the third option is the one most likely to be put into effect."[117]

Washington's Final Warning

In the days immediately preceding the October 5 vote, the attention of U.S. officials turned to forestalling any such temptation Pinochet might have to counter a victory for the no campaign by attempting to nullify the result, cracking down on the opposition in the guise of maintaining order or, perhaps, even staging an *auto-golpe*. Gelbard recollected that U.S. officials had been in contact with members of the junta and were getting "all kinds of signals that Matthei and Carabinero boss General Rodolfo Stange were reaching out to the opposition and were supportive of a true, transparent and legitimate democratic process in the referendum."[118] Not so Pinochet and the army. Uneasy about their commitment to the plebiscite process and willingness to respect an opposition victory, the State Department decided that on the day of voting, Acting Secretary John Whitehead (in Shultz's absence abroad) would summon Ambassador Errázuriz to his office and inform him that U.S. officials had "recently received profoundly disturbing reliable reports that the Chilean military, in particular the army, have made plans to permit and even instigate violence as a pretext for suspending or nullifying the plebiscite – if it looks like Pinochet is going to lose." Whitehead would then convey a strongly worded message for Errázuriz to transmit to Santiago: "Implementation of such a plan would seriously damage relations with the U.S. and utterly destroy Chile's reputation in the world."[119]

Deputy Assistant Secretary Skol sourced the Whitehead gambit to Elliott Abrams: "it was his from the word go." The meeting itself was "very frank, very head-on," and although Errázuriz categorically denied that there was any plot ("these are not the kinds of things that are transmitted to ambassadors," he said), there was no question that he forwarded the message to his superiors in Santiago. That message was, "Don't do it, cut it out or, if you do it, [the United States] will make it public and

---

[117] Transmittal Memo, Barnes to Abrams, October 1, 1988, ibid.
[118] Interview with Robert Gelbard.
[119] Telegram, Shultz (Whitehead) to AmEmb Santiago, October 1, 1988, DOS/FOIAe, III.

you will not be able to claim that you responded to a surprise chaotic situation."[120] Abrams instructed Barnes and senior Pentagon officials to pass on similar warnings to the Chilean military and requested the British to use their communication channels to the regime to do likewise.[121] "We knew that Pinochet was planning something," said Barnes's successor as Ambassador, Charles Gillespie, and they were told in no uncertain terms "that if they implemented a plan to jigger the results of the plebiscite . . . we were going to blow the whistle."[122] The same message was delivered via military-to-military channels, which was "absolutely standard procedure in these kinds of cases," according to Skol. "If you don't deliver it in more than one channel, people turn to their military counterparts who say, 'This must be the civilians in the State Department: we don't have to pay attention.'" A warning, he acknowledged, was as much as Washington could do in the circumstances:

When you make a threat, you make a threat that you can deliver, and of course we could deliver revelations. You don't weaken it by simultaneously saying, "We'll go to the UN Security Council, we'll do this, we'll do that." Dictators like Pinochet are perfectly capable of hunkering down for the short, medium, or even long term in most cases in response to economic or other threats, but this would blast open the whole ruse.[123]

Errázuriz's recollection of the meeting with Whitehead was suffused with indignation: "Those accusations were made to me several times and each time I told them, 'You are wrong. It is very easy to say these negative effects are going to happen, and I would ask you the day after the plebiscite when the government honors the results to give me an explanation of this, And they didn't give me any explanation – never."[124] The Chilean Foreign Ministry accused the United States of casting "a shadow over the plebiscite" and categorically denied the existence of any plan to stop it from taking place.[125] Years later, Errázuriz continued to harbor a grudge against Barnes over the entire incident, blaming him for seriously

[120] Telephone interview with Michael Skol.
[121] Memo, Abrams to Shultz, October 3, 1988, DOS/FOIAe, III. Also see Paper, "Presidential Evening Reading ('Plans to Disrupt Chile's Plebiscite')," October 3, 1988, Robert Pastorino-1987 (09/23/1988–12/12/1988) [Subject File], Box 92348, RRL.
[122] Charles A. Gillespie Jr. interview, FAOHC. The Department of Defense required no encouragement because its senior officials understood that the complete normalization of military-to-military ties was dependent on "a positive outcome to the plebiscite [i.e., Pinochet's defeat]." Ibid.
[123] Telephone interview with Michael Skol.
[124] Interview with Hernán Errázuriz.
[125] Briefing Memo, Arcos to Acting Secretary of State, October 4, 1988, DOS/FOIAe, III.

damaging bilateral ties by generating "mistrust in the State Department when he said that Pinochet did not want to hand over the government."[126]

While rumors circulated in Santiago about what Pinochet might do to cling to power, how much U.S. officials actually knew of his plans and how much was speculation or suspicion is unclear. The Country Team was constantly "on watch," remembered DCM George Jones, and there were "plans under way that we heard about through various means."[127] By the time of the Whitehead-Errázuriz meeting, Abrams was in possession of what he considered "crystal-clear proof that Pinochet was going to steal the result."[128] Pinochet's intention, said Michael Skol, was "to create a chaotic atmosphere, rioting, and then step in and cancel the results."[129] Evidence of the plan was so "persuasive," that had it been carried out, it "would have completely destroyed our relations with Chile."[130] The commander of Santiago's military garrison confided to a member of PDC President Aylwin's staff that Pinochet had ordered all military personnel removed from the capital by the end of polling day to leave the city vulnerable to violence and rioting – information that was transmitted to Ambassador Barnes by the Socialist Party's Heraldo Múñoz at the request of Aylwin and Ricardo Lagos.[131]

One day before the vote, ARA prepared a review of options available to the United States should Pinochet refuse to accept the outcome of the plebiscite and block the transition to democracy. They ranged from placing limits on Department of Agriculture cooperation with Chilean primary product exporters, to voting against MDB loans to Chile, to freezing Chilean government assets in the United States, to withdrawing most-favored nation trading status, to imposing selective or comprehensive trade embargoes. There was a cautionary proviso that any retaliatory sanctions should be devised in such a way as to "minimize the economic costs and maximize the political gains to the U.S." In particular, they "should not be adopted unless they can be maintained for an extended period without significant harm to U.S. economic interests."[132] No actual

[126] "Reagan's Role in Supporting the Pinochet Regime: Interview with Hernán Errázuriz," *Santiago Times*, June 14, 2004.
[127] Interview with George F. Jones.
[128] Interview with Robert Gelbard.
[129] Telephone interview with Michael Skol.
[130] Interview with Elliott Abrams.
[131] This account was confirmed during author interviews with Harry G. Barnes, Enrique Correa, and Heraldo Múñoz. Matthei and Stange had learned in advance of the plot to create chaos and "told us they weren't going to allow that" (Múñoz).
[132] Memo, Harrington to Howard, October 4, 1988, DOS/FOIAe, III.

contingency plans were drawn up and ready to be implemented should the plebiscite result be overturned or annulled by Pinochet. That was not how the State Department operated, said Schifter. "It rarely had contingency plans for anything. We would have faced it at that moment and said, 'What do we do now?' We weren't going to use force against Chile and what else could we have done? But our relations would certainly have gone into a deep spiral."[133]

To ensure a fair vote and minimize the possibility of Pinochet abrogating the result, the administration drew on the experience of the 1986 Philippine election, where Marcos's efforts to steal the election by manipulating the vote were much more difficult to achieve under the glare of international scrutiny. George Jones was convinced that, with U.S. encouragement, "had the eyes of the world not been on Chile and had there not been international observers in Chile for the plebiscite, then Pinochet would have gotten away with it. He would have manipulated the situation or stolen it. The United States had very hard evidence that he was trying to do that right up to the very last moment."[134] Intelligence reports referred to "contingency plans" drawn up by senior regime officials "to sabotage the plebiscite . . . and nullify the electoral process" if the opposition appeared likely to win the popular vote.[135] The general coordinator for the Command of the No, the Socialist Party's Enrique Correa, described the officers as tempted to disregard the vote as those most fearful of retribution for human rights abuses: they were simply "worried about their own fate. It was not a political decision."[136]

As the results came in, Pinochet's prospects of victory plummeted with each passing hour. Despite his overwhelming advantages and the restricted space to campaign allocated to the political opposition, when the plebiscite votes were counted, Pinochet had suffered a comprehensive defeat by approximately 56 percent to 44 percent. Just as provisions in the 1980 Constitution to guarantee the plebiscite's legitimacy had created space for Pinochet's opponents to organize and campaign against him, so the voter lists provided for in those same laws had made it difficult to rig the outcome.[137]

In a last gasp effort to hold off the inevitable, Pinochet delayed releasing the vote totals, even to his closest supporters, before consulting with

---

[133] Interviews with Richard Schifter and George F. Jones.
[134] George F. Jones interview, FAOHC.
[135] DIA, "Chile: Contingency Plans," October 4, 1988, NSA.
[136] Interview with Enrique Correa.
[137] See Huneeus, *The Pinochet Regime*, 401.

junta colleagues in La Moneda (the Presidential Palace). Hopeful that
the legitimate outcome could somehow be reversed or annulled, Pinochet
was unaware that Matthei and Stange had privately assured the U.S.
Embassy "that the results of the plebiscite were going to be respected."[138]
En route to the meeting on the evening of the election, and possessing
the opposition's parallel counting totals, General Matthei acknowledged
publicly to the waiting media that "it seems to me that the NO has
really won."[139] Matthei's concession statement, said George Jones, was
a "conscious decision on his part," and the timing meant that whatever
transpired in La Moneda, "Pinochet's hands were going to be tied by
what [the air force General] had said outside." Still, the "very angry"
dictator fought to the bitter end to nullify the results. When the other
junta members entered the meeting room, Pinochet handed each a copy
of a draft decree "suspending the plebiscite in essence and going back
to the drawing board, and they all refused to sign it. So, he threw up
his arms and said in effect that it was all over."[140] A Pentagon Defense
Intelligence Agency (DIA) report provided an almost identical account
of the meeting: Pinochet twice demanded that his colleagues – Matthei,
Stange, and army representative General Humberto Gordon – sign a
document giving him "extraordinary powers to meet the crisis of the
electoral defeat," which would allow him "to have the armed forces seize
the capital." Their resolute opposition left Pinochet "without alternative
but to accept a 'NO' win."[141] Matthei's defiant stance moved Robert
Gelbard to eulogize him as the "hero of the referendum."[142]

In his postplebiscite communiqués to Shultz, Ambassador Barnes
expressed considerable satisfaction over the U.S. contribution to the
plebiscite process and its outcome: the Communists had been isolated
from the democratic opposition and pushed to the political sidelines; the
Catholic Church wielded its influence to ensure a free and transparent
process; the democratic parties gained at least limited access to television, which was probably a "decisive factor" in the result; the opposition
coalition was unified in advocating a no vote and was the beneficiary of
a "substantial expansion of political rights"; limited human rights gains

---

[138] George F. Jones interview, FAOHC.
[139] Quoted in Kornbluh, *The Pinochet File*, 434.
[140] DIA, Information Report, January 1, 1989, NSA; George F. Jones interview, FAOHC.
[141] DIA, Information Report, "Chilean Junta Meeting: The Night of the Plebiscite," January 1, 1989, reprinted in Kornbluh, *The Pinochet File*, Document 13, 459–460. Gordon was former head of the CNI, the successor agency to DINA.
[142] Interview with Robert Gelbard.

occurred during the campaign; and the victorious democratic opposition was committed to maintaining the military's free market–foreign investment economic model in the transition to civilian rule. The outcome of the election had a contradictory impact on the armed forces: air force and Carabinero officers became more accessible to American diplomats, whereas liaising with army and navy personnel now became exceedingly difficult, as their senior ranks became "more and more deeply committed to Pinochet's effort to perpetuate himself in power."

Even though Barnes doubted that Pinochet could make a "political comeback," he urged Washington against operating on the assumption that he could now be "taken lightly." He was still powerful enough to create "turmoil" or carry out an *auto-golpe*. The key to limiting Pinochet's political opportunities, against the background of ebbing support among the rightist political parties and declining enthusiasm within the armed forces generally to see him contest any future presidential election, was the ability of the opposition to maintain "a moderate agenda and image." Ironically, the Ambassador concluded, the very constitution Pinochet created to perpetuate himself in power was proving to be his "iron cage."[143]

Keeping up the Pressure

If Barnes's view of the plebiscite and its outcome was generally favorable, his assessment of the transition process itself was more sobering. The democratic gains, he cautioned State's Seventh Floor, "could still be lost," and therefore it was incumbent on the administration to strive "to keep the process on track" and to avert a resurgence of "extremism [because] we are not out of the woods yet." The United States had to maintain a significant presence in Chile – via the NED, AID, and the United States Information Service – if democratic institutions had any chance of throwing down roots in a postdictatorial era. The no forces might have won a decisive victory, but the result had not "completely discredited" Pinochet. With the support of 44 percent of the electorate and the army leadership solidly behind him, despite the impact of the election defeat, he retained sufficient power to unleash a new round of repression if he decided that would be an advantageous move. At this problematic juncture, wrote Barnes, U.S. efforts needed to be directed, above all, toward deepening ties with the armed forces to "reinforce their commitment to democratic reform." Nor could Washington ignore the

---

[143] Telegram, Barnes to Shultz, October 26, 1988, DOS/FOIAe, III.

importance of shoring up the moderate opposition while simultaneously attempting to further marginalize the radical left from the centers of political influence and power.

Privately, tensions had emerged between the center-left parties in the coalition and the PDC over the latter's dominant position, and within the PDC between prospective candidates (the ex-President's son, Eduardo Frei Ruiz-Tagle, former PDC head Gabriel Valdés, Andrés Zaldívar and Patricio Aylwin) for the Chilean presidency. Of these, only Aylwin had categorically ruled out direct participation by the Communist Party in a future opposition election campaign. To promote the development of a "moderate center," Barnes deemed it important to cultivate ties between the opposition and the political right if the electorate was to be offered "a balanced choice in the upcoming elections and in consolidating a stable democratic system." Engaging with, and supporting, these groups would "be [just as] essential to attenuate incipient and in some instances open anti-American sentiment." Finally, the Ambassador appeared to imply that the State Department should take a more realistic approach toward dealing with the Communists than had hitherto been the case. "The Communist Party is a fact of political life," he observed, and should therefore be encouraged to shift away from clandestine to more open politics because it was "not apt to go away any time soon."[144]

Forty-eight hours after the plebiscite vote, Abrams traveled to London for a meeting with his British counterpart, David Gillmore. Both diplomats agreed Chile's political transition was not guaranteed – which made it doubly important to expand lines of communication with the army and to lobby sympathetic European governments to participate in efforts to keep the opposition unified "and the left in line." They discussed a "new strategy" for dealing with Chile's human rights problem in the UN, with the goal of producing a "forward looking resolution" acceptable to the Reagan administration ahead of the annual UNGA meeting. The two officials were confident that the current UN's mood would be more favorably disposed than in the past toward supporting a "milder, consensus" Chile resolution. That mood had resulted in the unanimous passage of resolutions "on perennially difficult issues," reflecting a new "general air of optimism" now permeating the global body.[145]

---

[144] Telegram, Barnes to Shultz, October 19, 1988, ibid. Also see Eugene Robinson, "Pinochet Grows Isolated; Chile's Opposition Begins to Fracture," *WP*, November 19, 1988, A19.

[145] Telegram, Shultz to AmEmb London and Santiago, October 12, 1988, DOS/FOIAe, III.

To this end, ARA's Southern Cone Office and HA began work on a plan to induce European governments to submit a brief resolution on Chile that would highlight the actual human rights gains made since the beginning of the year, identify those areas where abuses continued at unacceptable levels, and affirm the efforts of the Special Rapporteur. The Europeans would be asked to produce a final text based on "informal draft language" transmitted by Washington. Southern Cone Director Richard Howard was convinced that the Latin American democracies would line up behind such a resolution "and probably pre-empt or brush aside the unbalanced version we must expect from Mexico/Cuba." If a consensus developed in favor of a "moderate and accurate" resolution, the United States, if not prepared to cosponsor it, would at least cast a favorable vote.[146]

Despite the plebiscite outcome, some officials in ARA and HA saw no reason to immediately dump the U.S. policy of abstaining on Chile MDB loan requests until there was firm evidence that the "former pattern of gross violations [of human rights] has been terminated." By avoiding a premature shift, wrote Howard, "we conserve another small carrot" that can be used to press for new initiatives. By abstaining, the United States could buy much needed time to reassess bilateral ties during the actual transition to civilian rule. Besides, changing the vote now would require consultation with Congress, "perhaps sending the wrong signal both to the Hill and the GOC that it's 'business as usual' with Chile and that human rights is no longer a concern."[147] Abrams and Schifter, among others, took a different view that eventually prevailed: "Failing to support the loan in spite of the recent positive steps taken by the GOC could call into question our credibility in the IADB and thus may undermine our effectiveness in achieving real reforms in the institution."[148] Henceforth, the administration would support MDB loans to Chile, starting with a $35 million World Bank road construction loan. When Embassy officers transmitted the decision to the Chilean Human Rights Commission and the Vicariate each took a fairly relaxed view of the policy shift, indicating that they "understood the U.S. position perfectly [and] had no problem with it," most likely because of a belief that the loan would benefit the populace, not the dictatorship.[149]

---

[146] Memo, Howard to Abrams, October 21, 1988, ibid.
[147] Memo, Howard to Skol, October 20, 1988, ibid.
[148] Action Memo, ARA Abrams, Schifter HA, Larson EB to S/S, Oct 18, 1988. Robert Pastorino, Chile-1987 (09/23/1988–12/12/1988) [Subject File], Box 92348, RRL.
[149] Telegram, Barnes to Shultz, October 24, 1988, DOS/FOIAe, III.

Ahead of the annual UNGA vote on human rights in Chile, the USUN Mission was able to report that a "substantially more balanced" resolution had been put forward. The draft acknowledged the "important gains" achieved over recent months while simultaneously highlighting the persistence of "serious" human rights abuses, and it commented positively on the way in which the plebiscite had "stimulated increased political participation." The American delegation's enthusiasm for the draft was diminished in the absence of any reference to "terrorism from the political extremes" as a cause of some of the worst rights violations and by its failure to sufficiently acknowledge the successful plebiscite as a key step "toward the restoration of democratic procedures in Chile."[150] The final version expressed satisfaction at the lifting of states of emergency and the permission for greater political activity, retained its concern about widespread state-authored abuses, and urged the government to initiate a dialogue with the opposition to facilitate a full reestablishment of democracy.[151] In the event, the vote was carried 97–1, with the United States and fifty-four other member states registering abstentions.

In Santiago, Barnes's tour of duty was coming to an end. Back in mid-1987, Elliott Abrams attended a meeting of Western Hemisphere Chiefs of Mission, where an objective unrelated to the conference itself was to confirm a replacement for Barnes, who had expressed his intention to resign in 1988. One of the attendees, U.S. Ambassador to Colombia Charles Gillespie, was the replacement Abrams had in mind. After Gillespie accepted the reassignment to Santiago, Abrams revealed that there was one "hurdle that we have to get over." U.S. Ambassador to Uruguay Malcolm Wilkey, a Republican political appointee whose wife's family was part of the right-wing Chilean political elite, "wanted to go to Chile in the worst way [and] was making a major pitch for the job." As it happened, Secretary Shultz was determined to prevent this happening and successfully blocked Wilkey's effort.[152] The confirmation hearing before the SFRC, scheduled for mid-September 1988, was postponed for several weeks, reportedly because of objections raised by the ranking Republican member, Jesse Helms, that the Ambassador-designate had failed to

---

[150] Telegram, USUN Mission New York (Okun) to Shultz, November 31, 1988, ibid.
[151] "Situation of Human Rights and Fundamental Freedoms in Chile," A/RES/43/158, United Nations General Assembly, 43rd Session: Resolutions adopted on the Reports of the Third Committee, http://www.un.org/Depts/dhl/resguide/r43.htm.
[152] Charles A. Gillespie Jr. interview, FAOHC.

"sufficiently support" Pinochet and his government.[153] As for Pinochet, he was more than happy to see the end of Barnes, whom he accused of having done "nothing except make political propaganda against the government." Displaying his hostility to the very end, the Chilean autocrat refused the traditional presidential farewell for a departing Ambassador. "I did not shake his hand, I did see him off, [but] I did not say goodbye," said an obviously unrepentant Pinochet.[154]

Given that Barnes was simply following instructions, Pinochet's rebuff on his departure seemed a not-too-subtle manifestation of his anger at the shift in American policy. Clearly, managing Pinochet's denouement promised to be a formidable challenge for U.S. officials. With elections for a new President not due for more than twelve months, there was a slim possibility still that the Chilean ruler might halt the democracy process in its tracks. There was a greater likelihood that he would enact laws limiting a future civilian government's ability to deliver on popular expectations, creating the possibility of another cycle of unrest and confrontation. Even absent these outcomes, the restoration of normal bilateral ties would nonetheless require a deft diplomacy on Washington's part that would take into account the sensitivities of Pinochet and his colleagues, on one hand, while weighing up how to deal with the set of legislative sanctions against Chile that could not be removed overnight. This responsibility was about to be transferred to the incoming Bush administration.

[153] "Ambassadorial Nominations Languish," CQWR, September 17, 1988, 2624. Gillespie was finally confirmed on October 14 and arrived in Santiago in early December.
[154] Quoted in "Pinochet Criticizes U.S., Snubs Ambassador," AP, November 28, 1988.

7

Return to the Fold

The presidency of George H. Bush from January 1989 to January 1993 coincided with the collapse of the Soviet Union, the disintegration of its Eastern European bloc, and the emergence of a unipolar world where the United States was the only superpower. As momentous as these changes were, they did not result in a fundamental reevaluation of U.S. foreign policy goals. In appearance and style, the Bush administration initially leaned away from the emotionally charged and ideologically driven policy of the Reagan years to a more prudent and pragmatic approach in dealing with the Third World in particular. But Washington's new enthusiasm for solving outstanding problems through diplomacy rather than confrontation was, as events were to show, conditional and largely a function of the need to adapt to a new global reality that denied U.S. policy makers compelling national security arguments to justify interventionist policies and created opportunities for political settlements to a number of regional conflicts.

In his inaugural address, Bush embraced his predecessor's rhetoric about the need to support democracy and free market economies. The "day of the dictator is over," the new President declared, and the totalitarian era was passing: "great nations of the world are moving toward democracy [and] freedom [and] toward free markets through the door to prosperity."[1] For all that, the Bush White House would continue to emphasize the necessity of American global leadership, in the process subordinating the ambitions of competitor allies in Europe and Japan to Washington's interests. "American leadership," Bush insisted, meant

[1] George Bush, Inaugural Address, January 20, 1989, American Presidency Project.

"economic, political, and military" leadership and in all three respects embodied "a hard-nosed sense of American self-interest."[2] This dictated the maintenance of large, Cold War–sized military and intelligence budgets, now justified on the basis of the need to maintain worldwide stability (rather than the containment of communism) and to deal with new and continuing threats posed by rogue states, terrorism, and international drug trafficking. In the Third World, the collapse of the Soviet bloc gave an enormous boost to American power, first by eliminating any significant counterweight to U.S. objectives or power projections, and second by increasing the costs to those regimes seeking to pursue alternative economic and political strategies now more vulnerable to hostile initiatives by the dominant imperial state.

Entering the White House, Bush brought with him arguably the most impressive foreign policy credentials of any President since Dwight Eisenhower, having served as Ambassador to China and CIA Director under Gerald Ford, and then as Vice President to Ronald Reagan, when he played a key role in shaping Latin American policy.[3] His two senior foreign policy appointments – Secretary of State James Baker (Reagan's former White House Chief of Staff and Treasury Secretary) and NSC Adviser General Brent Scowcroft (a position he held in the Ford White House) – signaled a clear intention to avoid any sharp break with his predecessor's approach. The decision to revive an NSC structure that allocated control of key interagency committees to the NSC Adviser also drew on features of past Republican administrations, notably the process that operated under Nixon and Ford. What distinguished Bush's foreign policy bureaucracy was the absence of major personality conflicts and policy divisions.

The changed global power relationships and the Bush administration's own priorities did prefigure some shifts in policy emphasis and area concerns. Whereas Reagan was preoccupied with Eastern Europe and Central America, Bush wanted to focus attention on the Soviet Union and, especially during the first two years of his term in office, China and northeast Asia (his first overseas trip as President was to Tokyo, Seoul, and Beijing). Relations with Latin America had a twofold focus: furthering U.S. economic objectives through debt relief initiatives, free trade agreements (most notably with Mexico), and the announcement of an Enterprise for

---

[2] President George Bush, "America Must Remain Engaged," U.S. Department of State, *Dispatch*, November 21, 1992, 893–895.

[3] Walter LaFeber, *The American Age*, 2nd ed. (New York: W. W. Norton, 1994), 747.

the Americas aid program to assist the most heavily debt-burdened Latin regimes; and getting rid of the inherited, unfinished political problems of Nicaragua and Panama – finally achieving the Reagan objective of regime change in both countries via electoral intervention in one case and military intervention in the other.[4] Similarly, in outlining policy toward the Southern Cone, the Bush White House closely adhered to the basic parameters established by Reagan. In Chile, this meant a continuing support for the transition to a protected democracy and the restoration of a cooperative bilateral relationship with a new civilian government.

A Delicate Interregnum

Pinochet's defeat in the October 1988 plebiscite constituted a milestone in the redemocratization process in Chile, although it was not quite the devastating setback for the General that it may have first appeared. The terms of the 1980 Constitution allowed him another fourteen months as supreme ruler of Chile with sufficient power – and not inconsiderable support – to oversee the fine details of the transition and to hobble the powers of a new civilian government at best, or to further delay, or even cancel, the ultimate transfer of power at worst. Ambassador Harry Barnes's postplebiscite warning to his superiors in Washington that they were "not out of the woods yet" reflected less a concern about specific threats than a general sense that the transition was highly conditional. "What had happened with the plebiscite," said Barnes, "was in its own way a small miracle and one couldn't be sure, particularly in the knowledge of what was said to have happened in La Moneda [immediately following the vote] that somehow something might not happen without knowing for sure what that something might be or how it might happen."[5] Twenty-four hours after the October 5 vote, Pinochet had appeared on national

---

[4] In Nicaragua, Bush initially maintained Reagan's policy of hostility toward the Sandinista regime. At the same time, he lacked Reagan's emotional commitment to the insurgents so that Secretary of State James Baker was eventually able to persuade him of the need to get the "bleeding sore" of Central America off the national agenda by accepting the regional peace plan devised by Costa Rica's President Oscar Arias. James A. Baker III, *The Politics of Diplomacy: Revolution , War and Peace, 1989–1992.* New York: G.P. Putnam's Sons, 1995, 47; Baker, quoted in Michael R. Beschloss and Strobe Talbott, *At the Highest Levels* (London: Warner Books, 1993), 57. In the run-up to the February 1990 election, the Bush administration provided large-scale political and financial assistance to the presidential candidate of the major anti-Sandinista coalition that won the election, finally achieving Reagan's strategic objective.

[5] Interview with Harry G. Barnes.

television pointedly wearing a military uniform for the first time in several weeks. "Neither the tenets nor the constitutional itinerary outlined have been in play [in the plebiscite]," he declared.[6] Both the symbolism and the substance of the message were clear: the members of the triumphant no campaign should check both their euphoria and their ambition. There would be no hasty retreat by the armed forces from the political arena. Over the next few months, several military officials publicly cautioned that any decision by the armed forces to relinquish power was contingent on the maintenance of a stable security environment and the democratic opposition's agreement to adhere to the junta's political and economic reforms. The sharpest and most ominous statement was voiced by the new army Vice Commander, General Jorge Zincke, who was appointed by Pinochet after his plebiscite defeat. It was that if the opposition refused to play by the junta's rules, "we have the example of 1973."[7] Even if the military had no intention of going down that path, Aylwin was taking no chances. At a press conference less than twenty-four hours after his plebiscite victory, he "called for discussions with the armed forces on constitutional reforms and the democratic transition [but] stressed that the opposition is 'not proposing a rupture of the institutional structure.'"[8]

For the leaders of the no campaign (and U.S. officials), an immediate concern was how those who had voted against Pinochet would now respond. Would they, for instance, be emboldened to reach beyond their grasp and demand an earlier transition than Pinochet had planned and/or changes to the 1980 Constitution that he would not accept? PDC leader Patricio Aylwin singled out maintaining the political "truce" that had governed the plebiscite campaign as "the biggest problem" likely to confront the opposition: The no victory had raised popular expectations "which could be frustrated if we don't come up with early solutions." With Pinochet almost certain to contest every change, the possibility of a new cycle of protests and demonstrations was ever present. "The biggest challenge that we political leaders face," Aylwin said, "is controlling such pressures so that our political opportunity does not elude us."[9] Following the plebiscite victory, Aylwin wasted no time in announcing that the sixteen-party coalition that had managed the no campaign had reformed as the Concertación de Partidos por la Democracia (Coalition of Parties

---

[6] Quoted in Barros, *Constitutionalism and Dictatorship*, 308.
[7] Quoted in Constable and Valenzuela, *A Nation of Enemies*, 312.
[8] Telegram, Barnes to Shultz, October 7, 1988, Digital NSA.
[9] Quoted in Boeker, *Lost Illusions*, 48.

for Democracy, COPODE), and would support a single candidate in the presidential elections scheduled for December 1989. Who that candidate would be, whether he would be acceptable to the military, whether he could manage popular expectations, and whether he could bridge the various party and personality rivalries within the Concertación, were open questions. The only certainty – a virtual armed forces' precondition – was that the nominee must be a moderate. As the dominant party in the Concertación, a PDC member was almost certain to fill the position. Settling on a consensus candidate turned out to be no easy process. For months, the PDC was "caught up in a big mess" between competing presidential hopefuls.[10] It was not until February 1989 that the Party agreed that Aylwin would be its standard-bearer.[11] The Concertación policy platform had still to be determined and might be potentially unacceptable to the military. Finally, there remained the (limited) possibility that the radical left and those social movements it led would reject altogether the limitations imposed by the protected democracy model and mount a serious challenge to the Concertación/Pinochet transition scenario.[12]

On January 1, 1989, an NSC Policy Coordination Committee (PCC) "Discussion Paper on Chile" prepared for the incoming Bush administration set out the major objectives in the months prior to the scheduled December presidential and congressional elections: actively support the democratic process by "encouraging dialog between the civilians and the military"; ensure that the most likely presidential candidates are all strongly committed to the military regime's free market economic policies; and keep the pressure on for a satisfactory resolution to the Letelier case, which, it should be made clear, was "the key to reopening a security assistance program with Chile and to fully restoring military and political relationships." In pursuit of these goals, the discussion paper recommended a series of relatively modest initiatives: make provision

---

[10] Genaro Arriagada, Executive Director of the Concertación, quoted in Shirley Christian, "Foes of Pinochet Feuding over Vote," *NYT*, January 30, 1989, 1.

[11] Explanations for the choice of Aylwin ranged from his being the most favored second choice and thus "the logical consensus candidate of parties deeply divided over their first choice" to his leadership role in the plebiscite campaign. See Boeker, *Lost Illusions*, 40, 45.

[12] The Communist Party failed to rally significant support after the electoral success of the moderate opposition, the collapse of the Soviet Union and the unraveling of the Socialist bloc. In October 1990, the Party applied for formal legal recognition and contested municipal elections in June 1992, where it achieved a mere 6.62 percent of the vote. See Paul E. Sigmund, *The United States and Democracy in Chile* (Baltimore: Johns Hopkins University Press, 1993), 198.

for a "U.S. financial leader to 'remind' junta members that it would be impossible to negotiate on debt if elections results [were] overturned"; assist (by means unspecified) civilians in gaining control over the military; rebuild military-to-military contacts between Chile and the United States; and increase bilateral cooperation in combating international drug trafficking.[13]

Suspicion that Pinochet would not relinquish power willingly remained "very definitely" on the minds of some State Department officials, although "our position was exceedingly clear that we wouldn't tolerate that."[14] Assistant Secretary for Inter-American Affairs Elliott Abrams, however, was less concerned about the prospects of the transition being derailed in view of the electorate's decisive rejection of Pinochet in the plebiscite: "It didn't seem likely that you could really turn back at that point. We had a lot of faith in the opposition, in the Chilean elite, and the moderate left."[15] The decision by all other parties in the Concertación to support Aylwin's candidacy for the presidency further buoyed U.S. hopes of a best possible electoral outcome.

Following his confirmation hearing in October 1988, the new U.S. Ambassador to Chile, Charles Gillespie, held a number of meetings with senior officials in Washington that, in the broadest sense, focused on how to "encourage moderation and consensus-building dialogue from both the GOC and the opposition."[16] Gillespie received a revised "Letter of Instruction" from Shultz after his arrival in Santiago on December 7, although it offered nothing new in terms of the Embassy's role in fostering an "orderly transition" to democracy and the establishment of a civilian regime "friendly to major U.S. interests." But the letter did identify three priority objectives: expand contacts with the armed forces; encourage the democratic opposition "to distance itself from the Communist Party" and reaffirm its commitment to the free market economic model; and do not ease pressure on the regime to reach an acceptable (to Washington) resolution of the Letelier case, which remained an "obstacle

---

[13] NSC Policy Coordination Committee Discussion Paper, "Chile," January 1, 1989, DOS/FOIAe, 111. In late January, further confirmation of DINA's responsibility for the Letelier murders came to light when a retired Chilean diplomat, José Miguel Barros, revealed that senior Pinochet government officials told him in 1978 that the assassination had been directly ordered by DINA head Juan Manuel Contreras. See Shirley Christian, "Chilean Official Links a General, Long Suspect, to Letelier Killing," *NYT*, January 26, 1989, 1, 7.

[14] Telephone interview with Michael Skol.

[15] Interview with Elliott Abrams.

[16] Briefing Memo, Abrams to Shultz, October 27, 1988, DOS/FOIAe, III.

to the establishment of better relations."[17] To accelerate progress toward democracy and an improved human rights environment, the Embassy should engage with all the major political actors except the Communist Party – instructions, that by all accounts, Gillespie carried out to the letter. While maintaining excellent ties with the rightist political parties and their leading figures, such as Hernán Büchi, was a sine qua non, Gillespie was determined to be "really careful. We couldn't just come out and say we didn't want Büchi or Pinochet. We had to play an even hand but we had to make damn sure that nobody screwed up the process."[18] "The Concertación," said prominent Socialist Enrique Correa, "sealed a good relationship with the U.S. right from the start."[19]

The new Ambassador's attempt to play a kind of honest broker in Chile's transition process unexpectedly hit a hurdle in early March 1989 when the Santiago Embassy received two telephone calls warning that a shipment of grapes to the United States had been poisoned in protest at the Pinochet government policies. What resulted was a "nasty" incident in relations between the two countries that "wildly diverted" the Embassy from its main task of encouraging a smooth transition.[20] U.S. Food and Drug Administration (FDA) inspectors found two grapes laced with cyanide in a consignment of Chilean produce being unloaded in Philadelphia. The FDA immediately ordered that all Chilean grapes be taken off U.S. supermarket shelves and destroyed and placed a temporary ban on Chilean fruit imports. Authorities in the European Union, Japan, and Canada followed suit – placing at risk an industry that employed around 5 percent of Chileans and was responsible for generating $1 billion in export earnings.[21] "Here we thought we had just established the best possible U.S.-Chilean relations and laid the groundwork for Pinochet's departure and everything else, and this thing hits us in the

---

[17] Telegram, Shultz to AmEmb Santiago, December 15, 1988, ibid. Also see Charles A. Gillespie Jr. interview, FAOHC.

[18] Interview with Charles A. Gillespie Jr.

[19] Interview with Enrique Correa.

[20] Ibid.

[21] Philip Shenon, "Chilean Fruit Pulled from Shelves As U.S. Widens Inquiry on Poison," *NYT*, March 15, 1989, 1, 22. For a detailed sequence of events, see U.S. General Accounting Office, *Food Tampering: FDA's Actions on Chilean Fruit Based on Sound Evidence*, GAO/HRD-90-164, September 1990, 2–4, 23–25. Resorting to a rather cynical ploy, Secretary of State Baker and a number of other officials argued vigorously against the ban to give the appearance to the Chileans "that we had not lightly reached the decision to cut off the import of Chilean fruit and that the decision had not been unanimous." Charles A. Gillespie Jr. interview, FAOHC.

face," recalled Embassy DCM George Jones.[22] The poisoned grape incident quickly became "the hottest issue in Chile"[23] – in no small measure because of the actions of Richard Claro, President of Santa Rita Vineyards and a stockholder in the shipping company that transported grapes to the United States. Claro accused the American government of responsibility for the crisis and launched a well-financed media campaign to this effect, principally targeting the two most senior diplomats in the U.S. Embassy.[24] "It was unfortunate," said Jones, "because it certainly set back our relations with the Chilean right and the business community. There was such suspicion that we were doing this for political reasons and I talked myself blue in the face, and so did others, but it didn't do a bit of good."[25]

David Greenlee, who replaced George Jones as DCM in July, described "the anti-U.S. sentiment around the grape issue [as] vicious."[26] Gillespie himself said it was like operating in a "denied country."[27] If the FDA's actions caused outrage in some sectors of Chilean society, the government's response was more low key. Pinochet blamed the Communist Party for the poisoned grapes, and regime officials generally avoided public criticism of the United States, although a number of military officials suspected that this mini-crisis was concocted by Washington as a warning to the regime to stick to the transition timetable.[28]

What worried ARA officials most about the incident was not just the short-term impact on bilateral ties but the possible longer-term consequences "should the current wave of anti-Americanism not be managed carefully by the GOC and us." Several theories circulating in Chile interpreted the incident as part of a U.S. government plot to "topple Pinochet, weaken his regime and/or wreck the Chilean economy." To counter the vociferous criticism from the business community, Richard Howard suggested that the administration consider supporting "further IMF and World Bank assistance to Chile both for practical and PR

[22] George F. Jones interview, FAOHC.
[23] Memo, Howard to Skol, March 28, 1989, DOS/FOIAe, III.
[24] George F. Jones interview, FAOHC.
[25] Interview with George F. Jones.
[26] David Greenlee interview, FAOHC. One report described the level of anti-American sentiment in Chile over this issue of an order "not seen in Chile since the days of [the] Marxist Allende regime." "Background Information for Vice President's Meeting with Ambassador Gillespie," May 9, 1989, attachment to Memo, J. Stapleton Roy DOS to Carnes Lord, White House, May 8, 1990, DOS/FOIAe, III.
[27] Interview with Charles A. Gillespie Jr.
[28] See Ascanio Cavallo, *Los Hombres De La Transición* (Santiago: Editorial Andrés Bello, 1992), 65.

reasons." For this idea to be taken up would require the backing of Treasury, which, Howard acknowledged, "doubt[ed] the GOC actually need any new loans, and could get by with lesser actions such as an IMF decision to waiver reserve rules." Nonetheless, ARA urged Treasury staff "to offer to meet with the Chileans and to seek to work constructively with them to find realistic ways to deal with perceived economic problems."[29] In the process, this could diffuse attacks targeting the FDA's motivations in the grapes dispute by Senator Jesse Helms and other conservative Republicans on Capitol Hill.[30] The ban on Chilean fruit imports was lifted after five days; the losses sustained by Chilean exporters, originally estimated at $100 million, were subsequently revised upward of $350 million.[31]

Interior Minister Carlos Cáceres described the grapes crisis as the only incident in U.S.-Chilean ties that was "pretty difficult" to manage during the final year of Pinochet's rule.[32] That issue aside, Ambassador Charles Gillespie was one of those U.S. officials who harbored a "constant concern" that Pinochet might yet somehow renege on a transfer of power. Much of this anxiety was grounded in a very real fear that negotiations between the government and the opposition over constitutional reforms would test Pinochet's tolerance for a return to civilian rule. But, in what appeared to be a reluctant concession to the changing political reality in postplebiscite Chile, Pinochet announced that Cáceres had entered into discussion with opposition leaders on reforms to the 1980 Constitution. Although the Chilean leader authorized the talks, he still remained extremely ambivalent about any constitutional revisions. The U.S. Ambassador was in no doubt that Cáceres had only been able to convince Pinochet that the government should engage with the Concertación by arguing that "he [Cáceres] could manage the negotiations, and [the regime] wouldn't have to give up more than they had to."[33] The talks continued in fits and starts for several weeks, with Pinochet at one point threatening to close them down completely rather than accept any changes to the original document, and Cáceres and the new Foreign

---

[29] Memo, Howard to Skol, March 28, 1989, DOS/FOIAe, III.

[30] See Sigmund, *United States and Democracy in Chile*, 182.

[31] Memo, Howard to Skol, March 28, 1989, DOS/FOIAe, III; Report, DOS, "Sanctions against Chile: The End Game," July 23, 1990, ibid.

[32] Interview with Carlos Cáceres. Chilean attempts to extract compensation from the United States for the damage to the grape industry continued for years. See David R. Mares and Francisco Rojas Aravena, *The United States and Chile: Coming in from the Cold* (New York: Routledge, 2001), 99–101.

[33] Charles A. Gillespie Jr. interview, FAOHC. The right-wing Renovación Nacional Party decision to support the Concertación's reform agenda may have helped sway Pinochet.

Minister Hernán Errázuriz threatening to resign if he did terminate discussions. Eventually cooler junta heads prevailed – notably those of Admiral Jose Merino and air force General Fernando Matthei, who insisted that Pinochet accept a compromise outcome. The result was agreement on a list of fifty-four reforms that would be put to a plebiscite for approval in July.[34]

During the first quarter of 1989, Gillespie reported to Secretary of State James Baker that the Embassy hosted three "highly successful" visits by congressional delegations, "reinforcing support for our bipartisan policy" on the Hill, and continued to maintain "broad contacts with all major democratic parties" in Chile to improve their electoral prospects, strengthen their links to Washington, promote "consensus-building" policies, encourage them "to conserve the successful free-market-based economic policies of past years," and ensure that those likely to form a post-Pinochet government "adopt policies and outlooks favorable to U.S. interests." An equally important goal was to make it clear to the armed forces leadership that bilateral military ties could not be totally normalized until the U.S. Congress was "convinced that the transition to democracy is irreversible and that Chile is cooperating to resolve the Letelier murder case."[35] This task of convincing the Concertación to retain the military's economic model was probably the least onerous of the Embassy's objectives. Its conservative PDC presidential candidate Patricio Aylwin had already committed to maintaining the neoliberal framework, within which he hoped to make provision for a more active state role and a greater emphasis on social justice. The Socialist Party was not about to contest Aylwin's intent. Heraldo Múñoz explained, "We were in no condition to radically alter the [military's economic] model because what we had to show was that we would be able to govern well and concentrate on what was most important." There was no advantage in precipitating a conflict with the Chilean business community, he said, although there was a need to include "solidarity aspects and social equity."[36] His colleague Enrique Correa agreed: "We realized that we were not going to change the economic model in any major way. Our main goal was to generate social policies to increase social equity."[37]

---

[34] See Barros, *Constitutionalism and Dictatorship*, 309.
[35] Telegram, Gillespie to Shultz, April 4, 1989, DOS/FOIAe, III.
[36] Telephone interview with Heraldo Múñoz.
[37] Interview with Enrique Correa. During the presidential campaign, Aylwin ruled out a government under his leadership pursuing agrarian reform. See Oppenheim, *Politics in Chile*, 220.

Subtle Pressures

Keeping Congress onside was constantly on the minds of State Department officials. A memo from Richard Howard to Deputy Assistant Secretary Michael Skol made the point quite forcefully: "whatever flexibility we have in dealing with Chile is in part due to the strong bipartisan support our Chile policy enjoys in Congress."[38] This support was crucial if the combination of mild prodding and gentle encouragement – which was all that U.S. policy makers had available to them to ensure a smooth transition – was to succeed. To avoid any fracturing of this consensus required careful handling of criticism of the Pinochet regime in the UNHRC and the UNGA. In February, the U.S. Mission in Geneva had been instructed to seek passage of a "fair, balanced resolution on human rights in Chile [that took] into full account the progress that Chile has made and is making in returning to democratic rule." It was also told to restate the U.S. view that Chile "should not be singled out for special treatment" as a separate agenda item before the UNHRC.[39] To mobilize regional support, the American embassies in Mexico City and Bogotá were requested to approach their host governments and lobby them "on the need for a balanced resolution on Chile."[40] Secretary of State Baker was incensed over the preliminary draft of a Spanish/Mexican resolution that he termed "unbalanced and contain[ing] language and concepts which we find both harmful and unacceptable." The more specific objections were to its failure to be sufficiently positive about progress on human rights and the attribution of "extreme violence" only to the government without any reference to "leftist terrorists."[41]

On April 15, ARA's acting head Michael Kozak wrote to Baker that an Embassy informant had told the Ambassador that Pinochet was intent on "somehow thwart[ing] plans to hold presidential and congressional elections set for December 1989." Kozak himself was skeptical of this "intelligence" in light of Pinochet's and the army's "oft-stated pledge to uphold the terms of the 1980 Constitution and the progress already taken toward a transition to democracy in Chile, [making it] very difficult for Pinochet to carry out successfully whatever plan he may have threatened." Moreover, there would be minimal support for any such move within the

[38] Memo, Howard to Skol, March 28, 1989.
[39] Telegram, Baker (Armacost) to U.S. Mission, Geneva, February 17, 1989, DOS/FOIAe, III.
[40] Telegram, Baker (Armacost) to AmEmb Madrid and Rome, February 24, 1989, ibid.
[41] Telegram, Baker to U.S. Mission, Geneva, February 28, 1989, ibid.

electorate at large, and there was no certainty that the army itself "would agree to extra-constitutional steps to prolong his rule."[42]

Two weeks later, Kozak sent another memo to Baker outlining a 1989–1990 "Action Plan" for Chile. It was the product of months of discussion by an interagency working group established by ARA and had been approved at the Assistant Secretary level in both State and Defense. The overall objective of U.S. policy, the authors wrote, was to support an orderly return to democracy in Chile by March 11, 1990, and to employ U.S. influence and resources until that date "to encourage those who may form the new government to adopt policies and outlooks favorable to basic U.S. interests." The plan offered little that was new in the way of tactics, but it did set out the overall Bush administration approach in a comprehensive manner. First, U.S. policy should encourage the military regime to "keep the transition on track" and promote an ongoing dialogue between it and the democratic opposition. Second, positive human rights initiatives should elicit "favorable but balanced public responses" from Washington. Third, U.S. votes on Chile loan applications to the MDBs should be based on purely "economic and financial criteria" so long as the human rights situation did not worsen. Fourth, greater support for Chile should be provided in the UNGA and the UNHRC to foster human rights improvements. Fifth, measures should be taken that would ease the constraints on GSP and OPIC activities in Chile if the regime made "sufficient progress in the area of workers' rights." Sixth, bilateral ties with the Chilean armed forces should be normalized, focusing on liaison activities to influence their behavior and "encourag[ing] dialogue between military and democratic political leaders on the transition and on civil-military relations" once a post-Pinochet government was in place. Seventh, the United States should encourage all of the democratic parties, whether they voted yes or no in the plebiscite, to move to the political center and "distance [themselves] from the Communist Party." Finally, it was important to prod Chilean business and investment leaders

---

[42] Memo, Kozak to Baker, April 15, 1989, ibid. In his attempts to keep the transition process on track, Ambassador Gillespie paid special attention to a message about the Chilean military culture he had received time and again from Pinochet's supporters and opponents: the priority the armed forces attached to their sense of honor: "I said 'Okay, for lack of anything better to do we are going to play the honor tune every time we can,' so that if there was the slightest hint that something was going to happen, go wrong, or they were going to mess around, I and the spokespeople from the Embassy, visitors from Washington, would say, 'You know, the Chilean military is honorable institution, men of great honor and they will live up to their Constitution and to their obligations.'" Interview with Charles A. Gillespie Jr.

to "engage in a dialogue with the political parties on the need to conserve the successful economic policies of the past few years."[43] One Embassy official remembered the policy approach as being "very much like the work of a jeweller – to look at these angles all the time."[44]

For the time being, the relative lack of influence U.S. policy makers could exercise inside Chile meant that the greater part of their time and effort was expended simply on monitoring developments. In June, State's Bureau of Intelligence and Research (INR) reported that the plebiscite defeat had sent Pinochet into "a blue funk" and that his power was "slowly dissipating, with cracks beginning to appear in his façade of Army support." Although the thinking among senior Chilean military officers had been more cautious, it appeared that a number of generals "wanted to see Pinochet retire as both the President and Army Commander."[45] The INR discerned little enthusiasm among junior officers and enlisted men even before the October 1988 plebiscite vote for the idea of Pinochet remaining in power much longer. The dictator's response to indications of his dwindling support was characteristically aggressive and unequivocal, telling government officials that he would remain at the head of the army after December 1989 and "will not be subordinated" to any elected civilian President.[46] Although the PDC's Edgardo Boeninger remained "optimistic" about Chile's transition to democracy, he thought it necessary to inform senior State officials that the only "dark clouds" that could potentially create a problem were recent statements by senior army officials and Defense Minister Admiral Patricio Carvajal that they would not countenance the removal of Pinochet as Commander in Chief of the army by a future elected government.[47] In the wake of the October plebiscite, and throughout the early part of 1989, Pinochet toured military bases to shore up his support and reassure those in uniform that he would protect them from retribution over the 1973 coup and its aftermath.[48]

In a more detailed analysis of the political situation forwarded to Baker, Ambassador Gillespie was relatively upbeat. "There is no

---

[43] Memo, Kozak to Baker, April 30, 1989, DOS/FOIAe, III.
[44] Confidential telephone interview 3.
[45] Intelligence Report, DOS, INR, "Inter-American Highlights," no. 5, June 6, 1989, DOS/FOIAe, III.
[46] Quoted in "Pinochet Says As Army Chief He Will Not be Subordinated to President," AP, June 13, 1989.
[47] Telegram, Baker (Eagleburger) to AmEmb Santiago, July 6, 1989, DOS/FOIAe, III.
[48] See Helen Mary Spooner, *The General's Slow Retreat: Chile After Pinochet* (Berkeley: University of California, 2011), 32–33.

indication at this time that the military would support an *auto-golpe* or that Pinochet can circumvent the Constitution to run or, even if he did, that he would win the presidential election," he wrote. There was uncertainty over how the armed forces would relate to a civilian government: whether they would "actively support and encourage" it or adopt a more obstructionist posture "and undermine its ability to govern." Nonetheless, the Embassy was convinced that, despite the accumulated "animosity and distrust" on both sides, there was "sufficient good will" to believe that compromises on key issues such as Pinochet's role, human rights investigations, and the military's prerogatives within a democratic society were possible. Having been put forward as Concertación's presidential candidate, Patricio Aylwin continued to demonstrate "a pragmatism and reasonableness" that augured well for the resolution of all outstanding problems. Gillespie was particularly impressed by the agreement thrashed out on a constitutional reform package, which he termed a "major confidence-building step," and by Aylwin's negotiating skills. In his dealings with the military and the political parties, Aylwin had "proven to be a master at forging consensus."[49]

On July 30, Chileans overwhelmingly approved the constitutional reform package, with 86 percent of the electorate voting for the changes.[50] These included expanding the government's NSC (by adding the Comptroller General to balance the equal numbers of civilian and military members) and removing its ability to appeal to the armed forces to intervene in the political arena; increasing the number of elected senators from twenty-six to thirty-eight (to weaken the influence of the nine appointed senators plus four seats reserved for former commanders in chief); imposing limits on the executive's power under states of siege and emergency; and repealing a provision that for all practical purposes prevented the parties of the radical left from participating in political life (except for those engaged in or promoting violence or "totalitarianism"). The reforms also relaxed the procedures for approving constitutional amendments.[51]

The opposition did not achieve all of its sought-after concessions; importantly, the political and economic system introduced by the junta

49 Telegram, Gillespie to Baker, July 31, 1989, DOS/FOIAe, III.
50 Simon Collier and William F. Sater, *A History of Chile, 1808–2002*, 2nd ed. (Cambridge: Cambridge University Press, 2004), 381.
51 For a discussion of the tense negotiations over constitutional reform see Cavallo, *Los Hombres De La Transición*, 63ff. On the actual reforms, see Barros, *Constitutionalism and Dictatorship*, 310; Oppenheim, *Politics in Chile*, 182–183.

remained substantially intact. Additionally, the military retained power to determine its minimum annual budget, and the armed forces' Commander in Chief, not the civilian President, would still decide on promotions and retirements. When the Concertación released a forty-eight-page document in July outlining its own position with respect to these arrangements, Pinochet immediately denounced its alleged antimilitary bias. A second draft ordered by Aylwin failed to mollify the outgoing head of state, as it would have left the armed forces in a position of subordination to civilian rule and weakened the 1978 amnesty law. Eventually, the Concertación felt compelled to drop most of its goals contained in the document as they related to the armed forces.[52] However, the reforms that were passed at the end of the month did reduce, at least in a legal sense, the military's political influence over an elected government and confirmed the armed forces' agreement that the transition should run to script.

Amid these developments, the Bush administration remained alert to any public perception that it was either relaxed or comfortable with Pinochet's handling of the transition. In late July, reports surfaced that Pinochet was proposing a visit to New York to address the UNGA. The new Assistant Secretary of State for Inter-American Affairs, Bernard Aronson, moved quickly to stop the idea dead in its tracks, briefing a colleague about to meet Chile's Foreign Minister Errázuriz to discourage any such visit should the issue arise – which was likely. Aronson emphasized three points: such a trip would not improve Chile's global image; there was no possibility that it would "enhance prospects for the transition to democracy"; and scheduling a meeting between Pinochet and U.S. officials either in Washington or New York "would not serve any useful purpose." With the Chilean election campaign now in top gear, all it could do was "send incorrect and unhelpful signals."[53] According to Gillespie, American officials took the dramatic step of using the Letelier-Moffitt investigation to deter Pinochet by letting him know that "if he wanted to get off an airplane in the U.S. there might be people other than protocol officers waiting for him to do that."[54]

Three weeks later, Gillespie cabled Baker that, "with a few exceptions on the extremes, the significant [political] groups are not only no

[52] See Gregory B. Weeks, *The Military and Politics in Post-Authoritarian Chile* (Tuscaloosa: University of Alabama Press, 2003), 53–55.

[53] Briefing Memo, Aronson to Kimmitt, July 24, 1989, DOS/FOIAe, III.

[54] Interview with Charles A. Gillespie Jr. Pinochet was similarly persuaded not to attend a meeting of hemisphere-wide military commanders in Washington in 1991. See Spooner, *The General's Slow Retreat*, 67.

threat to U.S. interests, but are actually friendly toward them." The U.S. government could "reasonably expect to enjoy a good working relationship" with any of the declared presidential candidates. The Embassy, he added, had "been working hard to keep our lines of communication open to all democratic groups in Chile – right, center and left."[55] As Baker prepared to confer with Chilean Foreign Minister Errázuriz, Abrams advised him to focus on the positives – that the United States was "pleased" with the democratic transition process and the improved human rights environment – while cautioning that a complete normalization of ties was dependent on a resolution of the Letelier case, which would remain a sticking point in bilateral relations until after Pinochet left the presidency.[56] Meanwhile, Gillespie turned his attention to the task of establishing a more "constructive relationship" with the armed forces. The Ambassador noted that Chile had not been allocated any FMS funds for fiscal year 1990 and was only slated for $50,000 for International Military and Education Training (IMET). Although this amount was appropriate as long as Pinochet remained in power, "the projected 'zeroing out' of FMS for FY-91 would leave us with only IMET and rhetoric until late 1991 or 1992." The United States should reconsider, therefore, its decision not to provide security assistance funds for fiscal year 1991 to bolster U.S.-Chilean military ties under a new civilian government – provided, of course, that the transition scenario remained "on track" and the Letelier case was resolved "on acceptable terms."[57] That October, the Chilean Army finally took delivery of fifteen U.S. manufactured helicopters, the result of a secret deal negotiated the previous year and justified on the grounds that their "civilian configuration," and a design that prevented the attachment of weapons, made them exempt from the congressional military aid ban.[58]

Included in Gillespie's instructions was a directive to ensure that U.S. military activities in Chile were "carefully coordinated" with Washington's diplomatic moves "so we didn't send the wrong signals militarily." To support the democratic transition necessitated "help[ing] the Chileans establish the idea of civilian control over the military," which was a key objective in reestablishing military-to-military cooperation. The

55 Telegram, Gillespie to Baker, August 16, 1989, DOS/FOIAe, III.
56 Briefing Memo, Aronson to Shultz, "Meeting with Foreign Minister Errázuriz," September 27, drafted September 15, 1989, ibid.
57 Telegram, Gillespie to Baker, September 27, 1989, ibid.
58 Charles Gillespie Jr., quoted in Shirley Christian, "Despite Ban, Chilean Army Gets 15 U.S. Copters," *NYT*, October 1, 1989, 27.

Ambassador felt that this "wasn't going to be a major problem with the Air Force, only something of a problem with the Navy, but it was going to be very difficult with the Army."[59]

In mid-October, Gillespie transmitted a Country Team overview of the challenges facing the United States in Chile over the coming twelve months. It reflected a "substantial consensus" on what the key issues were and how best "to most effectively promote the U.S. interests at stake." On one subject there was complete unanimity: the key test of a new civilian President, most likely Patricio Aylwin, would be his ability to maintain unity among the multiparty Concertación while striving to achieve a "workable relationship" with the armed forces. Almost as important a challenge for the Bush administration would be how to balance support for the new government with the pursuit of a satisfactory resolution to the Letelier case – while making sure that the economic gains of recent years were maintained and consolidated. "The central question," wrote the Ambassador, "and one with wide-ranging implications for the hemisphere, is whether democracy can continue to deliver the economic goods." Such an outcome was not inevitable. While Aylwin's coalition appeared to "understand the importance" of this issue, it was "unclear [as] to what degree they will be able to preserve the economic model while also addressing long pent-up social demands."

Gillespie argued that Washington should seek to preserve its influence with the new government by backing "effective, results-oriented social policies and programs" which were "consistent with continued economic development." In the interim, the United States would have to act with considerable care in its relations with the Pinochet regime: "We must not deviate from our cool but correct approach ... Stroking or otherwise being perceived to be reaching out to the junta would exact a high cost, for no gain, not only here but in the U.S. Congress, where bipartisan support for our policy toward Chile still pertains." Encouraging democratic initiatives and responding positively to human rights gains must not give "any appearance of a warming of bilateral ties." The visit to Washington by a number of senior Aylwin political and economic advisers during the latter half of October, the Ambassador suggested, would provide the State Department and other involved agencies with an opportunity to disabuse the visitors of any "illusions" they might harbor about what an Aylwin-led government could expect in the way of U.S. support.[60] In a

[59] Interview with Charles A. Gillespie Jr.
[60] Telegram, Gillespie to Baker, October 16, 1989, DOS/FOIAe, III.

follow-up cable, DCM David Greenlee added that Washington should encourage the Concertación to "distance itself" from the Communist Party and should keep up pressure on Santiago to adhere to the Brady Plan (which incorporated the essential features of the 1985 Baker Plan but included a proposal for voluntary debt and debt service reduction) by inviting senior Treasury Department officials to visit Chile to meet with the new Minister of Finance once he was appointed.[61]

The Last Waltz

The actual conduct of the presidential election presented no real concern to U.S. officials. "It was all kind of scripted at that point," recalled an Embassy official. "There were certainly the beginnings of a pretty careful dance between the military and the civilians but no-one wanted to tear the scab and provoke something that wouldn't have been sustainable for either side."[62] By now Charles Gillespie was confident that, "having gotten through the [1988] plebiscite and the second referendum [July 1989], and seen the process, we would learn about any real hanky-panky if it happened on this occasion." Furthermore, in view of the closely monitored presidential election campaign by a slew of national and international organizations, "we didn't have to be *the* watchers all the time." The Embassy judged the Chilean Electoral Commission to be above board and honest and concluded that the vote itself was "going to be pretty straight."[63]

As election day neared, Bernard Aronson prepared to chair a PCC meeting to begin planning relations with a civilian government. His introductory remarks, drafted by ARA Southern Cone officer Keith Smith, noted that "Pinochet and the Army are hunkering down to protect themselves following the transfer of power," that Pinochet "had recently restructured the Army High Command to put in officers unquestionably loyal to him," and that he is currently "pushing through decrees to further insulate the military from civilian control." The outgoing head of state would undoubtedly adopt a tough posture toward the country's new leaders, Aronson said. Although the Generals' "bottom line is still unclear . . . the most visible crunch [will be] political [rather than military]." Aylwin had signaled his desire to begin negotiations with the

---

[61] Telegram, Greenlee to Baker, October 18, 1989, ibid.
[62] Confidential telephone interview 3.
[63] Interview with Charles A. Gillespie Jr. (our emphasis).

armed forces as soon as the election outcome was confirmed, the Assistant Secretary continued. This was well and good, but caution was the byword, as the "degree of ignorance, and uncertainty, on both sides is appalling."[64]

By common agreement, Aylwin's December victory over former Finance Minister Hernán Büchi – described by Gillespie as "Pinochet's candidate" – did not yet guarantee a smooth transfer of power from the military to a new civilian government.[65] Although the PDC leader received an outright majority of the popular vote (approximately 56 percent – almost double that of his opponent), recently enacted electoral laws had created a gerrymander that resulted in an overrepresentation of conservative candidates from rural areas in the Chamber of Deputies and in the Senate, even though the Concertación's legislative slate achieved in excess of 60 percent of the total vote.[66] The Constitution additionally allowed Pinochet to appoint nine of the forty-seven senators, which prevented the new government from achieving a majority of members and thereby enabling it to revoke such Pinochet-era initiatives as the 1978 Amnesty Law.[67]

In his first public comments on the result, Aylwin appealed to Pinochet to respect the interregnum between the election and the inauguration and "not to issue new laws and not to adopt important measures" without consultation – a request that was ignored.[68] The military continued to legislate in ways that would entrench its political and economic model (including a new wave of privatizations) and protect its institutional interests up until the day of Aylwin's inauguration.

The President-Elect appeared to not categorically rule out the future prosecution of armed forces officers for human rights abuses committed by the dictatorship,[69] spoke of the need for further constitutional reform

---

[64] Memo, Smith to Aronson, November 3, 1989, DOS/FOIAe, III.

[65] Charles A. Gillespie Jr. interview, FAOHC.

[66] The other two presidential candidates, Hernán Büchi and Francisco Errázuriz, a wealthy right-wing banker running a populist campaign, received 29 and 15 percent of the vote, respectively. The opposition won 72 of the 120 seats in the Chamber of Deputies, of which 69 were on the Concertación list, and its candidates won 22 of the 38 elected seats in the Senate. See Alan Angell, *Democracy after Pinochet* (London: Institute for the Study of the Americas, 2007), 47–48. The gerrymandering of congressional districts is commented on in Pamela Constable and Arturo Valenzuela, "Chile's Return to Democracy," *Foreign Affairs* 68, no. 5 (1989–1990), 176.

[67] Sigmund, *United States and Democracy in Chile*, 190.

[68] "Elections Conclude with Aylwin Victory," *FBIS: DR: LA*, December 18, 1989, 42.

[69] See "Aylwin on Armed Forces, Alliances," ibid., 44.

and changes to other laws, and expressed a belief that "it would not be good" for the country if Pinochet continued to hold the office of army Commander.[70] Maintaining his typically stubborn and uncompromising image, Pinochet seemed unaffected by the result and untroubled by Aylwin's assent to power, declaring that the armed forces had "fulfilled in a historic manner the task of restoring to Chile the essential basis of democracy" and reminding the electorate that progress could be made only "when personal selfishness and ideological interests are overcome, and when there is a firm willingness to implement realistic and coherent policies"[71] – a subtle criticism of both politics and politicians. He again declared that he had no intention of resigning as army Commander.[72] The potential for a clash between the old and the new leaders of Chile remained very much alive.

Any lingering doubts about the Concertación's economic outlook were soon put to rest with Aylwin's appointment of the conservative U.S.-trained economist and Christian Democrat Alejandro Foxley as Finance Minister in his new cabinet. Although critical of the negative consequences of the military's neoliberal economic model between 1977 and 1983, by the end of the 1980s, Foxley was lauding the regime for having successfully achieved the structural economic objectives outlined at the beginning of the junta's rule.[73] To outgoing Interior Minister Carlos Cáceres, this appointment was a clear signal about the direction of economic policy in the postmilitary era.[74] Neither did the Socialist Party's Carlos Ominami (a former member of the MIR), nominated to be Minister of the Economy, harbor any radical plans to challenge the military's neoliberal model. Acutely aware of the problems of runaway inflation besetting Argentina and Peru,[75] the emphasis was on fiscal austerity and

---

[70] "Chile: Aylwin Interviewed on Democratization, Cooperation," *FBIS: DR: LA*, December 19, 1989, 45.

[71] "President Pinochet Addresses Nation 15 December," *FBIS: DR: LA*, December 18, 1989, 44.

[72] "Pinochet to Continue as Army Commander," ibid., December 22, 1989, 38.

[73] See Alejandro Foxley, *Latin American Experiments in Neo-conservative Economics* (Berkeley: University of California Press, 1983), esp. 84–90; Petras and Leiva, *Democracy and Poverty in Chile*, 50–53.

[74] Interview with Carlos Cáceres. He would have undoubtedly been reassured of the new government's intentions by Cáceres's successful negotiations with Foxley over reform of the Chilean Central Bank. See Cavallo, *Los Hombres De La Transición*, 152–154.

[75] "If we repeated the cycle of our neighbors," said Foxley, "we will start with a very good first year, then a second year with a few problems, then a third year with an economic crisis, and finally a fourth year with a political crisis." Quoted in Eugene Robinson, "Pinochet's Legacy: Grandeur and Misery," *WP*, March, 11, 1990, A30.

cautious change under the rubric of growth with equity incorporating a social justice dimension. (Even so, after 1990, corporate taxes and the minimum wage were raised, the labor laws were reformed, and a stop was put to any further privatizations.[76])

In a February 1990 cable to the Santiago Embassy, Secretary Baker warned that the Chilean armed forces' professed commitment to a return to democracy masked considerable unease about the incoming government and that the army in particular had "contingency plans for another coup if, in their view, conditions warrant military intervention." Senior commanders had "made clear that they will not tolerate a return to Allende-era economic and social chaos [and nor] would they accept widespread prosecutions of military officers for human rights violations committed during the past 16 years." Even if these threats did not materialize, it was going to be exceedingly difficult to impose civilian control over the state's most powerful coercive institution due principally to "the hard-line orthodox attitudes" that predominated at the senior levels of the army and the navy. In contrast, the air force and national police were relatively more "flexible." That said, Baker was nonetheless convinced that the "greatest single threat" to Chilean redemocratization remained Pinochet himself, although one hopeful sign was that his popular support had declined "even among his fellow commanders."[77]

One week before Aylwin's inauguration, the CIA provided a secret assessment of his government's prospects. Applauding the President's appointment of "responsible and experienced politicians and economists" from his coalition to cabinet posts, it repeated Baker's warning that his "thorniest challenge will be the 'Pinochet problem.'" A number of legislative and administrative measures "rushed through" in the months prior to the election might "hamstring the new administration and Congress well into their first year, if not beyond." The government's ability to implement its program was almost certain to be constrained by the passage of laws preventing ministers from tampering with the bureaucracy and regulating the new Congress, the Central Bank, the Supreme Court, the judiciary, and the educational system. But it was Pinochet's actions to consolidate his position as head of the army and ensure its power and prerogatives would not be significantly eroded on returning to the barracks, which promised to most "complicate" Aylwin's ability to pursue his programs. "[By] promulgating laws and decrees on military matters, Pinochet ha[d]

---

[76] See Spooner, *The General's Slow Retreat*, 41–43; Collier and Sater, *A History of Chile*, 384.
[77] Telegram, Baker to AmEmb Santiago, DOS/FOIAe, III.

effectively reduced Aylwin's authority over the armed forces," the CIA
report warned. "New bills give the military fiscal authority to transfer or
appropriate state resources, protect its share of the national budget from
cuts, and limit Congress's right to investigate military abuses." Pinochet
had created other barriers as well to limit civilian control of the military,
including a requirement that any amendment to constitutional provisions
related to the role of the armed forces had to muster a two-thirds majority of both houses – more votes than the Concertación had in either
chamber.[78] In a more sinister development, all files from the Pinochet-era
state security agencies (DINA, CNI), which had been transferred to the
army for safekeeping, were conveniently destroyed in a fire.[79]

Before attending Aylwin's inauguration, U.S. Vice President Dan
Quayle paid a courtesy visit to Pinochet on the last day of his sixteen-year
rule. On emerging from their discussion, he quoted the General's assurance that relations with his successor would be problem-free and that
"when President Aylwin gave an order, that order would be complied
with."[80] Yet the inauguration, which took place in the half-finished congressional building 120 kilometers northwest of the capital in Valparaiso,
was a frosty affair. Only the Presidents of Argentina, Uruguay, and
Brazil attended the ceremony; visits by other heads of state awaited the
formal transfer of power when Aylwin returned to Santiago. Although
the political handover occurred on schedule, one opposition leader had
the feeling that Pinochet was "still lurking in the shadows."[81] The State
Department's Michael Skol invoked a more graphic image: "Chile's new
leaders emerged from the rat hole only to be surrounded by rats."[82]

Post-transition Bilateral Ties

If concerns about Pinochet and the military lingered among U.S. officials, there was no guarantee that relations with the Aylwin government
would be completely uncomplicated and trouble-free. For a start, there
were petty irritants: soon after Aylwin took office, Ambassador Gillespie

---

[78] CIA, Directorate of Intelligence, "Chile: Assessing President Aylwin and Transition to
   Democracy," March 5, 1990, NARA/FOIAe, III.
[79] Collier and Sater, *A History of Chile*, 383.
[80] Quoted in Rita Beamish, "Quayle: Pinochet Pledges to Obey New Government," AP,
   March 11, 1990.
[81] Telephone interview with Heraldo Múñoz.
[82] Telephone interview with Michael Skol. In the days after March 11, the presidential
   phone lines were tapped by the army. See Spooner, *The General's Slow Retreat*, 55.

complained that the new Foreign Minister, Enrique de Silva, treated him "like a hunk of ice"[83] because the latter's father had suffered from the poisoned grape controversy. But the one significant "troublespot" with the most potential to bedevil future U.S.-Chilean ties remained the Letelier case, which the CIA thought likely to "drag on for several months."[84] A State Department memo outlined just how vexed the Letelier case would be to unravel even with the cooperation of a sympathetic Chilean civilian government. It "strongly" opposed any precipitate action to eliminate the Kennedy amendment restricting arms sales and security assistance to Chile in the absence of significant progress on human rights and cooperation in prosecuting those responsible for the Letelier killings. To do so would be "extremely disruptive" to ongoing negotiations, deprive Aylwin of an important instrument of leverage over the armed forces to cooperate and not obstruct the investigation, and leave the White House "vulnerable" to domestic attack for having given away "whatever leverage we have to resolve the case." Indeed, any softening in Washington's position would create doubts in Santiago about the "credibility" of U.S. policy, "undercut our major policy goals in Chile," and weaken Aylwin's ability to impose limits on the activities of the armed forces.[85] The CIA also warned that bilateral ties could be affected by Santiago's presumption that its GSP trading benefits would be reinstated without delay, its expectation that the United States would turn on the economic and military aid spigots just as quickly, or a decision by the Aylwin government to restore diplomatic relations with Cuba "and perhaps even [Muammar Gaddafi's] Libya."

Aylwin's decisive election victory, his "responsible" ministerial appointments, the Concertación's unity and "solid position in Congress," and the new government's resolve "to reach an understanding with the military on its institutional role under civilian rule" were all reasons for optimism and the for CIA to predict that Aylwin would "probably muddle through during his first year in office."[86] Relations with Washington certainly began an upward trend following the transfer of power. Two months into Aylwin's term, U.S. officials had even begun talking about the eventual restoration of full military-to-military ties with Chile after

[83] Interview with Charles A. Gillespie Jr.

[84] CIA, Directorate of Intelligence, "Chile: Assessing President Aylwin," NARA/FOIAe, III.

[85] DOS, "Talking Points on Kennedy Amendment," February 22, 1990, DOS/FOIAe, III.

[86] CIA, Directorate of Intelligence, "Chile: Assessing President Aylwin," NARA/FOIAe, III.

the new government agreed to meet the U.S. request for compensation payments to the families of Letelier and Moffitt and submitted the issue to arbitration by an international panel of jurists set up under the 1914 Bryan-Suarez Mujica Treaty.[87] In a memo to Assistant Secretary of State Aronson, Keith Smith identified good reasons for normalizing defense ties, among them taking advantage of a potential multi-million-dollar market for military weapons and equipment sales, and reinforcing the armed services' support for the civilian regime. Obviously, Smith continued, contemplating a policy change of this magnitude had to take into account Capitol Hill's reluctance to move quickly in this area "prior to concrete actions on the Letelier case."[88] Ambassador Gillespie singled out Senator Edward Kennedy in particular as "very reluctant to see the gates of military assistance open again."[89]

Aylwin's management of the human rights problem was an encouraging sign to the Bush administration. The Embassy gave him "high marks" for setting up a Truth and Reconciliation ("Rettig") Commission early in his term to deal with abuses perpetrated under military rule. Underlining Aylwin's political skills, it "succeeded in cutting [Pinochet] down to size without damaging civil-military relations." Determined to accommodate all sides, however, the Commission's mandate was limited to uncovering the victims of terror, exhuming bodies, identifying the causes of death, paying compensation to victims and their families on the basis of non-judicial testimony, and issuing an advisory report. If the establishment of the Commission "mollified the left and gave hope to human rights victims and their families," its deliberately general and limited objectives "avoided a direct challenge to the military." The rationale was put in terms of stabilizing democracy that could only be achieved by not unnecessarily provoking the armed forces and their political allies.[90] In March 1990, the UN Special Rapporteur issued his last report on the human rights situation in Chile, and the mission was not renewed.[91] The

---

[87] In June, the panel determined that an ex gratia (admitting no guilt) payment of $2.6 million be made to the victims' families. At the time, the payment remained to be approved by the Chilean Congress.

[88] Memo, Smith to Aronson, May 4, 1990, DOS/FOIAe, III (emphasis original).

[89] Charles Gillespie Jr. interview, FAOHC.

[90] Telegram, AmEmb Santiago (Godard) to Baker, July 11, 1990, DOS/FOIAe, III. The only real challenge to the Commission's findings came from the army and the navy, who "objected to its lack of historical perspective." Memo, Aronson to Eagleburger, May 23, 1991, ibid.

[91] U.N. Commission on Human Rights, "Situation of Human Rights in Chile," March 7, 1990, E/CN.4/RES/199078, http://www.unhcr.org.

following month, the government completed negotiations with the Central Unica de Trabajadores (Central Workers' Confederation, CUT) on worker's rights. In an overture to the Chilean military, General Matthei was received by NSC Adviser Brent Scowcroft during a May visit to Washington, when he was awarded the Legion of Merit.[92]

During it first twelve months in office, the new civilian government fought an uphill struggle to overcome the restrictive constitutional and legal framework inherited from the dictatorship that would enable it to exert greater control over the armed forces, which continued to insist on operating as a self-governing institution virtually in extremis.[93] The armed forces in 1990 had greater political weight in the state and the political system than was the case before 1973 – a power they were not reluctant to use to put the government on notice that its status, and possibly survival, was conditioned on maintaining stability and order. This was at the heart of the protected democracy idea as espoused by Pinochet. Despite the absence of measures that impinged on the armed forces in any significant way during 1990, Pinochet "frequently threatened to repeat the '11th of September 1973' if national security were endangered." Such threats were primarily intended to deter a future government from pursuing criminal and other "investigations [that] threatened Pinochet's family, the Army, and the honor of the armed forces."[94]

The legal-judicial system inherited by the new regime further narrowed the possibilities for modifying the existing concentration of political and economic power. Prior to leaving office, the dictatorship offered generous pensions to supreme court justices to prematurely retire and replaced them with more unconditional loyalists. The agreements signed by the electoral politicians and Pinochet, for all practical purposes, froze for years to come the judicial system in the mold left by the authoritarian regime. As well, the agreements secured the jobs of the outgoing regime's

---

[92] Spooner, *The General's Slow Retreat*, 66–67.

[93] Of the nine proposed constitutional and legislative changes on the Aylwin government's democracy-expansion agenda, "only the direct democracy elections of local government" had been achieved by the mid-1990s. Alicia Frohmann, "Chile: External Actors and the Transition to Democracy," in *Beyond Sovereignty*, ed. Tom Farer (Baltimore: Johns Hopkins University Press, 1996), 246.

[94] Brian Loveman, "*Misión Cumplida*? Civil-Military Relations and the Chilean Political Transition," *Journal of InterAmerican Studies and World Affairs* 33, no. 3 (1991): 40, 36. As late as May 1991, senior State Department officials in the Bush administration were still concerned about the ability of the Aylwin government to "assert civilian authority over the armed forces without provoking a confrontation." Memo, Aronson to Eagleburger, May 23, 1991, DOS/FOIAe, III.

civil bureaucracy (new ministers could not hire "even their own secretaries and aides"), which meant that Aylwin's cabinet members now had to deal with departments staffed by individuals who were potentially opposed to the policies they would be responsible for carrying out – putting them in a position to use their discretionary powers to delay, distort, or undermine policies proposed by the new government. In the Interior Ministry, the new government was only able to make appointments to approximately 12 out of a total of 1,519 positions and an exceedingly modest 556 across the entire public sector.[95] Aylwin's Defense Minister, Patricio Rojas, complained that he had inherited a Department "with just empty boxes, no files at all," and that even his driver and security staff were all hangovers from the previous regime.[96]

In the economic sphere, before leaving office, Pinochet had issued a decree making the Central Bank an autonomous institution, thereby limiting the President's ability to mandate monetary policy. Finally, at the local or municipal government level, the outgoing regime was truly ascendant, as Pinochet had directly appointed 310 of the nation's 325 mayors, leaving only 15 to be chosen by Aylwin.[97]

The hard questions that promised to confront Washington and Santiago in the short and medium term were twofold: to what extent could a stable democracy be established in a situation where the military had been granted concessions that gave it the power to enter into the political arena at some future date; and could the culture of fear that characterized armed forces' rule be eliminated if the new governing class kept its commitment not to prosecute those responsible for the most brutal human rights abuses. In the longer term, how prepared was the new government to transform Chile into an authentic democracy by opening up the political system to greater participation and access to power by those most excluded and repressed during the Pinochet era? The institutional constraints within which the government was initially compelled to function, combined with the weight of the political right and designated senators (including the armed forces and the Carabineros) in Congress, meant that much of the Concertación program could not be approved. Nonetheless, it began the process of legally opening up the Chilean political system and restoring civil liberties that enlarged space for public expression, political organization, and electoral competition.

---

[95] See Angell, *Democracy after Pinochet*, 44.
[96] Quoted in Spooner, *The General's Slow Retreat*, 55.
[97] See Victor de la Fuente, "Chile Only Half Way to Democracy," *Guardian Weekly* (UK), October 14, 1990, 17.

Taking into account this uncertainty, Ambassador Gillespie advocated the removal of all U.S. sanctions on Chile ahead of President Bush's scheduled visit to Santiago in September 1990. This suggestion divided State Department officials. There was resistance to ending sanctions still in place until the Letelier case had been settled and was off the political radar, and because presidential certification (required by Congress under the Kennedy-Harkin legislation) had to be "defensible."[98] However, a Department report cautioned that if sanctions were not terminated by the time Bush touched down in Santiago, "the edge will be taken off his visit and he will be openly criticized by Chileans across the political spectrum." The report urged consultations with key congressional leaders on this issue, beginning with Kennedy, who was considered crucial to the outcome and who to date had "indicated he will be 'flexible and responsible' (his words) [and merely] wants to be reassured that our bilateral relations are not driven by military or security assistance matters."[99] In August, the *Miami Herald* reported that the administration had reduced its demands for certifying Chile to an agreement by Aylwin to submit the Letelier claims to a civilian court and appoint a special prosecutor. This shift was apparently linked to a feeling that a continuation of the arms embargo reflected badly on the "credibility" of the democratic government.[100]

Surprisingly, U.S. economic aid to Chile during the first year of civilian rule was quite limited. A State Department report conceded that the amount was inadequate, all the more so as the new government had taken "significant steps" to improve worker rights, had "undertaken a formal inquiry into the human rights abuses committed under the prior regime," had embraced the free market model (with some modifications), and was "one of the region's strongest supporters of the [Bush] Enterprise for the Americas Initiative and [would] soon sign a bilateral framework with the U.S. on trade and investment." In light of these outcomes, the lack of U.S. "reciprocity" was hard to deny, particularly the failure to restore GSP/OPIC benefits or to lift the Kennedy-Harkin sanctions.[101] Washington's parsimony compared unfavorably with a July 1990 decision by the IADB and World Bank to approve a $1.8 billion loan to fund a range of social programs.[102]

---

[98] Memo, Colson to Matheson, Young, July 18, 1990, DOS/FOIAe, III.
[99] Report, DOS, "Sanctions against Chile: The End Game," July 23, 1990, ibid.
[100] Christopher Marquis, "US May Lift Sanctions on Chile," *MH*, August 24, 1990, 14A.
[101] Report, DOS, "Justification for Restoration Via Waiver of OPIC Benefits to Chile," September 22, 1990, DOS/FOIAe, III.
[102] "IDB, World Bank to Grant $1.8 Billion in Loans," *FBIS: DR: LA*, July 24, 1990, 35.

Within State, a consensus was slowly building to restore Chile to the list of countries eligible for OPIC financing. By September, Secretary Baker had reached a view that the 1987 decision to suspend OPIC programs in Chile should be rescinded. Providing U.S. investors in Chile with access to OPIC financing was "one way for the U.S. to demonstrate support" for the new civilian government and simultaneously encourage much needed foreign capital to enter other sectors of its copper-dominated economy. Baker recommended issuance of a Presidential Determination stating that the revival of OPIC finance and insurance programs in Chile was "in the national economic interest."[103]

Relations with Chile were traveling through "some choppy waters right now," NSC Adviser Brent Scowcroft informed the White House on the eve of the first meeting between Aylwin and Bush in Washington on October 2 (the latter's earlier proposed trip to Chile had been rescheduled owing to a struggle with Congress over the administration's proposed fiscal year 1991 budget). Several issues were generating tension: not only the Letelier case, where the legislation regarding compensation and transference of jurisdiction from military to civilian courts, was winding its way through the Chilean Congress at a snail's pace, but also Santiago's entreaties to restore GSP benefits to Chile, and the reluctance on the part of the Chilean Congress to pass an effective pharmaceutical patent protection law, were pending. The USTR insisted on "holding GSP 'hostage'" until such a law was passed.[104] On a more positive note, the USTR no longer had any objections to a resumption of OPIC investment guarantee programs, although the office "strongly opposed" any commitments on a free trade agreement given Chile's small domestic market. On this issue, wrote Scowcroft, the NSC and Treasury advocated a compromise ("middle course") solution, making known to the Chileans that the United States supported an agreement "in principle." However, the time schedule would "have to be worked out," and Santiago must clearly understand that negotiations with Mexico took priority.[105]

The visit to Washington by the first democratically elected leader of Chile since 1973 was relatively low key and dominated by discussion of matter-of-fact obstacles to the full restoration of normal ties. During an

---

[103] Memo, Baker to President, September 25, 1990, DOS/FOIAe, III.
[104] Memo, Scowcroft to Bush, October 1, 1990, NARA/FOIAe, III. U.S. pharmaceutical companies complained that a patent protection law enacted by the outgoing military regime was inadequate as it only offered a term of fifteen years from filing (American companies were demanding twenty years) and did not protect patents in the pipeline.
[105] Ibid.

Oval Office meeting, Aylwin told Bush that failure to rescind the Kennedy-Harkin Amendment was fueling a belief among Pinochet supporters that "nothing" had changed with the restoration of civilian rule and that the United States retained "a bad opinion" of the Chilean armed forces. "For the government to achieve a higher degree of loyalty from the military we need to get [the] Amendment dropped," he pleaded. Doing so had the added advantage of minimizing Chilean congressional opposition to compensation payments to the Letelier and Moffitt families "without having it look like pressure" from outside.[106] But there was no immediate breakthrough forthcoming. At least there was one issue on which both Presidents could agree: signing off on the establishment of a Bilateral Council for Trade and Investment to begin the process of negotiating a free trade agreement.[107]

In late November, the *Boston Globe* reported that ties between Santiago and Washington were "so soured by economic and political disputes" that Aylwin government officials had discussed the possibility of requesting the U.S. President to drop Chile from his rescheduled South American trip. Privately, Chilean officials remained critical of what they viewed as a lack of urgency in the White House about normalizing bilateral ties "considering how thoroughly Chile has adhered to U.S. views on economic policy and democratic rule." Finance Minister Foxley complained publicly about eight months of U.S. foot dragging before receiving some indications that sanctions imposed on the military regime for human rights abuses might be soon lifted. He exhibited similar frustration over the implementation of Bush's Enterprise for the Americas Initiative: "I was in Washington four days after this was announced, and I publicly said, 'Chile is ready, ready to start negotiations along these lines. Well, several months have passed, and we are still waiting.'"[108] Ahead of Bush's arrival in Santiago, the administration finally restored Chile's eligibility for tariff concessions under the GSP.[109] And once Aylwin succeeded in having the Letelier case transferred to a civilian court, the legislative sanctions banning arms sales and defense cooperation was lifted – with the reluctant agreement of Edward Kennedy and other U.S. legislators who led the original battle to impose the sanctions in the absence of what

---

[106] Memo of Conversation with Aylwin, Oval Office, October 2, 1990, NARA/FOIAe, III.

[107] An actual free trade agreement was not signed between the two countries until 2003.

[108] Quoted in Tim Frasca, "Chileans Prepare Mixed Welcome for Bush Visit," *CSM*, December 6, 1990, 2.

[109] Owing to U.S. foot dragging, the decree reinstating GSP benefits was not signed until February 1991, which was another source of irritation inside the Chilean government.

they considered definitive movement toward a final resolution of these murders.[110]

Bush arrived at Santiago airport on December 6 and immediately departed for Valparaiso, where, addressing the Chilean Congress, he called Chile's peaceful transition from military dictatorship to democracy "every bit as far-reaching as the revolutions that changed the face of Eastern Europe."[111] Promising enhanced political and economic ties, he lauded Chile for moving more rapidly than any other Latin American nation "toward real free-market reform," which made it "a prime candidate" for Enterprise for the Americas Initiative debt relief funds.[112] One U.S. official called Bush's presence in Chile – extended at the Aylwin government's request from a twenty-three-hour stopover to an overnight visit – "the high point" of his tour of five Latin American countries (Chile, Argentina, Brazil, Uruguay, and Venezuela) because "this was the country we were going to build up the Latin American free trade area around."[113] For Ambassador Gillespie, the lifting of sanctions prior to the visit, along with settlement of the Letelier-Moffitt case to the satisfaction of both victims' families, meant that "relations with Chile were back to normal or were as normal as they could be."[114] The restoration of military ties was not long delayed. During a visit to Washington in March 1991, Defense Minister Patricio Rojas signed an agreement with the Pentagon covering a number of issues (excluding U.S. aid for internal order and security). Chile was readmitted into the FMS program and was slated

---

[110] Pamela Constable, "For New Chile, a Bush Gift," *BG*, December 7, 1990, 2. Manuel Contreras and one other former DINA officer were convicted for their role in the Letelier-Moffitt killings by a Chilean court in 1993 and sentenced to prison terms. The conviction was upheld by the Chilean Supreme Court on appeal in 1995 and the prison sentence of seven years enforced. Contreras was subsequently convicted on other charges relating to his time as head of DINA.

[111] Quoted in ibid.

[112] Quoted in Dan Balz, "Bush Lauds Free Market Economy in Chile, Promises Closer Relations," *WP*, December 7, 1990, A53. Just over six months later, Chile was the first beneficiary of these funds when the White House wrote off $15.7 million of its $39.3 million food aid debt and the administration signaled its intention to request Congress to approve a write-off of a much larger part of the country's $448 million debt owed to the U.S. government. Lauren Weiner, "Bush Forgives $15 Million in Debts to Reward Chile," *WT*, June 28, 1991, A8. Chile was also first recipient of an IADB private sector loan program, receiving $150 million to provide credit to the small business sector.

[113] Telephone interview with Michael Skol.

[114] Charles A. Gillespie Jr. interview, FAOHC. Compensation was finally paid to the Letelier and Moffitt families in January 1992.

to receive more than $1 million in U.S. military assistance for fiscal year 1992.[115]

The challenge the Bush White House inherited from its predecessor was twofold: to ensure the completion of the process of a democratic transition in Chile and to put the bilateral relationship on a positive footing. The first relied primarily on decisions taken by the Pinochet regime over which Washington's influence was limited. In reality, all Bush officials could do was encourage, as best they could, the key political and military actors to adhere to the letter and the spirit of the transition timetable. This meant publicly embracing the Aylwin coalition while carefully paying due regard to the sensibilities of the Chilean armed forces. During the interregnum between the 1988 plebiscite and the transfer of political power, a clear objective and astute management of the process by the State Department and its diplomats in Santiago produced an outcome hailed at both ends of Pennsylvania Avenue.

The second challenge proved a more difficult one. With the collapse of the Soviet Union and the end of the Cold War, Chile now ranked low on Bush's radar. Additionally, many Chileans still harbored resentment toward the United States over the 1973 coup and subsequent support provided to Pinochet. Given the tenuous nature of the transition, the Aylwin government had to proceed cautiously to meet the requirements the U.S. Congress had set down for the removal of sanctions. There were officials in Santiago and in Washington who continued to argue that sanctions had not yet exhausted their utility, remaining one of the few pressures Aylwin had at his disposal to keep the Chilean military in line. Nonetheless, while problems and challenges in the bilateral relationship remained to be addressed throughout the Bush presidency, these would be far outweighed by the political, economic, and military interests the restoration of democracy allowed the two countries now to share.

[115] Mares and Aravena, *United States and Chile*, 83.

Conclusion

Ronald Reagan entered the White House determined to jettison what he perceived as Jimmy Carter's hostile human rights policy toward autocratic regimes in Latin America and revert to a more traditional Cold War approach based on stability, security, and quiet diplomacy. The government of General Augusto Pinochet in Chile was greeted as an ideological (anticommunist) ally presiding over a model free market economy with little beyond lip service paid to its violent method of rule. Pinochet himself was showered with praise for having saved Chile from the chaos of the Allende years, and the military junta was offered all possible support to consolidate and maintain its hold on political power to counter any residual Marxist-terrorist threat.

During the latter half of Reagan's first term, however, a policy of cohabiting with "acceptable" dictators was becoming increasingly less viable, as public and congressional support for foreign alliances justified in the name of anticommunism had ebbed considerably and as military regimes across Latin America were revealed as unable to contain popular discontent because of their repressive political rule and/or their incompetence as economic managers. For Washington policy makers, this trend posed the problem of how to influence transitions from dictatorship to democracy in a way that conserved the institutional power and integrity of the armed forces and preserved U.S. strategic, political, and economic interests during and after a transition from military rule. Under Reagan, this translated into efforts to co-opt and shape political transitions in a manner that minimized losses and provided the best possible outcomes from the point of view of U.S. interests. What mattered was which sectors of the opposition movement would inherit power and thus oversee the direction of change: antisystem forces that conjured up images of major shifts in the distribution of political and class power, the restructuring of a capitalist economy, and the transformation of the state; or antiregime forces willing to accommodate and coexist with existing authoritarian/military state structures and compatible with U.S. interests.

Before the end of Reagan's first term, the junta's commitment to implementing a rightist revolution in Chile – political, economic, and social – had led to the "resurrection of civil society"[1] during 1983–1984, with the emergence of social movements (across the social class, occupational, and political spectra) offering a direct political challenge to the regime. The growing radicalization of the leadership of these movements and their forms of struggle had a major impact on the thinking of senior State Department officials, suggesting a compelling need to reevaluate the administration's approach to Chile and attempt to work with Pinochet to achieve a more sustainable long-term future for the country – that the time had arrived when it might be in the best interests of the United States to promote a return to democracy. Paralleling the growth of large-scale, antiregime civil disobedience was a continuing U.S. frustration over Pinochet's obstructionist posture in response to efforts to resolve the Letelier-Moffitt murder investigation. Above all, his stonewalling fueled congressional demands for stronger measures against the junta that the executive branch feared would further restrict its flexibility in responding to developments inside Chile. Regional developments further strengthened this thinking: transitions from dictatorship to democracy were occurring across much of Latin America to a point where Chile was beginning to stand out like a sore thumb and had become an international pariah with which the United States was most closely identified.[2] Although these factors were reason enough to justify questioning the existing approach of uncritical support for the Pinochet regime, those anticommunist ideologues who still retained considerable influence in the White House remained unconvinced that Washington should weaken ties with a major regional ally that, irrespective of bilateral tensions, continued to align with U.S. regional and global policies.

---

[1] Quoted in Guillermo O'Donnell, "Transitions to Democracy: Some Navigation Instruments," in *Democracy in the Americas*, ed. Robert A. Pastor (New York: Holmes and Meier, 1989), 70.

[2] For a comprehensive discussion of this trend, see Brian Loveman, "'Protected Democracies' and Military Guardianship: Political Transitions in Latin America, 1978–1993," *Journal of Inter-American Studies and World Affairs* 36, no. 1 (1994): 105–189.

Nonetheless, Reagan's broad policy statements during his time in office created opportunities for new thinking and debate, particularly within the State Department. The President's publicly declared support for freedom, democracy, and human rights generally – a position most comprehensively outlined during a June 1982 speech to the British Parliament and restated in his 1985 State of the Union address – gave his less ideologically driven officials an opportunity to contemplate policies beyond those advocated by hard-line anticommunist advisers and White House aides with long-standing personal, as well as political, ties to Reagan. Over time, the replacement or retirement of key ideologues, among them Secretary of State Alexander Haig and UN Ambassador Jeane Kirkpatrick, combined with the increasing trust the President placed in Haig's successor, George Shultz, provided opportunities to make the case for policy adjustments in bilateral ties with Chile. Contemplating William Clark's successor as NSC Adviser in October 1983, for instance, what was uppermost in Reagan's mind was the personal and policy disagreements that plagued his initial foreign policy team. Above all, he was reluctant to unnecessarily antagonize Shultz (and Chief of Staff James A. Baker III) by appointing another staunch ideologue to the post. Yet he had to contend with a solid chorus of support from administration hardliners actively promoting Reagan's UN Ambassador: "I'm being lobbied on behalf of Jeane Kirkpatrick for the NSC job," the President wrote in his diary. "I fear there would be bad chemistry with Geo[rge] S[hultz] & State. I lean toward [Clark's Deputy] Bud MacFarlane."[3] Although not part of the inner circle of advisers, and more of a pragmatist than his predecessor, MacFarlane was ultimately nominated to the position. This signaled the beginning of end of the ideologues' ascendancy and helped secure greater authority for Shultz in foreign policy matters generally. With MacFarlane's appointment, the Secretary's problems with the NSC, which, in the words of one of his senior advisers, had been constantly "biting at our ankles,"[4] certainly began to wane.

Following Kirkpatrick's decision to leave her post in 1985, Shultz moved to address two concerns in regard to Chile: that the country's political reforms were not keeping pace with its economic reforms and

---

[3] Brinkley, *The Reagan Diaries*, 187. Also see John M. Goshko, "Kirkpatrick Poses Personnel Problem," *WP*, November 10, 1984 A1, A5. The hostility between Kirkpatrick and Shultz peaked at the time of the Iran-Contra affair, when the Secretary attacked Kirkpatrick for supporting a scheme to siphon off funds from the sale of arms to Tehran to support the Nicaraguan anticommunist insurgency.
[4] Interview with Robert Gelbard.

that Pinochet's continuance in office could ultimately become destabilizing. He began advocating publicly for the need to combine support for anticommunist insurgencies and governments with increased attention to human rights, along with efforts to convince right-wing autocratic allies to undertake peaceful transitions to democracy. After twelve years of military rule, Chile was a prime candidate for this kind of message. Key personnel changes during Reagan's second term – the resignation of Defense Secretary Casper Weinberger, the death of CIA Director William Casey, and the growing influence of foreign policy advisers "more moderate and less driven by reflexive anti-communism"[5] – gave the Secretary of State ever more latitude to pursue his approach.

At the same time, Shultz did not have free rein to act on Chile as he saw fit. As late as December 1987, the Secretary's attempt to postpone a World Bank decision on a SAL to Chile was successfully opposed by the NSC, the Pentagon, the Department of Commerce, and even some sections within State. Following the World Bank vote, Shultz managed to persuade Reagan to put his name to a public statement in support of the complete restoration of democracy in Chile. While this constituted a significant victory for the Shultz approach, he suffered a perhaps more surprising setback only months later, failing to convince State's IO Bureau and its UN Mission (headed by Vernon Walters, a Reagan and Pinochet confidante) to support an effort to amend a draft Mexican resolution critical of Chile's human record before the March 1988 meeting of the UNHRC. The United States eventually abstained on the vote.[6]

If bureaucratic debates over policy options are part and parcel of U.S. foreign policy, the levels of intensity have varied depending on the stakes at risk. In the case of Chile, the disagreements lacked a good deal of vehemence precisely because no vital interests were perceived to be in danger. This eventually allowed for a more open policy debate and an increased tolerance for the articulation of different policy prescriptions. Other factors also provided reinforcement to those executive branch officials who

---

[5] Schaller, *Reckoning with Reagan*, 173. Shultz and Weinberger, for example, disagreed about virtually every major foreign policy issue, ranging from arms control to the use of military power to human rights to bilateral aid programs. See Cannon, *President Reagan*, 402–405. Actions that signaled a shift to this more pragmatic or politically expedient U.S. foreign policy included Reagan's 1987 decision to sign an Intermediate Range Nuclear Forces Treaty with the Soviet Union that eliminated all nuclear and conventional ground-launched missiles in Europe and to initiate discussions that culminated in the 1991 Strategic Arms Reduction Treaty.

[6] See Telegram, UN Mission, Geneva to Shultz, March 8, 1988, DOS/FOIAe, III. Walters had unsuccessfully opposed the abstention vote as well.

wanted to pursue a tougher policy toward Pinochet over the objections of reluctant colleagues: the rapid turnover of NSC Advisers during Reagan's final three years in office and the major distraction caused by the involvement of senior Council officials in the 1986–1987 Iran-Contra scandal; the Pentagon's marginal role in the Chile policy debate as a result of congressional restrictions on military aid and sales to the junta; and the continuing animosity toward Pinochet on Capitol Hill.

Winning the bureaucratic debate was not the only challenge confronting those Reagan officials in favor of promoting even this highly conditional democratic outcome in Chile; another was to maintain a consistent commitment to the new approach among key officeholders in the State Department from the Secretary through ARA to the Ambassador and the Country Team in Santiago. At each level, the ability to follow through on policy could be weakened or undermined by opposition to, or misinterpretation of, instructions or simply by a failure to act on them. Critical to the success of the democracy promotion strategy was Shultz's longevity as Secretary and his decision to appoint Elliott Abrams to replace Langhorne Motley as Assistant Secretary of State for Inter-American Affairs and Harry Barnes to replace James Theberge as U.S. Ambassador to Chile. Together with Abrams's deputy, Robert Gelbard, they formed a quartet in agreement on all aspects of the Shultz approach, which, in turn, made it that much harder for opponents in Washington to argue against it and that much more difficult for diplomats in the Santiago Embassy to ignore it.

Nonetheless, their efforts to influence the regime were complicated by the same reality that confronted Jimmy Carter in his attempt to encourage a greater respect for human rights in Chile: the options available to U.S. officials were few, and their exercise had to be proportionate to the ends they were intended to serve. That no key U.S. strategic, political, or economic interests were threatened in Chile in the 1980s meant that certain risks could be run in policy terms, but it also meant a self-limiting effect on what pressures could be brought to bear. So, too, did consideration of the wider flow-on effect of particular decisions taken, such as the implications of not supporting Chile's willingness to renegotiate its external debt obligations in 1982–1983, at a time when other Latin debtors were tempted to default. As well, since 1974, Congress had been cutting or severely limiting economic and military assistance – acts of punishment that denied the White House incentives with which to influence the regime's behavior.

Once Reagan was inaugurated for a second term as President, the bureaucratic debate over Chile policy moved decisively in favor of transmitting tougher signals to Santiago that Washington was opposed to Pinochet's indefinite rule and was keen to see practical steps taken to advance the return to democracy. At no time, however, did Reagan administration policy reflect a sustained and principled commitment to democracy promotion in Chile; rather, its application revealed a highly conditional and qualified support based on calculations that bilateral and regional U.S. interests would be best served by a political transition of this kind that would leave little to chance, much less to "democratic adventurism."[7] The revival of an inclusive, multiparty system that characterized Chile prior to 1973 was never considered an option warranting U.S. support and encouragement. This approach dovetailed perfectly with the junta's nonnegotiable preconditions for any future transfer of power: a civilian governing alternative that would preserve the essential objective of the September 1973 coup (ridding the country of its "Marxist cancer"), maintain the junta's political and economic structures, and forgo recriminations against the armed forces over their brutal governance.

The Reagan White House was under no circumstances prepared to countenance a redemocratization process that might result in an "unacceptable" segment of the opposition (left social movements and their

[7] While no comprehensive explanation of policy making can ignore the role of specific departments, interagency debates, and dominant personalities, it is always necessary to locate the bureaucratic conflicts within the larger framework (common assumptions) that shapes the universe within which the debates, disagreements, conflicts, and choice of policy options take place. Doing so enables the identification and explanation of the consistencies and continuities that have characterized American foreign policy toward the Third World since 1950. In the case of shifts and changes in Reagan's Chile policy, the discussions were typically over the most appropriate forms of action to take at particular times in pursuit of a broader consensual policy objective, which was a *particular* kind of democratization. See, for example, Reagan's stubborn reluctance to withdraw his support of the autocratic Marcos regime in the Philippines until virtually the eleventh hour, despite pressure from all his senior policy advisers to bite the bullet, which had little or nothing to do with any commitment to Philippine redemocratization. Indeed, he even went so far as to publicly declare that, notwithstanding Cory Aquino's clear-cut victory in the 1986 presidential election, she should accept the fraudulent Marcos vote count. James Mann, *Rise of the Vulcans* (New York: Penguin Books, 2004), 131–134; Amy Blitz, *The Contested State: American Foreign Policy and Regime Change in the Philippines* (Lanham: Rowman and Littlefield, 2000), 160–181; Walden Bello, "From Dictatorship to Elite Populism: The United States and the Philippine Crisis," in *Crisis and Confrontation: Ronald Reagan's Foreign Policy*, ed. Morris H. Morley, 214–250 (Totowa: Rowman and Littlefield, 1988).

militant political party allies) from heading a newly elected government and endangering democracy. Thus, in contrast to the requests for soft changes asked of the junta (practical measures consistent with the terms of its own transition plan), U.S. policy makers demanded a wide-ranging set of major concessions from the responsible opposition. In urging these antiregime forces to accept the 1978 amnesty law, and the basic parameters of the political and economic transformation outlined in the military Constitution of 1980, the United States was, at least implicitly, signaling that they must accept the legitimacy of the 1973 coup.[8] More explicitly, they had to relinquish what leverage they derived from street protests and strike action by breaking tactical alliances with the left, especially the Communist Party (a consistent U.S. theme was its insistence on isolating the Communist Party and keeping it at arm's length from the Concertación); agree to the regime's electoral timetable; and capitulate to the armed forces' demand for amnesty from prosecution for human rights abuses, thereby ensuring that they returned to the barracks with their status as the most powerful state institution fully intact. Should anything go wrong in a post-Pinochet Chile, U.S. policy makers still looked to the military as the fail-safe bulwark against a radical outcome. For this reason, though an elected civilian government was preferable to continued harsh military rule – particularly in view of the regional democracy trend – it must be one that would not give in to popular demands to seek justice in ways that could undermine the integrity of the armed forces or threaten U.S. interests in Chile and the rest of the hemisphere.

Although the prospect of driving a wedge between Pinochet and his generals – and splitting him from the ultimate source of his power – began to get increased consideration within the interagency policy debate, success in this area depended on an ability to convince other junta members that Pinochet's approach was counterproductive to the institution's interests and prerogatives and that a new approach would not weaken efforts to contain the "terrorist" threat. The Chilean military, however, would take a great deal of convincing that its time in power was coming to an end as it remained unshaken in its belief that it had both a moral and an historic responsibility to rebuild the country on a new foundation. As the NSC Staff Specialist on Latin America during the Carter administration observed, "everybody seemed to assume that once we decided we could

---

[8] The day following the 1973 coup, Patricio Aylwin publicly expressed his support for the military's destruction of Chilean democracy. See Jonathan Haslam, *The Nixon Administration and the Death of Allende's Chile* (London: Verso, 2005), 222.

just get rid of these guys they'd go and if you did a few things and they didn't go then obviously the U.S. didn't want that to happen. I don't know why people just assumed these guys were going to pack up when the United States told them."[9]

Aside from the sheer resilience of the Pinochet regime, there were the favorable 1978 and 1980 referenda votes – neither textbook exercises in electoral democracy, to be sure, but not totally fraudulent either – to reinforce the armed forces' claim that they had a mandate to finish the job. This meant not backing down and certainly not to be seen surrendering to the very political classes that, in their view, had brought Chile to the brink of disaster in 1973. Pinochet himself remained solidly entrenched in power. He retained the loyalty of the armed forces and the continuing support of a sizeable proportion of the country's upper and middle classes. Further adding to these bleak prospects for reform in Chile was a junta whose deliberations were largely kept secret from outsiders, a left-dominated extraparliamentary movement that had thus far been the only means of bringing any pressure to bear on the junta, but clearly not enough to contest its rule, and the disunited center-right opposition political party leaders whose fate – whatever U.S. policy makers might have hoped for – seemed to be merely to react to events and forces beyond their control. Whether State's new approach could be effectively implemented depended also on the level of satisfaction among key members of Congress regarding particular initiatives taken to advance the policy and the extent to which domestic perceptions of the administration's new turn could be effectively managed.

To achieve what Deputy Assistant Secretary of State for Inter-American Affairs James Michel termed the ultimate goal of facilitating "the emergence of a centrist political consensus and a soft transition into democracy,"[10] the United States had settled on a two-track approach by 1985–1986: on one hand prodding Pinochet as it searched for the right mix of quiet diplomacy, public criticism, and largely symbolic economic pressures to cajole him to implement his timetable for returning Chile to a restricted democratic political order, on the other coaxing antiregime social movements and political parties of the center-right, and 'acceptable' elements on the left, that Washington associated with moderation, dialogue, compromise, and limited reforms – over and above those of

[9] Interview with Robert Pastor.
[10] Quoted in Heraldo Múñoz and Carlos Portales, *Elusive Friendship* (Boulder: Westview Press, 1991), 61.

the antisystem left, viewed as synonymous with violence, polarization, chaos, radicalization, and other activities that endangered democracy – to acquiesce in the junta's transition plan.

If the Reagan administration confronted a less permeable operational environment in Chile than had Nixon and Kissinger in the 1970s (seeking to topple a regime that only held power in the executive branch of government), its efforts to broker a democratic transition were also complicated by self-imposed constraints. At the most general level, this meant a refusal to consider any sanctions that would seriously undermine the junta's neoliberal economic reforms or pose an open challenge to its hold on political power. Nonetheless, by publicly rejecting Pinochet's constant insistence that Chileans faced a stark choice between disorder and the stability provided by the military, and no longer willing to accommodate his reluctance to "fight terrorism" and "promote democracy" simultaneously, the White House, for the first time, was questioning the dictator's legitimacy. This restricted his room to maneuver – and boosted the status of the conservative/moderate opposition and those junta members (principally the air force's Fernando Matthei and the Carabineros's Rodolfo Stange) who had tired of the military's dalliance in politics.

Throughout much of the 1980s, Pinochet proved extremely reluctant to put in place the necessary architecture for a successful transition: an end to harassment of political opponents; lifting the states of siege and exception; legalizing political parties; effectively pursuing voter registration; and allowing the opposition access to the mass media. By pressing for action on these multiple fronts, the Reagan administration helped establish the groundwork for a successful transition. The Socialist Party's Ricardo Núñez spoke for many of his colleagues in stating that "the ability of the democratic forces to organize and demonstrate political will" could not have occurred in the absence of the U.S. role of "active spectator."[11] In other words, although never in a position to exercise the kind of influence over events in Chile that defined it as a major player behind the political shifts and changes – something the most vocal opponents of Pinochet on Capitol Hill never seemed to fully accept – the United States was hardly a passive observer.

As late as the eve of the October 1988 plebiscite that rejected his bid for a further term as head of state, Pinochet presented his junta colleagues with a plan to abrogate the result and continue to rule by force. This proposal was not only anathema to Washington but also

---

[11] Interview with Ricardo Núñez.

rejected by other members of the junta. Nevertheless, it raised serious questions about the depth of Pinochet's commitment to the laws he had introduced and whether he would have finally stepped down were it not for U.S. pressure and encouragement for a return to democracy, albeit of a kind that protected the traditional power, prerogatives, and neoliberal economic model of the armed forces.

Would greater flexibility in the executive branch's dealing with Chile – the constant request of U.S. officials during the Reagan years – have enabled a quicker result? Providing incentives to induce changes in the regime's behavior, to reward efforts to ease repression and introduce reforms, were unlikely to have influenced Pinochet's thinking. Whatever conceivable benefits Washington could have offered Pinochet would surely have been weighed against the costs to the junta's grip on power and his own reputation as someone who genuflected before no foreign power. "Pinochet had a very narrow world view which it was impossible to change," recalled Embassy DCM George Jones. Even so, some Reagan officials were reluctant to let go of a belief that "if we say the right things Pinochet will respond. The fact was that he would never respond except if he decided there was something in it for his goals."[12] As for other junta members – notably air force General Matthei, who was eager for access to sophisticated U.S. weaponry – they had little influence over Pinochet other than to block those of his initiatives that breached previously agreed-on decisions. Matthei reminded Washington of this on more than one occasion. There was also the example of Matthei's predecessor, General Gustavo Leigh, who had been unceremoniously removed in 1978 after becoming a little too independently minded for Pinochet's comfort.[13]

While senior Reagan officials, and especially Secretary of State George Shultz, were deeply averse to wielding high-impact economic sanctions as an instrument of foreign policy (which were never seriously considered when it came to Chile in any event), they would have been no more likely to produce a different outcome than increased flexibility in the application of Washington's policy. Pinochet was ruthless when it came to protecting his own interests both inside and outside of the junta. He showed no compunction in taking a leading role to set up Operation Condor in 1975, part of a joint effort by the Southern Cone military dictatorships

[12] Interview with George F. Jones.
[13] See Verónica Valdivia Ortiz de Zarate, *El Golpe Despues del Golpe. Leigh vs. Pinochet. Chile 1960–1980* (Santiago: LOM, 2003).

to coordinate intelligence operations and wage war against "subversives" who threatened "Christian civilization" at home and abroad. Then Assistant Secretary of State Harry Shlaudeman ranked Chile as considerably "more unrestrained" than the Brazilian and Argentina military rulers in efforts to physically eliminate regime opponents.[14] Nor did Pinochet show any remorse for authorizing an act of international terrorism on American soil in 1976 that resulted in the deaths of Orlando Letelier and Ronnie Moffitt. Constant Embassy warnings that Pinochet was capable of reacting to outside pressure by simply playing the nationalist card and drumming up anti-American sentiment were not entirely groundless. After all, the Chilean dictator had bluntly informed the U.S. Ambassador to Chile during the Carter presidency, George Landau, that he didn't need the Americans, and that he could and would turn to other sources of support if necessary.[15]

Although the restoration of democracy was more a function of decisions and timetables determined by Chile's internal dynamics than a response to imperial state pressures, the Reagan administration's contribution, as we have argued, was not without significance. It helped decompress a volatile situation in Chile by maintaining steady pressure on the regime to remain committed to its transition timetable and by coaxing and encouraging adherence to the 1980 Constitution among those junta members most eager to bring Pinochet's personalist rule to an end. Throughout the difficult days of the mid to late 1980s, the State Department and the Santiago Embassy shored up the moderate opposition by taking its leaders seriously as political players and by acknowledging them as a preferred government-in-waiting entitled to limited material and moral support. Last, but not least, Washington actively intervened, with funds and expertise, to ensure a free and fair vote in the 1988 plebiscite, which sounded the end of the dictatorship, and delivered unambiguous warnings of the dire consequences to bilateral relations and Chile's international image if Pinochet attempted to commit fraud or nullify the result.

In the end, the nonradical political opposition accepted Pinochet's imposed transition plan because they had no choice to do otherwise. As a consequence, the issue concerning the transition was largely redefined as a problem of "governability": the capacity of the new political class

[14] Memo, DOS, Shlaudeman to Kissinger, ARA Monthly Report (July), August 3, 1976, NSA.
[15] Pinochet had indicated to Landau that he would court the Chinese if he grew tired of dealing with the Americans. Interview with George W. Landau.

to sustain the confidence of the economic investors, maintain the allegiance of the armed forces, and contain the pent-up social demands of the popular classes. Undeniably, this represented a political victory for the forces that carried out the 1973 military coup and a personal triumph for Pinochet himself. The armed forces presided over a political transition at a time of its own choosing, with its internal cohesion, sense of honor, and institutional power unaffected, if not strengthened; the country was now governed by a popularly elected civilian regime dominated by the moderate and conservative opponents of military rule committed to maintaining the generals' neoliberal economic model; and those opposition forces posing the greatest threat to the state – the social movements and party sectors of the anti-system or radical left – were disarticulated and politically marginalized. If the Reagan White House played a less than decisive role in wresting political power from the armed forces, what ultimately transpired was the best possible outcome from the perspective of U.S. bilateral and regional interests in Chile.

Primary and Archival Sources

Interviews

Elliott Abrams, Washington, DC, October 28, 2007. DOS, Assistant Secretary for Human Rights and Humanitarian Affairs, 1981–1985; Assistant Secretary for Inter-American Affairs, 1985–1989.

David L. Aaron, Santa Monica, CA (telephone), September 5, 2007. NSC, Deputy Assistant for National Security Affairs, 1977–1981.

Harry G. Barnes Jr, Peacham, VT, October 27, 2007. DOS, U.S. Ambassador to Chile, 1985–1988.

John Bushnell, Falls Church, VA, September 22, 2006. DOS, Acting Deputy Assistant Secretary for Inter-American Affairs, 1979–1981.

Carlos Cáceres, Santiago, Chile, July 16, 2008. President, Central Bank, 1982–1983; Minister of Finance, 1983–1984; Minister of Interior, 1988–1989.

Steven Cohen, Washington, D.C., September 13, 2006. DOS, Deputy Assistant Secretary for Human Rights/Security Assistance, 1979–1980.

Confidential telephone interview 1, Washington, DC, September 5, 2007. DOS, U.S. Embassy, Santiago, and Department of State Chile Desk Officer during Reagan administration.

Confidential telephone interview 2, Springfield, VA, September 14, 2007. DOS, senior official, Latin American affairs, 1983–1988.

Confidential telephone interview 3, Washington, DC, September 25, 2007. DOS, senior official, U.S. Embassy, Santiago, 1989–1992.

Confidential telephone interview 4, Hilton Head, SC, April 19, 2007. DOS, U.S. Embassy, Santiago, during the transition from Carter to Reagan.

Enrique R. Correa, Santiago, Chile, July 17, 2008. Senior member, Socialist Party during 1980s; cofounder, Party of Democracy (PPD), 1987; member, Executive Committee of NO campaign, 1988.

Hernán Errázuriz, Santiago, Chile, July 14, 2008. President of Central Bank, 1983–1984; Ambassador to the United States, 1984–1988; Minister of Foreign Affairs, 1988–1990.

Robert Gelbard, Washington, DC, October 5, 2007. DOS, Deputy Assistant Secretary for South America, 1985–1988.

Charles A. Gillespie Jr., Washington, DC, September 14, 2007. DOS, U.S. Ambassador to Colombia, 1985–1988; U.S. Ambassador to Chile, 1988–1991.

Charles W. Grover, Bethesda, MD, September 15, 2006. DOS, Deputy Chief of Mission, U.S. Embassy, Santiago, 1978–1982.

Victor C. Johnson, Washington, DC, September 19, 2007. Staff Director, U.S. House of Representatives, Subcommittee on Western Hemisphere Affairs, 1981–1993.

George F. Jones, Fairfax, VA, September 17, 2007. DOS, Deputy Director, Office of Regional Political Programs, 1978–1982; Deputy Chief of Mission, U.S. Embassy, Santiago, 1985–1989.

George W. Landau, Peacham, VT, September 10, 2007. DOS, U.S. Ambassador to Chile, 1977–1982.

Paul M. Meo, Bethesda, MD, September 19, 2007. Senior World Bank Economic Official with Latin American responsibilities, principally with the Andean Group countries, including Chile, 1976–1987.

Langhorne Motley, Washington, DC, October 10, 2007. DOS, Assistant Secretary for Inter-American Affairs, 1982–1985.

Heraldo Múñoz, New York City, September 25, 2008. Cofounder, Party for Democracy, senior member of Chilean Socialist Party during 1980s, member of Executive Committee of NO campaign for the 1988 plebiscite.

Ricardo Núñez, Santiago, Chile, July 9, 2008. Socialist Party member; founder of the Socialist Convergence, 1980; Secretary-General, Socialist Party, and founder of Political Committee of Socialist Unity, 1986; founder, Party for Democracy, 1988; active role in NO campaign for 1988 plebiscite.

Robert Pastor, Washington, DC, September 18, 2006. NSC Staff, Senior Latin American Cluster/North/South Cluster, 1977–1981.

Richard Schifter, Bethesda, MD, September 17, 2007. DOS, U.S. Representative, United Nations Human Rights Committee, 1981–1985; Assistant Secretary for Human Rights and Humanitarian Affairs, 1985–1992.

Robert E. Service, Washington, DC, September 16, 2007. DOS, Office of Southern Cone Affairs, 1980–1982.

George P. Shultz, Stanford, CA, April 14, 2008. DOS, U.S. Secretary of State, 1982–1989.

Michael Skol, Cape Code, Maine, October 1, 2007. DOS, Deputy Director, Bureau of Inter-American Affairs, Office of Policy Planning, 1982–1985; Director, Office of Andean Affairs, 1987–1988; Deputy Assistant Secretary for Inter-American Affairs (South America), 1988–1990.

Robert Steven, Arlington, VA, April 16, 2007. DOS, Chile Desk Officer, 1977–1979.

James Swigert, Washington, DC, October 18, 2007. DOS, Chile Desk Officer, 1985–1987.

Gabriel Valdés, Santiago, Chile, July 15, 2008. President of Christian Democratic Party, 1982–1987; founder of Democratic Alliance, 1983.

Peter Whitney, Washington, DC, April 24, 2007. DOS, Chile Desk Officer, 1979–1981; Economic Officer, U.S. Embassy, Santiago, 1981–1983.

James M. Wilson, Jr. Washington, DC, September 15, 2006, DOS, Coordinator for Humanitarian Affairs, 1975; Assistant Secretary for Human Rights and Humanitarian Affairs, 1976–1978.

Manuscript, Archival, and Oral History Collections

American Presidency Project, http://www.presidency.ucsb.edu.

British Diplomatic Oral History Program, Churchill Archives Center, Cambridge, UK.

Declassified Documents Reference System, Washington, DC.

Foreign Affairs Oral History Collection, Association for Diplomatic Studies and Training, Arlington, VA.

Gerald R. Ford Library, Ann Arbor, MI.

International Monetary Fund Archives, Washington, DC.

Jimmy Carter Library, Atlanta, GA.

Margaret Thatcher Foundation, http://www.margaretthatcher.org.

National Security Archive, Washington, DC.

Ronald Reagan Library, Simi Valley, CA.

U.S. National Archives, College Park, MD.

World Bank Group Archives, Washington, DC.

Personal Papers

Robert Alexander, Rutgers University Library, Rutgers, NJ.

Harry G. Barnes, Manuscript Division, Library of Congress, Washington, DC.

Donald M. Fraser, Minnesota Historical Society, Minneapolis–St. Paul.

George Lister, Benson Latin American Library, University of Texas at Austin.

General Dennis P. McAuliffe, U.S. Army Military History Institute, Carlisle Barracks, PA.

James D. Theberge, Hoover Institution Archives, Stanford University, Palo Alto, CA.

U.S. Government Documents, Published and Unpublished

Congressional Record – Senate.

Congressional Record – House.

Foreign Broadcast Information Service, *Daily Report: Latin America.*

NSSD Number 2-85, January 9, 1985. "Economic Development for Central America," National Security Study Directives, 1981–1989. http://www.reagan.utexas.edu/archives/reference/NSSDs.html.

Public Papers of the Presidents of the United States, Ronald Reagan, 1982, January to July 2, 1982. Washington, DC: U.S. Government Printing Office, 1983.

U.S. Agency for International Development, *U.S. Overseas Loans and Grants and Assistance from International Organizations*, July 1, 1945–September 30, 1982, July 1, 1945–September 30, 1986.

U.S. Congress, House, Committee on Appropriations, Subcommittee on Foreign Operations and Related Agencies, *Foreign Assistance and Related Programs Appropriations for 1986, Part 3*, 99th Cong., 1st Sess., March 21, 1985.

U.S. Congress, House, Committee on Armed Services, *Report of the Delegation to Eastern Caribbean and South American Countries*, 98th Cong., 2d Sess., No. 16, Committee Print, February 1984.

U.S. Congress, House, Committee on Banking, Finance, and Urban Affairs, Subcommittee on International Development Institutions and Finance, *Current Directions for U.S. Policy toward Chile*, 100th Cong., 1st Sess., July 21, 1987.

U.S. Congress, House, *Human Rights Abuses in Chile: Time for United States Action*, 99th Cong., 2d Sess., July 30, 1986.

U.S. Congress, House, Transcript, *Briefing on Chile*, Executive Session, October 2, 1986.

U.S. Congress, House, *Human Rights and U.S. Policy in the Multilateral Development Banks*, 97th Cong., 1st Sess., July 21 and 23, 1981.

U.S. Congress, House, *Human Rights and U.S. Voting Policy in the Development Banks: The Case of Chile*, 99th Cong., 1st Sess., December 5, 1985.

U.S. Congress, House and Senate, Committee on Foreign Affairs, Subcommittee on Africa, *Human Rights Policies at the Multilateral Development Banks*, 98th Cong., 1st Sess., June 22, 1983.

U.S. Congress, House, Committee on Foreign Affairs, Subcommittee on Human Rights and International Organizations, *Implementation of Congressionally Mandated Human Rights Provisions, Volume 1*, 97th Cong., 1st Sess., July 14, 30, September 17, 1981.

U.S. Congress, House, Subcommittees on Human Rights and International Organizations, and the Western Hemisphere Affairs, *Human Rights in Argentina, Chile, Paraguay, and Uruguay*, 98th Cong., 1st Sess., October 21, 1983.

U.S. Congress, House, *U.S. Policy, Human Rights, and the Prospects for Democracy in Chile*, 100th Cong., 2d Sess., April 12, May 17, July 28, August 2, 3, 1988.

U.S. Congress, House, Subcommittee on International Economic Policy and Trade, *Reauthorization of the Overseas Private Investment Corporation*, 100th Cong., 2d Sess., March 15, 1985.

U.S. Congress, House, and on Inter-American Affairs, *U.S. Economic Sanctions against Chile*, 97th Cong., 1st Sess., March 10, 1981.

U.S. Congress, House, *Developing an American Consensus, Report by Howard H. Baker Jr.*, 97th Cong., 2d Sess., March 1982.

U.S. Congress, Senate, Committee on Foreign Relations, *Nomination of Ernest W. Lefever*, 97th Cong., 1st Sess., May 18, 19, June 4, 5, 1981.

U.S. Congress, Senate, *Official Transcript to Hear Testimony on Nomination of Harry G. Barnes to Be Ambassador to Chile*, June 17, 1985.

U.S. Congress, Senate, *Theberge Nomination to Be Ambassador*, Unpublished Transcript, December. 7, 1981.

U.S. Department of State Collections, Chile Declassification Project Collections, Electronic, State Chile, Tranche III.

U.S. Department of State Collections, Chile Declassification Project Collections, Electronic, CIA Creation Documents.

U.S. Department of State Collections, Chile Declassification Project Collections, Electronic, NARA, Chile III.

U.S. General Accounting Office, *Food Tampering: FDA's Actions on Chilean Fruit Based on Sound Evidence*, GAO/HRD-90-164, September 1990.

Index